Learning Spark SQL

Architect streaming analytics and machine learning solutions

Aurobindo Sarkar

BIRMINGHAM - MUMBAI

Learning Spark SQL

First published: August 2017

Production reference: 1010917

Published by Packt Publishing Ltd.
Livery Place
35 Livery Street
Birmingham
B3 2PB, UK.
ISBN 978-1-78588-835-9

www.packtpub.com

Credits

Author
Aurobindo Sarkar

Reviewer
Sumit Gupta

Commissioning Editor
Kunal Parikh

Acquisition Editor
Larissa Pinto

Content Development Editor
Arun Nadar

Technical Editor
Shweta Jadhav

Copy Editor
Shaila Kusanale

Project Coordinator
Ritika Manoj

Proofreader
Safis Editing

Indexer
Tejal Daruwale Soni

Graphics
Jason Monteiro

Production Coordinator
Shantanu Zagade

About the Author

Aurobindo Sarkar is currently the Country Head (India Engineering Center) for ZineOne Inc. With a career spanning over 24 years, he has consulted at some of the leading organizations in India, US, UK, and Canada. He specializes in real-time web-scale architectures, machine learning, deep learning, cloud engineering, and big data analytics. Aurobindo has been actively working as a CTO in technology start-ups for over 8 years now. As a member of the top leadership team at various start-ups, he has mentored founders and CxOs, provided technology advisory services, and led product architecture and engineering teams.

I would like to thank Packt for giving me the opportunity to write this book. Their patience, understanding, and support as I wrote, rewrote, revised, and improved upon the content of this book was massive in ensuring that the book remained current with the rapidly evolving versions of Spark.

I would especially like to thank Larissa Pinto, the acquisition editor (who first contacted me to write this book over a year ago) and Arun Nadar, the content development editor, who continuously, and patiently, worked with me to bring this book to a conclusion.

I would also like to thank my friends and colleagues who encouraged me throughout the journey.

Most of all, I want to thank my wife, Nitya, and kids, Somnath, Ravishankar, and Nandini, who understood, encouraged, and supported me, and sacrificed many family moments for me to be able to complete this book successfully. This one is for them…

About the Reviewer

Sumit Gupta is a seasoned professional, innovator, and technology evangelist with over 100 months of experience in architecting, managing, and delivering enterprise solutions revolving around a variety of business domains, such as hospitality, healthcare, risk management, insurance, and more. He is passionate about technology and has an overall hands-on experience of over 16 years in the software industry. He has been using big data and cloud technologies over the last 5 years to solve complex business problems.

Sumit has also authored *Neo4j Essentials*, *Building Web Applications with Python*, and *Neo4j, Real-Time Big Data Analytics*, and *Learning Real-time Processing with Spark Streaming*, all by Packt.

You can find him on LinkedIn at `sumit1001`.

www.PacktPub.com

For support files and downloads related to your book, please visit www.PacktPub.com. Did you know that Packt offers eBook versions of every book published, with PDF and ePub files available? You can upgrade to the eBook version at www.PacktPub.com and as a print book customer, you are entitled to a discount on the eBook copy. Get in touch with us at service@packtpub.com for more details.

At www.PacktPub.com, you can also read a collection of free technical articles, sign up for a range of free newsletters and receive exclusive discounts and offers on Packt books and eBooks.

https://www.packtpub.com/mapt

Get the most in-demand software skills with Mapt. Mapt gives you full access to all Packt books and video courses, as well as industry-leading tools to help you plan your personal development and advance your career.

Why subscribe?

- Fully searchable across every book published by Packt
- Copy and paste, print, and bookmark content
- On demand and accessible via a web browser

Customer Feedback

Thanks for purchasing this Packt book. At Packt, quality is at the heart of our editorial process. To help us improve, please leave us an honest review on this book's Amazon page at www.amazon.in/dp/1785888358.

If you'd like to join our team of regular reviewers, you can email us at customerreviews@packtpub.com. We award our regular reviewers with free eBooks and videos in exchange for their valuable feedback. Help us be relentless in improving our products!

Table of Contents

Preface   1

Chapter 1: Getting Started with Spark SQL   7

  What is Spark SQL?   8
  Introducing SparkSession   9
  Understanding Spark SQL concepts   15
    Understanding Resilient Distributed Datasets (RDDs)   15
    Understanding DataFrames and Datasets   17
    Understanding the Catalyst optimizer   21
      Understanding Catalyst optimizations   22
      Understanding Catalyst transformations   23
    Introducing Project Tungsten   27
  Using Spark SQL in streaming applications   30
    Understanding Structured Streaming internals   34
  Summary   36

Chapter 2: Using Spark SQL for Processing Structured and Semistructured Data   37

  Understanding data sources in Spark applications   38
    Selecting Spark data sources   39
  Using Spark with relational databases   40
  Using Spark with MongoDB (NoSQL database)   47
  Using Spark with JSON data   52
  Using Spark with Avro files   55
  Using Spark with Parquet files   57
  Defining and using custom data sources in Spark   58
  Summary   59

Chapter 3: Using Spark SQL for Data Exploration   61

  Introducing Exploratory Data Analysis (EDA)   62
  Using Spark SQL for basic data analysis   62
    Identifying missing data   64
    Computing basic statistics   65
    Identifying data outliers   69
  Visualizing data with Apache Zeppelin   70
  Sampling data with Spark SQL APIs   75

Sampling with the DataFrame/Dataset API   75
Sampling with the RDD API   76
Using Spark SQL for creating pivot tables   78
Summary   82

Chapter 4: Using Spark SQL for Data Munging   83
Introducing data munging   83
Exploring data munging techniques   85
Pre-processing of the household electric consumption Dataset   86
Computing basic statistics and aggregations   87
Augmenting the Dataset   88
Executing other miscellaneous processing steps   89
Pre-processing of the weather Dataset   90
Analyzing missing data   91
Combining data using a JOIN operation   94
Munging textual data   97
Processing multiple input data files   98
Removing stop words   100
Munging time series data   102
Pre-processing of the time-series Dataset   103
Processing date fields   105
Persisting and loading data   105
Defining a date-time index   107
Using the TimeSeriesRDD object   107
Handling missing time-series data   109
Computing basic statistics   109
Dealing with variable length records   110
Converting variable-length records to fixed-length records   111
Extracting data from "messy" columns   114
Preparing data for machine learning   117
Pre-processing data for machine learning   118
Creating and running a machine learning pipeline   119
Summary   121

Chapter 5: Using Spark SQL in Streaming Applications   123
Introducing streaming data applications   123
Building Spark streaming applications   124
Implementing sliding window-based functionality   126
Joining a streaming Dataset with a static Dataset   128
Using the Dataset API in Structured Streaming   131

Using output sinks   131
Using the Foreach Sink for arbitrary computations on output   132
Using the Memory Sink to save output to a table   133
Using the File Sink to save output to a partitioned table   133
Monitoring streaming queries   134
Using Kafka with Spark Structured Streaming   137
Introducing Kafka concepts   137
Introducing ZooKeeper concepts   138
Introducing Kafka-Spark integration   138
Introducing Kafka-Spark Structured Streaming   140
Writing a receiver for a custom data source   142
Summary   146

Chapter 6: Using Spark SQL in Machine Learning Applications   147

Introducing machine learning applications   147
Understanding Spark ML pipelines and their components   148
Understanding the steps in a pipeline application development process   149
Introducing feature engineering   150
Creating new features from raw data   151
Estimating the importance of a feature   152
Understanding dimensionality reduction   152
Deriving good features   153
Implementing a Spark ML classification model   154
Exploring the diabetes Dataset   156
Pre-processing the data   162
Building the Spark ML pipeline   167
Using StringIndexer for indexing categorical features and labels   167
Using VectorAssembler for assembling features into one column   171
Using a Spark ML classifier   172
Creating a Spark ML pipeline   173
Creating the training and test Datasets   173
Making predictions using the PipelineModel   174
Selecting the best model   175
Changing the ML algorithm in the pipeline   178
Introducing Spark ML tools and utilities   179
Using Principal Component Analysis to select features   179
Using encoders   180
Using Bucketizer   181
Using VectorSlicer   182
Using Chi-squared selector   183
Using a Normalizer   184
Retrieving our original labels   184

Implementing a Spark ML clustering model   186
Summary   192

Chapter 7: Using Spark SQL in Graph Applications   193

Introducing large-scale graph applications   194
Exploring graphs using GraphFrames   195
     Constructing a GraphFrame   195
     Basic graph queries and operations   196
     Motif analysis using GraphFrames   199
     Processing subgraphs   205
     Applying graph algorithms   206
     Saving and loading GraphFrames   209
Analyzing JSON input modeled as a graph   210
Processing graphs containing multiple types of relationships   218
Understanding GraphFrame internals   222
     Viewing GraphFrame physical execution plan   222
     Understanding partitioning in GraphFrames   222
Summary   227

Chapter 8: Using Spark SQL with SparkR   229

Introducing SparkR   229
Understanding the SparkR architecture   230
Understanding SparkR DataFrames   231
Using SparkR for EDA and data munging tasks   232
     Reading and writing Spark DataFrames   232
     Exploring structure and contents of Spark DataFrames   233
     Running basic operations on Spark DataFrames   236
     Executing SQL statements on Spark DataFrames   239
     Merging SparkR DataFrames   240
     Using User Defined Functions (UDFs)   242
Using SparkR for computing summary statistics   244
Using SparkR for data visualization   248
     Visualizing data on a map   261
     Visualizing graph nodes and edges   262
Using SparkR for machine learning   265
Summary   272

Chapter 9: Developing Applications with Spark SQL   273

Introducing Spark SQL applications   273
Understanding text analysis applications   274
     Using Spark SQL for textual analysis   275

Preprocessing textual data   275
Computing readability   280
Using word lists   283
Creating data preprocessing pipelines   284
Understanding themes in document corpuses   294
Using Naive Bayes classifiers   298
Developing a machine learning application   308
Summary   318

Chapter 10: Using Spark SQL in Deep Learning Applications   319
Introducing neural networks   320
Understanding deep learning   321
Understanding representation learning   321
Understanding stochastic gradient descent   323
Introducing deep learning in Spark   324
Introducing CaffeOnSpark   324
Introducing DL4J   324
Introducing TensorFrames   325
Working with BigDL   325
Tuning hyperparameters of deep learning models   327
Introducing deep learning pipelines   328
Understanding Supervised learning   328
Understanding convolutional neural networks   329
Using neural networks for text classification   333
Using deep neural networks for language processing   337
Understanding Recurrent Neural Networks   337
Introducing autoencoders   343
Summary   347

Chapter 11: Tuning Spark SQL Components for Performance   349
Introducing performance tuning in Spark SQL   349
Understanding DataFrame/Dataset APIs   350
Optimizing data serialization   351
Understanding Catalyst optimizations   354
Understanding the Dataset/DataFrame API   354
Understanding Catalyst transformations   357
Visualizing Spark application execution   361
Exploring Spark application execution metrics   367
Using external tools for performance tuning   368
Cost-based optimizer in Apache Spark 2.2   368
Understanding the CBO statistics collection   369

Statistics collection functions   371
    Filter operator   371
    Join operator   371
Build side selection   372
Understanding multi-way JOIN ordering optimization   373
Understanding performance improvements using whole-stage code generation   377
Summary   383
Chapter 12: Spark SQL in Large-Scale Application Architectures   385
Understanding Spark-based application architectures   386
Using Apache Spark for batch processing   388
Using Apache Spark for stream processing   389
Understanding the Lambda architecture   391
Understanding the Kappa Architecture   392
Design considerations for building scalable stream processing applications   393
Building robust ETL pipelines using Spark SQL   395
Choosing appropriate data formats   396
Transforming data in ETL pipelines   397
Addressing errors in ETL pipelines   404
Implementing a scalable monitoring solution   408
Deploying Spark machine learning pipelines   418
Understanding the challenges in typical ML deployment environments   421
Understanding types of model scoring architectures   422
Using cluster managers   424
Summary   428
Index   429

Preface

We will start this book with the basics of Spark SQL and its role in Spark applications. After the initial familiarization with Spark SQL, we will focus on using Spark SQL to execute tasks that are common to all big data projects, such as working with various types of data sources, exploratory data analysis, and data munging. We will also see how Spark SQL and SparkR can be leveraged to accomplish typical data science tasks at scale.

With the DataFrame/Dataset API and the Catalyst optimizer at the heart of Spark SQL, it is no surprise that it plays a key role in all applications based on the Spark technology stack. These applications include large-scale machine learning pipelines, large-scale graph applications, and emerging Spark-based deep learning applications. Additionally, we will present Spark SQL-based Structured Streaming applications that are deployed in complex production environments as continuous applications.

We will also review performance tuning in Spark SQL applications, including **cost-based optimization (CBO)** introduced in Spark 2.2. Finally, we will present application architectures that leverage Spark modules and Spark SQL in real-world applications. More specifically, we will cover key architectural components and patterns in large-scale Spark applications that architects and designers will find useful as building blocks for their own specific use cases.

What this book covers

Chapter 1, *Getting Started with Spark SQL*, gives you an overview of Spark SQL while getting you comfortable with the Spark environment through hands-on sessions.

Chapter 2, *Using Spark SQL for Processing Structured and Semistructured Data*, will help you use Spark to work with a relational database (MySQL), NoSQL database (MongoDB), semistructured data (JSON), and data storage formats commonly used in the Hadoop ecosystem (Avro and Parquet).

Chapter 3, *Using Spark SQL for Data Exploration*, demonstrates the use of Spark SQL to explore datasets, perform basic data quality checks, generate samples and pivot tables, and visualize data with Apache Zeppelin.

Chapter 4, *Using Spark SQL for Data Munging*, uses Spark SQL for performing some basic data munging/wrangling tasks. It also introduces you to a few techniques to handle missing data, bad data, duplicate records, and so on.

Chapter 5, *Using Spark SQL in Streaming Applications*, provides a few examples of using Spark SQL DataFrame/Dataset APIs to build streaming applications. Additionally, it also shows how to use Kafka in structured streaming applications.

Chapter 6, *Using Spark SQL in Machine Learning Applications*, focuses on using Spark SQL in machine learning applications. In this chapter, we will mainly explore the key concepts in feature engineering and implement machine learning pipelines.

Chapter 7, *Using Spark SQL in Graph Applications*, introduces you to GraphFrame applications. It provides examples of using Spark SQL DataFrame/Dataset APIs to build graph applications and apply the various graph algorithms into your graph applications.

Chapter 8, *Using Spark SQL with SparkR*, covers the SparkR architecture and SparkR DataFrames API. It provides code examples for using SparkR for Exploratory Data Analysis (EDA) and data munging tasks, data visualization, and machine learning.

Chapter 9, *Developing Applications with Spark SQL*, helps you build Spark applications using a mix of Spark modules. It presents examples of applications that combine Spark SQL with Spark Streaming, Spark Machine Learning, and so on.

Chapter 10, *Using Spark SQL in Deep Learning Applications*, introduces you to deep learning in Spark. It covers the basic concepts of a few popular deep learning models before you delve into working with BigDL and Spark.

Chapter 11, *Tuning Spark SQL Components for Performance*, presents you with the foundational concepts related to tuning a Spark application, including data serialization using encoders. It also covers the key aspects of the cost-based optimizer introduced in Spark 2.2 to optimize Spark SQL execution automatically.

Chapter 12, *Spark SQL in Large-Scale Application Architectures*, teaches you to identify the use cases where Spark SQL can be used in large-scale application architectures to implement typical functional and non-functional requirements.

What you need for this book

This book is based on Spark 2.2.0 (pre-built for Apache Hadoop 2.7 or later) and Scala 2.11.8. For one or two subsections, Spark 2.1.0 has also been used due to the unavailability of certain libraries and reported bugs (when used with Apache Spark 2.2). The hardware and OS specifications include minimum 8 GB RAM (16 GB strongly recommended), 100 GB HDD, and OS X 10.11.6 or later (or appropriate Linux versions recommended for Spark development).

Who this book is for

If you are a developer, engineer, or an architect and want to learn how to use Apache Spark in a web-scale project, then this is the book for you. It is assumed that you have prior knowledge of SQL querying. Basic programming knowledge with Scala, Java, R, or Python is all you need to get started with this book.

Conventions

In this book, you will find several text styles that distinguish between different kinds of information. Here are some examples of these styles and an explanation of their meaning.

Code words in text, database table names, folder names, filenames, file extensions, pathnames, dummy URLs, user input, and terminal commands as follows: "The model is trained by calling the `fit()` method on the training Dataset. "

A block of code is set as follows:

```
scala> val inDiaDataDF = spark.read.option("header",
true).csv("file:///Users/aurobindosarkar/Downloads/dataset_diabetes/diabeti
c_data.csv").cache()
```

Any command-line input or output is written as follows:

```
head -n 8000 input.txt > val.txt
tail -n +8000 input.txt > train.txt
```

New terms and **important words** are shown in bold. Words that you see on the screen, for example, in menus or dialog boxes, appear in the text like this: "Clicking the **Next** button moves you to the next screen."

Warnings or important notes appear like this.

Tips and tricks appear like this.

Reader feedback

Feedback from our readers is always welcome. Let us know what you think about this book-what you liked or disliked. Reader feedback is important for us as it helps us develop titles that you will really get the most out of.

To send us general feedback, simply email feedback@packtpub.com, and mention the book's title in the subject of your message.

If there is a topic that you have expertise in and you are interested in either writing or contributing to a book, see our author guide at www.packtpub.com/authors.

Customer support

Now that you are the proud owner of a Packt book, we have several things to help you to get the most from your purchase.

Downloading the example code

You can download the example code files for this book from your account at http://www.packtpub.com. If you purchased this book elsewhere, you can visit http://www.packtpub.com/support and register to have the files emailed directly to you.

You can download the code files by following these steps:

1. Log in or register to our website using your email address and password.
2. Hover the mouse pointer on the **SUPPORT** tab at the top.
3. Click on **Code Downloads & Errata**.
4. Enter the name of the book in the **Search** box.
5. Select the book for which you're looking to download the code files.
6. Choose from the drop-down menu where you purchased this book from.
7. Click on **Code Download**.

Once the file is downloaded, please make sure that you unzip or extract the folder using the latest version of:

- WinRAR / 7-Zip for Windows
- Zipeg / iZip / UnRarX for Mac
- 7-Zip / PeaZip for Linux

The code bundle for the book is also hosted on GitHub at `https://github.com/PacktPublishing/Learning-Spark-SQL`. We also have other code bundles from our rich catalog of books and videos available at `https://github.com/PacktPublishing/`. Check them out!

Downloading the color images of this book

We also provide you with a PDF file that has color images of the screenshots/diagrams used in this book. The color images will help you better understand the changes in the output. You can download this file from `https://www.packtpub.com/sites/default/files/downloads/LearningSparkSQL_ColorImages.pdf`.

Errata

Although we have taken every care to ensure the accuracy of our content, mistakes do happen. If you find a mistake in one of our books-maybe a mistake in the text or the code-we would be grateful if you could report this to us. By doing so, you can save other readers from frustration and help us improve subsequent versions of this book. If you find any errata, please report them by visiting `http://www.packtpub.com/submit-errata`, selecting your book, clicking on the **Errata Submission Form** link, and entering the details of your errata. Once your errata are verified, your submission will be accepted and the errata will be uploaded to our website or added to any list of existing errata under the Errata section of that title.

To view the previously submitted errata, go to `https://www.packtpub.com/books/content/support` and enter the name of the book in the search field. The required information will appear under the **Errata** section.

Piracy

Piracy of copyrighted material on the Internet is an ongoing problem across all media. At Packt, we take the protection of our copyright and licenses very seriously. If you come across any illegal copies of our works in any form on the Internet, please provide us with the location address or website name immediately so that we can pursue a remedy. Please contact us at copyright@packtpub.com with a link to the suspected pirated material. We appreciate your help in protecting our authors and our ability to bring you valuable content.

Questions

If you have a problem with any aspect of this book, you can contact us at questions@packtpub.com, and we will do our best to address the problem.

Getting Started with Spark SQL

1

Spark SQL is at the heart of all applications developed using Spark. In this book, we will explore Spark SQL in great detail, including its usage in various types of applications as well as its internal workings. Developers and architects will appreciate the technical concepts and hands-on sessions presented in each chapter, as they progress through the book.

In this chapter, we will introduce you to the key concepts related to Spark SQL. We will start with SparkSession, the new entry point for Spark SQL in Spark 2.0. Then, we will explore Spark SQL's interfaces RDDs, DataFrames, and Dataset APIs. Later on, we will explain the developer-level details regarding the Catalyst optimizer and Project Tungsten.

Finally, we will introduce an exciting new feature in Spark 2.0 for streaming applications, called Structured Streaming. Specific hands-on exercises (using publicly available Datasets) are presented throughout the chapter, so you can actively follow along as you read through the various sections.

More specifically, the sections in this chapter will cover the following topics along with practice hands-on sessions:

- What is Spark SQL?
- Introducing SparkSession
- Understanding Spark SQL concepts
  - Understanding RDDs, DataFrames, and Datasets
  - Understanding the Catalyst optimizer
  - Understanding Project Tungsten
- Using Spark SQL in continuous applications
- Understanding Structured Streaming internals

What is Spark SQL?

Spark SQL is one of the most advanced components of Apache Spark. It has been a part of the core distribution since Spark 1.0 and supports Python, Scala, Java, and R programming APIs. As illustrated in the figure below, Spark SQL components provide the foundation for Spark machine learning applications, streaming applications, graph applications, and many other types of application architectures.

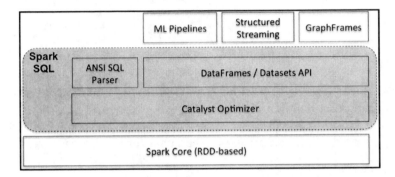

Such applications, typically, use Spark ML pipelines, Structured Streaming, and GraphFrames, which are all based on Spark SQL interfaces (DataFrame/Dataset API). These applications, along with constructs such as SQL, DataFrames, and Datasets API, receive the benefits of the Catalyst optimizer, automatically. This optimizer is also responsible for generating executable query plans based on the lower-level RDD interfaces.

We will explore ML pipelines in more detail in Chapter 6, *Using Spark SQL in Machine Learning Applications*. GraphFrames will be covered in Chapter 7, *Using Spark SQL in Graph Applications*. While, we will introduce the key concepts regarding Structured Streaming and the Catalyst optimizer in this chapter, we will get more details about them in Chapter 5, *Using Spark SQL in Streaming Applications*, and Chapter 11, *Tuning Spark SQL Components for Performance*.

In Spark 2.0, the DataFrame API has been merged with the Dataset API, thereby unifying data processing capabilities across Spark libraries. This also enables developers to work with a single high-level and type-safe API. However, the Spark software stack does not prevent developers from directly using the low-level RDD interface in their applications. Though the low-level RDD API will continue to be available, a vast majority of developers are expected to (and are recommended to) use the high-level APIs, namely, the Dataset and DataFrame APIs.

Additionally, Spark 2.0 extends Spark SQL capabilities by including a new ANSI SQL parser with support for subqueries and the SQL:2003 standard. More specifically, the subquery support now includes correlated/uncorrelated subqueries, and IN / NOT IN and EXISTS / NOT EXISTS predicates in WHERE / HAVING clauses.

At the core of Spark SQL is the Catalyst optimizer, which leverages Scala's advanced features, such as pattern matching, to provide an extensible query optimizer. DataFrames, Datasets, and SQL queries share the same execution and optimization pipeline; hence, there is no performance impact of using any one or the other of these constructs (or of using any of the supported programming APIs). The high-level DataFrame-based code written by the developer is converted to Catalyst expressions and then to low-level Java bytecode as it passes through this pipeline.

SparkSession is the entry point into Spark SQL-related functionality and we describe it in more detail in the next section.

Introducing SparkSession

In Spark 2.0, SparkSession represents a unified entry point for manipulating data in Spark. It minimizes the number of different contexts a developer has to use while working with Spark. SparkSession replaces multiple context objects, such as the SparkContext, SQLContext, and HiveContext. These contexts are now encapsulated within the SparkSession object.

In Spark programs, we use the builder design pattern to instantiate a SparkSession object. However, in the REPL environment (that is, in a Spark shell session), the SparkSession is automatically created and made available to you via an instance object called **Spark**.

At this time, start the Spark shell on your computer to interactively execute the code snippets in this section. As the shell starts up, you will notice a bunch of messages appearing on your screen, as shown in the following figure. You should see messages displaying the availability of a `SparkSession` object (as Spark), Spark version as 2.2.0, Scala version as 2.11.8, and the Java version as 1.8.x.

```
Aurobindos-MacBook-Pro-2:spark-2.2.0-bin-hadoop2.7 aurobindosarkar$ bin/spark-shell
Setting default log level to "WARN".
To adjust logging level use sc.setLogLevel(newLevel). For SparkR, use setLogLevel(newLevel).
17/08/19 19:45:38 WARN util.NativeCodeLoader: Unable to load native-hadoop library for your platform... using builtin-java classes where applicable
17/08/19 19:45:44 WARN metastore.ObjectStore: Failed to get database global_temp, returning NoSuchObjectException
Spark context Web UI available at http://192.168.8.100:4040
Spark context available as 'sc' (master = local[*], app id = local-1503152139834).
Spark session available as 'spark'.
Welcome to
      ____              __
     / __/__  ___ _____/ /__
    _\ \/ _ \/ _ `/ __/  '_/
   /___/ .__/\_,_/_/ /_/\_\   version 2.2.0
      /_/

Using Scala version 2.11.8 (Java HotSpot(TM) 64-Bit Server VM, Java 1.8.0_77)
Type in expressions to have them evaluated.
Type :help for more information.
```

The `SparkSession` object can be used to configure Spark's runtime config properties. For example, the two main resources that Spark and Yarn manage are the CPU and the memory. If you want to set the number of cores and the heap size for the Spark executor, then you can do that by setting the `spark.executor.cores` and the `spark.executor.memory` properties, respectively. In this example, we set these runtime properties to 2 cores and 4 GB, respectively, as shown:

```scala
scala> spark.conf.set("spark.executor.cores", "2")
scala> spark.conf.set("spark.executor.memory", "4g")
```

The `SparkSession` object can be used to read data from various sources, such as CSV, JSON, JDBC, stream, and so on. In addition, it can be used to execute SQL statements, register **User Defined Functions (UDFs)**, and work with Datasets and DataFrames. The following session illustrates some of these basic operations in Spark.

For this example, we use the breast cancer database created by Dr. William H. Wolberg, University of Wisconsin Hospitals, Madison. You can download the original Dataset from `https://archive.ics.uci.edu/ml/datasets/Breast+Cancer+Wisconsin+(Original)`. Each row in the dataset contains the sample number, nine cytological characteristics of breast fine needle aspirates graded 1 to 10, and the class `label`, benign `(2)` or malignant `(4)`.

First, we define a schema for the records in our file. The field descriptions are available at the Dataset's download site.

```scala
scala> import org.apache.spark.sql.types._
scala> val recordSchema = new StructType().add("sample",
"long").add("cThick", "integer").add("uCSize", "integer").add("uCShape",
"integer").add("mAdhes", "integer").add("sECSize", "integer").add("bNuc",
"integer").add("bChrom", "integer").add("nNuc", "integer").add("mitosis",
"integer").add("clas", "integer")
```

Next, we create a DataFrame from our input CSV file using the record schema defined in the preceding step:

```scala
val df = spark.read.format("csv").option("header",
false).schema(recordSchema).load("file:///Users/aurobindosarkar/Downloads/b
reast-cancer-wisconsin.data")
```

The newly created DataFrame can be displayed using the `show()` method:

```
scala> df.show()
+-------+------+------+-------+------+-------+----+------+----+-------+-----+
| sample|cThick|uCSize|uCShape|mAdhes|sECSize|bNuc|bChrom|nNuc|mitosis| clas|
+-------+------+------+-------+------+-------+----+------+----+-------+-----+
|1000025|     5|     1|      1|     1|      2|   1|     3|   1|      1|    2|
|1002945|     5|     4|      4|     5|      7|  10|     3|   2|      1|    2|
|1015425|     3|     1|      1|     1|      2|   2|     3|   1|      1|    2|
|1016277|     6|     8|      8|     1|      3|   4|     3|   7|      1|    2|
|1017023|     4|     1|      1|     3|      2|   1|     3|   1|      1|    2|
|1017122|     8|    10|     10|     8|      7|  10|     9|   7|      1|    4|
|1018099|     1|     1|      1|     1|      2|  10|     3|   1|      1|    2|
|1018561|     2|     1|      2|     1|      2|   1|     3|   1|      1|    2|
|1033078|     2|     1|      1|     1|      2|   1|     1|   1|      5|    2|
|1033078|     4|     2|      1|     1|      2|   1|     2|   1|      1|    2|
|1035283|     1|     1|      1|     1|      1|   1|     3|   1|      1|    2|
|1036172|     2|     1|      1|     1|      2|   1|     2|   1|      1|    2|
|1041801|     5|     3|      3|     3|      2|   3|     4|   4|      1|    4|
|1043999|     1|     1|      1|     1|      2|   3|     3|   1|      1|    2|
|1044572|     8|     7|      5|    10|      7|   9|     5|   5|      4|    4|
|1047630|     7|     4|      6|     4|      6|   1|     4|   3|      1|    4|
|1048672|     4|     1|      1|     1|      2|   1|     2|   1|      1|    2|
|1049815|     4|     1|      1|     1|      2|   1|     3|   1|      1|    2|
|1050670|    10|     7|      7|     6|      4|  10|     4|   1|      2|    4|
|1050718|     6|     1|      1|     1|      2|   1|     3|   1|      1|    2|
+-------+------+------+-------+------+-------+----+------+----+-------+-----+
only showing top 20 rows
```

The DataFrame can be registered as a SQL temporary view using the
`createOrReplaceTempView()` method. This allows applications to run SQL queries using
the `sql` function of the SparkSession object and return the results as a DataFrame.

Next, we create a temporary view for the DataFrame and execute a simple SQL statement
against it:

```scala
scala> df.createOrReplaceTempView("cancerTable")

scala> val sqlDF = spark.sql("SELECT sample, bNuc from cancerTable")
```

The contents of results DataFrame are displayed using the `show()` method:

```
scala> sqlDF.show()
+-------+----+
| sample|bNuc|
+-------+----+
|1000025|   1|
|1002945|  10|
|1015425|   2|
|1016277|   4|
|1017023|   1|
|1017122|  10|
|1018099|  10|
|1018561|   1|
|1033078|   1|
|1033078|   1|
|1035283|   1|
|1036172|   1|
|1041801|   3|
|1043999|   3|
|1044572|   9|
|1047630|   1|
|1048672|   1|
|1049815|   1|
|1050670|  10|
|1050718|   1|
+-------+----+
only showing top 20 rows
```

In the next code snippet, we show you the statements for creating a Spark Dataset using a `case` class and the `toDS()` method. Then, we define a UDF to convert the `clas` column, currently containing `2`'s and `4`'s to `0`'s and `1`'s respectively. We register the UDF using the `SparkSession` object and use it in a SQL statement:

```
scala> case class CancerClass(sample: Long, cThick: Int, uCSize: Int,
uCShape: Int, mAdhes: Int, sECSize: Int, bNuc: Int, bChrom: Int, nNuc: Int,
mitosis: Int, clas: Int)

scala> val cancerDS =
spark.sparkContext.textFile("file:///Users/aurobindosarkar/Documents/SparkB
ook/data/breast-cancer-wisconsin.data").map(_.split(",")).map(attributes =>
CancerClass(attributes(0).trim.toLong, attributes(1).trim.toInt,
attributes(2).trim.toInt, attributes(3).trim.toInt,
attributes(4).trim.toInt, attributes(5).trim.toInt,
attributes(6).trim.toInt, attributes(7).trim.toInt,
attributes(8).trim.toInt, attributes(9).trim.toInt,
attributes(10).trim.toInt)).toDS()

scala> def binarize(s: Int): Int = s match {case 2 => 0 case 4 => 1 }

scala> spark.udf.register("udfValueToCategory", (arg: Int) =>
binarize(arg))

scala> val sqlUDF = spark.sql("SELECT *, udfValueToCategory(clas) from
cancerTable")

scala> sqlUDF.show()
```

sample	cThick	uCSize	uCShape	mAdhes	sECSize	bNuc	bChrom	nNuc	mitosis	clas	UDF(clas)
1000025	5	1	1	1	2	1	3	1	1	2	0
1002945	5	4	4	5	7	10	3	2	1	2	0
1015425	3	1	1	1	2	2	3	1	1	2	0
1016277	6	8	8	1	3	4	3	7	1	2	0
1017023	4	1	1	3	2	1	3	1	1	2	0
1017122	8	10	10	8	7	10	9	7	1	4	1
1018099	1	1	1	1	2	10	3	1	1	2	0
1018561	2	1	2	1	2	1	3	1	1	2	0
1033078	2	1	1	1	2	1	1	1	5	2	0
1033078	4	2	1	1	2	1	2	1	1	2	0
1035283	1	1	1	1	1	1	3	1	1	2	0
1036172	2	1	1	1	2	1	2	1	1	2	0
1041801	5	3	3	3	2	3	4	4	1	4	1
1043999	1	1	1	1	2	3	3	1	1	2	0
1044572	8	7	5	10	7	9	5	5	4	4	1
1047630	7	4	6	4	6	1	4	3	1	4	1
1048672	4	1	1	1	2	1	2	1	1	2	0
1049815	4	1	1	1	2	1	3	1	1	2	0
1050670	10	7	7	6	4	10	4	1	2	4	1
1050718	6	1	1	1	2	1	3	1	1	2	0

only showing top 20 rows

`SparkSession` exposes methods (via the catalog attribute) of accessing the underlying metadata, such as the available databases and tables, registered UDFs, temporary views, and so on. Additionally, we can also cache tables, drop temporary views, and clear the cache. Some of these statements and their corresponding output are shown here:

```
scala> spark.catalog.currentDatabase

res5: String = default

scala> spark.catalog.isCached("cancerTable")

res6: Boolean = false

scala> spark.catalog.cacheTable("cancerTable")

scala> spark.catalog.isCached("cancerTable")

res8: Boolean = true

scala> spark.catalog.clearCache

scala> spark.catalog.isCached("cancerTable")

res10: Boolean = false

scala> spark.catalog.listDatabases.show()
```

name	description	locationUri
default	Default Hive data...	file:/Users/aurob...

You can also use the `take` method to display a specific number of records in the DataFrame:

```
scala> spark.catalog.listDatabases.take(1)
res13: Array[org.apache.spark.sql.catalog.Database] =
Array(Database[name='default', description='Default Hive database',
path='file:/Users/aurobindosarkar/Downloads/spark-2.2.0-bin-
hadoop2.7/spark-warehouse'])

scala> spark.catalog.listTables.show()
```

name	database	description	tableType	isTemporary
cancertable	null	null	TEMPORARY	true

We can drop the temp table that we created earlier with the following statement:

```scala
scala> spark.catalog.dropTempView("cancerTable")

scala> spark.catalog.listTables.show()
```

```
+----+--------+-----------+---------+-----------+
|name|database|description|tableType|isTemporary|
+----+--------+-----------+---------+-----------+
+----+--------+-----------+---------+-----------+
```

In the next few sections, we will describe RDDs, DataFrames, and Dataset constructs in more detail.

Understanding Spark SQL concepts

In this section, we will explore key concepts related to Resilient Distributed Datasets (RDD), DataFrames, and Datasets, Catalyst Optimizer and Project Tungsten.

Understanding Resilient Distributed Datasets (RDDs)

RDDs are Spark's primary distributed Dataset abstraction. It is a collection of data that is immutable, distributed, lazily evaluated, type inferred, and cacheable. Prior to execution, the developer code (using higher-level constructs such as SQL, DataFrames, and Dataset APIs) is converted to a DAG of RDDs (ready for execution).

You can create RDDs by parallelizing an existing collection of data or accessing a Dataset residing in an external storage system, such as the file system or various Hadoop-based data sources. The parallelized collections form a distributed Dataset that enable parallel operations on them.

You can create a RDD from the input file with number of partitions specified, as shown:

```scala
scala> val cancerRDD =
sc.textFile("file:///Users/aurobindosarkar/Downloads/breast-cancer-
wisconsin.data", 4)

scala> cancerRDD.partitions.size
res37: Int = 4
```

You can implicitly convert the RDD to a DataFrame by importing the `spark.implicits` package and using the `toDF()` method:

```
scala> import spark.implicits._scala>
val cancerDF = cancerRDD.toDF()
```

To create a DataFrame with a specific schema, we define a Row object for the rows contained in the DataFrame. Additionally, we split the comma-separated data, convert it to a list of fields, and then map it to the Row object. Finally, we use the `createDataFrame()` to create the DataFrame with a specified schema:

```
def row(line: List[String]): Row = { Row(line(0).toLong, line(1).toInt,
line(2).toInt, line(3).toInt, line(4).toInt, line(5).toInt, line(6).toInt,
line(7).toInt, line(8).toInt, line(9).toInt, line(10).toInt) }
val data = cancerRDD.map(_.split(",").to[List]).map(row)
val cancerDF = spark.createDataFrame(data, recordSchema)
```

Further, we can easily convert the preceding DataFrame to a Dataset using the `case` class defined earlier:

```
scala> val cancerDS = cancerDF.as[CancerClass]
```

RDD data is logically divided into a set of partitions; additionally, all input, intermediate, and output data is also represented as partitions. The number of RDD partitions defines the level of data fragmentation. These partitions are also the basic units of parallelism. Spark execution jobs are split into multiple stages, and as each stage operates on one partition at a time, it is very important to tune the number of partitions. Fewer partitions than active stages means your cluster could be under-utilized, while an excessive number of partitions could impact the performance due to higher disk and network I/O.

The programming interface to RDDs support two types of operations: transformations and actions. The transformations create a new Dataset from an existing one, while the actions return a value or result of a computation. All transformations are evaluated lazily--the actual execution occurs only when an action is executed to compute a result. The transformations form a lineage graph instead of actually replicating data across multiple machines. This graph-based approach enables an efficient fault tolerance model. For example, if an RDD partition is lost, then it can be recomputed based on the lineage graph.

You can control data persistence (for example, caching) and specify placement preferences for RDD partitions and then use specific operators for manipulating them. By default, Spark persists RDDs in memory, but it can spill them to disk if sufficient RAM isn't available. Caching improves performance by several orders of magnitude; however, it is often memory intensive. Other persistence options include storing RDDs to disk and replicating them across the nodes in your cluster. The in-memory storage of persistent RDDs can be in the form of deserialized or serialized Java objects. The deserialized option is faster, while the serialized option is more memory-efficient (but slower). Unused RDDs are automatically removed from the cache but, depending on your requirements; if a specific RDD is no longer required, then you can also explicitly release it.

Understanding DataFrames and Datasets

A DataFrame is similar to a table in a relational database, a pandas dataframe, or a data frame in R. It is a distributed collection of rows that is organized into columns. It uses the immutable, in-memory, resilient, distributed, and parallel capabilities of RDD, and applies a schema to the data. DataFrames are also evaluated lazily. Additionally, they provide a **domain-specific language** (**DSL**) for distributed data manipulation.

Conceptually, the DataFrame is an alias for a collection of generic objects `Dataset[Row]`, where a row is a generic untyped object. This means that syntax errors for DataFrames are caught during the compile stage; however, analysis errors are detected only during runtime.

DataFrames can be constructed from a wide array of sources, such as structured data files, Hive tables, databases, or RDDs. The source data can be read from local filesystems, HDFS, Amazon S3, and RDBMSs. In addition, other popular data formats, such as CSV, JSON, Avro, Parquet, and so on, are also supported. Additionally, you can also create and use custom data sources.

The DataFrame API supports Scala, Java, Python, and R programming APIs. The DataFrames API is declarative, and combined with procedural Spark code, it provides a much tighter integration between the relational and procedural processing in your applications. DataFrames can be manipulated using Spark's procedural API, or using relational APIs (with richer optimizations).

In the early versions of Spark, you had to write arbitrary Java, Python, or Scala functions that operated on RDDs. In this scenario, the functions were executing on opaque Java objects. Hence, the user functions were essentially black boxes executing opaque computations using opaque objects and data types. This approach was very general and such programs had complete control over the execution of every data operation. However, as the engine did not know the code you were executing or the nature of the data, it was not possible to optimize these arbitrary Java objects. In addition, it was incumbent on the developers to write efficient programs that were dependent on the nature of their specific workloads.

In Spark 2.0, the main benefit of using SQL, DataFrames, and Datasets is that it's easier to program using these high-level programming interfaces while reaping the benefits of improved performance, automatically. You have to write significantly fewer lines of code and the programs are automatically optimized and efficient code is generated for you. This results in better performance while significantly reducing the burden on developers. Now, the developer can focus on the "what" rather than the "how" of something that needs to be accomplished.

The Dataset API was first added to Spark 1.6 to provide the benefits of both RDDs and the Spark SQL's optimizer. A Dataset can be constructed from JVM objects and then manipulated using functional transformations such as map, filter, and so on. As the Dataset is a collection of strongly-typed objects specified using a user-defined case class, both syntax errors and analysis errors can be detected at compile time.

The unified Dataset API can be used in both Scala and Java. However, Python does not support the Dataset API yet.

In the following example, we present a few basic DataFrame/Dataset operations. For this purpose, we will use two restaurant listing datasets that are typically used in duplicate records detection and record linkage applications. The two lists, one each from Zagat's and Fodor's restaurant guides, have duplicate records between them. To keep this example simple, we have manually converted the input files to a CSV format. You can download the original dataset from http://www.cs.utexas.edu/users/ml/riddle/data.html.

First, we define a case class for the records in the two files:

```
scala> case class RestClass(name: String, street: String, city: String,
phone: String, cuisine: String)
```

Next, we create Datasets from the two files:

```
scala> val rest1DS =
spark.sparkContext.textFile("file:///Users/aurobindosarkar/Documents/SparkB
ook/data/zagats.csv").map(_.split(",")).map(attributes =>
RestClass(attributes(0).trim, attributes(1).trim, attributes(2).trim,
attributes(3).trim, attributes(4).trim)).toDS()

scala> val rest2DS =
spark.sparkContext.textFile("file:///Users/aurobindosarkar/Documents/SparkB
ook/data/fodors.csv").map(_.split(",")).map(attributes =>
RestClass(attributes(0).trim, attributes(1).trim, attributes(2).trim,
attributes(3).trim, attributes(4).trim)).toDS()
```

We define a UDF to clean up and transform the phone numbers in the second Dataset to match the format in the first file:

```
scala> def formatPhoneNo(s: String): String = s match {case s if
s.contains("/") => s.replaceAll("/", "-").replaceAll("- ", "-
").replaceAll("--", "-") case _ => s }

scala> val udfStandardizePhoneNos = udf[String, String]( x =>
formatPhoneNo(x) )

scala> val rest2DSM1 = rest2DS.withColumn("stdphone",
udfStandardizePhoneNos(rest2DS.col("phone")))
```

```
scala> rest2DSM1.show()
+--------------------+--------------------+------------+------------+------------+------------+
|                name|              street|        city|       phone|     cuisine|    stdphone|
+--------------------+--------------------+------------+------------+------------+------------+
|Adriano's Ristorante|2930 Beverly Glen...| Los Angeles|310/475-9807|     Italian|310-475-9807|
|Arnie Morton's of...|435 S. La Cienega...| Los Angeles|310/246-1501|    American|310-246-1501|
|   Art's Delicatessen| 12224 Ventura Blvd.| Studio City|818/762-1221|    American|818-762-1221|
|   Barney Greengrass| 9570 Wilshire Blvd.|Beverly Hills|310/777-5877|    American|310-777-5877|
|          Beaurivage|26025 Pacific Coa...|      Malibu|310/456-5733|      French|310-456-5733|
|       Bistro Garden|      176 N. Canon Dr.| Los Angeles|310/550-3900|  Californian|310-550-3900|
|        Border Grill|            4th St.| Los Angeles|310/451-1655|     Mexican|310-451-1655|
|        Broadway Deli|   3rd St. Promenade| Santa Monica|310/451-0616|    American|310-451-0616|
|            Ca'Brea| 346 S. La Brea Ave.| Los Angeles|213/938-2863|     Italian|213-938-2863|
|           Ca'del Sol| 4100 Cahuenga Blvd.| Los Angeles|818/985-4669|     Italian|818-985-4669|
|          Cafe Bizou| 14016 Ventura Blvd.| Sherman Oaks|818/788-3536|      French|818-788-3536|
|          Cafe Pinot|     700 W. Fifth St.| Los Angeles|213/239-6500|  Californian|213-239-6500|
|California Pizza ...|   207 S. Beverly Dr.| Los Angeles|310/275-1101|  Californian|310-275-1101|
|           Campanile| 624 S. La Brea Ave.| Los Angeles|213/938-1447|    American|213-938-1447|
|            Canter's| 419 N. Fairfax Ave.| Los Angeles|213/651-2030|    American|213-651-2030|
|                Cava|            3rd St.| Los Angeles|213/658-8898|Mediterranean|213-658-8898|
|        Cha Cha Cha|   656 N. Virgil Ave.| Los Angeles|213/664-7723|   Caribbean|213-664-7723|
|           Chan Dara|310 N. Larchmont ...| Los Angeles|213/467-1052|       Asian|213-467-1052|
|      Chinois on Main|       2709 Main St.| Santa Monica|310/392-9025|      French|310-392-9025|
|              Citrus|   6703 Melrose Ave.| Los Angeles|213/857-0034|  Californian|213-857-0034|
+--------------------+--------------------+------------+------------+------------+------------+
only showing top 20 rows
```

Next, we create temporary views from our Datasets:

```scala
scala> rest1DS.createOrReplaceTempView("rest1Table")

scala> rest2DSM1.createOrReplaceTempView("rest2Table")
```

We can get a count of the number of duplicates, by executing a SQL statement on these tables that returns the count of the number of records with matching phone numbers:

```scala
scala> spark.sql("SELECT count(*) from rest1Table, rest2Table where
rest1Table.phone = rest2Table.stdphone").show()
```

```
+--------+
|count(1)|
+--------+
|     112|
+--------+
```

Next, we execute a SQL statement that returns a DataFrame containing the rows with matching phone numbers:

```scala
scala> val sqlDF = spark.sql("SELECT a.name, b.name, a.phone, b.stdphone
from rest1Table a, rest2Table b where a.phone = b.stdphone")
```

The results listing the name and the phone number columns from the two tables can be displayed to visually verify, if the results are possible duplicates:

```
scala> sqlDF.show()
+--------------------+--------------------+------------+------------+
|                name|                name|       phone|    stdphone|
+--------------------+--------------------+------------+------------+
|      Buckhead Diner|      Buckhead Diner|404-262-3336|404-262-3336|
|Lespinasse (New Y...|          Lespinasse|212-339-6719|212-339-6719|
| Tavern on the Green| Tavern on the Green|212-873-3200|212-873-3200|
|    Brasserie Le Coze|    Brasserie Le Coze|404-266-1440|404-266-1440|
|          Bacchanalia|          Bacchanalia|404-365-0410|404-365-0410|
|         Pinot Bistro|         Pinot Bistro|818-990-0500|818-990-0500|
|Hedgerose Heights...|Hedgerose Heights...|404-233-7673|404-233-7673|
|               Jo Jo|               Jo Jo|212-223-5656|212-223-5656|
|Ritz-Carlton Cafe...|Restaurant  Ritz-...|404-659-0400|404-659-0400|
|Ritz-Carlton Rest...|Restaurant  Ritz-...|404-659-0400|404-659-0400|
|          Montrachet|          Montrachet|212-219-2777|212-219-2777|
|             Abruzzi|             Abruzzi|404-261-8186|404-261-8186|
|          River Cafe|     River Caf&eacute;|718-522-5200|718-522-5200|
|    Cafe des Artistes|Caf&eacute; des A...|212-877-3500|212-877-3500|
|     Bone's Restaurant|              Bone's|404-237-2663|404-237-2663|
|            Matsuhisa|            Matsuhisa|310-659-9639|310-659-9639|
|      PlumpJack Cafe|PlumpJack Caf&eac...|415-563-4755|415-563-4755|
|             Aquavit|             Aquavit|212-307-7311|212-307-7311|
|       Heera of India|       Heera of India|404-876-4408|404-876-4408|
|              Lutece|       Lut&egrave;ce|212-752-2225|212-752-2225|
+--------------------+--------------------+------------+------------+
only showing top 20 rows
```

In the next section, we will shift our focus to Spark SQL internals, more specifically, to the Catalyst optimizer and Project Tungsten.

Understanding the Catalyst optimizer

The Catalyst optimizer is at the core of Spark SQL and is implemented in Scala. It enables several key features, such as schema inference (from JSON data), that are very useful in data analysis work.

The following figure shows the high-level transformation process from a developer's program containing DataFrames/Datasets to the final execution plan:

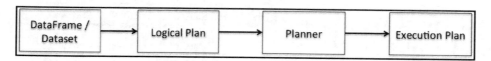

The internal representation of the program is a query plan. The query plan describes data operations such as aggregate, join, and filter, which match what is defined in your query. These operations generate a new Dataset from the input Dataset. After we have an initial version of the query plan ready, the Catalyst optimizer will apply a series of transformations to convert it to an optimized query plan. Finally, the Spark SQL code generation mechanism translates the optimized query plan into a DAG of RDDs that is ready for execution. The query plans and the optimized query plans are internally represented as trees. So, at its core, the Catalyst optimizer contains a general library for representing trees and applying rules to manipulate them. On top of this library, are several other libraries that are more specific to relational query processing.

Catalyst has two types of query plans: **Logical** and **Physical Plans**. The Logical Plan describes the computations on the Datasets without defining how to carry out the specific computations. Typically, the Logical Plan generates a list of attributes or columns as output under a set of constraints on the generated rows. The Physical Plan describes the computations on Datasets with specific definitions on how to execute them (it is executable).

Let's explore the transformation steps in more detail. The initial query plan is essentially an unresolved Logical Plan, that is, we don't know the source of the Datasets or the columns (contained in the Dataset) at this stage and we also don't know the types of columns. The first step in this pipeline is the analysis step. During analysis, the catalog information is used to convert the unresolved Logical Plan to a resolved Logical Plan.

In the next step, a set of logical optimization rules is applied to the resolved Logical Plan, resulting in an optimized Logical Plan. In the next step the optimizer may generate multiple Physical Plans and compare their costs to pick the best one. The first version of the **Cost-based Optimizer (CBO)**, built on top of Spark SQL has been released in Spark 2.2. More details on cost-based optimization are presented in Chapter 11, *Tuning Spark SQL Components for Performance*.

All three--**DataFrame**, **Dataset** and SQL--share the same optimization pipeline as illustrated in the following figure:

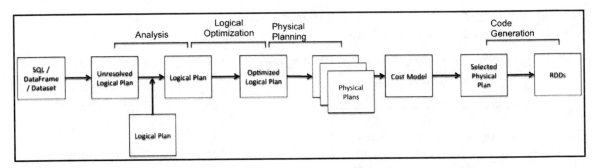

Understanding Catalyst optimizations

In Catalyst, there are two main types of optimizations: Logical and Physical:

- **Logical Optimizations**: This includes the ability of the optimizer to push filter predicates down to the data source and enable execution to skip irrelevant data. For example, in the case of Parquet files, entire blocks can be skipped and comparisons on strings can be turned into cheaper integer comparisons via dictionary encoding. In the case of RDBMSs, the predicates are pushed down to the database to reduce the amount of data traffic.

- **Physical Optimizations**: This includes the ability to choose intelligently between broadcast joins and shuffle joins to reduce network traffic, performing lower-level optimizations, such as eliminating expensive object allocations and reducing virtual function calls. Hence, and performance typically improves when DataFrames are introduced in your programs.

The Rule Executor is responsible for the analysis and logical optimization steps, while a set of strategies and the Rule Executor are responsible for the physical planning step. The Rule Executor transforms a tree to another of the same type by applying a set of rules in batches. These rules can be applied one or more times. Also, each of these rules is implemented as a transform. A transform is basically a function, associated with every tree, and is used to implement a single rule. In Scala terms, the transformation is defined as a partial function (a function defined for a subset of its possible arguments). These are typically defined as case statements to determine whether the partial function (using pattern matching) is defined for the given input.

The Rule Executor makes the Physical Plan ready for execution by preparing scalar subqueries, ensuring that the input rows meet the requirements of the specific operation and applying the physical optimizations. For example, in the sort merge join operations, the input rows need to be sorted as per the join condition. The optimizer inserts the appropriate sort operations, as required, on the input rows before the sort merge join operation is executed.

Understanding Catalyst transformations

Conceptually, the Catalyst optimizer executes two types of transformations. The first one converts an input tree type to the same tree type (that is, without changing the tree type). This type of transformation includes converting one expression to another expression, one Logical Plan to another Logical Plan, and one Physical Plan to another Physical Plan. The second type of transformation converts one tree type to another type, for example, from a Logical Plan to a Physical Plan. A Logical Plan is converted to a Physical Plan by applying a set of strategies. These strategies use pattern matching to convert a tree to the other type. For example, we have specific patterns for matching logical project and filter operators to physical project and filter operators, respectively.

A set of rules can also be combined into a single rule to accomplish a specific transformation. For example, depending on your query, predicates such as filter can be pushed down to reduce the overall number of rows before executing a join operation. In addition, if your query has an expression with constants in your query, then constant folding optimization computes the expression once at the time of compilation instead of repeating it for every row during runtime. Furthermore, if your query requires a subset of columns, then column pruning can help reduce the columns to the essential ones. All these rules can be combined into a single rule to achieve all three transformations.

In the following example, we measure the difference in execution times on Spark 1.6 and Spark 2.2. We use the iPinYou Real-Time Bidding Dataset for Computational Advertising Research in our next example. This Dataset contains the data from three seasons of the iPinYou global RTB bidding algorithm competition. You can download this Dataset from the data server at University College London at http://data.computational-advertising.org/.

First, we define the `case` classes for the records in the bid transactions and the region files:

```scala
scala> case class PinTrans(bidid: String, timestamp: String, ipinyouid:
String, useragent: String, IP: String, region: String, city: String,
adexchange: String, domain: String, url:String, urlid: String, slotid:
String, slotwidth: String, slotheight: String, slotvisibility: String,
slotformat: String, slotprice: String, creative: String, bidprice: String)

scala> case class PinRegion(region: String, regionName: String)
```

Next, we create the DataFrames from one of the bids files and the region file:

```scala
scala> val pintransDF =
spark.sparkContext.textFile("file:///Users/aurobindosarkar/Downloads/make-
ipinyou-data-master/original-
data/ipinyou.contest.dataset/training1st/bid.20130314.txt").map(_.split("\t
")).map(attributes => PinTrans(attributes(0).trim, attributes(1).trim,
attributes(2).trim, attributes(3).trim, attributes(4).trim,
attributes(5).trim, attributes(6).trim, attributes(7).trim,
attributes(8).trim, attributes(9).trim, attributes(10).trim,
attributes(11).trim, attributes(12).trim, attributes(13).trim,
attributes(14).trim, attributes(15).trim, attributes(16).trim,
attributes(17).trim, attributes(18).trim)).toDF()

scala> val pinregionDF =
spark.sparkContext.textFile("file:///Users/aurobindosarkar/Downloads/make-
ipinyou-data-master/original-
data/ipinyou.contest.dataset/region.en.txt").map(_.split("\t")).map(attribu
tes => PinRegion(attributes(0).trim, attributes(1).trim)).toDF()
```

Next, we borrow a simple benchmark function (available in several Databricks sample notebooks) to measure the execution time:

```scala
scala> def benchmark(name: String)(f: => Unit) {
 val startTime = System.nanoTime
 f
 val endTime = System.nanoTime
 println(s"Time taken in $name: " + (endTime - startTime).toDouble /
1000000000 + " seconds")
```

```
        }
```

We use the SparkSession object to set the whole-stage code generation parameter off (this roughly translates to the Spark 1.6 environment). We also measure the execution time for a `join` operation between the two DataFrames:

```
scala> spark.conf.set("spark.sql.codegen.wholeStage", false)
scala> benchmark("Spark 1.6") {
   |    pintransDF.join(pinregionDF, "region").count()
   |  }
Time taken in Spark 1.6: 3.742190552 seconds
```

Next, we set the whole-stage code generation parameter to true and measure the execution time. We note that the execution time is much lower for the same code in Spark 2.2:

```
scala> spark.conf.set("spark.sql.codegen.wholeStage", true)
scala> benchmark("Spark 2.2") {
   |    pintransDF.join(pinregionDF, "region").count()
   |  }
Time taken in Spark 2.2: 1.881881579 seconds
```

We use the `explain()` function to print out the various stages in the Catalyst transformations pipeline. We will explain the following output in more detail in Chapter 11, *Tuning Spark SQL Components for Performance*:

```
scala> pintransDF.join(pinregionDF,
"region").selectExpr("count(*)").explain(true)
```

```
== Parsed Logical Plan ==
'Project [unresolvedalias('count(1), Some(<function1>))]
+- Project [region#416, bidid#411, timestamp#412, ipinyouid#413,
useragent#414, IP#415, city#417, adexchange#418, domain#419, url#420,
urlid#421, slotid#422, slotwidth#423, slotheight#424, slotvisibility#425,
slotformat#426, slotprice#427, creative#428, bidprice#429, regionName#455]
   +- Join Inner, (region#416 = region#454)
      :- SerializeFromObject [staticinvoke(class
org.apache.spark.unsafe.types.UTF8String, StringType,
.
.
.
$line61.$read$$iw$$iw$PinTrans, true)).bidprice, true) AS bidprice#429]
      :   +- ExternalRDD [obj#410]
      +- SerializeFromObject [staticinvoke(class
org.apache.spark.unsafe.types.UTF8String, StringType, fromString,
assertnotnull(assertnotnull(input[0, $line62.$read$$iw$$iw$PinRegion,
true])).region, true) AS region#454, staticinvoke(class
org.apache.spark.unsafe.types.UTF8String, StringType, fromString,
assertnotnull(assertnotnull(input[0, $line62.$read$$iw$$iw$PinRegion,
true])).regionName, true) AS regionName#455]
         +- ExternalRDD [obj#453]
```

```
== Analyzed Logical Plan ==
count(1): bigint
Aggregate [count(1) AS count(1)#583L]
+- Project [region#416, bidid#411, timestamp#412, ipinyouid#413,
useragent#414, IP#415, city#417, adexchange#418, domain#419, url#420,
urlid#421, slotid#422, slotwidth#423, slotheight#424, slotvisibility#425,
slotformat#426, slotprice#427, creative#428, bidprice#429, regionName#455]
   +- Join Inner, (region#416 = region#454)
      :- SerializeFromObject [staticinvoke(class
org.apache.spark.unsafe.types.UTF8String, StringType,
.
.
.
$line61.$read$$iw$$iw$PinTrans, true])).bidprice, true) AS bidprice#429]
      :  +- ExternalRDD [obj#410]
      +- SerializeFromObject [staticinvoke(class
org.apache.spark.unsafe.types.UTF8String, StringType, fromString,
assertnotnull(assertnotnull(input[0, $line62.$read$$iw$$iw$PinRegion,
true])).region, true) AS region#454, staticinvoke(class
org.apache.spark.unsafe.types.UTF8String, StringType, fromString,
assertnotnull(assertnotnull(input[0, $line62.$read$$iw$$iw$PinRegion,
true])).regionName, true) AS regionName#455]
         +- ExternalRDD [obj#453]
```

```
== Optimized Logical Plan ==
Aggregate [count(1) AS count(1)#583L]
+- Project
   +- Join Inner, (region#416 = region#454)
      :- Project [region#416]
      :  +- Filter isnotnull(region#416)
      :     +- SerializeFromObject [staticinvoke(class
org.apache.spark.unsafe.types.UTF8String, StringType,
.
.
.
$line61.$read$$iw$$iw$PinTrans, true])).bidprice, true) AS bidprice#429]
      :           +- ExternalRDD [obj#410]
      +- Project [region#454]
         +- Filter isnotnull(region#454)
            +- SerializeFromObject [staticinvoke(class
org.apache.spark.unsafe.types.UTF8String, StringType, fromString,
assertnotnull(input[0, $line62.$read$$iw$$iw$PinRegion, true]).region, true)
AS region#454, staticinvoke(class org.apache.spark.unsafe.types.UTF8String,
StringType, fromString, assertnotnull(input[0,
$line62.$read$$iw$$iw$PinRegion, true]).regionName, true) AS regionName#455]
               +- ExternalRDD [obj#453]
```

```
== Physical Plan ==
*HashAggregate(keys=[], functions=[count(1)], output=[count(1)#583L])
+- Exchange SinglePartition
   +- *HashAggregate(keys=[], functions=[partial_count(1)],
output=[count#585L])
      +- *Project
         +- *SortMergeJoin [region#416], [region#454], Inner
            :- *Sort [region#416 ASC NULLS FIRST], false, 0
            :  +- Exchange hashpartitioning(region#416, 200)
            :     +- *Project [region#416]
            :        +- *Filter isnotnull(region#416)
            :           +- *SerializeFromObject [staticinvoke(class
org.apache.spark.unsafe.types.UTF8String, StringType,
.
.
.
$line61.$read$$iw$$iw$PinTrans, true]).bidprice, true) AS bidprice#429]
            :                 +- Scan ExternalRDDScan[obj#410]
            +- *Sort [region#454 ASC NULLS FIRST], false, 0
               +- Exchange hashpartitioning(region#454, 200)
                  +- *Project [region#454]
                     +- *Filter isnotnull(region#454)
                        +- *SerializeFromObject [staticinvoke(class
org.apache.spark.unsafe.types.UTF8String, StringType, fromString,
assertnotnull(input[0, $line62.$read$$iw$$iw$PinRegion, true]).region, true)
AS region#454, staticinvoke(class org.apache.spark.unsafe.types.UTF8String,
StringType, fromString, assertnotnull(input[0,
$line62.$read$$iw$$iw$PinRegion, true]).regionName, true) AS regionName#455]
                           +- Scan ExternalRDDScan[obj#453]
```

In the next section, we present developer-relevant details of Project Tungsten.

Introducing Project Tungsten

Project Tungsten was touted as the largest change to Spark's execution engine since the project's inception. The motivation for Project Tungsten was the observation that CPU and memory, rather than I/O and network, were the bottlenecks in a majority of Spark workloads.

The CPU is the bottleneck now because of the improvements in hardware (for example, SSDs and striped HDD arrays for storage), optimizations done to Spark's I/O (for example, shuffle and network layer implementations, input data pruning for disk I/O reduction, and so on) and improvements in data formats (for example, columnar formats like Parquet, binary data formats, and so on). In addition, large-scale serialization and hashing tasks in Spark are CPU-bound operations.

Spark 1.x used a query evaluation strategy based on an iterator model (referred to as the Volcano model). As each operator in a query presented an interface that returned a tuple at a time to the next operator in the tree, this interface allowed query execution engines to compose arbitrary combinations of operators. Before Spark 2.0, a majority of the CPU cycles were spent in useless work, such as making virtual function calls or reading/writing intermediate data to CPU cache or memory.

Project Tungsten focuses on three areas to improve the efficiency of memory and CPU to push the performance closer to the limits of the underlying hardware. These three areas are memory management and binary processing, cache-aware computation, and code generation. Additionally, the second generation Tungsten execution engine, integrated in Spark 2.0, uses a technique called whole-stage code generation. This technique enables the engine to eliminate virtual function dispatches and move intermediate data from memory to CPU registers, and exploits the modern CPU features through loop unrolling and SIMD. In addition, the Spark 2.0 engine also speeds up operations considered too complex for code generation by employing another technique, called vectorization.

Whole-stage code generation collapses the entire query into a single function. Further, it eliminates virtual function calls and uses CPU registers for storing intermediate data. This in turn, significantly improves CPU efficiency and runtime performance. It achieves the performance of hand-written code, while continuing to remain a general-purpose engine.

In vectorization, the engine batches multiple rows together in a columnar format and each operator iterates over the data within a batch. However, it still requires putting intermediate data in-memory rather than keeping them in CPU registers. As a result, vectorization is only used when it is not possible to do whole-stage code generation.

Tungsten memory management improvements focus on storing Java objects in compact binary format to reduce GC overhead, denser in-memory data format to reduce spillovers (for example, the Parquet format), and for operators that understand data types (in the case of DataFrames, Datasets, and SQL) to work directly against binary format in memory rather than serialization/deserialization and so on.

Code generation exploits modern compilers and CPUs for implementing improvements. These include faster expression evaluation and DataFrame/SQL operators, and a faster serializer. Generic evaluation of expressions is very expensive on the JVM, due to virtual function calls, branches based on expression type, object creation, and memory consumption due to primitive boxing. By generating custom bytecode on the fly, these overheads are largely eliminated.

Here, we present the Physical Plan for our join operation between the bids and the region DataFrames from the preceding section with whole-stage code generation enabled. In the `explain()` output, when an operator is marked with a star *, then it means that the whole-stage code generation is enabled for that operation. In the following physical plan, this includes the Aggregate, Project, `SortMergeJoin`, Filter, and Sort operators. Exchange, however, does not implement whole-stage code generation because it is sending data across the network:

```
scala> pintransDF.join(pinregionDF,
"region").selectExpr("count(*)").explain()
```

```
== Physical Plan ==
*HashAggregate(keys=[], functions=[count(1)])
+- Exchange SinglePartition
   +- *HashAggregate(keys=[], functions=[partial_count(1)])
      +- *Project
         +- *SortMergeJoin [region#416], [region#454], Inner
            :- *Sort [region#416 ASC NULLS FIRST], false, 0
            :  +- Exchange hashpartitioning(region#416, 200)
            :     +- *Project [region#416]
            :        +- *Filter isnotnull(region#416)
            :           +- *SerializeFromObject [staticinvoke(class
org.apache.spark.unsafe.types.UTF8String, StringType, fromString,
.
.
.
StringType, fromString, assertnotnull(input[0, $line61.$read$$iw$$iw$PinTrans,
true]).bidprice, true) AS bidprice#429]
            :              +- Scan ExternalRDDScan[obj#410]
            +- *Sort [region#454 ASC NULLS FIRST], false, 0
               +- Exchange hashpartitioning(region#454, 200)
                  +- *Project [region#454]
                     +- *Filter isnotnull(region#454)
                        +- *SerializeFromObject [staticinvoke(class
org.apache.spark.unsafe.types.UTF8String, StringType, fromString,
assertnotnull(input[0, $line62.$read$$iw$$iw$PinRegion, true]).region, true)
AS region#454, staticinvoke(class org.apache.spark.unsafe.types.UTF8String,
StringType, fromString, assertnotnull(input[0,
$line62.$read$$iw$$iw$PinRegion, true]).regionName, true) AS regionName#455]
                           +- Scan ExternalRDDScan[obj#453]
```

Project Tungsten hugely benefits DataFrames and Datasets (for all programming APIs--Java, Scala, Python, and R) and Spark SQL queries. Also, for many of the data processing operators, the new engine is orders of magnitude faster.

In the next section, we shift our focus to a new Spark 2.0 feature, called Structured Streaming, that supports Spark-based streaming applications.

Using Spark SQL in streaming applications

Streaming applications are getting increasingly complex, because such computations don't run in isolation. They need to interact with batch data, support interactive analysis, support sophisticated machine learning applications, and so on. Typically, such applications store incoming event stream(s) on long-term storage, continuously monitor events, and run machine learning models on the stored data, while simultaneously enabling continuous learning on the incoming stream. They also have the capability to interactively query the stored data while providing exactly-once write guarantees, handling late arriving data, performing aggregations, and so on. These types of applications are a lot more than mere streaming applications and have, therefore, been termed as continuous applications.

Before Spark 2.0, streaming applications were built on the concept of DStreams. There were several pain points associated with using DStreams. In DStreams, the timestamp was when the event actually came into the Spark system; the time embedded in the event was not taken into consideration. In addition, though the same engine can process both the batch and streaming computations, the APIs involved, though similar between RDDs (batch) and DStream (streaming), required the developer to make code changes. The DStream streaming model placed the burden on the developer to address various failure conditions, and it was hard to reason about data consistency issues. In Spark 2.0, Structured Streaming was introduced to deal with all of these pain points.

Structured Streaming is a fast, fault-tolerant, exactly-once stateful stream processing approach. It enables streaming analytics without having to reason about the underlying mechanics of streaming. In the new model, the input can be thought of as data from an append-only table (that grows continuously). A trigger specifies the time interval for checking the input for the arrival of new data. As shown in the following figure, the query represents the queries or the operations, such as map, filter, and reduce on the input, and result represents the final table that is updated in each trigger interval, as per the specified operation. The output defines the part of the result to be written to the data sink in each time interval.

The output modes can be complete, delta, or append, where the complete output mode means writing the full result table every time, the delta output mode writes the changed rows from the previous batch, and the append output mode writes the new rows only, respectively:

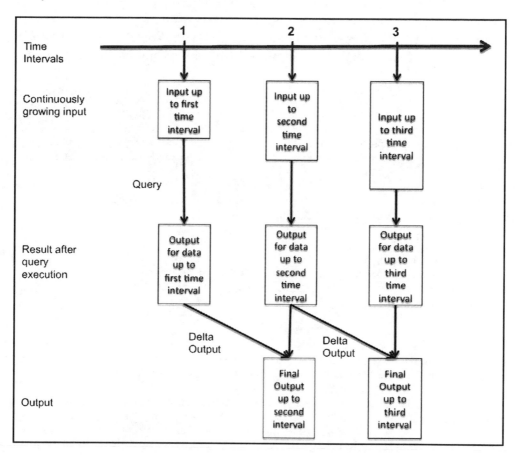

In Spark 2.0, in addition to the static bounded DataFrames, we have the concept of a continuous unbounded DataFrame. Both static and continuous DataFrames use the same API, thereby unifying streaming, interactive, and batch queries. For example, you can aggregate data in a stream and then serve it using JDBC. The high-level streaming API is built on the Spark SQL engine and is tightly integrated with SQL queries and the DataFrame/Dataset APIs. The primary benefit is that you use the same high-level Spark DataFrame and Dataset APIs, and the Spark engine figures out the incremental and continuous execution required for operations.

Additionally, there are query management APIs that you can use to manage multiple, concurrently running, and streaming queries. For instance, you can list running queries, stop and restart queries, retrieve exceptions in case of failures, and so on. We will get more details regarding Structured Streaming in Chapter 5, *Using Spark SQL in Streaming Applications*.

In the example code below, we use two bid files from the iPinYou Dataset as the source for our streaming data. First, we define our input records schema and create a streaming input DataFrame:

```scala
scala> import org.apache.spark.sql.types._
scala> import org.apache.spark.sql.functions._
scala> import scala.concurrent.duration._
scala> import org.apache.spark.sql.streaming.ProcessingTime
scala> import org.apache.spark.sql.streaming.OutputMode.Complete

scala> val bidSchema = new StructType().add("bidid",
StringType).add("timestamp", StringType).add("ipinyouid",
StringType).add("useragent", StringType).add("IP",
StringType).add("region", IntegerType).add("city",
IntegerType).add("adexchange", StringType).add("domain",
StringType).add("url:String", StringType).add("urlid: String",
StringType).add("slotid: String", StringType).add("slotwidth",
StringType).add("slotheight", StringType).add("slotvisibility",
StringType).add("slotformat", StringType).add("slotprice",
StringType).add("creative", StringType).add("bidprice", StringType)

scala> val streamingInputDF =
spark.readStream.format("csv").schema(bidSchema).option("header",
false).option("inferSchema", true).option("sep",
"\t").option("maxFilesPerTrigger",
1).load("file:///Users/aurobindosarkar/Downloads/make-ipinyou-data-
master/original-data/ipinyou.contest.dataset/bidfiles")
```

Next, we define our query with a time interval of 20 seconds and the output mode as Complete:

```scala
scala> val streamingCountsDF = streamingInputDF.groupBy($"city").count()

scala> val query =
streamingCountsDF.writeStream.format("console").trigger(ProcessingTime(20.s
econds)).queryName("counts").outputMode(Complete).start()
```

In the output, you will observe that the count of bids from each region gets updated in each time interval as new data arrives. You will need to drop new bid files (or start with multiple bid files, as they will get picked up for processing one at a time based on the value of maxFilesPerTrigger) from the original Dataset into the bidfiles directory to see the updated results:

```
-------------------------------------------
Batch: 0
-------------------------------------------
+----+-----+
|city|count|
+----+-----+
| 148|21104|
| 243| 3207|
|  31| 1386|
| 137|  564|
|  85|30907|
| 251|  933|
|  65| 8247|
|  53| 1244|
| 255|  618|
| 133| 1069|
| 296|  613|
| 322|  320|
|  78|  290|
| 362|   29|
| 321|  543|
| 375| 6125|
| 108| 5937|
| 155| 2927|
| 193| 1347|
| 211| 1453|
+----+-----+
only showing top 20 rows
```

```
-------------------------------------------
Batch: 1
-------------------------------------------
+----+-----+
|city|count|
+----+-----+
| 148|41789|
| 243| 6733|
|  31| 2844|
|  85|63244|
| 251| 1968|
| 137| 1163|
|  65|17408|
| 255| 1351|
|  53| 2433|
| 296| 1209|
| 133| 2190|
| 322|  648|
|  78|  604|
| 321| 1113|
| 362|   58|
| 375|11748|
| 108|12641|
| 155| 5982|
| 193| 2913|
|  34| 2707|
+----+-----+
only showing top 20 rows
```

Additionally, you can also query the system for active streams, as follows:

```
scala> spark.streams.active.foreach(println)
Streaming Query - counts [state = ACTIVE]
```

Finally, you can stop the execution of your streaming application using the `stop()` method, as shown:

```
//Execute the stop() function after you have finished executing the code in
the next section.
scala> query.stop()
```

In the next section, we conceptually describe how Structured Streaming works internally.

Understanding Structured Streaming internals

To enable the Structured Streaming functionality, the planner polls for new data from the sources and incrementally executes the computation on it before writing it to the sink. In addition, any running aggregates required by your application are maintained as in-memory states backed by a **Write-Ahead Log** (**WAL**). The in-memory state data is generated and used across incremental executions. The fault tolerance requirements for such applications include the ability to recover and replay all data and metadata in the system. The planner writes offsets to a fault-tolerant WAL on persistent storage, such as HDFS, before execution as illustrated in the figure:.

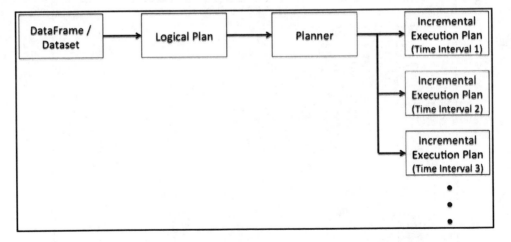

In case the planner fails on the current incremental execution, the restarted planner reads from the WAL and re-executes the exact range of offsets required. Typically, sources such as Kafka are also fault-tolerant and generate the original transactions data, given the appropriate offsets recovered by the planner. The state data is usually maintained in a versioned, key-value map in Spark workers and is backed by a WAL on HDFS. The planner ensures that the correct version of the state is used to re-execute the transactions subsequent to a failure. Additionally, the sinks are idempotent by design, and can handle the re-executions without double commits of the output. Hence, an overall combination of offset tracking in WAL, state management, and fault-tolerant sources and sinks provide the end-to-end exactly-once guarantees.

We can list the Physical Plan for our example of Structured Streaming using the `explain` method, as shown:

```scala
scala> spark.streams.active(0).explain
```

```
== Physical Plan ==
*HashAggregate(keys=[city#1033], functions=[count(1)])
+- StateStoreSave [city#1033],
OperatorStateId(/private/var/folders/tj/prwqrjj16jn4k5jh6g91rwtc0000gn/T/tempo
rary-570c0fdf-55ff-40cb-88eb-d00c01ed3f22/state,0,1), Complete, 0
   +- *HashAggregate(keys=[city#1033], functions=[merge_count(1)])
      +- StateStoreRestore [city#1033],
OperatorStateId(/private/var/folders/tj/prwqrjj16jn4k5jh6g91rwtc0000gn/T/tempo
rary-570c0fdf-55ff-40cb-88eb-d00c01ed3f22/state,0,1)
         +- *HashAggregate(keys=[city#1033], functions=[merge_count(1)])
            +- Exchange hashpartitioning(city#1033, 200)
               +- *HashAggregate(keys=[city#1033],
functions=[partial_count(1)])
                  +- *FileScan csv [city#1033] Batched: false, Format: CSV,
Location: InMemoryFileIndex[file:/Users/aurobindosarkar/Downloads/make-
ipinyou-data-master/original-data/ip..., PartitionFilters: [], PushedFilters:
[], ReadSchema: struct<city:int>
```

We will explain the preceding output in more detail in Chapter 11, *Tuning Spark SQL Components for Performance*.

Summary

In this chapter, we introduced you to Spark SQL, SparkSession (primary entry point to Spark SQL), and Spark SQL interfaces (RDDs, DataFrames, and Dataset). We then described some of the internals of Spark SQL, including the Catalyst and Project Tungsten-based optimizations. Finally, we explored how to use Spark SQL in streaming applications and the concept of Structured Streaming. The primary goal of this chapter was to give you an overview of Spark SQL while getting you comfortable with the Spark environment through hands-on sessions (using public Datasets).

In the next chapter, we will get into the details of using Spark SQL to explore structured and semi-structured data typical to big data applications.

2

Using Spark SQL for Processing Structured and Semistructured Data

In this chapter, we will familiarize you with using Spark SQL with different types of data sources and data storage formats. Spark provides easy and standard structures (that is, RDDs and DataFrames/Datasets) to work with both structured and semistructured data. We include some of the data sources that are most commonly used in big data applications, such as, relational data, NoSQL databases, and files (CSV, JSON, Parquet, and Avro). Spark also allows you to define and use custom data sources. A series of hands-on exercises in this chapter will enable you to use Spark with different types of data sources and data formats.

In this chapter, you shall learn the following topics:

- Understanding data sources in Spark applications
- Using JDBC to work with relational databases
- Using Spark with MongoDB (NoSQL database)
- Working with JSON data
- Using Spark with Avro and Parquet Datasets

Understanding data sources in Spark applications

Spark can connect to many different data sources, including files, and SQL and NoSQL databases. Some of the more popular data sources include files (CSV, JSON, Parquet, AVRO), MySQL, MongoDB, HBase, and Cassandra.

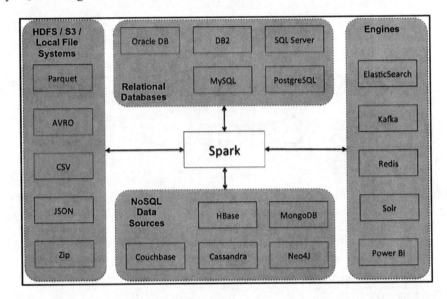

In addition, it can also connect to special purpose engines and data sources, such as ElasticSearch, Apache Kafka, and Redis. These engines enable specific functionality in Spark applications such as search, streaming, caching, and so on. For example, Redis enables deployment of cached machine learning models in high performance applications. We discuss more on Redis-based application deployment in Chapter 12, *Spark SQL in Large-Scale Application Architectures*. Kafka is extremely popular in Spark streaming applications, and we will cover more details on Kafka-based streaming applications in Chapter 5, *Using Spark SQL in Streaming Applications*, and Chapter 12, *Spark SQL in Large-Scale Application Architectures*. The DataSource API enables Spark connectivity to a wide variety of data sources including custom data sources.

 Refer to the Spark packages website https://spark-packages.org/ to work with various data sources, algorithms, and specialized Datasets.

In Chapter 1, *Getting Started with Spark SQL,* we used CSV and JSON files on our filesystem as input data sources and used SQL to query them. However, using Spark SQL to query data residing in files is not a replacement for using databases. Initially, some people used HDFS as a data source because of the simplicity and the ease of using Spark SQL for querying such data. However, the execution performance can vary significantly based on the queries being executed and the nature of the workloads. Architects and developers need to understand which data stores to use in order to best meet their processing requirements. We discuss some high-level considerations for selecting Spark data sources below.

Selecting Spark data sources

Filesystems are a great place to dump large volumes of data and for supporting general purpose processing of large Datasets. Some of the benefits you will get by using files are inexpensive storage, flexible processing, and scale. The decision to store large-scale data in files is usually driven by the prohibitive costs of storing the same on commercial databases. Additionally, file storage is also preferred when the nature of the data does not benefit from typical database optimizations, for example, unstructured data. Additionally, workloads, such as machine learning applications, with iterative in-memory processing requirements and distributed algorithms may be better suited to run on distributed file systems.

The types of data you would typically store on filesystems are archival data, unstructured data, massive social media and other web-scale Datasets, and backup copies of primary data stores. The types of workloads best supported on files are batch workloads, exploratory data analysis, multistage processing pipelines, and iterative workloads. Popular use cases for using files include ETL pipelines, splicing data across varied data sources, such as log files, CSV, Parquet, zipped file formats, and so on. In addition, you can choose to store the same data in multiple formats optimized for your specific processing requirements.

What's not so great about Spark connected to a filesystem are use cases involving frequent random accesses, frequent inserts, frequent/incremental updates, and reporting or search operations under heavy load conditions across many users. These use cases are discussed in more detail as we move on.

Queries selecting a small subset of records from your distributed storage are supported in Spark but are not very efficient, because it would typically require Spark to go through all your files to find your result row(s). This may be acceptable for data exploration tasks but not for sustained processing loads from several concurrent users. If you need to frequently and randomly access your data, using a database can be a more effective solution. Making the data available to your users using a traditional SQL database and creating indexes on the key columns can better support this use case. Alternatively, key-value NoSQL stores can also retrieve the value of a key a lot more efficiently.

As each insert creates a new file, the inserts are reasonably fast however querying becomes low as the Spark jobs will need to open all these files and read from them to support queries. Again, a database used to support frequent inserts may be a much better solution. Alternatively, you can also routinely compact your Spark SQL table files to reduce the overall number of files. Use the `Select *` and `coalesce` DataFrame commands to write the data out from a DataFrame created from multiple input files to a single / combined output file.

Other operations and use cases, such as frequent/incremental updates, reporting, and searching are better handled using databases or specialized engines. Files are not optimized for updating random rows. However, databases are ideal for executing efficient update operations. You can connect Spark to HDFS and use BI tools, such as Tableau, but it is better to dump the data to a database for serving concurrent users under load. Typically, it is better to use Spark to read the data, perform aggregations, and so on, and then write the results out to a database that serves end users. In the search use case, Spark will need to go through each row to find and return the search results, thereby impacting performance. In this case, using the specialized engines such as ElasticSearch and Apache Solr may be a better solution than using Spark.

In cases where the data is heavily skewed, or for executing faster joins on a cluster, we can use cluster by or bucketing techniques to improve performance.

Using Spark with relational databases

There is a huge debate on whether relational databases fit into big data processing scenarios. However, it's undeniable that vast quantities of structured data in enterprises live in such databases, and organizations rely heavily on the existing RDBMSs for their critical business transactions.

A vast majority of developers are most comfortable working with relational databases and the rich set of tools available from leading vendors. Increasingly, cloud service providers, such as Amazon AWS, have made administration, replication, and scaling simple enough for many organizations to transition their large relational databases to the cloud.

Some good big data use cases for relational databases include the following:

- Complex OLTP transactions
- Applications or features that need ACID compliance
- Support for standard SQL
- Real-time ad hoc query functionality
- Systems implementing many complex relationships

 For an excellent coverage of NoSQL and relational use cases, refer to the blog titled **What the heck are you actually using NoSQL for?** at `http://highscalability.com/blog/2010/12/6/what-the-heck-are-you-actually-using-nosql-for.html`.

In Spark, it is easy to work with relational data and combine it with other data sources in different forms and formats:

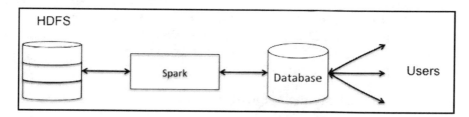

As an example that illustrates using Spark with a MySQL database, we will implement a use-case in which we split the data between HDFS and MySQL. The MySQL database will be targeted to support interactive queries from concurrent users, while the data on HDFS will be targeted for batch processing, running machine learning applications, and for making the data available to BI tools. In this example, we assume that the interactive queries are against the current month's data only. Hence, we will retain only the current month's data in MySQL and write out the rest of data to HDFS (in JSON format).

The implementation steps, we will follow are:

1. Create MySQL database.
2. Define a table.
3. Create a user ID and grant privileges.

4. Start Spark shell with MySQL JDBC driver.

5. Create a RDD from input data file, separate the header, define a schema, and create a DataFrame.

6. Create a new column for timestamps.

7. Separate the data into two DataFrames based on the timestamp value (data for the current month and rest of data previous months).

8. Drop the original invoiceDate column and then rename the timestamp column to invoiceDate.

9. Write out the DataFrame containing current month data to the MySQL table.

10. Write out the DataFrame containing data (other than current month data) to HDFS (in JSON format).

 If you do not have MySQL already installed and available, you can download it from `https://www.mysql.com/downloads/`. Follow the installation instructions for your specific OS to install the database. Also, download the JDBC connector available on the same website.

After you have your MySQL database server up and running, fire up the MySQL shell. In the following steps, we will create a new database and define a transactions table. We use a transnational dataset that contains all the transactions occurring between 01/12/2010 and 09/12/2011 for a UK-based and registered nonstore online retail. The dataset has been contributed by Dr Daqing Chen, Director: Public Analytics group, School of Engineering, London South Bank University and is available at `https://archive.ics.uci.edu/ml/datasets/Online+Retail`.

You should see a screen similar to the following when you start the MySQL shell:

```
Aurobindos-MacBook-Pro-2:Downloadsaurobindosarkar$ mysql -u root -p
Enter password:
Welcome to the MySQL monitor.  Commands end with ; or \g.
Your MySQL connection id is 7
Server version: 5.6.27 Homebrew

Copyright (c) 2000, 2015, Oracle and/or its affiliates. All rights reserved.

Oracle is a registered trademark of Oracle Corporation and/or its
affiliates. Other names may be trademarks of their respective
owners.

Type 'help;' or '\h' for help. Type '\c' to clear the current input statement.

mysql>
```

1. Create a new database called `retailDB` to store our customer transactions data:

```
mysql> create database retailDB;
Connect to retailDB as follows:
mysql> use retailDB;
```

2. Here, we define a transactions table with `transactionID` as the primary key. In a production scenario, you would also create indexes on other fields, such as `CustomerID`, to support queries more efficiently:

```
mysql>create table transactions(transactionID integer not null
auto_increment, invoiceNovarchar(20), stockCodevarchar(20),
description varchar(255), quantity integer, unitPrice double,
customerIDvarchar(20), country varchar(100), invoiceDate
Timestamp, primary key(transactionID));
```

Next, we verify the transactions table schema using the `describe` command to ensure that it is exactly how we want it:

```
mysql> describe transactions;
```

```
+---------------+--------------+------+-----+-------------------+-----------------------------+
| Field         | Type         | Null | Key | Default           | Extra                       |
+---------------+--------------+------+-----+-------------------+-----------------------------+
| transactionID | int(11)      | NO   | PRI | NULL              | auto_increment              |
| invoiceNo     | varchar(20)  | YES  |     | NULL              |                             |
| stockCode     | varchar(20)  | YES  |     | NULL              |                             |
| description   | varchar(255) | YES  |     | NULL              |                             |
| quantity      | int(11)      | YES  |     | NULL              |                             |
| unitPrice     | double       | YES  |     | NULL              |                             |
| customerID    | varchar(20)  | YES  |     | NULL              |                             |
| country       | varchar(100) | YES  |     | NULL              |                             |
| invoiceDate   | timestamp    | NO   |     | CURRENT_TIMESTAMP | on update CURRENT_TIMESTAMP |
+---------------+--------------+------+-----+-------------------+-----------------------------+
9 rows in set (0.01 sec)
```

3. Create a user ID `retaildbuser` and grant all privileges to it. We will use this user from our Spark shell for connecting and executing our queries.

```
mysql> CREATE USER 'retaildbuser'@'localhost' IDENTIFIED BY
       'mypass';
mysql> GRANT ALL ON retailDB.* TO 'retaildbuser'@'localhost';
```

4. Start the Spark shell with the classpath containing the path to the MySQL JDBC driver, as follows:

```
SPARK_CLASSPATH=/Users/aurobindosarkar/Downloads/mysql-connector-
java-5.1.38/mysql-connector-java-5.1.38-bin.jar bin/spark-shell
```

5. Create a RDD containing all the rows from our downloaded Dataset:

```
scala> import org.apache.spark.sql.types._
scala> import org.apache.spark.sql.Row
scala> import java.util.Properties

scala>val inFileRDD =
sc.textFile("file:///Users/aurobindosarkar/Downloads/UCI Online
Retail.txt")
```

6. Separate the header from the rest of the data:

```
scala>val allRowsRDD = inFileRDD.map(line
=>line.split("\t").map(_.trim))
scala>val header = allRowsRDD.first
scala>val data = allRowsRDD.filter(_(0) != header(0))
```

7. Define the fields and define a schema for our data records, as follows:

```
scala>val fields = Seq(
| StructField("invoiceNo", StringType, true),
| StructField("stockCode", StringType, true),
| StructField("description", StringType, true),
| StructField("quantity", IntegerType, true),
| StructField("invoiceDate", StringType, true),
| StructField("unitPrice", DoubleType, true),
| StructField("customerID", StringType, true),
| StructField("country", StringType, true)
| )
scala>val schema = StructType(fields)
```

8. Create an RDD of Row objects, create a DataFrame using the previously created schema:

```
scala>val rowRDD = data.map(attributes => Row(attributes(0),
attributes(1), attributes(2), attributes(3).toInt, attributes(4),
attributes(5).toDouble, attributes(6), attributes(7)))

scala>val r1DF = spark.createDataFrame(rowRDD, schema)
```

9. Add a column called `ts` (a timestamp column) to the DataFrame, as follows:

```scala
scala>val ts =
unix_timestamp($"invoiceDate","dd/MM/yyHH:mm").cast("timestamp")
scala>val r2DF = r1DF.withColumn("ts", ts)
scala>r2DF.show()
```

```
|invoiceNo|stockCode|     description|quantity|  invoiceDate|unitPrice|customerID|        country|              ts|
+---------+---------+----------------+--------+-------------+---------+----------+---------------+----------------+
|   536365|   85123A|WHITE HANGING HEA...|       6|01/12/10 8:26|     2.55|     17850|United Kingdom|2010-12-01 08:26:...|
|   536365|    71053| WHITE METAL LANTERN|       6|01/12/10 8:26|     3.39|     17850|United Kingdom|2010-12-01 08:26:...|
|   536365|   84406B|CREAM CUPID HEART...|       8|01/12/10 8:26|     2.75|     17850|United Kingdom|2010-12-01 08:26:...|
|   536365|   84029G|KNITTED UNION FLA...|       6|01/12/10 8:26|     3.39|     17850|United Kingdom|2010-12-01 08:26:...|
|   536365|   84029E|RED WOOLLY HOTTIE...|       6|01/12/10 8:26|     3.39|     17850|United Kingdom|2010-12-01 08:26:...|
|   536365|    22752|SET 7 BABUSHKA NE...|       2|01/12/10 8:26|     7.65|     17850|United Kingdom|2010-12-01 08:26:...|
|   536365|    21730|GLASS STAR FROSTE...|       6|01/12/10 8:26|     4.25|     17850|United Kingdom|2010-12-01 08:26:...|
|   536366|    22633|HAND WARMER UNION...|       6|01/12/10 8:28|     1.85|     17850|United Kingdom|2010-12-01 08:28:...|
|   536366|    22632|HAND WARMER RED P...|       6|01/12/10 8:28|     1.85|     17850|United Kingdom|2010-12-01 08:28:...|
|   536367|    84879|ASSORTED COLOUR B...|      32|01/12/10 8:34|     1.69|     13047|United Kingdom|2010-12-01 08:34:...|
|   536367|    22745|POPPY'S PLAYHOUSE...|       6|01/12/10 8:34|      2.1|     13047|United Kingdom|2010-12-01 08:34:...|
|   536367|    22748|POPPY'S PLAYHOUSE...|       6|01/12/10 8:34|      2.1|     13047|United Kingdom|2010-12-01 08:34:...|
|   536367|    22749|FELTCRAFT PRINCES...|       8|01/12/10 8:34|     3.75|     13047|United Kingdom|2010-12-01 08:34:...|
|   536367|    22310|IVORY KNITTED MUG...|       6|01/12/10 8:34|     1.65|     13047|United Kingdom|2010-12-01 08:34:...|
|   536367|    84969|BOX OF 6 ASSORTED...|       6|01/12/10 8:34|     4.25|     13047|United Kingdom|2010-12-01 08:34:...|
|   536367|    22623|BOX OF VINTAGE JI...|       3|01/12/10 8:34|     4.95|     13047|United Kingdom|2010-12-01 08:34:...|
|   536367|    22622|BOX OF VINTAGE AL...|       2|01/12/10 8:34|     9.95|     13047|United Kingdom|2010-12-01 08:34:...|
|   536367|    21754|HOME BUILDING BLO...|       3|01/12/10 8:34|     5.95|     13047|United Kingdom|2010-12-01 08:34:...|
|   536367|    21755|LOVE BUILDING BLO...|       3|01/12/10 8:34|     5.95|     13047|United Kingdom|2010-12-01 08:34:...|
|   536367|    21777|RECIPE BOX WITH M...|       4|01/12/10 8:34|     7.95|     13047|United Kingdom|2010-12-01 08:34:...|
+---------+---------+----------------+--------+-------------+---------+----------+---------------+----------------+
only showing top 20 rows
```

10. Create a table object and execute appropriate SQLs to separate the table data into two DataFrames based on the timestamps:

```scala
scala> r2DF.createOrReplaceTempView("retailTable")
scala>val r3DF = spark.sql("select * from retailTable where ts<
'2011-12-01'")
scala>val r4DF = spark.sql("select * from retailTable where ts>=
'2011-12-01'")
```

11. Drop the `invoiceDate` column in our new DataFrame.

```scala
scala>val selectData = r4DF.select("invoiceNo", "stockCode",
"description", "quantity", "unitPrice", "customerID", "country",
"ts")
```

12. Rename the `ts` column to `invoiceDate`, as follows:

```
scala>val writeData = selectData.withColumnRenamed("ts",
"invoiceDate")
scala>writeData.show()
```

```
scala>writeData.show()
+---------+---------+--------------------+--------+---------+----------+--------------+--------------------+
|invoiceNo|stockCode|         description|quantity|unitPrice|customerID|       country|         invoiceDate|
+---------+---------+--------------------+--------+---------+----------+--------------+--------------------+
|  C579889|    23245|SET OF 3 REGENCY ...|      -8|     4.15|     13853|United Kingdom|2011-12-01 08:12:...|
|  C579890|    84947|ANTIQUE SILVER TE...|      -1|     1.25|     15197|United Kingdom|2011-12-01 08:14:...|
|  C579890|    23374|RED SPOT PAPER GI...|      -1|     0.82|     15197|United Kingdom|2011-12-01 08:14:...|
|  C579890|    84945|MULTI COLOUR SILV...|      -2|     0.85|     15197|United Kingdom|2011-12-01 08:14:...|
|  C579891|    23485|BOTANICAL GARDENS...|      -1|     25.0|     13644|United Kingdom|2011-12-01 08:18:...|
|  C579891|    23186|FRENCH STYLE STOR...|      -6|     0.29|     13644|United Kingdom|2011-12-01 08:18:...|
|  C579892|    23461|SWEETHEART BIRD H...|      -4|     4.15|     13310|United Kingdom|2011-12-01 08:23:...|
|  C579893|    37449|CERAMIC CAKE STAN...|      -2|     9.95|     13468|United Kingdom|2011-12-01 08:25:...|
|  C579894|    23012|GLASS APOTHECARY ...|      -1|     3.95|     13098|United Kingdom|2011-12-01 08:26:...|
|  C579894|    23568|EGG CUP HENRIETTA...|      -1|     1.25|     13098|United Kingdom|2011-12-01 08:26:...|
|  C579894|    23319|BOX OF 6 MINI 50'...|      -6|     2.08|     13098|United Kingdom|2011-12-01 08:26:...|
|  C579895|    23374|RED SPOT PAPER GI...|      -5|     0.82|     14329|United Kingdom|2011-12-01 08:27:...|
|  C579896|    23456|MEDIUM PARLOUR PI...|      -2|     4.15|     13971|United Kingdom|2011-12-01 08:27:...|
|  C579897|    23382|BOX OF 6 CHRISTMA...|      -2|     3.75|     17636|United Kingdom|2011-12-01 08:29:...|
|  C579897|    23256|CHILDRENS CUTLERY...|      -1|     4.15|     17636|United Kingdom|2011-12-01 08:29:...|
|  C579897|    23203|JUMBO BAG VINTAGE...|      -1|     2.08|     17636|United Kingdom|2011-12-01 08:29:...|
|  C579897|    22470|HEART OF WICKER L...|      -2|     2.95|     17636|United Kingdom|2011-12-01 08:29:...|
|  C579898|    22153|ANGEL DECORATION ...|      -1|     0.42|     14299|United Kingdom|2011-12-01 08:32:...|
|  C579898|    22969|HOMEMADE JAM SCEN...|      -1|     1.45|     14299|United Kingdom|2011-12-01 08:32:...|
|   579899|    23301|GARDENERS KNEELIN...|      24|     1.65|     15687|United Kingdom|2011-12-01 08:33:...|
+---------+---------+--------------------+--------+---------+----------+--------------+--------------------+
only showing top 20 rows
```

13. Create a variable to point to the database URL. Additionally, create a `Properties` object to hold the user ID and password required for connecting to `retailDB`. Next, connect to the MySQL database and insert the records from the "current month" into the transactions table:

```
scala>val dbUrl = "jdbc:mysql://localhost:3306/retailDB"
scala>val prop = new Properties()
scala>prop.setProperty("user", "retaildbuser")
scala>prop.setProperty("password", "mypass")
scala>writeData.write.mode("append").jdbc(dbUrl, "transactions",
prop)
```

14. Select the columns of interest from the DataFrame (containing data other than for the current month), and write them out to the HDFS filesystem in JSON format:

```
scala>val selectData = r3DF.select("invoiceNo", "stockCode",
"description", "quantity", "unitPrice", "customerID", "country",
"ts")

scala>val writeData = selectData.withColumnRenamed("ts",
"invoiceDate")
scala>writeData.select("*").write.format("json")
.save("hdfs://localhost:9000/Users/r3DF")
```

Using Spark with MongoDB (NoSQL database)

In this section, we will use Spark with one of the most popular NoSQL databases - MongoDB. MongoDB is a distributed document database that stores data in JSON-like format. Unlike the rigid schemas in relational databases, the data structure in MongoDB is a lot more flexible and the stored documents can have arbitrary fields. This flexibility combined with high availability and scalability features make it a good choice for storing data in many applications. It is also free and open-source software.

 If you do not have MongoDB already installed and available, then you can download it from `https://www.mongodb.org/downloads`. Follow the installation instructions for your specific OS to install the database.

The New York City schools directory dataset for this example has been taken from the New York City Open Data website and can be downloaded from `https://nycplatform.socrata.com/data?browseSearch=scope=agency=cat=educationtype=datasets`.

After you have your MongoDB database server up and running, fire up the MongoDB shell. In the following steps, we will create a new database, define a collection, and insert New York City school's data using the MongoDB import utility from the command line.

You should see a screen similar to the following when you start the MongoDB shell:

```
Aurobindos-MacBook-Pro-2:Downloadsaurobindosarkar$ mongo
MongoDB shell version: 3.2.0
connecting to: test
Welcome to the MongoDB shell.
For interactive help, type "help".
For more comprehensive documentation, see
        http://docs.mongodb.org/
Questions? Try the support group
        http://groups.google.com/group/mongodb-user
Server has startup warnings:
2015-12-27T17:40:17.264+0530 I CONTROL  [initandlisten]
2015-12-27T17:40:17.264+0530 I CONTROL  [initandlisten] ** WARNING: soft rlimits too low. Number of files is
256, should be at least 1000
>
```

Next, execute the use `<DATABASE>` command to select an existing database or create a new one, if it does not exist.

If you make a mistake while creating a new collection, you can use the `db.dropDatabase()` and/or `db.collection.drop()` commands to delete the dababase and/or the collection, respectively, and then recreate it with the required changes.

```
>use nycschoolsDB
switched to dbnycschoolsDB
```

The `mongoimport` utility needs to be executed from the command prompt (and not in the `mongodb` shell):

```
mongoimport --host localhost --port 27017 --username <your user name here>
--password "<your password here>" --collection schools --db nycschoolsDB --
file <your download file name here>
```

You can list the imported collection and print a record to validate the import operation, as follows:

```
>show collections
 schools
 >db.schools.findOne()
```

```
{
    "_id" : ObjectId("57f9e1598a793a2f1013dfed"),
    "dbn" : "17K548",
    "school_name" : "Brooklyn School for Music & Theatre",
    "boro" : "Brooklyn",
    "building_code" : "K440",
    "phone_number" : "718-230-6250",
    "fax_number" : "718-230-6262",
    "grade_span_min" : 9,
    "grade_span_max" : 12,
    "expgrade_span_min" : "",
    "expgrade_span_max" : "",
    "bus" : "B41, B43, B44-SBS, B45, B48, B49, B69",
    "subway" : "2, 3, 4, 5, F, S to Botanic Garden ; B, Q to Prospect Park",
    "primary_address_line_1" : "883 Classon Avenue",
    "city" : "Brooklyn",
    "state_code" : "NY",
    "zip" : 11225,
    "website" : "Bkmusicntheatre.com",
    "total_students" : 399,
    "campus_name" : "Prospect Heights Educational Campus",
     "school_type" : "",
```

```
"overview_paragraph" : "Brooklyn School for Music & Theatre (BSMT) uses our
academic program to accommodate the intellectual, social, emotional and
physical needs of creative high school students. Our vision is to provide a
model professional environment where respect is mutual, ideas are shared and
learning is not limited to the classroom. We prepare students for higher
education and professional careers in the music and theatre industries.",
    "program_highlights" : "We offer highly competitive positions in our
Drama, Chorus and Dance Company wherein students receive small group
instruction focused on sharpening and furthering their skills while developing
their professional portfolio for auditions in their chosen field.",
    "language_classes" : "Spanish",
    "advancedplacement_courses" : "English Language and Composition, United
States History",
    "online_ap_courses" : "",
    "online_language_courses" : "",
    "extracurricular_activities" : "Variety of clubs: Chess, The Step Team,
Fashion, Tech Team, Women's Group; Extensive arts after-school program: Dance
Company, Drama Company and Chorus Company, back stage crew program that trains
students in running the lights, sound, video and all back stage and pit crew
responsibilities; Saturday and After-school classes for Regents Preparation;
School Leadership Team; Student Government; at least three annual major
school-wide productions; two annual talent shows",
    "psal_sports_boys" : "Baseball, Basketball & JV Basketball, Cross
Country, Indoor Track, Outdoor Track, Soccer, Volleyball",
    "psal_sports_girls" : "Basketball, Cross Country, Indoor Track, Outdoor
Track, Soccer, Softball",
    "psal_sports_coed" : "",
    "school_sports" : "",
```

```
"partner_cbo" : "F.Y.R.EZONE (Finding Your Rhythm thru Education) is an
entertainment company built on high academic expectations and is committed to
meaningful learning. We are vested in the "whole" child. Our engaging teaching
and effective programs will be challenged and guided to academic success.
FYREZONE is committed to enhancing self-esteem, self awareness, preventing
drop-out, and most importantly instilling a confidence that can take them
through their Junior High, High School, college years.",
    "partner_hospital" : "",
    "partner_highered" : "",
    "partner_cultural" : "In 2002, Roundabout Theatre was selected by New
York City Department of Education to help design, develop, and operate
Brooklyn School for Music and Theatre. Since the school's development,
Roundabout has provided year-long programs connecting the process of theatre
production to project-based learning objectives and curriculum standards.
Step-in-School Inc is an enrichment programs that works to teach Step, aligned
with all of its historic, artistic and physio-educational components.
Additionally, Step-in-School works to connect the developmental assets of this
art form to college preparatory services and youth professional
developmental.",
    "partner_nonprofit" : "One To World's Global Classroom connects New York
City youth with trained, international university scholars through interactive
workshops that engage students in learning about world cultures and global
issues. Through face-to-face interactions and meaningful cross-cultural
exchange with international leaders of tomorrow, today's New York City K-12
students develop the skills, awareness and understanding to become global
citizens in their communities, both locally and worldwide.",
```

```
"partner_corporate" : "",
    "partner_financial" : "",
    "partner_other" : "",
    "addtl_info1" : "",
    "addtl_info2" : "",
    "start_time" : "8:10 AM",
    "end_time" : "3:00 PM",
    "se_services" : "This school will provide students with disabilities the
supports and services indicated on their IEPs.",
    "ell_programs" : "ESL",
    "school_accessibility_description" : "Functionally Accessible",
    "number_programs" : 1,
    "priority01" : "Priority to Brooklyn students or residents",
    "priority02" : "Then to New York City residents",
    "priority03" : "",
    "priority04" : "",
    "priority05" : "",
    "priority06" : "",
    "priority07" : "",
    "priority08" : "",
    "priority09" : "",
    "priority10" : "",
    "Location 1" : "883 Classon Avenue\nBrooklyn, NY
11225\n(40.67029890700047, -73.96164787599963)"
}
```

You can download the `mongo-spark-connector` jar for Spark 2.2 (`mongo-spark-connector_2.11-2.2.0-assembly.jar`) from `http://repo1.maven.org/maven2/org/mongodb/spark/mongo-spark-connector_2.11/2.2.0/`.

Next, start the Spark shell with the `mongo-spark-connector_2.11-2.2.0-assembly.jar` file specified on the command line:

```
./bin/spark-shell --jars /Users/aurobindosarkar/Downloads/mongo-spark-
connector_2.11-2.2.0-assembly.jar
scala> import org.apache.spark.sql.SQLContext
scala> import org.apache.spark.{SparkConf, SparkContext}
scala> import com.mongodb.spark.MongoSpark
scala> import com.mongodb.spark.config.{ReadConfig, WriteConfig}
```

Next, we define the URIs for `read` and `write` operations from Spark:

```
scala>val readConfig = ReadConfig(Map("uri" ->
"mongodb://localhost:27017/nycschoolsDB.schools?readPreference=primaryPrefe
rred"))

scala>val writeConfig = WriteConfig(Map("uri" ->
"mongodb://localhost:27017/nycschoolsDB.outCollection"))
```

Define a `case` class for the school record, as follows:

```scala
scala> case class School(dbn: String, school_name: String, boro: String,
building_code: String, phone_number: String, fax_number: String,
grade_span_min: String, grade_span_max: String, expgrade_span_min: String,
expgrade_span_max: String, bus: String, subway: String,
primary_address_line_1: String, city: String, state_code: String, zip: String,
website: String, total_students: String, campus_name: String, school_type:
String, overview_paragraph: String, program_highlights: String,
language_classes: String, advancedplacement_courses: String,
online_ap_courses: String, online_language_courses: String,
extracurricular_activities: String, psal_sports_boys: String,
psal_sports_girls: String, psal_sports_coed: String, school_sports: String,
partner_cbo: String, partner_hospital: String, partner_highered: String,
partner_cultural: String, partner_nonprofit: String, partner_corporate:
String, partner_financial: String, partner_other: String, addtl_info1: String,
addtl_info2: String, start_time: String, end_time: String, se_services:
String, ell_programs: String, school_accessibility_description: String,
number_programs: String, priority01: String, priority02: String, priority03:
String, priority04: String, priority05: String, priority06: String,
priority07: String, priority08: String, priority09: String, priority10:
String, Location_1: String)
```

Next, you can create a DataFrame from our collection and display a record from our newly created DataFrame.

```scala
scala>val schoolsDF = MongoSpark.load(sc, readConfig).toDF[School]

scala>schoolsDF.take(1).foreach(println)
```

```
[17K548,Brooklyn School for Music & Theatre,Brooklyn,K440,718-230-6250,718-
230-6262,9,12,,,B41, B43, B44-SBS, B45, B48, B49, B69,2, 3, 4, 5, F, S to
Botanic Garden ; B, Q to Prospect Park,883 Classon
Avenue,Brooklyn,NY,11225,Bkmusicntheatre.com,399,Prospect Heights Educational
Campus,,Brooklyn School for Music & Theatre (BSMT) uses our academic program
to accommodate the intellectual, social, emotional and physical needs of
creative high school students. Our vision is to provide a model professional
environment where respect is mutual, ideas are shared and learning is not
limited to the classroom. We prepare students for higher education and
professional careers in the music and theatre industries.,We offer highly
competitive positions in our Drama, Chorus and Dance Company wherein students
receive small group instruction focused on sharpening and furthering their
skills while developing their professional portfolio for auditions in their
chosen field.,Spanish,English Language and Composition, United States
History,,,Variety of clubs: Chess, The Step Team, Fashion, Tech Team, Women's
Group; Extensive arts after-school program: Dance Company, Drama Company and
Chorus Company, back stage crew program that trains students in running the
lights, sound, video and all back stage and pit crew responsibilities;
Saturday and After-school classes for Regents Preparation;
```

```
School Leadership Team; Student Government; at least three annual major
school-wide productions; two annual talent shows,Baseball, Basketball & JV
Basketball, Cross Country, Indoor Track, Outdoor Track, Soccer,
Volleyball,Basketball, Cross Country, Indoor Track, Outdoor Track, Soccer,
Softball,,,F.Y.R.EZONE (Finding Your Rhythm thru Education) is an
entertainment company built on high academic expectations and is committed to
meaningful learning. We are vested in the "whole" child. Our engaging teaching
and effective programs will be challenged and guided to academic success.
FYREZONE is committed to enhancing self-esteem, self awareness, preventing
drop-out, and most importantly instilling a confidence that can take them
through their Junior High, High School, college years.,,,In 2002, Roundabout
Theatre was selected by New York City Department of Education to help design,
develop, and operate Brooklyn School for Music and Theatre. Since the school's
development, Roundabout has provided year-long programs connecting the process
of theatre production to project-based learning objectives and curriculum
standards. Step-in-School Inc is an enrichment programs that works to teach
Step, aligned with all of its historic, artistic and physio-educational
components. Additionally, Step-in-School works to connect the developmental
assets of this art form to college preparatory services and youth professional
developmental.,One To World's Global Classroom connects New York City youth
with trained, international university scholars through interactive workshops
that engage students in learning about world cultures and global issues.
Through face-to-face interactions and meaningful cross-cultural exchange with
international leaders of tomorrow, today's New York City K-12 students develop
the skills, awareness and understanding to become global citizens in their
communities, both locally and worldwide.,,,,,,8:10 AM,3:00 PM,This school will
provide students with disabilities the supports and services indicated on
their IEPs.,ESL,Functionally Accessible,1,Priority to Brooklyn students or
residents,Then to New York City residents,,,,,,,,,null]
```

 Note: The following sections will be updated with the latest versions of the connector packages later.

In the next several sections, we describe using Spark with several popular big data file formats.

Using Spark with JSON data

JSON is a simple, flexible, and compact format used extensively as a data-interchange format in web services. Spark's support for JSON is great. There is no need for defining the schema for the JSON data, as the schema is automatically inferred. In addition, Spark greatly simplifies the query syntax required to access fields in complex JSON data structures. We will present detailed examples of JSON data in Chapter 12, *Spark SQL in Large-Scale Application Architectures*.

The dataset for this example contains approximately 1.69 million Amazon reviews for the electronics category, and can be downloaded from: `http://jmcauley.ucsd.edu/data/amazon/`.

We can directly read a JSON dataset to create Spark SQL DataFrame. We will read in a sample set of order records from a JSON file:

```
scala>val reviewsDF =
spark.read.json("file:///Users/aurobindosarkar/Downloads/reviews_Electronic
s_5.json")
```

You can print the schema of the newly created DataFrame to verify the fields and their characteristics using the `printSchema` method.

```
scala> reviewsDF.printSchema()
```

```
root
 |-- asin: string (nullable = true)
 |-- helpful: array (nullable = true)
 |    |-- element: long (containsNull = true)
 |-- overall: double (nullable = true)
 |-- reviewText: string (nullable = true)
 |-- reviewTime: string (nullable = true)
 |-- reviewerID: string (nullable = true)
 |-- reviewerName: string (nullable = true)
 |-- summary: string (nullable = true)
 |-- unixReviewTime: long (nullable = true)
```

Once, the JSON Dataset is converted to a Spark SQL DataFrame, you can work with it extensively in a standard way. Next, we will execute an SQL statement to select certain columns from our orders that are received from customers in a specific age bracket:

```
scala>reviewsDF.createOrReplaceTempView("reviewsTable")
scala>val selectedDF = spark.sql("SELECT asin, overall, reviewTime,
reviewerID, reviewerName FROM reviewsTable WHERE overall >= 3")
```

Display the results of the SQL execution (stored in another DataFrame) using the `show` method, as follows:

```scala
scala> selectedDF.show()
```

```
+----------+-------+-----------+-------------+-----------------+
|      asin|overall| reviewTime|   reviewerID|     reviewerName|
+----------+-------+-----------+-------------+-----------------+
|0528881469|    5.0| 06  2, 2013|A094DHGC771SJ|          amazdnu|
|0528881469|    3.0| 09  9, 2010|A3N7T0DY83Y4IG|    C. A. Freeman|
|0594451647|    5.0| 01  3, 2014|A2JXAZZI9PHK9Z|Billy G. Noland "...|
|0594451647|    5.0| 05  4, 2014|AAZ084UMH8VZ2|D. L. Brown "A Kn...|
|0594451647|    4.0|07 11, 2014| AEZ3CR6BKIROJ|    Mark Dietter|
|0594451647|    5.0|01 20, 2014|A3BY5KCNQZXV5U|          Matenai|
|0594481813|    4.0|04 16, 2014| A7S2B0I67WNWB|           AllyMG|
|0594481813|    5.0| 05  5, 2014|A3HICVLF4PFFMN|  Amazon Customer|
|0594481813|    5.0|06 24, 2013|ANSKSPEEAKY7S|             Gena|
|0594481813|    3.0|05 25, 2013|A2QBZA4S1ROX9Q|             Jake|
|0594481813|    5.0| 03  9, 2013|ANY6JUFM0GH8U|     J. Clement|
|0594481813|    3.0|08 31, 2013|AT09WGFUM934H|             John|
|0594481813|    3.0|09 18, 2013|AGAKHE014LQFU|        Nicodimus|
|0594481813|    4.0|06 27, 2013|A1S6B5QFWGVL5U|      T. Vaughan|
|0972683275|    5.0|07 12, 2014|A20XXTXWF2TCPY|             null|
|0972683275|    5.0|04 30, 2013|A2IDCSC6NVONIZ|          2Cents!|
|0972683275|    5.0|12 16, 2011|A1EDI0X3GI1SK7|              AGW|
|0972683275|    4.0|11 23, 2013|A3BMUBUC1N77U8|         ahoffoss|
|0972683275|    4.0|08 30, 2010| AVRFGGCCCR6QU|Alberto Dieguez "...|
|0972683275|    5.0|05 12, 2013|A3UOSOCRKS3WIH|    Allen Coberly|
+----------+-------+-----------+-------------+-----------------+
only showing top 20 rows
```

We can access the array elements of the `helpful` column in the `reviewDF` DataFrame (using DSL) as shown:

```scala
scala> val selectedJSONArrayElementDF = reviewsDF.select($"asin",
$"overall", $"helpful").where($"helpful".getItem(0) < 3)

scala>selectedJSONArrayElementDF.show()
```

```
+----------+-------+-------+
|      asin|overall|helpful|
+----------+-------+-------+
|0528881469|    5.0| [0, 0]|
|0528881469|    1.0| [0, 0]|
|0594451647|    2.0| [0, 0]|
|0594451647|    5.0| [0, 0]|
|0594451647|    4.0| [0, 0]|
|0594481813|    4.0| [2, 2]|
|0594481813|    5.0| [0, 0]|
|0594481813|    5.0| [1, 1]|
|0594481813|    3.0| [0, 1]|
|0594481813|    5.0| [2, 2]|
|0594481813|    3.0| [0, 0]|
|0594481813|    4.0| [2, 2]|
|0972683275|    5.0| [0, 0]|
|0972683275|    5.0| [1, 1]|
|0972683275|    5.0| [0, 1]|
|0972683275|    4.0| [0, 0]|
|0972683275|    5.0| [0, 0]|
|0972683275|    4.0| [0, 0]|
|0972683275|    4.0| [0, 0]|
|0972683275|    5.0| [1, 1]|
+----------+-------+-------+
only showing top 20 rows
```

An example of writing out a DataFrame as a JSON file was presented in an earlier section where we selected the columns of interest from the DataFrame (containing data other than for the current month), and wrote them out to the HDFS filesystem in JSON format.

Using Spark with Avro files

Avro is a very popular data serialization system that provides a compact and fast binary data format. Avro files are self-describing because the schema is stored along with the data.

You can download `spark-avro connector` JAR from https://mvnrepository.com/artifact/com.databricks/spark-avro_2.11/3.2.0.

 We will switch to Spark 2.1 for this section. At the time of writing this book due to a documented bug in the `spark-avro connector` library, we are getting exceptions while writing Avro files (using `spark-avro connector 3.2`) with Spark 2.2.

Start Spark shell with the spark-avro JAR included in the session:

```
Aurobindos-MacBook-Pro-2:spark-2.1.0-bin-hadoop2.7 aurobindosarkar$
bin/spark-shell --jars /Users/aurobindosarkar/Downloads/spark-
avro_2.11-3.2.0.jar
```

We will use the JSON file from the previous section containing the Amazon reviews data to create the `Avro` file. Create a DataFrame from the input JSON file and display the number of records:

```
scala> import com.databricks.spark.avro._
scala> val reviewsDF =
spark.read.json("file:///Users/aurobindosarkar/Downloads/reviews_Electronic
s_5.json")

scala> reviewsDF.count()
res4: Long = 1689188
```

Next, we filter all the reviews with an overall rating of less than 3, `coalesce` the output to a single file, and write out the resulting DataFrame to an `Avro` file:

```
scala> reviewsDF.filter("overall <
3").coalesce(1).write.avro("file:///Users/aurobindosarkar/Downloads/amazon_
reviews/avro")
```

Next, we show how to read an `Avro` file by creating a DataFrame from the `Avro` file created in the previous step and display the number of records in it:

```scala
scala> val reviewsAvroDF =
spark.read.avro("file:///Users/aurobindosarkar/Downloads/amazon_reviews/avr
o/part-00000-c6b6b423-70d6-440f-acbe-0de65a6a7f2e.avro")

scala> reviewsAvroDF.count()
res5: Long = 190864
```

Next, we select a few columns and display five records from the results DataFrame by specifying `show(5)`:

```scala
scala> reviewsAvroDF.select("asin", "helpful", "overall", "reviewTime",
"reviewerID", "reviewerName").show(5)
```

```
+----------+--------+-------+-----------+--------------+--------------------+
|      asin| helpful|overall| reviewTime|    reviewerID|        reviewerName|
+----------+--------+-------+-----------+--------------+--------------------+
|0528881469|[12, 15]|    1.0|11 25, 2010| AMO214LNFCEI4|    Amazon Customer|
|0528881469| [9, 10]|    2.0|11 24, 2010|A1H8PY3QHMQQA0|Dave M. Shaw "mac...|
|0528881469|  [0, 0]|    1.0|09 29, 2011|A24EV6RXELQZ63|        Wayne Smith|
|0594451647|  [0, 0]|    2.0|04 27, 2014|A2P5U7BDKKT7FW|          Christian|
|0972683275|  [0, 2]|    2.0|12 17, 2012|A2LR9WP2JGDT8E|          E. Coronel|
+----------+--------+-------+-----------+--------------+--------------------+
only showing top 5 rows
```

Next, we specify compression options for `Avro` files by setting the Spark session configuration values:

```scala
scala> spark.conf.set("spark.sql.avro.compression.codec", "deflate")
scala> spark.conf.set("spark.sql.avro.deflate.level", "5")
```

Now, when we write the DataFrame, the `Avro` file is stored in a compressed format:

```scala
scala> val reviewsAvroDF =
spark.read.avro("file:////Users/aurobindosarkar/Downloads/amazon_reviews/av
ro/part-00000-c6b6b423-70d6-440f-acbe-0de65a6a7f2e.avro")
```

You can also write out the DataFrame partitioned by a specific column. Here, we partition based on the `overall` column (containing `values < 3` in each row):

```scala
scala>
reviewsAvroDF.write.partitionBy("overall").avro("file:////Users/aurobindosa
rkar/Downloads/amazon_reviews/avro/partitioned")
```

The screenshot of the Avro files from this session are shown here. Notice the sizes of the compressed version (67 MB) versus the original file (97.4 MB) . Additionally, notice the two separate directories created for the partitioned (by overall values) Avro files.

▼ 📁 amazon_reviews	Today, 12:33 AM	--
▼ 📁 avro	Today, 1:05 AM	--
📄 .DS_Store	Today, 1:05 AM	6 KB
▼ 📁 partitioned	Today, 1:05 AM	--
📄 _SUCCESS	Today, 1:05 AM	Zero bytes
▶ 📁 overall=1.0	Today, 1:05 AM	--
▶ 📁 overall=2.0	Today, 1:05 AM	--
▼ 📁 compressed	Today, 1:01 AM	--
📄 _SUCCESS	Today, 1:01 AM	Zero bytes
📄 .part-00000-4b5a2d8b-c6f1-4c0c-9d4b-be10d2224e36.avro.crc	Today, 1:01 AM	523 KB
📄 part-00000-4b5a2d8b-c6f1-4c0c-9d4b-be10d2224e36.avro	Today, 1:01 AM	67 MB
📄 _SUCCESS	Today, 12:20 AM	Zero bytes
📄 .part-00000-c6b6b423-70d6-440f-acbe-0de65a6a7f2e.avro.crc	Today, 12:20 AM	761 KB
📄 part-00000-c6b6b423-70d6-440f-acbe-0de65a6a7f2e.avro	Today, 12:20 AM	97.4 MB

For more details on spark-avro, refer: https://github.com/databricks/spark-avro

Using Spark with Parquet files

Apache Parquet is a popular columnar storage format. It is used in many big data applications in the Hadoop ecosystem. Parquet supports very efficient compression and encoding schemes that can give a significant boost to the performance of such applications. In this section, we show you the simplicity with which you can directly read Parquet files into a standard Spark SQL DataFrame.

Here, we use the reviewsDF created previously from the Amazon reviews contained in a JSON formatted file and write it out in the Parquet format to create the Parquet file. We use coalesce(1) to create a single output file:

```scala
scala> reviewsDF.filter("overall <
3").coalesce(1).write.parquet("file:///Users/aurobindosarkar/Downloads/amaz
on_reviews/parquet")
```

In the next step, we create a DataFrame from the Parquet file using just one statement:

```scala
scala> val reviewsParquetDF =
spark.read.parquet("file:///Users/aurobindosarkar/Downloads/amazon_reviews/
parquet/part-00000-3b512935-ec11-48fa-8720-e52a6a29416b.snappy.parquet")
```

After the DataFrame is created, you can operate on it as you normally would with the DataFrames created from any other data source. Here, we register the DataFrame as a temp view and query it using SQL:

```scala
scala> reviewsParquetDF.createOrReplaceTempView("reviewsTable")
scala> val reviews1RatingsDF = spark.sql("select asin, overall, reviewerID,
reviewerName from reviewsTable where overall < 2")
```

Here, we specify two parameters to display the records in the resulting DataFrame. The first parameter specifies the number of records to display and a value of false for the second parameter shows the full values in the columns (with no truncation).

```scala
scala> reviews1RatingsDF.show(5, false)
```

```
+----------+-------+-------------+-----------------------------+
|asin      |overall|reviewerID   |reviewerName                 |
+----------+-------+-------------+-----------------------------+
|0528881469|1.0    |AMO214LNFCEI4|Amazon Customer              |
|0528881469|1.0    |A24EV6RXELQZ63|Wayne Smith                 |
|0972683275|1.0    |A2JMN2JA9LSHVL|Eric G. Gruner             |
|0972683275|1.0    |A38FGQVJM18OWV|George S. Mitchell "gsmitchell"|
|0972683275|1.0    |A15K7HV1XD6YWR|Musawir Karim              |
+----------+-------+-------------+-----------------------------+
only showing top 5 rows
```

Defining and using custom data sources in Spark

You can define your own data sources and combine the data from such sources with data from other more standard data sources (for example, relational databases, Parquet files, and so on). In Chapter 5, *Using Spark SQL in Streaming Applications*, we define a custom data source for streaming data from public APIs available from **Transport for London** (**TfL**) site.

Refer to the video *Spark DataFrames Simple and Fast Analysis of Structured Data - Michael Armbrust (Databricks)* at https://www.youtube.com/watch? v=xWkJCUcD55w for a good example of defining a data source for Jira and creating a Spark SQL DataFrame from it.

Summary

In this chapter, we demonstrated using Spark with various data sources and data formats. We used Spark to work with a relational database (MySQL), NoSQL database (MongoDB), semistructured data (JSON), and data storage formats commonly used in the Hadoop ecosystem (Avro and Parquet). This sets you up very nicely for the more advanced Spark application-oriented chapters to follow.

In the next chapter, we will shift our focus from the mechanics of working with Spark to how Spark SQL can be used to explore data, perform data quality checks, and visualize data.

3

Using Spark SQL for Data Exploration

In this chapter, we will introduce you to using Spark SQL for exploratory data analysis. We will introduce preliminary techniques to compute some basic statistics, identify outliers, and visualize, sample, and pivot data. A series of hands-on exercises in this chapter will enable you to use Spark SQL along with tools such as Apache Zeppelin for developing an intuition about your data.

In this chapter, we shall look at the following topics:

- What is Exploratory Data Analysis (EDA)
- Why is EDA important?
- Using Spark SQL for basic data analysis
- Visualizing data with Apache Zeppelin
- Sampling data with Spark SQL APIs
- Using Spark SQL for creating pivot tables

Introducing Exploratory Data Analysis (EDA)

Exploratory Data Analysis (EDA), or **Initial Data Analysis (IDA)**, is an approach to data analysis that attempts to maximize insight into data. This includes assessing the quality and structure of the data, calculating summary or descriptive statistics, and plotting appropriate graphs. It can uncover underlying structures and suggest how the data should be modeled. Furthermore, EDA helps us detect outliers, errors, and anomalies in our data, and deciding what to do about such data is often more important than other, more sophisticated analysis. EDA enables us to test our underlying assumptions, discover clusters and other patterns in our data, and identify the possible relationships between various variables. A careful EDA process is vital to understanding the data and is sometimes sufficient to reveal such poor data quality that using a more sophisticated model-based analysis is not justified.

Typically, the graphical techniques used in EDA are simple, consisting of plotting the raw data and simple statistics. The focus is on the structures and models revealed by the data or best fit the data. EDA techniques include scatter plots, box plots, histograms, probability plots, and so on. In most EDA techniques, we use all of the data, without making any underlying assumptions. The analyst builds intuition, or gets a "feel", for the Dataset as a result of such exploration. More specifically, the graphical techniques allow us to efficiently select and validate appropriate models, test our assumptions, identify relationships, select estimators, detect outliers, and so on.

EDA involves a lot of trial and error, and several iterations. The best way is to start simple and then build in complexity as you go along. There is a major trade-off in modeling between the simple and the more accurate ones. Simple models may be much easier to interpret and understand. These models can get you to 90% accuracy very quickly, versus a more complex model that might take weeks or months to get you an additional 2% improvement. For example, you should plot simple histograms and scatter plots to quickly start developing an intuition for your data.

Using Spark SQL for basic data analysis

Interactively, processing and visualizing large data is challenging as the queries can take a long time to execute and the visual interface cannot accommodate as many pixels as data points. Spark supports in-memory computations and a high degree of parallelism to achieve interactivity with large distributed data. In addition, Spark is capable of handling petabytes of data and provides a set of versatile programming interfaces and libraries. These include SQL, Scala, Python, Java and R APIs, and libraries for distributed statistics and machine learning.

For data that fits into a single computer, there are many good tools available, such as R, MATLAB, and others. However, if the data does not fit into a single machine, or if it is very complicated to get the data to that machine, or if a single computer cannot easily process the data, then this section will offer some good tools and techniques for data exploration.

In this section, we will go through some basic data exploration exercises to understand a sample Dataset. We will use a Dataset that contains data related to direct marketing campaigns (phone calls) of a Portuguese banking institution. The marketing campaigns were based on phone calls to customers. We'll use the `bank-additional-full.csv` file that contains 41,188 records and 20 input fields, ordered by date (from May 2008 to November 2010). The Dataset has been contributed by S. Moro, P. Cortez, and P. Rita, and can be downloaded from `https://archive.ics.uci.edu/ml/datasets/Bank+Marketing`.

1. As a first step, let's define a schema and read in the CSV file to create a DataFrame. You can use `:paste` command to paste initial set of statements in your Spark shell session (use *Ctrl+D* to exit the paste mode), as shown:

```scala
scala> :paste
// Entering paste mode (ctrl-D to finish)

import org.apache.spark.sql.types._
import spark.implicits._

val age = StructField("age", DataTypes.IntegerType)
val job = StructField("job", DataTypes.StringType)
val marital = StructField("marital", DataTypes.StringType)
val edu = StructField("edu", DataTypes.StringType)
val credit_default = StructField("credit_default", DataTypes.StringType)
val housing = StructField("housing", DataTypes.StringType)
val loan = StructField("loan", DataTypes.StringType)
val contact = StructField("contact", DataTypes.StringType)
val month = StructField("month", DataTypes.StringType)
val day = StructField("day", DataTypes.StringType)
val dur = StructField("dur", DataTypes.DoubleType)
val campaign = StructField("campaign", DataTypes.DoubleType)
val pdays = StructField("pdays", DataTypes.DoubleType)
val prev = StructField("prev", DataTypes.DoubleType)
val pout = StructField("pout", DataTypes.StringType)
val emp_var_rate = StructField("emp_var_rate", DataTypes.DoubleType)
val cons_price_idx = StructField("cons_price_idx", DataTypes.DoubleType)
val cons_conf_idx = StructField("cons_conf_idx", DataTypes.DoubleType)
val euribor3m = StructField("euribor3m", DataTypes.DoubleType)
val nr_employed = StructField("nr_employed", DataTypes.DoubleType)
val deposit = StructField("deposit", DataTypes.StringType)

val fields = Array(age, job, marital, edu, credit_default, housing, loan, contact, month, day, dur, campaign, pdays, prev, pout,
emp_var_rate, cons_price_idx, cons_conf_idx, euribor3m, nr_employed, deposit)

val schema = StructType(fields)

val df = spark.read.schema(schema).option("sep", ";").option("header", true).csv("file:///Users/aurobindosarkar/Downloads/bank-
additional/bank-additional-full.csv")

// Exiting paste mode, now interpreting.
```

2. After the DataFrame has been created, we first verify the number of records:

```
scala> df.count()
res0: Long = 41188
```

3. We can also define a `case` class called `Call` for our input records, and then create a strongly-typed Dataset, as follows:

```
scala> case class Call(age: Double, job: String, marital: String, edu: String, credit_default: String, housing: String, loan: String, contact: String, month: String, day: String, dur: Double, campaign: Double, pdays: Double, prev: Double, pout: String, emp_var_rate: Double, cons_price_idx: Double, cons_conf_idx: Double, euribor3m: Double, nr_employed: Double, deposit: String)

scala> val ds = df.as[Call]

scala> ds.printSchema()
root
 |-- age: integer (nullable = true)
 |-- job: string (nullable = true)
 |-- marital: string (nullable = true)
 |-- edu: string (nullable = true)
 |-- credit_default: string (nullable = true)
 |-- housing: string (nullable = true)
 |-- loan: string (nullable = true)
 |-- contact: string (nullable = true)
 |-- month: string (nullable = true)
 |-- day: string (nullable = true)
 |-- dur: double (nullable = true)
 |-- campaign: double (nullable = true)
 |-- pdays: double (nullable = true)
 |-- prev: double (nullable = true)
 |-- pout: string (nullable = true)
 |-- emp_var_rate: double (nullable = true)
 |-- cons_price_idx: double (nullable = true)
 |-- cons_conf_idx: double (nullable = true)
 |-- euribor3m: double (nullable = true)
 |-- nr_employed: double (nullable = true)
 |-- deposit: string (nullable = true)
```

In the next section, we will begin our data exploration by identifying missing data in our Dataset.

Identifying missing data

Missing data can occur in Datasets due to reasons ranging from negligence to a refusal on the part of respondents to provide a specific data point. However, in all cases, missing data is a common occurrence in real-world Datasets. Missing data can create problems in data analysis and sometimes lead to wrong decisions or conclusions. Hence, it is very important to identify missing data and devise effective strategies to deal with it.

In this section, we analyze the numbers of records with missing data fields in our sample Dataset. In order to simulate missing data, we will edit our sample Dataset by replacing fields containing "unknown" values with empty strings.

First, we created a DataFrame/Dataset from our edited file, as shown:

```
scala> val dfMissing = spark.read.schema(schema).option("sep", ";").option("header", true).csv("file:///Users/aurobindosarkar/
Downloads/bank-additional/bank-additional-full-with-missing.csv")

scala> val dfMissing = spark.read.schema(schema).option("sep", ";").option("header", true).csv("file:///Users/aurobindosarkar/
Downloads/bank-additional/bank-additional-full-with-missing.csv")

scala> val dsMissing = dfMissing.as[Call]
```

The following two statements give us a count of rows with certain fields having missing data:

```
scala> dsMissing.groupBy("marital").count().show()
+--------+-----+
| marital|count|
+--------+-----+
|    null|   80|
|divorced| 4612|
| married|24928|
|  single|11568|
+--------+-----+


scala> dsMissing.groupBy("job").count().show()
+-------------+-----+
|          job|count|
+-------------+-----+
|   management| 2924|
|      retired| 1720|
|         null|  330|
|self-employed| 1421|
|      student|  875|
|  blue-collar| 9254|
| entrepreneur| 1456|
|       admin.|10422|
|   technician| 6743|
|     services| 3969|
|    housemaid| 1060|
|   unemployed| 1014|
+-------------+-----+
```

In Chapter 4, *Using Spark SQL for Data Munging*, we will look at effective ways of dealing with missing data. In the next section, we will compute some basic statistics for our sample Dataset to improve our understanding of the data.

Computing basic statistics

Computing basic statistics is essential for a good preliminary understanding of our data. First, for convenience, we create a case class and a Dataset containing a subset of fields from our original DataFrame. In the following example, we choose some of the numeric fields and the outcome field, that is, the "term deposit subscribed" field:

```
scala> case class CallStats(age: Int, dur: Double, campaign: Double, prev:
Double, deposit: String)

scala> val dsSubset = ds.select($"age", $"dur", $"campaign", $"prev",
$"deposit")

scala> dsSubset.show(5)
+---+---+--------+----+-------+
|age|dur|campaign|prev|deposit|
+---+---+--------+----+-------+
| 56|261|       1|   0|     no|
| 57|149|       1|   0|     no|
| 37|226|       1|   0|     no|
| 40|151|       1|   0|     no|
| 56|307|       1|   0|     no|
+---+---+--------+----+-------+
only showing top 5 rows

scala> val dsCallStats = dsSubset.as[CallStats]

scala> dsCallStats.cache()
```

Next, we use `describe()` compute the `count`, `mean`, `stdev`, `min`, and `max` values for the numeric columns in our Dataset. The `describe()` command gives a way to do a quick sense-check on your data. For example, the counts of rows of each of the columns selected matches the total number records in the DataFrame (no null or invalid rows),whether the average and range of values for the age column matching your expectations, and so on. Based on the values of the means and standard deviations, you can get select certain data elements for deeper analysis. For example, assuming normal distribution, the mean and standard deviation values for age suggest most values of age are in the range 30 to 50 years, for other columns the standard deviation values may be indicative of a skew in the data (as the standard deviation is greater than the mean).

```
scala> dsSubset.describe().show()
+-------+------------------+-----------------+------------------+-------------------+
|summary|               age|              dur|          campaign|               prev|
+-------+------------------+-----------------+------------------+-------------------+
|  count|             41188|            41188|             41188|              41188|
|   mean| 40.02406040594348|258.2850101971448|2.567592502670681|0.17296299893172767|
| stddev|10.421249980934057|259.27924883646455|2.770013542902331|0.49490107983928927|
|    min|                17|                0|                 1|                  0|
|    max|                98|             4918|                56|                  7|
+-------+------------------+-----------------+------------------+-------------------+
```

Further, we can use the stat package to compute additional statistics such as covariance and Pearson's correlation coefficient. The covariance indicates the joint variability of two random variables. As we are in the EDA phase, these measures can give us indicators of how one variable varies vis-a-vis another one. For example, the sign of the covariance indicates the direction of variability between the two variables. In the following example, the covariance between age and duration of the last contact move in opposite directions, that is as age increases the duration decreases. Correlation gives a magnitude for the strength of this relationship between these two variables.

```
scala> val cov = dsSubset.stat.cov("age","dur")
cov: Double = -2.3391469421267863

scala> val corr = dsSubset.stat.corr("age","dur")
corr: Double = -8.657050101409879E-4
```

We can create cross tabulations or crosstabs between two variables to evaluate interrelationships between them. For example, in the following example we create a crosstab between age and marital status represented as a 2x2 contingency table. From the table, we understand, for a given age the breakup of the total number of individuals across the various marital statuses. We can also extract items that occur most frequently in data columns of the DataFrame. Here, we choose the education level as the column and specify a support level of 0.3, that is, we want to find education levels that occur with a frequency greater than 0.3 (observed 30% of the time, at a minimum) in the DataFrame. Lastly, we can also compute approximate quantiles of the numeric columns in the DataFrame. Here, we compute the same for the age column with specified quantile probabilities of 0.25, 0.5 and 0.75, (a value of 0 is the minimum, 1 is the maximum, and 0.5 is the median).

```
scala> ds.stat.crosstab("age", "marital").orderBy("age_marital").show(10)
+-----------+--------+-------+------+-------+
|age_marital|divorced|married|single|unknown|
+-----------+--------+-------+------+-------+
|         17|       0|      0|     5|      0|
|         18|       0|      0|    28|      0|
|         19|       0|      0|    42|      0|
|         20|       0|      1|    64|      0|
|         21|       0|      8|    94|      0|
|         22|       0|     16|   121|      0|
|         23|       0|     30|   196|      0|
|         24|       4|     78|   381|      0|
|         25|      17|    150|   429|      2|
|         26|      13|    196|   489|      0|
+-----------+--------+-------+------+-------+
only showing top 10 rows

scala> val freq = df.stat.freqItems(Seq("edu"), 0.3)

scala> freq.collect()(0)
res137: org.apache.spark.sql.Row = [WrappedArray(high.school,
university.degree, professional.course)]

scala> val quantiles = df.stat.approxQuantile("age", Array(0.25,0.5,0.75),0.0)
quantiles: Array[Double] = Array(32.0, 38.0, 47.0)
```

Next, we use the typed aggregation functions to summarize our data to understand it better. In the following statement, we aggregate the results by whether a term deposit was subscribed along with the total customers contacted, average number of calls made per customer, the average duration of the calls, and the average number of previous calls made to such customers. The results are rounded to two decimal points:

```scala
scala> import org.apache.spark.sql.expressions.scalalang.typed.{
     |       count => typedCount,
     |       avg => typedAvg,
     |       sum => typedSum}

scala> (dsCallStats.groupByKey(callstats =>
callstats.deposit).agg(typedCount[CallStats](_.age).name("A"),typedAvg[CallSta
ts](_.campaign).name("B"),typedAvg[CallStats](_.dur).name("C"),typedAvg[CallSt
ats](_.prev).name("D")).withColumnRenamed("value", "E")).select($"E".name("TD
Subscribed?"), $"A".name("Total Customers"), round($"B", 2).name("Avg
calls(curr)"), round($"C", 2).name("Avg dur"), round($"D", 2).name("Avg
calls(prev)")).show()
```

TD Subscribed?	Total Customers	Avg calls(curr)	Avg dur	Avg calls(prev)
no	36548	2.63	220.84	0.13
yes	4640	2.05	553.19	0.49

Similarly, executing the following statement gives similar results by customer's age:

```scala
scala> (dsCallStats.groupByKey(callstats =>
callstats.age).agg(typedCount[CallStats](_.age).name("A"),typedAvg[CallStats](
_.campaign).name("B"),typedAvg[CallStats](_.dur).name("C"),typedAvg[CallStats]
(_.prev).name("D")).withColumnRenamed("value", "E")).select($"E".name("Age"),
$"A".name("Total Customers"), round($"B", 2).name("Avg calls(curr)"),
round($"C", 2).name("Avg dur"), round($"D", 2).name("Avg
calls(prev)")).orderBy($"age").show(5)
```

Age	Total Customers	Avg calls(curr)	Avg dur	Avg calls(prev)
17	5	2.2	420.0	1.8
18	28	1.32	321.79	0.75
19	42	2.29	271.5	0.67
20	65	2.35	288.49	0.63
21	102	2.03	264.25	0.28

```
only showing top 5 rows
```

After getting a better understanding of our data by computing basic statistics, we shift our focus to identifying outliers in our data.

Identifying data outliers

An outlier or an anomaly is an observation of the data that deviates significantly from other observations in the Dataset. These erroneous outliers can be due to errors in the data-collection or variability in measurement. They can impact the results significantly so it is imperative to identify them during the EDA process.

However, these techniques define outliers as points, which do not lie in clusters. The user has to model the data points using statistical distributions, and the outliers are identified depending on how they appear in relation to the underlying model. The main problem with these approaches is that during EDA, the user typically does not have enough knowledge about the underlying data distribution.

EDA, using a modeling and visualizing approach, is a good way of achieving a deeper intuition of our data. Spark MLlib supports a large (and growing) set of distributed machine learning algorithms to make this task simpler. For example, we can apply clustering algorithms and visualize the results to detect outliers in a combination columns. In the following example, we use the last contact duration, in seconds (duration), number of contacts performed during this campaign, for this client (campaign), number of days that have passed by after the client was last contacted from a previous campaign (pdays) and the previous: number of contacts performed before this campaign and for this client (prev) values to compute two clusters in our data by applying the k-means clustering algorithm:

```scala
scala> import org.apache.spark.mllib.linalg.Vectors

scala> import org.apache.spark.mllib.clustering.KMeans

scala> val vectors = df.rdd.map(r =>
Vectors.dense(r.getDouble(10),r.getDouble(11), r.getDouble(12),
r.getDouble(13)))

scala> vectors.cache()
res13: vectors.type = MapPartitionsRDD[71] at map at <console>:80

scala> val kMeansModel = KMeans.train(vectors, 2, 20)

scala> kMeansModel.clusterCenters.foreach(println)
[182.0339819280448,2.590526082377072,965.4441765064582,0.17010366428294252]
[796.6381604696674,2.405675146771037,941.5154598825832,0.19315068493150686]
```

Other distributed algorithms useful for EDA include classification, regression, dimensionality reduction, correlation, and hypothesis testing. More details on using Spark SQL and these algorithms are covered in Chapter 6, *Using Spark SQL in Machine Learning Applications*.

Visualizing data with Apache Zeppelin

Typically, we will generate many graphs to verify our hunches about the data. A lot of these quick and dirty graphs used during EDA are, ultimately, discarded. Exploratory data visualization is critical for data analysis and modeling. However, we often skip exploratory visualization with large data because it is hard. For instance, browsers cannot typically cannot handle millions of data points. Hence, we have to summarize, sample, or model our data before we can effectively visualize it.

Traditionally, BI tools provided extensive aggregation and pivoting features to visualize the data. However, these tools typically used nightly jobs to summarize large volumes of data. The summarized data was subsequently downloaded and visualized on the practitioner's workstations. Spark can eliminate many of these batch jobs to support interactive data visualization.

In this section, we will explore some basic data visualization techniques using Apache Zeppelin. Apache Zeppelin is a web-based tool that supports interactive data analysis and visualization. It supports several language interpreters and comes with built-in Spark integration. Hence, it is quick and easy to get started with exploratory data analysis using Apache Zeppelin:

1. You can download Appache Zeppelin from `https://zeppelin.apache.org/`. Unzip the package on your hard drive and start Zeppelin using the following command:

   ```
   Aurobindos-MacBook-Pro-2:zeppelin-0.6.2-bin-all aurobindosarkar$
   bin/zeppelin-daemon.sh start
   ```

2. You should see the following message:

   ```
   Zeppelin start                                              [  OK  ]
   ```

3. You should be able to see the Zeppelin home page at:
   `http://localhost:8080/:`

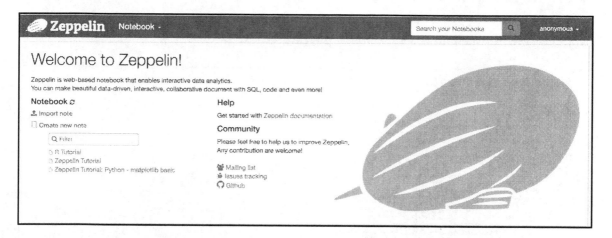

4. Click on the **Create new note** link and specify a path and name for your notebook, as shown:

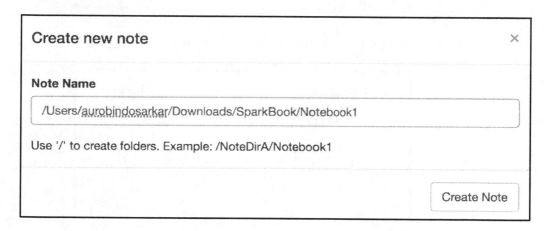

5. In the next step, we paste the same code as in the beginning of this chapter to create a DataFrame for our sample Dataset:

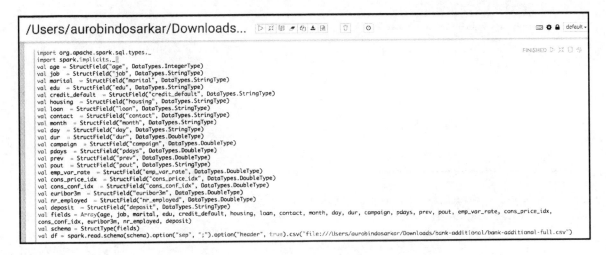

6. We can execute typical DataFrame operations, as follows:

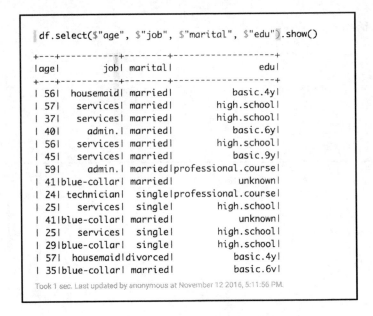

7. Next, we create a table from our DataFrame and execute some SQL on it. The results of the SQL statements' execution can be charted by clicking on the appropriate chart-type required. Here, we create bar charts as an illustrative example of summarizing and visualizing data:

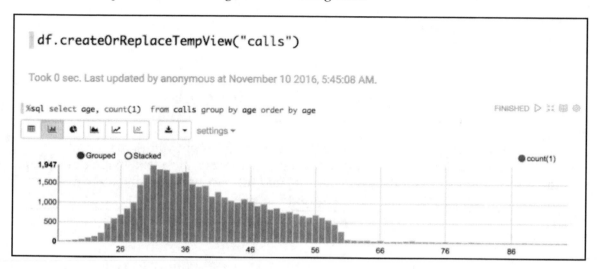

8. We can create a scatter plot, as shown in the following figure:

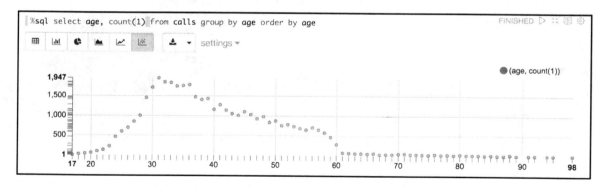

You can also read the coordinate values of each of the points plotted:

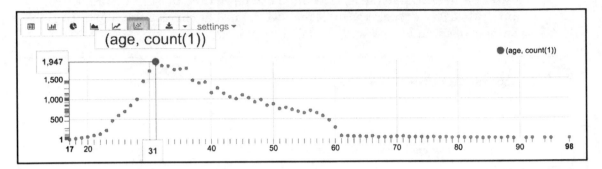

9. Additionally, we can create a textbox that accepts input values to make the experience interactive. In the following figure, we create a textbox that can accept different values for the age parameter and the bar chart is updated accordingly:

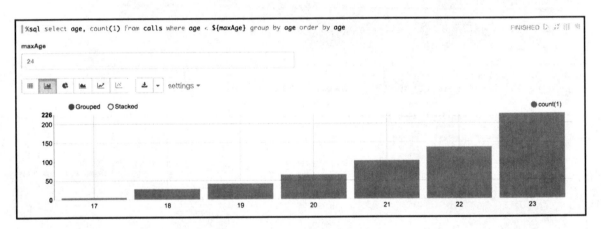

10. Similarly, we can also create drop-down lists where the user can select the appropriate option:

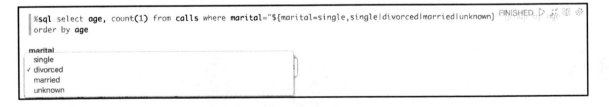

And, the table of values or chart automatically gets updated:

```
%sql select age, count(1) from calls where marital="${marital=single,single|divorced|married|unknown}    FINISHED  ▷ ⅍ 圖 ⚙
order by age
```

marital

single	⇕

⊞ ᵬᵢᵢ ◔ ▰ ⬈ ᵢⱽ   ⤓ ▾

age	count(1)
17	5
18	28
19	42
20	64
21	94

We will explore more advanced visualizations using Spark SQL and SparkR in `Chapter 8,` *Using Spark SQL with SparkR*. In the next section, we will explore the methods used to generate samples from our data.

Sampling data with Spark SQL APIs

Often, we need to visualize individual data points to understand the nature of our data. Statisticians use sampling techniques extensively for data analysis. Spark supports both approximate and exact sample generation. Approximate sampling is faster and is often good enough in most cases.

In this section, we will explore Spark SQL APIs used for generating samples. We will work through some examples of generating approximate and exact stratified samples, with and without replacement, using the DataFrame/Dataset API and RDD-based methods.

Sampling with the DataFrame/Dataset API

We can use the `sampleBy` to create a stratified sample without replacement. We can specify the fractions for the percentages of each value to be selected in the sample.

The size of the sample and the number of record of each type are shown here:

```scala
scala> import scala.collection.immutable.Map

scala> val fractions = Map("unknown" -> .10, "divorced" -> .15, "married" ->
0.5, "single" -> .25)

scala> val dsStratifiedSample = ds.stat.sampleBy("marital", fractions, 36L)

scala> dsStratifiedSample.count()
res15: Long = 16014
```

Next, we create a sample with replacement that selects a fraction of rows (10% of the total records) using a random seed. Using `sample` is not guaranteed to provide the exact fraction of the total number of records in the Dataset. We also print out the numbers of each type of records in the sample:

```scala
scala> val dsSampleWithReplacement = ds.sample(true, .10)

scala>
dsSampleWithReplacement.groupBy("marital").count().orderBy("marital").show()
+--------+-----+
| marital|count|
+--------+-----+
|divorced|  472|
| married| 2496|
|  single| 1162|
| unknown|    8|
+--------+-----+
```

In the next section, we will explore sampling methods using RDDs.

Sampling with the RDD API

In this section, we use RDDs for creating stratified samples with and without replacement.

First, we create an RDD from our DataFrame:

```
scala> import org.apache.spark.mllib.linalg.Vector
import org.apache.spark.mllib.linalg.Vector

scala> val rowsRDD = df.rdd.map(r => (r.getAs[String](2), List(r.getInt(0),
r.getString(1), r.getString(2), r.getString(3), r.getString(4),
r.getString(5), r.getString(6), r.getString(7), r.getString(8),
r.getString(9), r.getDouble(10), r.getDouble(11), r.getDouble(12),
r.getDouble(13), r.getString(14), r.getDouble(15), r.getDouble(16),
r.getDouble(17), r.getDouble(18), r.getDouble(19), r.getString(20))))

scala> rowsRDD.take(2).foreach(println)
(married,List(56, housemaid, married, basic.4y, no, no, no, telephone, may,
mon, 261.0, 1.0, 999.0, 0.0, nonexistent, 1.1, 93.994, -36.4, 4.857, 5191.0,
no))
(married,List(57, services, married, high.school, unknown, no, no, telephone,
may, mon, 149.0, 1.0, 999.0, 0.0, nonexistent, 1.1, 93.994, -36.4, 4.857,
5191.0, no))
```

We can specify the fractions of each record-type in our sample, as illustrated:

```
scala> val fractions = Map("unknown" -> .10, "divorced" -> .15, "married" ->
0.5, "single" -> .25)
```

In the following illustration, we use the `sampleByKey` and `sampleByKeyExact` methods to create our samples. The former is an approximate sample while the latter is an exact sample. The first parameter specifies whether the sample is generated with or without replacement:

```
scala> val rowsSampleRDD = rowsRDD.sampleByKey(true, fractions, 1)

scala> val rowsSampleRDDExact = rowsRDD.sampleByKeyExact(true, fractions, 1)
```

Next, we print out the total number of records in the population and in each of the samples. You will notice that the `sampleByKeyExact` gives you exact numbers of records as per the specified fractions:

```
scala> println(rowsRDD.countByKey)
Map(married -> 24928, unknown -> 80, single -> 11568, divorced -> 4612)

scala> println(rowsSampleRDD.countByKey)
Map(married -> 12500, unknown -> 11, single -> 2920, divorced -> 702)

scala> println(rowsSampleRDDExact.countByKey)
Map(married -> 12464, unknown -> 8, single -> 2892, divorced -> 692)
```

The sample method can be used to create a random sample containing the specified fraction of records in the sample. Next, we create a sample with replacement, containing 10% of the total records:

```scala
scala> val rowsRandomSampleRDD = rowsRDD.sample(true, .1)

scala> println(rowsRandomSampleRDD.countByKey)
Map(married -> 2524, unknown -> 6, single -> 1198, divorced -> 472)
```

Other statistical operations, such as hypothesis testing, random data generation, visualizing probability distributions, and so on, will be covered in the later chapters. In the next section, we will explore our data using Spark SQL for creating pivot tables.

Using Spark SQL for creating pivot tables

Pivot tables create alternate views of your data and are commonly used during data exploration. In the following example, we demonstrate pivoting using Spark DataFrames:

```scala
scala> val sourceDF = df.select($"job", $"marital", $"edu", $"housing",
$"loan", $"contact", $"month", $"day", $"dur", $"campaign", $"pdays", $"prev",
$"pout", $"deposit")
```

The following example pivots on housing loan taken and computes the numbers by marital status:

```scala
scala>
sourceDF.groupBy("marital").pivot("housing").agg(count("housing")).sort("marit
al").show()
+---------+-----+-------+-----+
| marital|   no|unknown|  yes|
+---------+-----+-------+-----+
|divorced| 2092|    121| 2399|
| married|11389|    588|12951|
|  single| 5097|    280| 6191|
| unknown|   44|      1|   35|
+---------+-----+-------+-----+
```

In the next example, we create a DataFrame with appropriate column names for the total and average number of calls:

```
scala> sourceDF.groupBy("job").pivot("marital", Seq("unknown", "divorced",
"married", "single")).agg(round(sum("campaign"), 2), round(avg("campaign"),
2)).sort("job").toDF("Job", "U-Tot", "U-Avg", "D-Tot", "D-Avg", "M-Tot", "M-
Avg", "S-Tot", "S-Avg").show()
```

Job	U-Tot	U-Avg	D-Tot	D-Avg	M-Tot	M-Avg	S-Tot	S-Avg
admin.	24.0	1.71	3398.0	2.65	13807.0	2.63	10113.0	2.61
blue-collar	54.0	3.86	1893.0	2.6	17051.0	2.55	4678.0	2.56
entrepreneur	11.0	3.67	485.0	2.71	2664.0	2.49	532.0	2.62
housemaid	17.0	5.67	396.0	2.46	2089.0	2.69	296.0	2.49
management	16.0	5.33	866.0	2.62	5192.0	2.49	1166.0	2.33
retired	17.0	3.4	865.0	2.49	3110.0	2.44	268.0	2.88
self-employed	11.0	2.2	341.0	2.56	2525.0	2.79	904.0	2.39
services	33.0	5.5	1345.0	2.53	5903.0	2.57	2990.0	2.63
student	1.0	1.0	19.0	2.11	112.0	2.73	1709.0	2.07
technician	21.0	1.75	2113.0	2.73	9348.0	2.55	5897.0	2.58
unemployed	11.0	2.2	303.0	2.44	1701.0	2.68	585.0	2.33
unknown	39.0	4.33	29.0	2.23	633.0	2.71	173.0	2.34

In the following example, we create a DataFrame with appropriate column names for the total and average duration of calls for each job category:

```
scala> sourceDF.groupBy("job").pivot("marital", Seq("unknown", "divorced",
"married", "single")).agg(round(sum("dur"), 2), round(avg("dur"),
2)).sort("job").toDF("Job", "U-Tot", "U-Avg", "D-Tot", "D-Avg", "M-Tot", "M-
Avg", "S-Tot", "S-Avg").show()
```

Job	U-Tot	U-Avg	D-Tot	D-Avg	M-Tot	M-Avg	S-Tot	S-Avg
admin.	4753.0	339.5	325183.0	254.05	1335988.0	254.33	984517.0	254.07
blue-collar	4860.0	347.14	198377.0	272.5	1750593.0	261.79	494245.0	270.82
entrepreneur	1146.0	382.0	41972.0	234.48	287624.0	268.56	52576.0	259.0
housemaid	355.0	118.33	40625.0	252.33	193334.0	248.82	31168.0	261.92
management	477.0	159.0	82252.0	248.5	540274.0	258.63	128635.0	256.76
retired	2247.0	449.4	89253.0	256.47	352288.0	276.52	26997.0	290.29
self-employed	2475.0	495.0	38910.0	292.56	236205.0	261.29	97756.0	257.93
services	1440.0	240.0	137672.0	258.78	576591.0	251.35	309879.0	272.54
student	155.0	155.0	3177.0	353.0	9279.0	226.32	235612.0	285.94
technician	3988.0	332.33	179986.0	232.54	925448.0	252.17	577894.0	252.69
unemployed	756.0	151.2	30969.0	249.75	161178.0	254.22	60041.0	239.21
unknown	2366.0	262.89	2105.0	161.92	48628.0	207.81	25994.0	351.27

In the following example, we show pivoting to compute average call duration for each job category, while also specifying a subset of marital status:

```
scala> sourceDF.groupBy("job").pivot("marital", Seq("divorced",
"married")).agg(round(avg("dur"), 2)).sort("job").show()
+-------------+--------+--------+
|          job|divorced|married |
+-------------+--------+--------+
|       admin.|  254.05|  254.33|
|  blue-collar|   272.5|  261.79|
| entrepreneur|  234.48|  268.56|
|     housemaid|  252.33|  248.82|
|   management|   248.5|  258.63|
|      retired|  256.47|  276.52|
|self-employed|  292.56|  261.29|
|     services|  258.78|  251.35|
|      student|   353.0|  226.32|
|   technician|  232.54|  252.17|
|   unemployed|  249.75|  254.22|
|      unknown|  161.92|  207.81|
+-------------+--------+--------+
```

The following example is the same as the preceding one, except that we split the average call duration values by the housing loan field as well in this case:

```
scala> sourceDF.groupBy("job", "housing").pivot("marital", Seq("divorced",
"married")).agg(round(avg("dur"), 2)).sort("job").show
+-------------+-------+--------+--------+
|          job|housing|divorced|married |
+-------------+-------+--------+--------+
|       admin.|     no|  251.43|  257.44|
|       admin.|    yes|   259.6|  251.86|
|       admin.|unknown|  193.11|  251.27|
|  blue-collar|     no|  272.92|  268.64|
|  blue-collar|unknown|  211.15|   233.1|
|  blue-collar|    yes|  275.48|  256.89|
| entrepreneur|unknown|   302.2|   189.9|
| entrepreneur|    yes|   271.8|  279.45|
| entrepreneur|     no|  191.42|  259.84|
|     housemaid|    yes|  239.06|  233.45|
|     housemaid|unknown|   166.2|   342.9|
|     housemaid|     no|  275.84|  259.95|
|   management|    yes|  253.36|  256.95|
|   management|     no|  244.96|  260.18|
|   management|unknown|   230.5|  264.98|
|      retired|unknown|  231.25|  238.11|
|      retired|    yes|  250.91|  284.82|
|      retired|     no|  265.21|  270.03|
|self-employed|    yes|  303.29|  264.08|
|self-employed|unknown|  186.67|  228.27|
+-------------+-------+--------+--------+
only showing top 20 rows
```

Next, we show how you can create a DataFrame of pivot table of term deposits subscribed by month, save it to disk, and read it back into a RDD:

```
scala> import org.apache.spark.sql._

scala> val saveDF = sourceDF.groupBy("deposit").pivot("month", Seq("jan",
"feb", "mar", "apr", "may", "jun", "jul", "aug", "sep", "oct", "nov",
"dec")).agg(count("deposit")).sort("deposit").na.fill(0)

scala> val writer: DataFrameWriter[Row] = saveDF.write

scala>
writer.format("csv").mode("overwrite").save("file:///Users/aurobindosarkar/Dow
nloads/saveDF")

scala> val dataRDD =
sc.textFile("file:///Users/aurobindosarkar/Downloads/saveDF/*.csv").map(_.spli
t(","))
```

Further, we use the RDD in the preceding step to compute quarterly totals of customers who subscribed and did not subscribe to term loans:

```
scala> val labels = List("deposit", "jan", "feb", "mar", "apr", "may", "jun",
"jul", "aug", "sep", "oct", "nov", "dec")

scala> val labelQ2 = List("apr", "may", "jun")
scala> val labelQ3 = List("jul", "aug", "sep")

scala> val indexQ2 = labelQ2.map(x => labels.indexOf(x))
scala> val indexQ3 = labelQ3.map(x => labels.indexOf(x))

scala> dataRDD.map(x => indexQ2.map(i => x(i).toDouble).sum).collect
res133: Array[Double] = Array(19735.0, 1984.0)

scala> dataRDD.map(x => indexQ3.map(i => x(i).toDouble).sum).collect
res134: Array[Double] = Array(12362.0, 1560.0)
```

We will introduce a detailed analysis of other types of data, including streaming data, large-scale graphs, time-series data, and so on, later in this book.

Summary

In this chapter, we demonstrated using Spark SQL for exploring Datasets, performing basic data quality checks, generating samples and pivot tables, and visualizing data with Apache Zeppelin.

In the next chapter, we will shift our focus to data munging/wrangling. We will introduce techniques to handle missing data, bad data, duplicate records, and so on. We will also use extensive hands-on sessions for demonstrating the use of Spark SQL for common data munging tasks.

4
Using Spark SQL for Data Munging

In this code-intensive chapter, we will present key data munging techniques used to transform raw data to a usable format for analysis. We start with some general data munging steps that are applicable in a wide variety of scenarios. Then, we shift our focus to specific types of data including time-series data, text, and data preprocessing steps for Spark MLlib-based machine learning pipelines. We will use several Datasets to illustrate these techniques.

In this chapter, we shall learn:

- What is data munging?
- Explore data munging techniques
- Combine data using joins
- Munging on textual data
- Munging on time-series data
- Dealing with variable length records
- Data preparation for machine learning pipelines

Introducing data munging

Raw data is typically messy and requires a series of transformations before it becomes useful for modeling and analysis work. Such Datasets can have missing data, duplicate records, corrupted data, incomplete records, and so on. In its simplest form, data munging, or data wrangling, is basically the transformation of raw data into a usable format. In most projects, this is the most challenging and time-consuming step.

However, without data munging your project can reduce to a garbage-in, garbage-out scenario.

Typically, you will execute a bunch of functions and processes such as subset, filter, aggregate, sort, merge, reshape, and so on. In addition, you will also do type conversions, add new fields/columns, rename fields/columns, and so on.

A large project can comprise of several different kinds of data with varying degrees of data quality. There can be a mix of numerical, textual, time-series, structured, and unstructured data including audio and video data used together or separately for analysis. A substantial part of such projects consist of cleansing and transformation steps combined with some statistical analyses and visualization.

We will use several Datasets to demonstrate the key data munging techniques required for preparing the data for subsequent modeling and analyses. These Datasets and their sources are listed as follows:

- **Individual household electric power consumption Dataset**: The original source for the Dataset provided by Georges Hebrail, Senior Researcher, EDF R&D, Clamart, France and Alice Berard, TELECOM ParisTech Master of Engineering Internship at EDF R&D, Clamart, France. The Dataset consists of measurements of electric power consumption in one household at one-minute intervals for a period of nearly four years. This Dataset is available for download from the UCI Machine Learning Repository from the following URL:

    ```
    https://archive.ics.uci.edu/ml/datasets/
    Individual+household+electric+power+consumption.
    ```

- **Machine Learning based ZZAlpha Ltd Stock Recommendations 2012-2014 Dataset**: This Dataset contains recommendations made, for various US traded stock portfolios, the morning of each day during a three year period from Jan 1, 2012 to Dec 31, 2014. This Dataset can be downloaded from the following URL:

    ```
    https://archive.ics.uci.edu/ml/datasets/
    Machine+Learning+based+ZZAlpha+Ltd.+Stock+Recommendations+2012-2014.
    ```

- **Paris weather history Dataset**: This Dataset contains the daily weather report for Paris. We downloaded historical data covering the same time period as in the household electric power consumption Dataset. This Dataset can downloaded from the following URL:

    ```
    https://www.wunderground.com/history/airport/LFPG.
    ```

- **Original 20 newsgroups data**: This data set consists of 20,000 messages taken from 20 Usenet newsgroups. The original owner and donor of this Dataset was Tom Mitchell, School of Computer Science, Carnegie Mellon University. Approximately a thousand Usenet articles were taken from each of the 20 newsgroups. Each newsgroup is stored in a subdirectory and each article stored as a separate file. The Dataset can be downloaded from the following URL:

  ```
  http://kdd.ics.uci.edu/databases/20newsgroups/20newsgroups.html.
  ```

- **Yahoo finance data**: This Dataset comprises of historical daily stock prices for six stocks for one year duration (from 12/04/2015 to 12/04/2016). The data for each of the ticker symbols chosen can been downloaded from the following site:

  ```
  http://finance.yahoo.com/.
  ```

Exploring data munging techniques

In this section, we will introduce several data munging techniques using household electric consumption and weather Datasets. The best way to learn these techniques is to practice the various ways to manipulate the data contained in various publically available Datasets (in addition to the ones used here). The more you practice, the better you will get at it. In the process, you will probably evolve your own style, and develop several toolsets and techniques to achieve your munging objectives. At a minimum, you should get very comfortable working with and moving between RDDs, DataFrames, and Datasets, computing counts, distinct counts, and various aggregations to cross-check your results and match your intuitive understanding the Datasets. Additionally, it is also important to develop the ability to make decisions based on the pros and cons of executing any given munging step.

We will attempt to accomplish the following objectives in this section:

1. Pre-process the household electric consumption Dataset--read the input Dataset, define case class for the rows, count the number of records, remove the header and rows with missing data values, and create a DataFrame.
2. Compute basic statistics and aggregations
3. Augment the Dataset with new information relevant to the analysis
4. Execute other miscellaneous processing steps, if required
5. Pre-process the weather Dataset--similar to step 1
6. Analyze missing data
7. Combine the Datasets using JOIN and analyze the results

Start the Spark shell, at this time, and follow along as you read through this and the subsequent sections.

Import all required classes used in this section:

```
scala> import org.apache.spark.sql.types._
scala> import spark.implicits._
scala> import org.apache.spark.sql.functions.{from_unixtime, unix_timestamp}
scala> import org.apache.spark.sql.functions.udf
scala> import org.apache.spark.sql.{Row, Column, DataFrame}
scala> import scala.collection.mutable.WrappedArray
scala> import com.google.common.collect.ImmutableMap

scala> import org.apache.spark.rdd.RDD
```

Pre-processing of the household electric consumption Dataset

Create a `case` class for household electric power consumption called `HouseholdEPC`:

```
scala> case class HouseholdEPC(date: String, time: String, gap: Double, grp: Double, voltage: Double, gi: Double, sm_1: Double, sm_2: Double, sm_3: Double)
```

Read the input Dataset into a RDD and count the number of rows in it.

```
scala> val hhEPCRdd =
sc.textFile("file:///Users/aurobindosarkar/Downloads/household_power_consumption.txt")
```

```
scala> hhEPCRdd.count()
res71: Long = 2075260
```

Next, remove the header and all other rows containing missing values, (represented as ?'s in the input), as shown in the following steps:

```
scala> val header = hhEPCRdd.first()

header: String =
Date;Time;Global_active_power;Global_reactive_power;Voltage;Global_intensity;Sub_metering_1;Sub_metering_2;Sub_metering_3
```

```
scala> val data = hhEPCRdd.filter(row => row != header).filter(rows => !rows.contains("?"))
```

In the next step, convert the RDD [String] to a RDD with the case class, we defined earlier, and convert the RDD a DatFrame of HouseholdEPC objects.

```scala
scala> val hhEPCClassRdd = data.map(_.split(";")).map(p =>
HouseholdEPC(p(0).trim().toString,p(1).trim().toString,p(2).toDouble,p(3).toDo
uble,p(4).toDouble,p(5).toDouble,p(6).toDouble,p(7).toDouble,p(8).toDouble))

scala> val hhEPCDF = hhEPCClassRdd.toDF()
```

Display a few sample records in the DataFrame, and count the number of rows in it to verify that the number of rows in the DataFrame matches the expected number of rows in your input Dataset.

```scala
scala> hhEPCDF.show(5)
+----------+--------+-----+-----+--------+----+----+----+----+
|      date|    time|  gap|  grp|voltage|  gi|sm_1|sm_2|sm_3|
+----------+--------+-----+-----+--------+----+----+----+----+
|16/12/2006|17:24:00|4.216|0.418| 234.84|18.4| 0.0| 1.0|17.0|
|16/12/2006|17:25:00| 5.36|0.436| 233.63|23.0| 0.0| 1.0|16.0|
|16/12/2006|17:26:00|5.374|0.498| 233.29|23.0| 0.0| 2.0|17.0|
|16/12/2006|17:27:00|5.388|0.502| 233.74|23.0| 0.0| 1.0|17.0|
|16/12/2006|17:28:00|3.666|0.528| 235.68|15.8| 0.0| 1.0|17.0|
+----------+--------+-----+-----+--------+----+----+----+----+
only showing top 5 rows

scala> hhEPCDF.count()
res73: Long = 2049280
```

Computing basic statistics and aggregations

Next, compute and display some basic statistics for the numeric columns in the DataFrame to get a feel for the data, we will be working with.

```scala
scala> hhEPCDF.describe().show()
```

We can also display the basic statistics for some or all of the columns rounded to four decimal places. We can also rename each of the columns by prefixing a r to the column names to differentiate them from the original column names.

```scala
scala> hhEPCDF.describe().select($"summary", $"gap", $"grp", $"voltage",
$"gi", $"sm_1", $"sm_2", $"sm_3", round($"gap", 4).name("rgap"), round($"grp",
4).name("rgrp"), round($"voltage", 4).name("rvoltage"), round($"gi",
4).name("rgi"), round($"sm_1", 4).name("rsm_1"), round($"sm_2",
4).name("rsm_2"), round($"sm_3", 4).name("rsm_3")).drop("gap", "grp",
"voltage", "gi", "sm_1", "sm_2", "sm_3").show()
```

summary	rgap	rgrp	rvoltage	rgi	rsm_1	rsm_2	rsm_3
count	2049280.0	2049280.0	2049280.0	2049280.0	2049280.0	2049280.0	2049280.0
mean	1.0916	0.1237	240.8399	4.6278	1.1219	1.2985	6.4584
stddev	1.0573	0.1127	3.24	4.4444	6.153	5.822	8.4372
min	0.076	0.0	223.2	0.2	0.0	0.0	0.0
max	11.122	1.39	254.15	48.4	88.0	80.0	31.0

In addition, we count the distinct number of days, for which the data is contained in the DataFrame using an aggregation function:

```scala
scala> val numDates =
hhEPCDF.groupBy("date").agg(countDistinct("date")).count()
numDates: Long = 1433
```

Augmenting the Dataset

We can augment the DataFrame with new columns for the day of the week, day of the month, month and year information. For example, we may be interested in studying power consumption on weekdays versus weekends. This can help achieve a better understanding of the data through visualization or pivoting based on these fields.

```scala
scala> val hhEPCDatesDf = hhEPCDF.withColumn("dow",
from_unixtime(unix_timestamp($"date", "dd/MM/yyyy"),
"EEEEE")).withColumn("day", dayofmonth(to_date(unix_timestamp($"date",
"dd/MM/yyyy").cast("timestamp")))).withColumn("month",
month(to_date(unix_timestamp($"date",
"dd/MM/yyyy").cast("timestamp")))).withColumn("year",
year(to_date(unix_timestamp($"date", "dd/MM/yyyy").cast("timestamp"))))

scala> hhEPCDatesDf.show(5)
```

date	time	gap	grp	voltage	gi	sm_1	sm_2	sm_3	dow	day	month	year
16/12/2006	17:24:00	4.216	0.418	234.84	18.4	0.0	1.0	17.0	Saturday	16	12	2006
16/12/2006	17:25:00	5.36	0.436	233.63	23.0	0.0	1.0	16.0	Saturday	16	12	2006
16/12/2006	17:26:00	5.374	0.498	233.29	23.0	0.0	2.0	17.0	Saturday	16	12	2006
16/12/2006	17:27:00	5.388	0.502	233.74	23.0	0.0	1.0	17.0	Saturday	16	12	2006
16/12/2006	17:28:00	3.666	0.528	235.68	15.8	0.0	1.0	17.0	Saturday	16	12	2006

```
only showing top 5 rows
```

Executing other miscellaneous processing steps

If required we can choose to execute a few more steps to help cleanse the data further, study more aggregations, or to convert to a typesafe data structure, and so on.

We can drop the time column and aggregate the values in various columns using aggregation functions such as sum and average on the values of each day's readings. Here, we rename the columns with a d prefix to represent daily values.

```scala
scala> val delTmDF = hhEPCDF.drop("time")

scala> val finalDayDf1 =
delTmDF.groupBy($"date").agg(sum($"gap").name("A"),sum($"grp").name("B"),avg($
"voltage").name("C"),sum($"gi").name("D"), sum($"sm_1").name("E"),
sum($"sm_2").name("F"), sum($"sm_3").name("G")).select($"date", round($"A",
2).name("dgap"), round($"B", 2).name("dgrp"), round($"C", 2).name("dvoltage"),
round($"C", 2).name("dgi"), round($"E", 2).name("dsm_1"), round($"F",
2).name("dsm_2"), round($"G", 2).name("dsm_3")).withColumn("day",
dayofmonth(to_date(unix_timestamp($"date",
"dd/MM/yyyy").cast("timestamp")))).withColumn("month",
month(to_date(unix_timestamp($"date",
"dd/MM/yyyy").cast("timestamp")))).withColumn("year",
year(to_date(unix_timestamp($"date", "dd/MM/yyyy").cast("timestamp"))))
```

We display a few sample records from this DataFrame:

```scala
scala> finalDayDf1.show(5)
```

```
+----------+-------+------+--------+------+------+------+-------+---+-----+----+
|      date|   dgap|  dgrp|dvoltage|   dgi| dsm_1| dsm_2| dsm_3|day|month|year|
+----------+-------+------+--------+------+------+------+-------+---+-----+----+
| 30/1/2007| 1707.8|180.93|  241.84|241.84|1123.0|1424.0| 8149.0| 30|    1|2007|
| 13/2/2007|1414.55|134.68|  241.17|241.17|   0.0|2828.0| 6256.0| 13|    2|2007|
|19/11/2007|1723.65|112.03|  242.77|242.77|1089.0| 253.0|10750.0| 19|   11|2007|
| 12/1/2008|2871.41|162.72|  239.96|239.96|5594.0|2621.0|11116.0| 12|    1|2008|
| 26/2/2008| 507.12| 84.59|  239.53|239.53|   0.0| 295.0| 2013.0| 26|    2|2008|
+----------+-------+------+--------+------+------+------+-------+---+-----+----+
only showing top 5 rows
```

Here, we group the readings by year and month, and then count the number of readings and display them for each of the months. The first month's number of readings is low as the data was captured in half a month.

```
scala> val readingsByMonthDf = hhEPCDatesDf.groupBy($"year",
$"month").count().orderBy($"year", $"month")

scala> readingsByMonthDf.count()
res77: Long = 48

scala> readingsByMonthDf.show(5)
+----+-----+-----+
|year|month|count|
+----+-----+-----+
|2006|   12|21992|
|2007|    1|44638|
|2007|    2|40318|
|2007|    3|44639|
|2007|    4|39477|
+----+-----+-----+
only showing top 5 rows
```

We can also convert our DataFrame to a Dataset using a `case` class, as follows:

```
scala> case class HouseholdEPCDTmDay(date: String, day: String, month: String,
year: String, dgap: Double, dgrp: Double, dvoltage: Double, dgi: Double,
dsm_1: Double, dsm_2: Double, dsm_3: Double)

scala> val finalDayDs1 = finalDayDf1.as[HouseholdEPCDTmDay]
```

At this stage, we have completed all the steps for pre-processing the household electric consumption Dataset. We now shift our focus to processing the weather Dataset.

Pre-processing of the weather Dataset

First, we define a `case` class for the weather readings.

```
scala> case class DayWeather(CET: String, Max_TemperatureC: Double,
Mean_TemperatureC: Double, Min_TemperatureC: Double, Dew_PointC: Double,
MeanDew_PointC: Double, Min_DewpointC: Double, Max_Humidity: Double,
Mean_Humidity: Double, Min_Humidity: Double, Max_Sea_Level_PressurehPa:
Double, Mean_Sea_Leve_PressurehPa: Double, Min_Sea_Level_PressurehPa: Double,
Max_VisibilityKm: Double, Mean_VisibilityKm: Double, Min_VisibilitykM: Double,
Max_Wind_SpeedKmph: Double, Mean_Wind_SpeedKmph: Double, Max_Gust_SpeedKmph:
Double, Precipitationmm: Double, CloudCover: Double, Events: String,
WindDirDegrees: Double)
```

Next, we read in the four files of the daily weather readings (downloaded from the Paris Weather website) approximately matching the same duration as the household electric power consumption readings.

```
scala> val dwRdd1 =
sc.textFile("file:///Users/aurobindosarkar/Downloads/Paris_Weather/Paris_Weather_Year_1.c
sv")
scala> val dwRdd2 =
sc.textFile("file:///Users/aurobindosarkar/Downloads/Paris_Weather/Paris_Weather_Year_2.c
sv")
scala> val dwRdd3 =
sc.textFile("file:///Users/aurobindosarkar/Downloads/Paris_Weather/Paris_Weather_Year_3.c
sv")
scala> val dwRdd4 =
sc.textFile("file:///Users/aurobindosarkar/Downloads/Paris_Weather/Paris_Weather_Year_4.c
sv")

scala> println("Number 0f Readings - Year 1: " + dwRdd1.count())
Number 0f Readings - Year 1: 366

scala> println("Number 0f Readings - Year 2: " + dwRdd2.count())
Number 0f Readings - Year 2: 367

scala> println("Number 0f Readings - Year 3: " + dwRdd3.count())
Number 0f Readings - Year 3: 366

scala> println("Number 0f Readings - Year 4: " + dwRdd4.count())
Number 0f Readings - Year 4: 377
```

Remove the headers from each of the input files shown as follows. We have shown the output of header values so you get a sense of the various weather reading parameters captured in these Datasets:

```
scala> val header = dwRdd1.first()

header: String = CET,Max TemperatureC,Mean TemperatureC,Min TemperatureC,Dew
PointC,MeanDew PointC,Min DewpointC,Max Humidity, Mean Humidity, Min Humidity,
Max Sea Level PressurehPa, Mean Sea Level PressurehPa, Min Sea Level
PressurehPa, Max VisibilityKm, Mean VisibilityKm, Min VisibilitykM, Max Wind
SpeedKm/h, Mean Wind SpeedKm/h, Max Gust SpeedKm/h,Precipitationmm,
CloudCover, Events,WindDirDegrees

scala> val data1 = dwRdd1.filter(row => row != header)
scala> val data2 = dwRdd2.filter(row => row != header)
scala> val data3 = dwRdd3.filter(row => row != header)
scala> val data4 = dwRdd4.filter(row => row != header)
```

Analyzing missing data

If we wanted to get a sense of the number of rows containing one or more missing fields in the RDD, we can create a RDD with these rows:

```scala
scala> val emptyFieldRowsRDD = data1.map(_.split(",")).filter(!_.contains(""))

scala> emptyFieldRowsRDD.count()
res81: Long = 139
```

We can also do the same, if our data was available in a DataFrame as shown:

```scala
scala> val csvDF = spark.read.format("csv").option("header",
true).option("inferSchema",
true).load("file:///Users/aurobindosarkar/Downloads/Paris_Weather/Paris_Weathe
r_Year_1.csv")

scala> csvDF.select($"CET", $" Events").show()
+--------------------+-----------------+
|                 CET|           Events|
+--------------------+-----------------+
|2006-11-16 00:00:...|             Rain|
|2006-11-17 00:00:...|             Rain|
|2006-11-18 00:00:...|             Rain|
|2006-11-19 00:00:...|             Rain|
|2006-11-20 00:00:...|             Rain|
|2006-11-21 00:00:...|Rain-Thunderstorm|
|2006-11-22 00:00:...|             Rain|
|2006-11-23 00:00:...|             Rain|
|2006-11-24 00:00:...|             Rain|
|2006-11-25 00:00:...|             Rain|
|2006-11-26 00:00:...|                 |
|2006-11-27 00:00:...|             Rain|
|2006-11-28 00:00:...|             Rain|
|2006-11-29 00:00:...|              Fog|
|2006-11-30 00:00:...|              Fog|
|2006-12-01 00:00:...|                 |
|2006-12-02 00:00:...|             Rain|
|2006-12-03 00:00:...|             Rain|
|2006-12-04 00:00:...|             Rain|
|2006-12-05 00:00:...|             Rain|
+--------------------+-----------------+
only showing top 20 rows
```

A quick check of the Dataset reveals that most of the rows with missing data also have missing values for the Events and Max Gust Speed Km/h columns. Filtering on these two column values actually, captures all the rows with missing field values. It also matches the results for missing values in the RDD.

```scala
scala> val dropRowsWithEmptyFieldsDF = csvDF.filter($" Events" =!=
"").filter($" Max Gust SpeedKm/h" =!= "")
scala> dropRowsWithEmptyFieldsDF.count()
res80: Long = 139
```

As there are many rows that contain one or more missing fields, we choose to retain these rows to ensure we do not lose valuable information. In the following function, we insert 0 in all the missing fields of an RDD.

```scala
scala> def processRdd(data: RDD[String]): RDD[DayWeather] = { val dwClassRdd =
data.map(_.split(",")).map(c => c.map(f => f match { case x if x.isEmpty() =>
"0"; case x => x })).map(p => DayWeather(p(0).trim().toString, p(1).toDouble,
p(2).toDouble, p(3).toDouble, p(4).toDouble, p(5).toDouble, p(6).toDouble,
p(7).toDouble, p(8).toDouble, p(9).toDouble, p(10).toDouble, p(11).toDouble,
p(12).toDouble, p(13).toDouble, p(14).toDouble, p(15).toDouble,
p(16).toDouble, p(17).toDouble, p(18).toDouble, p(19).toDouble,
p(20).toDouble, p(21).trim().toString, p(22).toDouble)); dwClassRdd; }

scala> val dwClassRdd1 = processRdd(data1)
scala> val dwClassRdd2 = processRdd(data2)
scala> val dwClassRdd3 = processRdd(data3)
scala> val dwClassRdd4 = processRdd(data4)

scala> dwClassRdd1.take(5).foreach(println)
DayWeather(2006-11-
16,17.0,14.0,12.0,13.0,10.0,8.0,100.0,77.0,63.0,1004.0,1002.0,1001.0,10.0,10.0
,4.0,40.0,23.0,60.0,0.0,6.0,Rain,185.0)
DayWeather(2006-11-
17,14.0,11.0,9.0,11.0,8.0,7.0,94.0,83.0,72.0,1009.0,1007.0,1004.0,10.0,10.0,10
.0,32.0,18.0,58.0,0.0,5.0,Rain,202.0)
DayWeather(2006-11-
18,13.0,10.0,8.0,9.0,6.0,3.0,100.0,78.0,54.0,1019.0,1014.0,1007.0,10.0,10.0,10
.0,34.0,18.0,52.0,0.0,6.0,Rain,215.0)
DayWeather(2006-11-
19,10.0,8.0,5.0,9.0,6.0,4.0,100.0,90.0,76.0,1022.0,1018.0,1013.0,10.0,9.0,5.0,
26.0,11.0,0.0,0.0,5.0,Rain,284.0)
DayWeather(2006-11-
20,12.0,8.0,5.0,12.0,7.0,4.0,100.0,92.0,81.0,1021.0,1012.0,1003.0,10.0,9.0,3.0
,34.0,21.0,52.0,0.0,6.0,Rain,196.0)
```

We can replace 0 inserted in the previous step with an NA in the string fields, as follows:

```
scala> val dwDS1 = dwClassRdd1.toDF().na.replace(Seq("CET", "Events"),Map("0" ->
"NA")).as[DayWeather]
scala> val dwDS2 = dwClassRdd2.toDF().na.replace(Seq("CET", "Events"),Map("0" ->
"NA")).as[DayWeather]
scala> val dwDS3 = dwClassRdd3.toDF().na.replace(Seq("CET", "Events"),Map("0" ->
"NA")).as[DayWeather]
scala> val dwDS4 = dwClassRdd4.toDF().na.replace(Seq("CET", "Events"),Map("0" ->
"NA")).as[DayWeather]
```

At this stage, we can combine the rows of the four Datasets into a single Dataset using the union operation.

```
scala> val finalDs2 = dwDS1.union(dwDS2).union(dwDS3).union(dwDS4)

scala> finalDs2.count()
res83: Long = 1472
```

At this stage, the processing of our second Dataset containing weather data is complete. In the next section, we combine these pre-processed Datasets using a join operation.

Combining data using a JOIN operation

In this section, we will introduce the JOIN operation, in which the daily household electric power consumption is combined with the weather data. We have assumed the locations of readings taken for the household electric power consumption and the weather readings are in close enough proximity to be relevant.

Next, we use the join operation to combine the daily household electric power consumption Dataset with the weather Dataset.

```
scala> val joinedDF =
finalDayDs1.join(finalDs2).where(unix_timestamp(finalDayDs1("date"),
"dd/MM/yyyy") === unix_timestamp(finalDs2("CET"), "yyyy-MM-dd"))
```

Verify the number of rows in the final DataFrame obtained with the number of rows expected subsequent to the join operation shown as follows:

```
scala> joinedDF.count()
res84: Long = 1433
```

You can compute a series of correlations between various columns in the newly joined Dataset containing columns from each of the two original Datasets to get a feel for the strength and direction of relationships between the columns, as follows:

```
scala> val corr = joinedDF.stat.corr("Mean_TemperatureC","dgap")
corr: Double = -0.5407030887973712

scala> println("Mean_TemperatureC to grp : Correlation = %.4f".format(corr))
Mean_TemperatureC to grp : Correlation = -0.5407

scala> val corr = joinedDF.stat.corr("Mean_TemperatureC","dgrp")
corr: Double = 0.47091563055684876

scala> println("Mean_TemperatureC to dgrp : Correlation = %.4f".format(corr))
Mean_TemperatureC to dgrp : Correlation = 0.4709

scala> val corr = joinedDF.stat.corr("Mean_Humidity","dgap")
corr: Double = 0.3420834803263318

scala> val corr = joinedDF.stat.corr("Mean_Humidity","dgrp")
corr: Double = -0.2778028625600493

scala> val corr = joinedDF.stat.corr("Max_TemperatureC","dsm_1")
corr: Double = -0.12588773465430714

scala> val corr = joinedDF.stat.corr("Max_TemperatureC","dsm_2")
corr: Double = -0.12267913849215695

scala> val corr = joinedDF.stat.corr("Max_TemperatureC","dsm_3")
corr: Double = -0.37749055597177456
```

Similarly, you can join the Datasets grouped by year and month to get a higher-level summarization of the data.

```
scala> val joinedMonthlyDF = joinedDF.groupBy("year",
"month").agg(sum($"dgap").name("A"),sum($"dgrp").name("B"),avg($"dvoltage").na
me("C"),sum($"dgi").name("D"), sum($"dsm_1").name("E"),
sum($"dsm_2").name("F"), sum($"dsm_3").name("G")).select($"year", $"month",
round($"A", 2).name("mgap"), round($"B", 2).name("mgrp"), round($"C",
2).name("mvoltage"), round($"C", 2).name("mgi"), round($"E", 2).name("msm_1"),
round($"F", 2).name("msm_2"), round($"G", 2).name("msm_3")).orderBy("year",
"month")
```

In order to visualize the summarized data, we can execute the preceding statements in an Apache Zeppelin notebook. For instance, we can plot the monthly **Global Reactive Power (GRP)** values by transforming `joinedMonthlyDF` into a table and then selecting the appropriate columns from it, as follows:

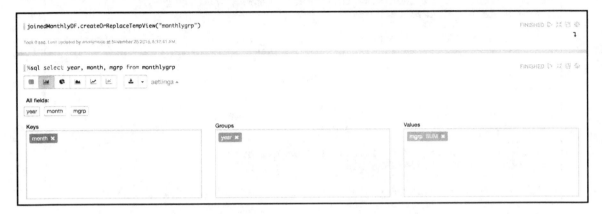

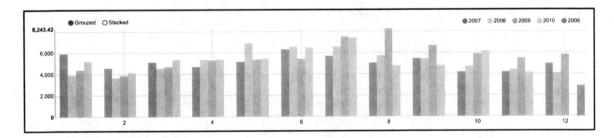

Similarly, if you want to analyze readings by the day of the week then follow, the steps as shown:

```scala
scala> val joinedDayDF =
finalDayDs1.join(finalDs2).where(unix_timestamp(finalDayDs1("date"),
"dd/MM/yyyy") === unix_timestamp(finalDs2("CET"), "yyyy-MM-dd"))

scala> joinedDayDF.count()
res87: Long = 1433

scala> val joinedDayDowDF = joinedDayDF.withColumn("dow",
from_unixtime(unix_timestamp($"date", "dd/MM/yyyy"), "EEEEE"))
```

Finally, we print the schema of the joined Dataset (augmented with the day of the week column) so you can further explore the relationships between various fields of this DataFrame:

```
scala> joinedDayDowDF.printSchema()
root
 |-- date: string (nullable = true)
 |-- dgap: double (nullable = true)
 |-- dgrp: double (nullable = true)
 |-- dvoltage: double (nullable = true)
 |-- dgi: double (nullable = true)
 |-- dsm_1: double (nullable = true)
 |-- dsm_2: double (nullable = true)
 |-- dsm_3: double (nullable = true)
 |-- day: integer (nullable = true)
 |-- month: integer (nullable = true)
 |-- year: integer (nullable = true)
 |-- CET: string (nullable = true)
 |-- Max_TemperatureC: double (nullable = false)
 |-- Mean_TemperatureC: double (nullable = false)
 |-- Min_TemperatureC: double (nullable = false)
 |-- Dew_PointC: double (nullable = false)
 |-- MeanDew_PointC: double (nullable = false)
 |-- Min_DewpointC: double (nullable = false)
 |-- Max_Humidity: double (nullable = false)
 |-- Mean_Humidity: double (nullable = false)
 |-- Min_Humidity: double (nullable = false)
 |-- Max_Sea_Level_PressurehPa: double (nullable = false)
 |-- Mean_Sea_Leve_PressurehPa: double (nullable = false)
 |-- Min_Sea_Level_PressurehPa: double (nullable = false)
 |-- Max_VisibilityKm: double (nullable = false)
 |-- Mean_VisibilityKm: double (nullable = false)
 |-- Min_VisibilitykM: double (nullable = false)
 |-- Max_Wind_SpeedKmph: double (nullable = false)
 |-- Mean_Wind_SpeedKmph: double (nullable = false)
 |-- Max_Gust_SpeedKmph: double (nullable = false)
 |-- Precipitationmm: double (nullable = false)
 |-- CloudCover: double (nullable = false)
 |-- Events: string (nullable = true)
 |-- WindDirDegrees: double (nullable = false)
 |-- dow: string (nullable = true)
```

In the next section, we shift our focus to munging textual data.

Munging textual data

In this section, we explore data munging techniques for typical text analysis situations. Many text-based analyses tasks require computing word counts, removing stop words, stemming, and so on. In addition, we will also explore how you can process multiple files, one at a time, from HDFS directories.

First, we import all the classes that will be used in this section:

```scala
scala> import org.apache.spark.sql.types.{StructType, StructField, StringType}
scala> import org.apache.spark.sql.DataFrame
scala> import spark.implicits._
```

Processing multiple input data files

In the next few steps, we initialize a set of variables for defining the directory containing the input files, and an empty RDD. We also create a list of filenames from the input HDFS directory. In the following example, we will work with files contained in a single directory; however, the techniques can easily be extended across all 20 newsgroup sub-directories.

```scala
scala> val path = "hdfs://localhost:9000/20_newsgroups/comp.graphics"
scala> val data = spark.sparkContext.wholeTextFiles(path)
scala> var output : org.apache.spark.rdd.RDD[(String, String, Int)] =
sc.emptyRDD
scala> val files = data.map { case (filename, content) => filename}
```

Next, we write a function to compute the word counts for each file and collect the results in an `ArrayBuffer`:

```scala
scala> def Process(filename: String):
org.apache.spark.rdd.RDD[(String, String, Int)]= {
     |      println("Processing:" + filename)
     |      val fpath = filename.split('/').last;
     |      val lines = spark.sparkContext.textFile(filename);
     |      val counts = lines.flatMap(line => line.split("
")).map(word => word).map(word => (word, 1)).reduceByKey(_ + _);
     |      val word_counts = counts.map( x => (fpath,x._1, x._2));
     |      word_counts
     | }

scala> val buf =
scala.collection.mutable.ArrayBuffer.empty[org.apache.spark.rdd.RDD[(
String, String, Int)]]

scala> files.collect.foreach( filename => { buf += Process(filename);
})
```

We have included a print statement to display the file names as they are picked up for processing, as follows:

```
Processing:hdfs://localhost:9000/20_newsgroups/comp.graphics/37261
Processing:hdfs://localhost:9000/20_newsgroups/comp.graphics/37913
Processing:hdfs://localhost:9000/20_newsgroups/comp.graphics/37914
                               .
                               .
                               .
Processing:hdfs://localhost:9000/20_newsgroups/comp.graphics/40008
Processing:hdfs://localhost:9000/20_newsgroups/comp.graphics/40027
Processing:hdfs://localhost:9000/20_newsgroups/comp.graphics/40062
```

We add the rows into a single RDD using the `union` operation:

```
scala> output = spark.sparkContext.union(buf.toList);
```

We could have directly executed the union step as each file is processed, as follows:

```
files.collect.foreach( filename => { output = output.union(Process(filename));
})
```

However, using `RDD.union()` creates a new step in the lineage graph requiring an extra set of stack frames for each new RDD. This can easily lead to a Stack Overflow condition. Instead, we use `SparkContext.union()` which executes the `union` operation all at once without the extra memory overheads.

We can cache and print sample rows from our output RDD as follows:

```
scala> output.cache()

scala> output.take(5).foreach(println)
(37261,sent,1)
(37261,sponsoring,1)
(37261,deadline,1)
(37261,seminar),1)
(37261,Short,1)
```

In the next section, we show you ways of filtering out stop words. For simplicity, we focus only on well-formed words in the text. However, you can easily add conditions to filter out special characters and other anomalies in our data using String functions and regexes (for a detailed example, refer Chapter 9, *Developing Applications with Spark SQL).*

Removing stop words

In our example, we create a set of stop words and filter them out from the words in contained in each file. Normally, a Spark operation executing on a remote node works on a separate copy of the variables used in the function. We can use a broadcast variable to maintain a read-only, cached copy of the set of stop words at each node in the cluster instead of shipping a copy of it with the tasks to be executed on the nodes. Spark attempts to distribute the broadcast variables efficiently to reduce the overall communication overheads. Further more, we also filter out empty lists returned by the function as a result of our filtering process and stop words removal.

```scala
scala> val stopWords = sc.broadcast(Set("as", "able", "about",
"above", "according", "accordingly", "across", "actually", "..."))

scala> def processLine(s: String, stopWords: Set[String]):
List[String] = {
    |        s.toLowerCase()
    |          .split("\\s+")
    |          .filter(x => x.matches("[A-Za-z]+"))
    |          .filter(!stopWords.contains(_))
    |          .toList
    | }

scala> val groupedRDD = output.map{ case (x, y, z) => (x,
(processLine(y.trim(), stopWords.value)).mkString, z)}.filter{case
(x, y, z) => !y.equals("")}

scala> groupedRDD.take(20).foreach(println)
(37261,sent,1)
(37261,sponsoring,1)
(37261,deadline,1)
(37261,short,1)
(37261,materials,1)
(37261,june,2)
(37261,include,1)
(37261,reality,2)
(37261,organizations,1)
(37261,type,1)
(37261,reality,1)
(37261,voice,1)
(37261,visualization,3)
(37261,naval,2)
(37261,please,1)
(37261,visualization,1)
(37261,viewgraphs,1)
(37261,solicited,1)
(37261,proposed,1)
(37261,purpose,1)
```

We can extract the words from each of the tuples in the RDD and create a DataFrame containing them, as follows:

```scala
scala> val words = groupedRDD.map{ case (x, y, z) => y}
scala> val wordsDF = words.toDF
```

In the following example, we show another method for filtering out the stop words from our list of words. In order to improve the word matches between the two lists, we process the stop words file in a similar manner to the words extracted from the input files. We read the file containing stop words, remove leading and trailing spaces, convert to lower case, replace special characters, filter out empty words, and, finally, create a DataFrame (containing the stop words).

> We use the list of stop words available at
> `http://algs4.cs.princeton.edu/35applications/stopwords.txt` in our example.

```scala
scala> val stopwords =
sc.textFile("file:///Users/aurobindosarkar/Downloads/sparkworks/Spark
Book/data/stopwords.txt")
```

Here, we use a `regex` to filter out special characters contained in the file.

```scala
scala> val regex = "[,.:;'\"\\?\\-!\\(\\)]".r

scala> val stopwordsDF = stopwords.flatMap(line =>
line.split("[\\s]")).map(word =>
regex.replaceAllIn(word.trim.toLowerCase, "")).filter(word =>
!word.isEmpty).toDF()

scala> stopwordsDF.count()
res4: Long = 544
```

Next, we compare the number of words in our list before and after the removal of the stop words from our original list of words. The final number of words remaining suggests that a majority of words in our input files were stop words.

```scala
scala> words.count()
res5: Long = 88268

scala> val cleanwords = wordsDF.except(stopwordsDF)

scala> cleanwords.count()
res7: Long = 10245
```

For a more detailed coverage of text data processing (of an annual 10-K financial filing document and other document corpuses) including building pre-processing data pipelines, identifying themes in document corpuses, using Naïve Bayes classifiers, and developing a machine learning application, refer Chapter 9, *Developing Applications with Spark SQL.*

In the next section, we shift our focus to munging time-series data using the spark-time-series library from Cloudera.

Munging time series data

Time series data is a sequence of values linked to a timestamp. In this section, we use Cloudera's spark-ts package for analyzing time-series data.

 Refer to *Cloudera Engineering Blog, A New Library for Analyzing Time-Series Data with Apache Spark,* for more details on time-series data and its processing using spark-ts. This blog is available at: https://github.com/sryza/spark-timeseries.

The spark-ts package can be downloaded and built using instructions available at:

https://github.com/sryza/spark-timeseries.

We will attempt to accomplish the following objectives in the following sub-sections:

- Pre-processing of the time-series Dataset
- Processing date fields
- Persisting and loading data
- Defining a date-time index
- Using the TimeSeriesRDD object
- Handling missing time-series data
- Computing basic statistics

For this section, specify inclusion of the spark-ts.jar file while starting the Spark shell as shown:

```
bin/spark-shell --jars /Users/aurobindosarkar/Downloads/spark-timeseries-
master/target/sparkts-0.4.0-SNAPSHOT-jar-with-dependencies.jar
```

We download Datasets containing pricing and volume data for six stocks over a one year period from the Yahoo Finance site. We will need to pre-process the data before we can use the `spark-ts` package for time-series data analysis.

Import the classes required in this section.

```
scala> import java.sql.Timestamp
scala> import java.time.{LocalDateTime, ZoneId, ZonedDateTime}
scala> import com.cloudera.sparkts._
scala> import com.cloudera.sparkts.stats.TimeSeriesStatisticalTests
scala> import org.apache.spark.{SparkContext, SparkConf}
scala> import org.apache.spark.sql.{DataFrame, Row, SQLContext}
scala> import org.apache.spark.sql.types._
```

Pre-processing of the time-series Dataset

Read the data from the input data files and define a `case` class Stock containing the fields in the Dataset plus a field to hold the ticker symbol.

```
scala> val amznRDD =
sc.textFile("file:///Users/aurobindosarkar/Downloads/yahoo/tableAMZN.csv")
scala> val orclRDD =
sc.textFile("file:///Users/aurobindosarkar/Downloads/yahoo/tableORCL.csv")
scala> val ibmRDD =
sc.textFile("file:///Users/aurobindosarkar/Downloads/yahoo/tableIBM.csv")
scala> val cscoRDD =
sc.textFile("file:///Users/aurobindosarkar/Downloads/yahoo/tableCSCO.csv")
scala> val googRDD =
sc.textFile("file:///Users/aurobindosarkar/Downloads/yahoo/tableGOOG.csv")
scala> val msftRDD =
sc.textFile("file:///Users/aurobindosarkar/Downloads/yahoo/tableMSFT.csv")

scala> case class Stock(ticker: String, datestr: String, open: Double, high:
Double, low: Double, close: Double, volume: Int, adjclose: Double)
```

Next, we remove the header from each of the files, map our RDD row using the `case` class, include a string for the ticker symbol, and convert the RDD to a DataFrame.

```
scala> val header = amznRDD.first()

scala> val amznData = amznRDD.filter(row => row !=
header).map(_.split(",")).map(p => Stock("AMZN", p(0).trim().toString,
p(1).toDouble, p(2).toDouble, p(3).toDouble, p(4).toDouble, p(5).toInt,
p(6).toDouble)).toDF.as[Stock]

scala> val orclData = orclRDD.filter(row => row !=
header).map(_.split(",")).map(p => Stock("ORCL", p(0).trim().toString,
p(1).toDouble, p(2).toDouble, p(3).toDouble, p(4).toDouble, p(5).toInt,
p(6).toDouble)).toDF.as[Stock]

scala> val ibmData = ibmRDD.filter(row => row !=
header).map(_.split(",")).map(p => Stock("IBM", p(0).trim().toString,
p(1).toDouble, p(2).toDouble, p(3).toDouble, p(4).toDouble, p(5).toInt,
p(6).toDouble)).toDF.as[Stock]

scala> val cscoData = cscoRDD.filter(row => row !=
header).map(_.split(",")).map(p => Stock("CSCO", p(0).trim().toString,
p(1).toDouble, p(2).toDouble, p(3).toDouble, p(4).toDouble, p(5).toInt,
p(6).toDouble)).toDF.as[Stock]

scala> val googData = googRDD.filter(row => row !=
header).map(_.split(",")).map(p => Stock("GOOG", p(0).trim().toString,
p(1).toDouble, p(2).toDouble, p(3).toDouble, p(4).toDouble, p(5).toInt,
p(6).toDouble)).toDF.as[Stock]

scala> val msftData = msftRDD.filter(row => row !=
header).map(_.split(",")).map(p => Stock("MSFT", p(0).trim().toString,
p(1).toDouble, p(2).toDouble, p(3).toDouble, p(4).toDouble, p(5).toInt,
p(6).toDouble)).toDF.as[Stock]
```

Next, we combine the rows from each of our DataFrames using `union`.

```
scala> val allData =
amznData.union(orclData).union(ibmData).union(cscoData).union(googData).union(msftData)
```

Processing date fields

In the next step, we separate out the date column into three separate fields containing the day, month, and the year information.

```
scala> val allWithDMY = allData.withColumn("day",
dayofmonth(to_date(unix_timestamp($"datestr", "yyyy-MM-
dd").cast("timestamp")))).withColumn("month",
month(to_date(unix_timestamp($"datestr", "yyyy-MM-
dd").cast("timestamp")))).withColumn("year",
year(to_date(unix_timestamp($"datestr", "yyyy-MM-dd").cast("timestamp"))))
```

Persisting and loading data

At this stage, we can persist our DataFrame to a CSV file using the `DataFrameWriter` class. The overwrite mode lets you overwrite the file, if it is already present from a previous execution of the `write` operation:

```
scala>
allWithDMY.write.mode("overwrite").csv("file:///Users/aurobindosarkar/Downloads/dtDF")
```

For loading the time series Dataset written to disk in the previous step, we define a function to load our observations from a file and return a DataFrame:

```scala
scala> def loadObservations(sqlContext: SQLContext, path: String): DataFrame =
{
    |        val rowRdd = sqlContext.sparkContext.textFile(path).map { line =>
    |        val tokens = line.split(',');
    |        val dt = ZonedDateTime.of(tokens(10).toInt, tokens(9).toInt,
tokens(8).toInt, 0, 0, 0, 0, ZoneId.systemDefault());
    |        val ticker = tokens(0).toString;
    |        val open = tokens(2).toDouble;
    |        val high = tokens(3).toDouble;
    |        val low = tokens(4).toDouble;
    |        val close = tokens(5).toDouble;
    |        val volume = tokens(6).toInt;
    |        val adjclose = tokens(7).toDouble;
    |        Row(Timestamp.from(dt.toInstant), ticker, open, high, low, close,
volume, adjclose);
    |        }
    |        val fields = Seq(StructField("timestamp", TimestampType, true),
StructField("ticker", StringType, true), StructField("open", DoubleType,
true), StructField("high", DoubleType, true), StructField("low", DoubleType,
true), StructField("close", DoubleType, true), StructField("volume",
IntegerType, true), StructField("adjclose", DoubleType, true));
    |        val schema = StructType(fields);
    |        sqlContext.createDataFrame(rowRdd, schema);
    |    }
```

```scala
scala> val tickerObs = loadObservations(spark.sqlContext,
"file:///Users/aurobindosarkar/Downloads/dtDF")

scala> tickerObs.show(5)
+-------------------+------+---------+---------+---------+---------+-------+---------+
|          timestamp|ticker|     open|     high|      low|    close| volume| adjclose|
+-------------------+------+---------+---------+---------+---------+-------+---------+
|2016-12-02 00:00:...|  AMZN|743.400024| 748.48999|736.700012|740.340027|3499200|740.340027|
|2016-12-01 00:00:...|  AMZN|752.409973|753.369995|738.030029|743.650024|4626500|743.650024|
|2016-11-30 00:00:...|  AMZN|     762.0|768.090027|    750.25|750.570007|4580100|750.570007|
|2016-11-29 00:00:...|  AMZN|     768.0|769.890015|761.320007| 762.52002|3266500| 762.52002|
|2016-11-28 00:00:...|  AMZN| 776.98999|    777.0| 764.23999|766.77002|4380900| 766.77002|
+-------------------+------+---------+---------+---------+---------+-------+---------+
only showing top 5 rows
```

Defining a date-time index

We define a date-time index for the period for which we have the data so that each record (for a specific ticker symbol) includes a time series represented as an array of 366 positions for each of the days in the year (plus one extra day as we have downloaded the data from 12/04/2015 to 12/04/2016). The Business Day Frequency specifies that the data is available for the business days of the year only.

```scala
scala> val zone = ZoneId.systemDefault()
zone: java.time.ZoneId = Asia/Kolkata

scala> val dtIndex =
DateTimeIndex.uniformFromInterval(ZonedDateTime.of(LocalDateTime.parse("2015-
12-04T00:00:00"), zone), ZonedDateTime.of(LocalDateTime.parse("2016-12-
04T00:00:00"), zone), new BusinessDayFrequency(1))
```

Using the TimeSeriesRDD object

The main abstraction in the `spark-ts` library is a RDD called `TimeSeriesRDD`. The data is a set of observations represented as a tuple of (timestamp, key, value). The key is a label used to identify the time series. In the following example, our tuple is (timestamp, ticker, close). Each series in the RDD has the ticker symbol as the key and the daily closing price of the stock as the value.

```scala
scala> val tickerTsrdd =
TimeSeriesRDD.timeSeriesRDDFromObservations(dtIndex, tickerObs,
"timestamp", "ticker", "close")
```

We can cache and display the number of rows in the RDD which should be equal to the number of stocks in our example:

```scala
scala> tickerTsrdd.cache()

scala> println(tickerTsrdd.count())
6
```

Display a couple of rows from the RDD to see the data in each row:

```
scala> tickerTsrdd.take(2).foreach(println)

(GOOG,[766.809998,763.25,762.369995,751.609985,749.460022,738.869995,747.77002,743.400024,758.090027,749
.429993,739.309998,747.77002,750.0,750.309998,748.400024,NaN,762.51001,776.599976,771.0,758.880005,NaN,7
41.840027,742.580017,743.619995,726.390015,714.469971,716.030029,726.070007,700.559998,714.719971,694.45
0012,NaN,701.789978,698.450012,706.590027,725.25,711.669983,713.039978,699.98999,730.960022,742.950012,7
52.0,764.650024,726.950012,708.01001,683.570007,682.73999,678.109985,684.119995,683.109985,682.400024,Na
N,691.0,708.400024,697.349976,700.909973,706.460022,695.849976,699.559998,705.75,705.070007,697.77002,71
8.809998,718.849976,712.419983,710.890015,695.159973,693.969971,705.23999,712.820007,726.820007,730.4899
9,728.330017,736.090027,737.780029,737.599976,742.090027,740.75,738.059998,735.299988,NaN,733.530029,744
.77002,750.530029,744.950012,749.909973,745.289978,737.799988,745.690002,740.280029,739.150024,736.09997
6,743.090027,751.719971,753.200012,759.0,766.609985,753.929993,752.669983,759.140015,718.77002,723.15002
4,708.140015,705.840027,691.02002,693.01001,698.210022,692.359985,695.700012,701.429993,711.119995,712.9
00024,723.179993,715.289978,713.309998,710.830017,716.48999,706.22998,706.630005,700.320007,709.73999,70
4.23999,720.090027,725.27002,724.119995,732.659973,NaN,735.719971,734.150024,730.400024,722.340027,716.5
49988,716.650024,728.280029,728.580017,719.409973,718.359985,718.27002,718.919983,710.359985,691.719971,
693.710022,695.940002,697.460022,701.869995,675.219971,668.26001,680.039978,684.109985,692.099976,699.21
0022,NaN,694.950012,697.77002,695.359985,705.630005,715.090027,720.640015,716.97998,720.950012,719.84997
6,733.780029,736.960022,741.190002,738.630005,742.73999,739.77002,738.419983,741.77002,745.909973,768.78
9978,772.880005,771.070007,773.179993,771.609985,782.219971,781.76001,784.26001,784.679993,784.849976,78
3.219971,782.440002,777.140015,779.909973,777.5,775.419983,772.150024,772.080017,769.640015,769.409973,7
69.539978,772.150024,769.090027,767.049988,768.780029,771.460022,NaN,780.080017,780.349976,775.320007,75
9.659973,769.02002,759.690002,762.48999,771.76001,768.880005,765.700012,771.409973,776.219971,787.210022
,786.900024,774.210022,783.01001,781.559998,775.01001,777.289978,772.559998,776.429993,776.469971,776.85
9985,775.080017,785.940002,783.070007,786.140015,778.190002,778.530029,779.960022,795.26001,801.5,796.96
9971,799.369995,813.109985,807.669983,799.070007,795.349976,795.369995,784.539978,783.609985,768.700012,
762.130005,762.02002,782.52002,790.51001,785.309998,762.559998,754.02002,736.080017,758.48999,764.47998,
771.22998,760.539978,769.200012,768.27002,760.98999,NaN,761.679993,768.23999,770.840027,758.039978,747.9
19983,750.5])
(IBM,[140.429993,139.550003,138.050003,136.610001,136.779999,134.570007,135.929993,137.789993,139.289993
,136.75,134.899994,135.5,137.929993,138.539993,138.25,NaN,137.610001,139.779999,139.339996,137.619995,Na
N,135.949997,135.850006,135.169998,132.860001,131.630005,133.229996,132.899994,131.169998,132.910004,130
.029999,NaN,128.110001,121.860001,122.910004,122.5,122.080002,122.589996,120.959999,122.220001,124.79000
1,124.830002,122.940002,124.720001,127.650002,128.570007,126.980003,124.07,120.190002,117.849998,121.040
001,NaN,122.739998,126.099998,132.449997,133.080002,133.770004,132.399994,132.800003,134.5,132.029999,13
1.029999,134.369995,136.300003,137.800003,137.800003,140.149994,139.070007,140.410004,140.190002,142.360
001,142.779999,142.960007,144.789993,147.039993,147.089996,148.630005,148.100006,145.399994,147.949997,N
aN,148.399994,149.330002,148.410004,151.449997,152.520004,152.070007,150.0,150.020004,148.25,149.350006,
149.25,149.630005,151.229996,151.160004,151.720001,152.529999,144.0,146.110001,149.300003,148.5,148.8099
98,149.080002,150.470001,147.070007,145.940002,145.270004,144.130005,144.25,146.470001,147.289993,147.33
9996,149.970001,148.949997,148.839996,147.720001,149.460007,148.0,147.339996,144.929993,147.25,146.77000
4,148.309998,151.690002,152.440002,152.839996,NaN,153.740005,152.509995,153.5,152.889999,152.729996,153.
330002,154.0,153.419998,152.369995,151.279999,151.059998,150.679993,151.059998,151.990005,153.610001,154
.050003,152.919998,155.350006,146.589996,143.5,145.699997,148.460007,151.779999,152.350006,NaN,151.67999
3,152.369995,152.600006,154.460007,155.330002,157.039993,158.020004,160.279999,159.779999,159.860001,159
.580002,161.360001,160.449997,162.070007,162.649994,162.119995,161.830002,161.369995,160.619995,161.4499
97,160.580002,160.669998,161.550003,163.5,162.039993,161.770004,162.080002,163.529999,161.949997,161.880
005,160.699997,160.440002,161.360001,160.039993,160.0,160.259995,159.050003,158.630005,158.320007,159.72
0001,159.399994,158.880005,159.539993,159.550003,NaN,160.350006,161.639999,159.0,155.690002,158.289993,1
55.809998,154.050003,155.660004,153.839996,154.869995,154.449997,155.529999,156.110001,154.979996,153.97
9996,156.770004,158.289993,158.110001,158.850006,157.610001,156.460007,157.080002,156.880005,155.669998,
157.020004,154.789993,154.289993,153.720001,154.449997,154.770004,150.720001,151.259995,151.520004,149.6
30005,150.570007,150.880005,151.809998,153.300006,152.610001,153.690002,152.789993,151.949997,152.369995
,152.429993,155.720001,155.169998,154.809998,160.220001,161.270004,158.210007,158.669998,159.289993,159.
800003,160.389999,162.770004,162.669998,161.979996,NaN,163.139999,164.520004,163.529999,162.220001,159.8
20007,160.020004])
```

Handling missing time-series data

Next, we check the RDD for missing data. The missing data is marked with NaN values. Computing basic statistics with NaN values present will give errors. Hence, we need to replace these missing values with approximations. Our example data does not contain any missing fields. However, as an exercise, we delete a few values from the input datasets to simulate these NaN values in the RDD, and then impute these values using linear interpolation. Other approximations available include next, previous, and nearest values.

We fill in the approximate values for the missing values, as follows:

```scala
scala> val filled = tickerTsrdd.fill("linear")
```

Computing basic statistics

Finally, we compute the mean, standard deviation, max and min values for each of our series, as follows:

```scala
scala> val stats = filled.seriesStats()

scala> stats.foreach(println)

(count: 261, mean: 28.518161, stdev: 2.328072, max: 31.870001, min: 22.510000)
(count: 261, mean: 691.321877, stdev: 90.598730, max: 844.359985, min: 482.070007)
(count: 261, mean: 740.845729, stdev: 32.360211, max: 813.109985, min: 668.260010)
(count: 261, mean: 39.054598, stdev: 1.973492, max: 41.770000, min: 33.939999)
(count: 261, mean: 148.243046, stdev: 11.410119, max: 164.520004, min: 117.849998)
(count: 261, mean: 54.719253, stdev: 3.231158, max: 61.119999, min: 48.430000)
```

There are many other useful functions available for exploratory data analysis and data munging using the TimeSeriesRDD object. These include collecting the RDD as a local time series, finding specific time series, various filters and slicing functionality, sorting and re-partitioning the data, writing out the time series to CSV files, and many more.

Dealing with variable length records

In this section, we will explore a way of dealing with variable length records. Our approach essentially converts each of the rows to a fixed length record equal to the maximum length record. In our example, as each row represents a portfolio and there is no unique identifier, this method is useful for manipulating data into the familiar fixed length records case. We will generate the requisite number of fields to equal the maximum number of stocks in the largest portfolio. This will lead to empty fields where the number of stocks is less than the maximum number of stocks in any portfolio. Another way to deal with variable length records is to use the explode() function to create new rows for each stock in a given portfolio (for an example of using the explode() function, refer Chapter 9, *Developing Applications with Spark SQL).*

To avoid repeating all the steps from previous examples to read in all the files, we have combined the data into a single input file in this example.

First, we import the classes required and read the input file into an RDD:

```scala
scala> import org.apache.spark.sql.types._

scala> import spark.implicits._

scala> import org.apache.spark.sql.functions.{from_unixtime, unix_timestamp}

scala> import org.apache.spark.sql.functions.udf

scala> import org.apache.spark.sql.{Row, Column, DataFrame}

scala> import scala.collection.mutable.WrappedArray

scala> import org.apache.spark.rdd.RDD

scala> val inputRDD =
sc.textFile("file:///Users/aurobindosarkar/Downloads/ZZAlpha1/combined.txt")
```

We count the total number of portfolios and print a few records from the RDD. You can see that while the first and the second portfolios contain one stock each, the third one contains two stocks.

```
scala> inputRDD.count()

res0: Long = 481261

scala> inputRDD.take(5).foreach(println)
Jan 03 2012_006 Big_100_1_LONG_SHORT_F.pdf, L, DB 0.888 =35.23/39.67, Avg of 1 = 0.888
Jan 03 2012_006 Big_100_1_LONG_SHORT_F.pdf, S, LLY 0.956 =40.11/41.95, Avg of 1 = 0.956
Jan 03 2012_006 Big_100_2_LONG_SHORT_F.pdf, L, DB 0.888 =35.23/39.67, SU 1.068
=31.78/29.77, Avg of 2 = 0.978
Jan 03 2012_006 Big_100_2_LONG_SHORT_F.pdf, S, LLY 0.956 =40.11/41.95, MO 1.005
=28.79/28.65, Avg of 2 = 0.981
Jan 03 2012_006 Big_100_5_LONG_SHORT_F.pdf, L, DB 0.888 =35.23/39.67, MON 1.107
=78.97/71.32, OXY 1.021 =98.73/96.73, RY 1.001 =51.84/51.77, SU 1.068 =31.78/29.77, Avg
of 5 = 1.017
```

Converting variable-length records to fixed-length records

In our example Dataset, there are no fields missing, hence, we can use the number of commas in each row to derive the varying number stock-related fields in each of the portfolios. Alternatively, this information can be extracted from the strings contained in last field of the RDD.

Next, we create a UDF to count the number of stocks indirectly by counting the number of commas in each row. We use `describe` to find the maximum number of commas across all rows in the dataset.

```
scala> def countSubstring( str:String, substr:String ) =
substr.r.findAllMatchIn(str).length

scala> def nSubs(substr: String) = udf((x: String) => countSubstring(x,
substr))

scala> val nCommas = inputRDD.toDF().withColumn("commas",
nSubs(",")($"value"))

scala> nCommas.describe().select($"summary", $"commas").where(($"summary" ===
"count") || ($"summary" === "max")).show()
+-------+------+
|summary|commas|
+-------+------+
|  count|481261|
|    max|    22|
+-------+------+
```

In the next step, we augment the DataFrame with a column containing the number of commas.

```
scala> nCommas.take(5).foreach(println)
[Jan 03 2012_006 Big_100_1_LONG_SHORT_F.pdf, L, DB 0.888 =35.23/39.67, Avg of 1 =
0.888,3]
[Jan 03 2012_006 Big_100_1_LONG_SHORT_F.pdf, S, LLY 0.956 =40.11/41.95, Avg of 1 =
0.956,3]
[Jan 03 2012_006 Big_100_2_LONG_SHORT_F.pdf, L, DB 0.888 =35.23/39.67, SU 1.068
=31.78/29.77, Avg of 2 = 0.978,4]
[Jan 03 2012_006 Big_100_2_LONG_SHORT_F.pdf, S, LLY 0.956 =40.11/41.95, MO 1.005
=28.79/28.65, Avg of 2 = 0.981,4]
[Jan 03 2012_006 Big_100_5_LONG_SHORT_F.pdf, L, DB 0.888 =35.23/39.67, MON 1.107
=78.97/71.32, OXY 1.021 =98.73/96.73, RY 1.001 =51.84/51.77, SU 1.068 =31.78/29.77, Avg
of 5 = 1.017,7]
```

Then we write a function to insert the correct number of commas in each row at the appropriate location:

```
scala> def insertSubstring( str:String, substr:String, times: Int ): String =
{ val builder = StringBuilder.newBuilder; builder.append(str.substring(0,
str.lastIndexOf(substr)+1));builder.append(substr * (22-
times));builder.append(str.substring(str.lastIndexOf(substr)+1));
builder.toString;}

scala> def nInserts(substr: String) = udf((x: String, times: Int) =>
insertSubstring(x, substr, times))
```

Next, we drop the number of commas column, as it is not required in the subsequent steps:

```
scala> val fixedLengthDf = nCommas.withColumn("record",
nInserts(",")($"value", $"commas")).drop("value", "commas")
```

```
scala> fixedLengthDf.take(5).foreach(println)
[Jan 03 2012_006 Big_100_1_LONG_SHORT_F.pdf, L, DB 0.888 =35.23/39.67,,,,,,,,,,,,,,,,,,,
Avg of 1 = 0.888]
[Jan 03 2012_006 Big_100_1_LONG_SHORT_F.pdf, S, LLY 0.956
=40.11/41.95,,,,,,,,,,,,,,,,,,, Avg of 1 = 0.956]
[Jan 03 2012_006 Big_100_2_LONG_SHORT_F.pdf, L, DB 0.888 =35.23/39.67, SU 1.068
=31.78/29.77,,,,,,,,,,,,,,,,,, Avg of 2 = 0.978]
[Jan 03 2012_006 Big_100_2_LONG_SHORT_F.pdf, S, LLY 0.956 =40.11/41.95, MO 1.005
=28.79/28.65,,,,,,,,,,,,,,,,,, Avg of 2 = 0.981]
[Jan 03 2012_006 Big_100_5_LONG_SHORT_F.pdf, L, DB 0.888 =35.23/39.67, MON 1.107
=78.97/71.32, OXY 1.021 =98.73/96.73, RY 1.001 =51.84/51.77, SU 1.068
=31.78/29.77,,,,,,,,,,,,,,,,, Avg of 5 = 1.017]
```

At this stage, if you want to get rid of duplicate rows in the DataFrame, then you can use the `dropDuplicates` method shown as follows:

```
scala> fixedLengthDf.count()
res5: Long = 481261

scala> val dupRemovedDf = fixedLengthDf.dropDuplicates()

scala> dupRemovedDf.count()
res6: Long = 478057
```

In the next step, we define a `case` class for the `Portfolio` with the maximum number of stocks in the largest portfolio.

```
scala> case class Portfolio(datestr: String, ls: String, stock1: String,
stock2: String, stock3: String, stock4: String, stock5: String, stock6:
String, stock7: String, stock8: String, stock9: String, stock10: String,
stock11: String, stock12: String, stock13: String, stock14: String, stock15:
String, stock16: String, stock17: String, stock18: String, stock19: String,
stock20: String, avgstr: String )
```

Next, we convert the RDD into a DataFrame. For convenience, we will demonstrate the operations using fewer stock-related columns; however, the same can be extended to fields for other stocks in the portfolio:

```
scala> val rowsRdd = dupRemovedDf.rdd.map{ row: Row =>
row.getString(0).split(",") }

scala> val dfFixed = rowsRdd.map(s => Portfolio(s(0), s(1), s(2), s(3), s(4),
s(5), s(6), s(7), s(8), s(9), s(10), s(11), s(12), s(13), s(14), s(15), s(16),
s(17), s(18), s(19), s(20), s(21), s(22))).toDF()

scala> dfFixed.count()
res7: Long = 478057
```

```
scala> dfFixed.select("datestr", "ls", "stock1", "stock2", "avgstr").show(5)
+--------------------+---+--------------------+--------------------+----------------+
|             datestr| ls|              stock1|              stock2|          avgstr|
+--------------------+---+--------------------+--------------------+----------------+
|Jan 03 2012_006 B...|  L| DB 0.888 =35.23/...|                    | Avg of 1 = 0.888|
|Jan 03 2012_006 B...|  S| LLY 0.956 =40.11...|                    | Avg of 1 = 0.956|
|Jan 03 2012_006 B...|  L| DB 0.888 =35.23/...| SU 1.068 =31.78/...| Avg of 2 = 0.978|
|Jan 03 2012_006 B...|  S| LLY 0.956 =40.11...| MO 1.005 =28.79/...| Avg of 2 = 0.981|
|Jan 03 2012_006 B...|  L| DB 0.888 =35.23/...| MON 1.107 =78.97...| Avg of 5 = 1.017|
+--------------------+---+--------------------+--------------------+----------------+
only showing top 5 rows
```

We can replace empty fields for stocks in the smaller portfolios with NA , as follows:

```
scala> val df2 = dfFixed.na.replace("stock2",ImmutableMap.of("",
"NA")).select("datestr", "ls", "stock1", "stock2", "avgstr")

scala> df2.show(5)
+-------------------+---+--------------------+--------------------+-----------------+
|            datestr| ls|              stock1|              stock2|           avgstr|
+-------------------+---+--------------------+--------------------+-----------------+
|Jan 03 2012_006 B...|  L| DB 0.888 =35.23/...|                  NA| Avg of 1 = 0.888|
|Jan 03 2012_006 B...|  S| LLY 0.956 =40.11...|                  NA| Avg of 1 = 0.956|
|Jan 03 2012_006 B...|  L| DB 0.888 =35.23/...| SU 1.068 =31.78/...| Avg of 2 = 0.978|
|Jan 03 2012_006 B...|  S| LLY 0.956 =40.11...| MO 1.005 =28.79/...| Avg of 2 = 0.981|
|Jan 03 2012_006 B...|  L| DB 0.888 =35.23/...| MON 1.107 =78.97...| Avg of 5 = 1.017|
+-------------------+---+--------------------+--------------------+-----------------+
only showing top 5 rows
```

Extracting data from "messy" columns

In this section, we continue on from the previous section, however, we will work with a single stock to demonstrate the data manipulations required to modify the data fields to a state where we end up with cleaner and richer data than we started with.

As most of the fields contain several pieces of information, we will execute a series of statements to separate them out into their own independent columns:

```
scala> val df3 = dfFixed.select("datestr", "ls", "stock1", "avgstr")

scala> df3.take(5).foreach(println)
[Jan 03 2012_006 Big_100_1_LONG_SHORT_F.pdf, L, DB 0.888 =35.23/39.67, Avg of 1 = 0.888]
[Jan 03 2012_006 Big_100_1_LONG_SHORT_F.pdf, S, LLY 0.956 =40.11/41.95, Avg of 1 = 0.956]
[Jan 03 2012_006 Big_100_2_LONG_SHORT_F.pdf, L, DB 0.888 =35.23/39.67, Avg of 2 = 0.978]
[Jan 03 2012_006 Big_100_2_LONG_SHORT_F.pdf, S, LLY 0.956 =40.11/41.95, Avg of 2 = 0.981]
[Jan 03 2012_006 Big_100_5_LONG_SHORT_F.pdf, L, DB 0.888 =35.23/39.67, Avg of 5 = 1.017]
```

In the next step, we remove the first underscore with a space in the `datestr` column. This results in separating out the date field:

```
scala> def replaceFirstSubstring( str:String, substr:String, repl: String):
String = { val result = str.replaceFirst(substr, repl); result;}

scala> def nRepls(substr: String, repl: String) = udf((x: String) =>
replaceFirstSubstring(x, substr, repl))

scala> val df4 = df3.withColumn("cleanDatestr", nRepls("_", "
")($"datestr")).drop("datestr").withColumnRenamed("cleanDatestr",
"datestr").select("datestr", "ls", "stock1", "avgstr")

scala> df4.take(5).foreach(println)
[Jan 03 2012 006 Big_100_1_LONG_SHORT_F.pdf, L, DB 0.888 =35.23/39.67, Avg of 1 = 0.888]
[Jan 03 2012 006 Big_100_1_LONG_SHORT_F.pdf, S, LLY 0.956 =40.11/41.95, Avg of 1 = 0.956]
[Jan 03 2012 006 Big_100_2_LONG_SHORT_F.pdf, L, DB 0.888 =35.23/39.67, Avg of 2 = 0.978]
[Jan 03 2012 006 Big_100_2_LONG_SHORT_F.pdf, S, LLY 0.956 =40.11/41.95, Avg of 2 = 0.981]
[Jan 03 2012 006 Big_100_5_LONG_SHORT_F.pdf, L, DB 0.888 =35.23/39.67, Avg of 5 = 1.017]
```

Next, we separate out the information in the stock column, as it contains several pieces of useful information including the ticker symbol, ratio of the selling price and purchase price, and the selling price and purchase price. First, we get rid of the = in the stock column by replacing it with an empty string:

```
scala> val df4A = df4.withColumn("temp1", nRepls("=",
"")($"stock1")).withColumn("temp", nRepls("/", " ")($"temp1")).drop("temp1",
"stock1")

scala> df4A.take(5).foreach(println)
[Jan 03 2012 006 Big_100_1_LONG_SHORT_F.pdf, L, Avg of 1 = 0.888, DB 0.888   35.23 39.67]
[Jan 03 2012 006 Big_100_1_LONG_SHORT_F.pdf, S, Avg of 1 = 0.956, LLY 0.956   40.11 41.95]
[Jan 03 2012 006 Big_100_2_LONG_SHORT_F.pdf, L, Avg of 2 = 0.978, DB 0.888   35.23 39.67]
[Jan 03 2012 006 Big_100_2_LONG_SHORT_F.pdf, S, Avg of 2 = 0.981, LLY 0.956   40.11 41.95]
[Jan 03 2012 006 Big_100_5_LONG_SHORT_F.pdf, L, Avg of 5 = 1.017, DB 0.888   35.23 39.67]
```

Next, the values in each column separated by spaces in each column are converted into an array of the values:

```
scala> def splitString( str:String, sep:String): Array[String] = { val result
= str.split(sep); result;}

scala> def splitStr(sep: String) = udf((x: String) => splitString(x.trim(),
sep))

scala> val df5 = df4A.withColumn("temp1", splitStr("
")($"datestr")).withColumn("temp2", splitStr("
")($"temp")).withColumn("avgarray", splitStr(" ")($"avgstr")).drop("datestr",
"temp").select("temp1", "ls", "temp2", "avgarray")
```

```
scala> df5.show(5)
+--------------------+---+--------------------+--------------------+
|               temp1| ls|               temp2|            avgarray|
+--------------------+---+--------------------+--------------------+
|[Jan, 03, 2012, 0...|  L|[DB, 0.888, 35.23...|[Avg, of, 1, =, 0...|
|[Jan, 03, 2012, 0...|  S|[LLY, 0.956, 40.1...|[Avg, of, 1, =, 0...|
|[Jan, 03, 2012, 0...|  L|[DB, 0.888, 35.23...|[Avg, of, 2, =, 0...|
|[Jan, 03, 2012, 0...|  S|[LLY, 0.956, 40.1...|[Avg, of, 2, =, 0...|
|[Jan, 03, 2012, 0...|  L|[DB, 0.888, 35.23...|[Avg, of, 5, =, 1...|
+--------------------+---+--------------------+--------------------+
only showing top 5 rows
```

Next, we use a UDF to pick certain elements from the arrays in each column into their own separate columns.

```scala
scala> def retArrayIndex( str:Array[String], index:Int): String = { val result
= str(index); result;}

scala> def retArrayVal(index: Int) = udf((x: WrappedArray[String]) =>
retArrayIndex(x.toArray[String], index))

scala> val df6 = df5.withColumn("month",
retArrayVal(0)($"temp1")).withColumn("dom",
retArrayVal(1)($"temp1")).withColumn("year",
retArrayVal(2)($"temp1")).withColumn("y4",
retArrayVal(3)($"temp1")).withColumn("file",
retArrayVal(4)($"temp1")).withColumn("ticker",
retArrayVal(0)($"temp2")).withColumn("S/P Ratio",
retArrayVal(1)($"temp2")).withColumn("SP",
retArrayVal(2)($"temp2")).withColumn("PP",
retArrayVal(3)($"temp2")).withColumn("nStocks",
retArrayVal(2)($"avgarray")).drop("temp1", "temp2", "avgarray")

scala> df6.show(5)
+---+-----+---+----+---+--------------------+------+---------+-----+-----+-------+
| ls|month|dom|year| y4|                file|ticker|S/P Ratio|   SP|   PP|nStocks|
+---+-----+---+----+---+--------------------+------+---------+-----+-----+-------+
|  L|  Jan| 03|2012|006|Big_100_1_LONG_SH...|    DB|    0.888|35.23|39.67|      1|
|  S|  Jan| 03|2012|006|Big_100_1_LONG_SH...|   LLY|    0.956|40.11|41.95|      1|
|  L|  Jan| 03|2012|006|Big_100_2_LONG_SH...|    DB|    0.888|35.23|39.67|      2|
|  S|  Jan| 03|2012|006|Big_100_2_LONG_SH...|   LLY|    0.956|40.11|41.95|      2|
|  L|  Jan| 03|2012|006|Big_100_5_LONG_SH...|    DB|    0.888|35.23|39.67|      5|
+---+-----+---+----+---+--------------------+------+---------+-----+-----+-------+
only showing top 5 rows
```

The file column is not particularly useful for our analysis, except for extracting the information at the beginning of the filename that denotes the pool of stocks from which the stocks for any given portfolio were picked. We do that next, as follows:

```scala
scala> def extractUptoSecondSubstring( str:String, sub:String): String = { val
result = str.substring(0, str.indexOf(sub, str.indexOf(sub) + 1)); result;}

scala> def extractStr(sub: String) = udf((x: String) =>
extractUptoSecondSubstring(x.trim(), sub))

scala> val df6A = df6.withColumn("type",
extractStr("_")($"file")).drop("file").select("month", "dom", "year", "y4",
"type", "ls", "ticker", "S/P Ratio", "SP", "PP", "nStocks")
```

The following is the final version of the DataFrame that is ready for further analysis. In this example, we have worked with a single stock however you can easily extend the same techniques to all stocks in any given portfolio to arrive at the final, clean and rich, DataFrame ready for querying, modeling, and analysis.

```
scala> df6A.show(5)
+-----+---+----+---+-------+---+------+---------+-----+-----+-------+
|month|dom|year| y4|   type| ls|ticker|S/P Ratio|   SP|   PP|nStocks|
+-----+---+----+---+-------+---+------+---------+-----+-----+-------+
|  Jan| 03|2012|006|Big_100|  L|    DB|    0.888|35.23|39.67|      1|
|  Jan| 03|2012|006|Big_100|  S|   LLY|    0.956|40.11|41.95|      1|
|  Jan| 03|2012|006|Big_100|  L|    DB|    0.888|35.23|39.67|      2|
|  Jan| 03|2012|006|Big_100|  S|   LLY|    0.956|40.11|41.95|      2|
|  Jan| 03|2012|006|Big_100|  L|    DB|    0.888|35.23|39.67|      5|
+-----+---+----+---+-------+---+------+---------+-----+-----+-------+
only showing top 5 rows
```

In the next section, we briefly introduce the steps required for preparing data for use with Spark MLlib machine learning algorithms for classification problems.

Preparing data for machine learning

In this section, we introduce the process of preparing the input data prior to applying Spark MLlib algorithms. Typically, we need to have two columns called label and features for using Spark MLlib classification algorithms. We will illustrate this with the following example described:

We import the required classes for this section:

```
scala> import org.apache.spark.ml.Pipeline
scala> import
org.apache.spark.ml.classification.{RandomForestClassificationModel,
RandomForestClassifier}
scala> import
org.apache.spark.ml.evaluation.MulticlassClassificationEvaluator
scala> import org.apache.spark.ml.feature.{IndexToString, StringIndexer,
VectorIndexer}
scala> import org.apache.spark.ml.linalg.Vectors
```

Pre-processing data for machine learning

We define a set of UDFs used in this section. These include, for example, checking whether a string contains a specific substring or not, and returning a 0.0 or 1.0 value to create the label column. Another UDF is used to create a features vector from the numeric fields in the DataFrame.

For example, we can convert the day of week field to a numeric value by binning shown as follows:

```scala
scala> def containsSubstring( str:String, substr:String): Double = {
if (str.contains(substr)) 1 else 0}

scala> def udfContains(substr: String) = udf((x: String) =>
containsSubstring(x, substr))
scala> def udfVec() = udf[org.apache.spark.ml.linalg.Vector, String,
Int, Double, Double, Double] { (a, b, c, d, e) => val x = a match {
case "Monday" => 1; case "Tuesday" => 2; case "Wednesday" => 3; case
"Thursday" => 4; case "Friday" => 5; case "Saturday" => 6; case
"Sunday" => 7; }; Vectors.dense(x, b, c, d, e);}
```

In our example, we create a label from the Events column of the household electric consumption Dataset based on whether it rained on given a day or not. For illustrative purposes, we use the columns from the household's electric power consumption readings in the joined DataFrame from before, even though readings from weather Dataset are probably a better predictor of rain.

```scala
scala> val joinedRained = joinedDayDowDF.withColumn("label",
udfContains("Rain")($"Events")).withColumn("features",
udfVec()($"dow", $"month", $"dsm_1", $"dsm_2", $"dsm_3"))

scala> val labelIndexer = new
StringIndexer().setInputCol("label").setOutputCol("indexedLabel").fit
(joinedRained)

scala> val featureIndexer = new
VectorIndexer().setInputCol("features").setOutputCol("indexedFeatures
").setMaxCategories(7).fit(joinedRained)
```

Finally, we can also split our DataFrame to create training and test Datasets containing 70% and 30% of the readings, chosen randomly, respectively. These Datasets are used for training and testing machine learning algorithms.

```scala
scala> val Array(trainingData, testData) =
joinedRained.randomSplit(Array(0.7, 0.3))
```

Creating and running a machine learning pipeline

In this section, we present an example of a machine learning pipeline that uses the indexers and the training data to train a Random Forest model. We will not present detailed explanations for the steps, as our primary purpose here is to only demonstrate how the preparatory steps in the previous section are actually used.

```
scala> val rf = new
RandomForestClassifier().setLabelCol("indexedLabel").setFeaturesCol("indexe
dFeatures").setNumTrees(10)

scala> // Convert indexed labels back to original labels.
scala> val labelConverter = new
IndexToString().setInputCol("prediction").setOutputCol("predictedLabel").se
tLabels(labelIndexer.labels)

scala> // Chain indexers and forest in a Pipeline.
scala> val pipeline = new Pipeline().setStages(Array(labelIndexer,
featureIndexer, rf, labelConverter))

scala> // Train model. This also runs the indexers.
scala> val model = pipeline.fit(trainingData)

scala> // Make predictions.
scala> val predictions = model.transform(testData)

scala> // Select example rows to display.
scala> predictions.select("predictedLabel", "label", "features").show(5)
```

```
+--------------+-----+--------------------+
|predictedLabel|label|            features|
+--------------+-----+--------------------+
|           0.0|  1.0|[5.0,8.0,336.0,26...|
|           1.0|  0.0|[4.0,7.0,837.0,47...|
|           0.0|  1.0|[6.0,4.0,2007.0,3...|
|           0.0|  1.0|[2.0,7.0,1292.0,3...|
|           0.0|  0.0|[6.0,5.0,2278.0,2...|
+--------------+-----+--------------------+
only showing top 5 rows
```

```scala
scala> // Select (prediction, true label) and compute test error.
scala> val evaluator = new
MulticlassClassificationEvaluator().setLabelCol("indexedLabel").setPredicti
onCol("prediction").setMetricName("accuracy")

scala> val accuracy = evaluator.evaluate(predictions)
accuracy: Double = 0.5341463414634147

scala> println("Test Error = " + (1.0 - accuracy))
Test Error = 0.46585365853658534

scala> val rfModel =
model.stages(2).asInstanceOf[RandomForestClassificationModel]

scala> println("Learned classification forest model:\n" +
rfModel.toDebugString)
```

```
Learned classification forest model:
RandomForestClassificationModel (uid=rfc_8dbd03c1c4e1) with 10 trees
  Tree 0 (weight 1.0):
    If (feature 3 <= 2492.0)
     If (feature 2 <= 4307.0)
      If (feature 3 <= 689.0)
       If (feature 0 in {1.0,2.0,4.0,5.0,6.0})
        If (feature 1 <= 10.0)
         Predict: 0.0
        Else (feature 1 > 10.0)
         Predict: 1.0
  .

  .
  .
Tree 9 (weight 1.0):
    If (feature 3 <= 689.0)
     If (feature 3 <= 258.0)
      If (feature 1 <= 8.0)
       If (feature 4 <= 5457.0)
        If (feature 4 <= 1980.0)
         Predict: 0.0
        Else (feature 4 > 1980.0)
         Predict: 0.0
```

More details on specific data structures and operations including vectors, processing categorical variables, and so on, for Spark MLlib processing, are covered in Chapter 6, *Using Spark SQL in Machine Learning Applications,* and Chapter 9, *Developing Applications with Spark SQL.* Additionally, techniques for preparing data for graph applications are presented in Chapter 7, *Using Spark SQL in Graph Applications.*

Summary

In this chapter, we explored using Spark SQL for performing some basic data munging/wrangling tasks. We covered munging textual data, working with variable length records, extracting data from "messy" columns, combining data using JOIN, and preparing data for machine learning applications. In addition, we used `spark-ts` library to work with time-series data.

In the next chapter, we will shift our focus to Spark Streaming applications. We will introduce you to using Spark SQL in such applications. We will also include extensive hands-on sessions for demonstrating the use of Spark SQL in implementing the common use cases in Spark Streaming applications.

5
Using Spark SQL in Streaming Applications

In this chapter, we will present typical use cases for using Spark SQL in streaming applications. Our focus will be on structured streaming using the Dataset/DataFrame APIs introduced in Spark 2.0. Additionally, we will introduce and work with Apache Kafka, as it is an integral part of many web-scale streaming application architectures. Streaming applications typically involve real-time, context-aware responses to incoming data or messages. We will use several examples to illustrate the key concepts and techniques to build such applications.

In this chapter, we will learn these topics:

- What is a streaming data application?
- Typical streaming use cases
- Using Spark SQL DataFrame/Dataset APIs to build streaming applications
- Using Kafka in Structured Streaming applications
- Creating a receiver for a custom data source

Introducing streaming data applications

Traditional batch applications typically ran for hours, processing all or most of the data stored in relational databases. More recently, Hadoop-based systems have been used to support MapReduce-based batch jobs to process very large volumes of distributed data. In contrast, stream processing occurs on streaming data that is continuously generated. Such processing is used in a wide variety of analytics applications that compute correlations between events, aggregate values, sample incoming data, and so on.

Stream processing typically ingests a sequence of data and incrementally computes statistics and other functions on a record-by-record/event-by-event basis, or over sliding time windows, on the fly.

Increasingly, streaming data applications are applying machine learning algorithms and **Complex Event Processing** (**CEP**) algorithms to provide strategic insights and the ability to quickly and intelligently react to rapidly changing business conditions. Such applications can scale to handle very high volumes of streaming data and respond appropriately on a real-time basis. Additionally, many organizations are implementing architectures containing both a real-time layer and a batch layer. In such implementations, it is very important to maintain a single code base, as far as possible, for these two layers (for examples such architectures, refer Chapter 12, *Spark SQL in Large-Scale Application Architectures*). Spark Structured Streaming APIs helps us achieve such objectives in a scalable, reliable, and fault-tolerant manner.

Some of the real-world uses cases for streaming applications include processing of sensor data in IoT applications, stock market applications such as risk management and algorithmic trading, network monitoring, surveillance applications, in-the-moment customer engagement in e-commerce applications, fraud detection, and so on.

As a result, many platforms have emerged that provide the infrastructure needed to build streaming data applications, including Apache Kafka, Apache Spark Streaming, Apache Storm, Amazon Kinesis Streams, and others.

In this chapter, we will explore stream processing using Apache Spark and Apache Kafka. Over the next few sections, we will explore Spark Structured Streaming in detail using Spark SQL DataFrame/Dataset APIs.

Building Spark streaming applications

In this section, we will primarily focus on the newly introduced structured streaming feature (in Spark 2.0). Structured streaming APIs are GA with Spark 2.2 and using them is the preferred method for building streaming Spark applications. Several updates to Kafka-based processing components including performance improvements have also been released in Spark 2.2. We introduced structured streaming in Chapter 1, *Getting Started with Spark SQL*. In this chapter, we will get deeper into the topic and present several code examples to showcase its capabilities.

As a quick recap, structured streaming provides a fast, scalable, fault-tolerant, end-to-end exactly-once stream processing without the developer having to reason about the underlying streaming mechanisms.

It is built on the Spark SQL engine, and the streaming computations can be expressed in the same way batch computations are expressed on static data. It provides several data abstractions including Streaming Query, Streaming Source, and Streaming Sink to simplify streaming applications without getting into the underlying complexities of data streaming. Programming APIs are available in Scala, Java, and Python, and you can use the familiar Dataset / DataFrame API to implement your applications.

In Chapter 1, *Getting Started with Spark SQL*, we used the IPinYou Dataset to create a streaming DataFrame and then defined a streaming query on it. We showed the results getting updated in each time interval. Here, we recreate our streaming DataFrame, and then execute various functions on it to showcase the types of computations possible on the streaming input data.

First, we start the Spark shell and import the necessary classes required for the hands-on part of this chapter. We will be using file sources to simulate the incoming data in most of our examples:

```
scala> import org.apache.spark.sql.types._
scala> import org.apache.spark.sql.functions._
scala> import scala.concurrent.duration._
scala> import org.apache.spark.sql.streaming.ProcessingTime
scala> import org.apache.spark.sql.streaming.OutputMode.Complete
scala> import spark.implicits._
```

Next, we define the schema for the bid records in our source files, as shown:

```
scala> val bidSchema = new StructType().add("bidid",
StringType).add("timestamp", StringType).add("ipinyouid",
StringType).add("useragent", StringType).add("IP",
StringType).add("region", IntegerType).add("cityID",
IntegerType).add("adexchange", StringType).add("domain",
StringType).add("turl", StringType).add("urlid", StringType).add("slotid",
StringType).add("slotwidth", StringType).add("slotheight",
StringType).add("slotvisibility", StringType).add("slotformat",
StringType).add("slotprice", StringType).add("creative",
StringType).add("bidprice", StringType)
```

In the next step, we will define a streaming data source based on the input CSV file. We specify the schema defined in the previous step and other required parameters (using options). We also limit the number of files processed to one per batch:

```
scala> val streamingInputDF =
spark.readStream.format("csv").schema(bidSchema).option("header",
false).option("inferSchema", true).option("sep",
"\t").option("maxFilesPerTrigger",
1).load("file:///Users/aurobindosarkar/Downloads/make-ipinyou-data-
```

```
master/original-data/ipinyou.contest.dataset/bidfiles")
```

You can print the schema of the streaming DataFrame as you would in the case of a static one:

```
scala> streamingInputDF.printSchema()
root
|-- bidid: string (nullable = true)
|-- timestamp: string (nullable = true)
|-- ipinyouid: string (nullable = true)
|-- useragent: string (nullable = true)
|-- IP: string (nullable = true)
|-- region: integer (nullable = true)
|-- cityID: integer (nullable = true)
|-- adexchange: string (nullable = true)
|-- domain: string (nullable = true)
|-- turl: string (nullable = true)
|-- urlid: string (nullable = true)
|-- slotid: string (nullable = true)
|-- slotwidth: string (nullable = true)
|-- slotheight: string (nullable = true)
|-- slotvisibility: string (nullable = true)
|-- slotformat: string (nullable = true)
|-- slotprice: string (nullable = true)
|-- creative: string (nullable = true)
|-- bidprice: string (nullable = true)
```

Implementing sliding window-based functionality

In this subsection, we will cover the sliding window operation on streaming data.

As the timestamp data is not in the correct format, we will define a new column and convert the input timestamp string to the right format and type for our processing:

```
scala> val ts = unix_timestamp($"timestamp",
"yyyyMMddHHmmssSSS").cast("timestamp")

scala> val streamingCityTimeDF = streamingInputDF.withColumn("ts",
ts).select($"cityID", $"ts")
```

Next, we will define a streaming query that writes the output to the standard output. We will define aggregations over a sliding window where we group the data by window and city ID, and compute the count of each group.

For a more detailed description of structured streaming programming, refer to http://spark.apache.org/docs/latest/structured-streaming-programming-guide.html.

Here, we count the number of bids within 10-minute windows updating every five minutes, that is, bids received in 10-minutes windows sliding every five minutes. The streaming query using a window is as shown:

```scala
scala> val windowedCounts = streamingCityTimeDF.groupBy(window($"ts", "10 minutes", "5 minutes"),
$"cityID").count().writeStream.outputMode("complete").format("console").start()
```

The output is written to the standard output because we used a Console Sink as specified by the console keyword in the format parameter. The output contains columns for the window, the city ID, and the computed counts, as follows. We see two batches as we have placed two files in our input directory:

```
scala> ----------------------------------------------------
Batch: 0
----------------------------------------------------
+--------------------+------+-----+
|              window|cityID|count|
+--------------------+------+-----+
|[2013-03-11 13:10...|    64|   14|
|[2013-03-11 02:25...|   282|   15|
|[2013-03-11 02:20...|   281|    6|
|[2013-03-11 14:20...|    21|   14|
|[2013-03-11 14:00...|    83|   21|
|[2013-03-11 13:40...|   253|    9|
|[2013-03-11 13:10...|   326|    1|
|[2013-03-11 00:30...|    36|    3|
|[2013-03-11 01:40...|    31|    1|
|[2013-03-11 00:15...|   241|   16|
|[2013-03-11 01:45...|   247|    2|
|[2013-03-11 02:05...|   148|   13|
|[2013-03-11 17:10...|    91|   20|
|[2013-03-11 17:25...|   280|   23|
|[2013-03-11 02:30...|    23|   15|
|[2013-03-11 17:50...|   285|   19|
|[2013-03-11 08:05...|   210|   20|
|[2013-03-11 00:45...|    19|   10|
|[2013-03-11 22:55...|   238|   27|
|[2013-03-11 13:15...|    63|    5|
+--------------------+------+-----+
only showing top 20 rows
```

```
-------------------------------------------------
Batch: 1
-------------------------------------------------
+--------------------+------+-----+
|              window|cityID|count|
+--------------------+------+-----+
|[2013-03-11 02:20...|   281|    6|
|[2013-03-11 14:00...|    83|   21|
|[2013-03-11 13:40...|   253|    9|
|[2013-03-12 10:55...|   378|    2|
|[2013-03-11 00:30...|    36|    3|
|[2013-03-11 01:40...|    31|    1|
|[2013-03-11 00:15...|   241|   16|
|[2013-03-12 08:25...|   292|    7|
|[2013-03-12 11:00...|   359|   15|
|[2013-03-12 23:25...|   251|   16|
|[2013-03-12 19:50...|   285|   15|
|[2013-03-11 02:05...|   148|   13|
|[2013-03-11 02:30...|    23|   15|
|[2013-03-11 17:50...|   285|   19|
|[2013-03-11 08:05...|   210|   20|
|[2013-03-11 00:45...|    19|   10|
|[2013-03-11 22:55...|   238|   27|
|[2013-03-12 10:55...|   287|   18|
|[2013-03-12 13:00...|    94|  136|
|[2013-03-12 15:30...|     6|    4|
+--------------------+------+-----+
only showing top 20 rows
```

Joining a streaming Dataset with a static Dataset

In this subsection, we will give an example of joining a streaming Dataset with a static one. We will join Datasets based on the `cityID` to achieve user-friendly output that contains the city name instead of the `cityID`. First, we define a schema for our city records and create static DataFrame from the CSV file containing the city IDs and their corresponding city names:

```scala
scala> val citySchema = new StructType().add("cityID",
StringType).add("cityName", StringType)

scala> val staticDF =
spark.read.format("csv").schema(citySchema).option("header",
false).option("inferSchema", true).option("sep",
"\t").load("file:///Users/aurobindosarkar/Downloads/make-ipinyou-data-
master/original-data/ipinyou.contest.dataset/city.en.txt")
```

Next, we will join the streaming and the static DataFrames, as shown:

```scala
scala> val joinedDF = streamingCityTimeDF.join(staticDF, "cityID")
```

We will execute our previous streaming query with the column for city names specified instead of city IDs in the joined DataFrame:

```
scala> val windowedCityCounts = joinedDF.groupBy(window($"ts", "10
minutes", "5 minutes"),
$"cityName").count().writeStream.outputMode("complete").format("console").s
tart()
```

The results are as follows. Here, we see a single batch of output data, as we have removed one of the input files from our source directory. For the rest of this chapter, we will limit processing to a single input file to conserve space:

```
scala> -------------------------------------------------
Batch: 0
-------------------------------------------------

+--------------------+----------------+-----+
|              window|        cityName|count|
+--------------------+----------------+-----+
|[2013-03-11 11:05...|         bazhong|    1|
|[2013-03-11 19:30...|        shaoxing|  135|
|[2013-03-11 01:15...|         nanping|    4|
|[2013-03-11 21:40...|         xiangfan|   23|
|[2013-03-11 18:55...|          wuzhou|   18|
|[2013-03-11 03:20...|         jiuquan|    5|
|[2013-03-11 20:20...|       liangshan|   31|
|[2013-03-11 19:20...|        shaoyang|   18|
|[2013-03-11 04:40...|         nanyang|   13|
|[2013-03-11 09:25...|taizhou_jiangsu|    3|
|[2013-03-11 07:10...|            yaan|    2|
|[2013-03-11 07:30...|         suining|    8|
|[2013-03-11 22:35...|         lvliang|   36|
|[2013-03-11 14:20...|        zhongwei|    3|
|[2013-03-11 05:55...|         bazhong|    1|
|[2013-03-11 12:50...|          ziyang|   21|
|[2013-03-11 02:25...|         taizhou|   23|
|[2013-03-11 03:50...|           benxi|    3|
|[2013-03-11 08:05...|        neijiang|   25|
|[2013-03-11 14:20...|          fuyang|   33|
+--------------------+----------------+-----+
only showing top 20 rows
```

Next, we create a new DataFrame with a timestamp column and a few selected columns from a previously created DataFrame:

```scala
scala> val streamingCityNameBidsTimeDF = streamingInputDF.withColumn("ts",
ts).select($"ts", $"bidid", $"cityID", $"bidprice",
$"slotprice").join(staticDF, "cityID")
```

As we are not computing aggregations, and simply want the streaming bids to be appended to the results, we use the outputMode "append" instead of "complete", as follows:

```scala
scala> val cityBids = streamingCityNameBidsTimeDF.select($"ts", $"bidid",
$"bidprice", $"slotprice",
$"cityName").writeStream.outputMode("append").format("console").start()
```

```
scala> -------------------------------------------------
Batch: 0
-------------------------------------------------
+-------------------+--------------+--------+---------+---------+
|                 ts|         bidid|bidprice|slotprice| cityName|
+-------------------+--------------+--------+---------+---------+
|2013-03-11 17:21:01|f2ce7b51f499eae08...|     300|        5| changzhi|
|2013-03-11 17:21:01|dabbf5f389089c39d...|     300|       59|   ningbo|
|2013-03-11 17:21:01|55cc617434cd07963...|     300|        5|  unknown|
|2013-03-11 17:21:01|de10b3396b222f60f...|     300|        5| shenyang|
|2013-03-11 17:21:01|375afd6a39e551874...|     300|       52| changzhi|
|2013-03-11 17:21:01|67f35f322a4936370...|     300|        5|   leshan|
|2013-03-11 17:21:01|1dbfbeafe74bbd9e0...|     300|      295|   leshan|
|2013-03-11 17:21:01|6d1f7c8008fd440b9...|     300|        5|    jinan|
|2013-03-11 17:21:01|c3872ff374277ad36...|     300|        8| shenzhen|
|2013-03-11 17:21:01|5530617cd63368116...|     300|       52|     wuxi|
|2013-03-11 17:21:01|8927586d9cbdd83a2...|     300|        5|  nanjing|
|2013-03-11 17:21:01|bec9fd1c23f5f3908...|     300|        5|  chengdu|
|2013-03-11 17:21:01|a35a52d81f0f78ed7...|     300|        5|guangzhou|
|2013-03-11 17:21:01|184bf096e7fa66a12...|     300|      148|   zhuhai|
|2013-03-11 17:21:01|cbe88409742e18f86...|     300|        5| mianyang|
|2013-03-11 17:21:01|97c5e98e080d43a5f...|     300|        5| jincheng|
|2013-03-11 17:21:01|ccd41a3c166b0c110...|     300|        5|   daqing|
|2013-03-11 17:21:01|dfadede03a58b6dfd...|     300|        5|      aba|
|2013-03-11 17:21:01|be059b6aa9289bb46...|     300|        5| mianyang|
|2013-03-11 17:21:01|d6afb0b0a9f486164...|     300|        5|  nanjing|
+-------------------+--------------+--------+---------+---------+
only showing top 20 rows
```

Using the Dataset API in Structured Streaming

So far, we have used untyped APIs with DataFrames. In order to use typed APIs, we can switch from using DataFrames to Datasets. Most streaming operations are supported by the DataFrame/Dataset APIs; however, a few operations such as multiple streaming aggregations and distinct operations not supported, yet. And others such as outer JOINs and sorting are conditionally supported.

 For a complete list of unsupported and conditionally supported operations, refer to http://spark.apache.org/docs/latest/structured-streaming-programming-guide.html.

Here, we present a few examples of using typed APIs.

First, we will define a case class called Bid:

```scala
scala> case class Bid(bidid: String, timestamp: String, ipinyouid: String,
useragent: String, IP: String, region: Integer, cityID: Integer,
adexchange: String, domain: String, turl: String, urlid: String, slotid:
String, slotwidth: String, slotheight: String, slotvisibility: String,
slotformat: String, slotprice: String, creative: String, bidprice: String)
```

We can define a streaming Dataset from a streaming DataFrame using the case class defined in the previous step:

```scala
scala> val ds = streamingInputDF.as[Bid]
```

Using output sinks

You can direct the streaming output data to various output sinks including File, Foreach, Console, and Memory sinks. Typically, the Console and Memory sinks are used for debugging purposes. As we have already used Console sink in earlier sections; here we will discuss the usage of other sinks in more detail.

Using the Foreach Sink for arbitrary computations on output

If you want to perform arbitrary computations on the output, then you can use the Foreach Sink. For this purpose, you will need to implement the ForeachWriter interface, as shown. In our example, we simply print the record, but you can also perform other computations, as per your requirements:

```
import org.apache.spark.sql.ForeachWriter

val writer = new ForeachWriter[String] {
    override def open(partitionId: Long, version: Long) = true
    override def process(value: String) = println(value)
    override def close(errorOrNull: Throwable) = {}
}
```

In the next step, we will implement an example using the Foreach sink defined in the previous step. Specify the ForeachWriter implemented in the preceding step as shown:

```
scala> val dsForeach = ds.filter(_.adexchange ==
"3").map(_.useragent).writeStream.foreach(writer).start()
```

As a result, the user-agent information is displayed as shown:

```
scala> Mozilla/5.0 (Windows NT 5.1) AppleWebKit/537.1 (KHTML, like Gecko)
Chrome/21.0.1180.89 Safari/537.1
Mozilla/5.0 (Windows NT 5.1) AppleWebKit/537.1 (KHTML, like Gecko)
Chrome/21.0.1180.89 Safari/537.1
Mozilla/4.0 (compatible; MSIE 7.0; Windows NT 5.1; InfoPath.2)
                          .

                          .

                          .

Mozilla/4.0 (compatible; MSIE 7.0; Windows NT 5.1; Trident/4.0; .NET CLR
2.0.50727)
Mozilla/4.0 (compatible; MSIE 7.0; Windows NT 5.1; Trident/4.0; .NET CLR
2.0.50727)
Mozilla/4.0 (compatible; MSIE 8.0; Windows NT 6.1; Trident/4.0; FDM; .NET4.0C)
```

Using the Memory Sink to save output to a table

If you want to save the output data as a table, you can use the Memory Sink; this can be useful for interactive querying. We define a streaming DataFrame as before. However, we specify the format parameter as `memory` and the table name. Finally, we execute a SQL query on our table, as shown:

```scala
scala> val aggAdexchangeDF =
streamingInputDF.groupBy($"adexchange").count()

scala> val aggQuery =
aggAdexchangeDF.writeStream.queryName("aggregateTable").outputMode("complet
e").format("memory").start()

scala> spark.sql("select * from aggregateTable").show()
```

```
+-----------+-------+
|adexchange|  count|
+-----------+-------+
|         3| 839458|
|         1|1049105|
|         2|1540938|
+-----------+-------+
```

Using the File Sink to save output to a partitioned table

We can also save the output as partitioned tables. For instance, we can partition the output by time and store them as Parquet files on HDFS. Here, we show an example of storing our output to Parquet files using a File Sink. It is mandatory to specify the checkpoint directory location in the given command:

```scala
scala> val cityBidsParquet = streamingCityNameBidsTimeDF.select($"bidid",
$"bidprice", $"slotprice",
$"cityName").writeStream.outputMode("append").format("parquet").option("pat
h", "hdfs://localhost:9000/pout").option("checkpointLocation",
"hdfs://localhost:9000/poutcp").start()
```

You can check the HDFS filesystem for the output Parquet files and the checkpoint files, as shown:

```
Aurobindos-MacBook-Pro-2:~ aurobindosarkar$ hdfs dfs -ls /pout
```

```
Found 17 items
drwxr-xr-x   - aurobindosarkar supergroup          0 2017-08-25 00:03
/pout/_spark_metadata
-rw-r--r--   1 aurobindosarkar supergroup    5028115 2017-08-25 00:03
/pout/part-00000-30859feb-965e-41be-b257-bb872b3c0f44-c000.snappy.parquet
-rw-r--r--   1 aurobindosarkar supergroup    5147398 2017-08-25 00:03
/pout/part-00000-6927b229-fcd0-4411-9de8-41a7b77359dd-c000.snappy.parquet
-rw-r--r--   1 aurobindosarkar supergroup    4956498 2017-08-25 00:03
/pout/part-00001-403362a0-1141-4602-8e94-241442546ed8-c000.snappy.parquet
-rw-r--r--   1 aurobindosarkar supergroup    5095930 2017-08-25 00:03
/pout/part-00001-a8c5de46-5e42-425f-920e-f3bad5c05fbf-c000.snappy.parquet
-rw-r--r--   1 aurobindosarkar supergroup    5064670 2017-08-25 00:03
/pout/part-00002-90f4e91d-45a6-40e5-b833-ff0014e989ca-c000.snappy.parquet
-rw-r--r--   1 aurobindosarkar supergroup    5110948 2017-08-25 00:03
/pout/part-00002-eafe9de5-c376-4a1d-a2bb-c9cf006b60d1-c000.snappy.parquet
-rw-r--r--   1 aurobindosarkar supergroup    5179985 2017-08-25 00:03
/pout/part-00003-6a053817-36e3-44f8-9220-74bfa33d8fd2-c000.snappy.parquet
-rw-r--r--   1 aurobindosarkar supergroup    4863236 2017-08-25 00:03
/pout/part-00003-facee78e-9be9-4d95-b850-8e053f1db48d-c000.snappy.parquet
-rw-r--r--   1 aurobindosarkar supergroup    4991215 2017-08-25 00:03
/pout/part-00004-333d8dcb-8b63-4c46-b5e9-6b989003d9c3-c000.snappy.parquet
-rw-r--r--   1 aurobindosarkar supergroup    5077441 2017-08-25 00:03
/pout/part-00004-746821ad-4657-426e-aef6-94baa672e10d-c000.snappy.parquet
-rw-r--r--   1 aurobindosarkar supergroup    4971655 2017-08-25 00:03
/pout/part-00005-0cc84880-6058-4038-85d7-83089d100036-c000.snappy.parquet
-rw-r--r--   1 aurobindosarkar supergroup    5170948 2017-08-25 00:03
/pout/part-00005-78629915-701e-4c2e-a6d0-aad09e1eea54-c000.snappy.parquet
-rw-r--r--   1 aurobindosarkar supergroup    4973106 2017-08-25 00:03
/pout/part-00006-930e03a4-7ab4-4061-87da-f626abf6bd1c-c000.snappy.parquet
-rw-r--r--   1 aurobindosarkar supergroup    5037874 2017-08-25 00:03
/pout/part-00006-f86ca876-dbe0-4a1b-80af-65a4990026db-c000.snappy.parquet
-rw-r--r--   1 aurobindosarkar supergroup    4866992 2017-08-25 00:03
/pout/part-00007-1a0cecb0-53bd-4fb4-8804-47dd7e5612d5-c000.snappy.parquet
-rw-r--r--   1 aurobindosarkar supergroup    4649468 2017-08-25 00:03
/pout/part-00007-6b85aebd-80d6-4d4f-8a8e-ab605155f7b0-c000.snappy.parquet
```

```
Aurobindos-MacBook-Pro-2:~ aurobindosarkar$ hdfs dfs -ls /poutcp
```

```
Found 4 items
drwxr-xr-x   - aurobindosarkar supergroup          0 2017-08-25 00:03
/poutcp/commits
-rw-r--r--   1 aurobindosarkar supergroup         45 2017-08-25 00:03
/poutcp/metadata
drwxr-xr-x   - aurobindosarkar supergroup          0 2017-08-25 00:03
/poutcp/offsets
drwxr-xr-x   - aurobindosarkar supergroup          0 2017-08-25 00:03
/poutcp/sources
```

In the next section, we will explore some useful features for managing and monitoring streaming queries.

Monitoring streaming queries

At this stage, if you list the active streaming queries in the system, you should see the following output:

```
scala> spark.streams.active.foreach(x => println("ID:"+ x.id + "
Run ID:"+ x.runId + "                    Status: "+ x.status))

ID:0ebe31f5-6b76-46ea-a328-cd0c637be49c
Run ID:6f203d14-2a3a-4c9f-9ea0-8a6783d97873
Status: {
  "message" : "Waiting for data to arrive",
  "isDataAvailable" : false,
  "isTriggerActive" : false
}
ID:519cac9a-9d2f-4a01-9d67-afc15a6b03d2
Run ID:558590a7-cbd3-42b8-886b-cdc32bb4f6d7
Status: {
  "message" : "Waiting for data to arrive",
  "isDataAvailable" : false,
  "isTriggerActive" : false
}
ID:1068bc38-8ba9-4d5e-8762-bbd2abffdd51
Run ID:bf875a27-c4d8-4631-9ea2-d51a0e7cb232
Status: {
  "message" : "Waiting for data to arrive",
  "isDataAvailable" : false,
  "isTriggerActive" : false
}
ID:d69c4005-21f1-487a-9fe5-d804ca86f0ff
Run ID:a6969c1b-51da-4986-b5f3-a10cd2397784
Status: {
  "message" : "Waiting for data to arrive",
  "isDataAvailable" : false,
  "isTriggerActive" : false
}
ID:1fa9e48d-091a-4888-9e69-126a2f1c081a
Run ID:34dc2c60-eebc-4ed6-bf25-decd6b0ad6c3
Status: {
  "message" : "Waiting for data to arrive",
  "isDataAvailable" : false,  "isTriggerActive" : false
}
ID:a7ff2807-dc23-4a14-9a9c-9f8f1fa6a6b0
Run ID:6c8f1a83-bb1c-4dd7-8974
83042a286bae
Status: {
  "message" : "Waiting for data to arrive",
  "isDataAvailable" : false,
```

```
        "isTriggerActive" : false
    }
```

We can also monitor and manage a specific streaming query, for example, the windowedCounts **query (a** StreamingQuery **object), as shown:**

```
scala> // get the unique identifier of the running query that persists
across restarts from checkpoint data
scala> windowedCounts.id
res6: java.util.UUID = 0ebe31f5-6b76-46ea-a328-cd0c637be49c

scala> // get the unique id of this run of the query, which will be
generated at every start/restart
scala> windowedCounts.runId
res7: java.util.UUID = 6f203d14-2a3a-4c9f-9ea0-8a6783d97873

scala> // the exception if the query has been terminated with error
scala> windowedCounts.exception
res8: Option[org.apache.spark.sql.streaming.StreamingQueryException] = None

scala> // the most recent progress update of this streaming query
scala> windowedCounts.lastProgress
res9: org.apache.spark.sql.streaming.StreamingQueryProgress =
```

```
{
  "id" : "0ebe31f5-6b76-46ea-a328-cd0c637be49c",
  "runId" : "6f203d14-2a3a-4c9f-9ea0-8a6783d97873",
  "name" : null,
  "timestamp" : "2017-08-25T18:38:28.421Z",
  "numInputRows" : 0,
  "inputRowsPerSecond" : 0.0,
  "processedRowsPerSecond" : 0.0,
  "durationMs" : {
    "getOffset" : 2,
    "triggerExecution" : 2
  },
  "stateOperators" : [ {
    "numRowsTotal" : 156570,
    "numRowsUpdated" : 0
  } ],
  "sources" : [ {
    "description" :
"FileStreamSource[file:/Users/aurobindosarkar/Downloads/make-ipinyou-data-
master/original-data/ipinyou.contest.dataset/bidfiles]",
    "startOffset" : {
      "logOffset" : 1
    },
    "endOffset" : {
      "logOffset" : 1
    },
    "numInputRows" : 0,
    "inputRowsPerSecond" : 0.0,
  ...
```

To stop the streaming query execution, you can execute the `stop()` command, as follows:

```scala
scala> windowedCounts.stop()
```

In the next section, we will shift our focus using Kafka as the source of incoming data streams in our structured streaming applications.

Using Kafka with Spark Structured Streaming

Apache Kafka is a distributed streaming platform. It enables you to publish and subscribe to data streams, and process and store them as they get produced. Kafka's widespread adoption by the industry for web-scale applications is because of its high throughput, low latency, high scalability, high concurrency, reliability, and fault-tolerance features.

Introducing Kafka concepts

Kafka is typically used to build real-time streaming data pipelines to move data between systems, reliably, and also to transform and react to the streams of data. Kafka is run as a cluster on one or more servers.

Some of the key concepts of Kafka are described here:

- **Topic**: High-level abstraction for a category or stream name to which messages are published. A topic can have 0, 1, or many consumers who subscribe to the messages published to it. Users define a new topic for each new category of messages.

- **Producers**: Clients that publish messages to a topic.

- **Consumers**: Clients that consume messages from a topic.

- **Brokers**: One or more servers where message data is replicated and persisted.

Additionally, the producers and consumers can simultaneously write to and read from multiple topics. Each Kafka topic is partitioned and messages written to each partition are sequential. The messages in the partitions have an offset that uniquely identifies each message within the partition.

The reference site for Apache Kafka installation, tutorials, and examples is
`https://kafka.apache.org/`.

The partitions of a topic are distributed and each Broker handles requests for a share of the partitions. Each partition is replicated across a configurable number of Brokers. The Kafka cluster retains all published messages for a configurable period of time. Apache Kafka uses Apache ZooKeeper as a coordination service for its distributed processes.

Introducing ZooKeeper concepts

ZooKeeper is a distributed, open-source coordination service for distributed applications. It relieves the developer from having to implement coordination services from scratch. It uses a shared hierarchical namespace to allow distributed processes to coordinate with each other and avoid errors related to race conditions and deadlocks.

 The reference site for Apache ZooKeeper installation and tutorials is
`https://zookeeper.apache.org/`.

ZooKeeper data is kept in memory and, hence, it has very high throughput and low latency. It is replicated over a set of hosts to provide high availability. ZooKeeper provides a set of guarantees, including sequential consistency and atomicity.

Introducing Kafka-Spark integration

We present a simple example here to familiarize you with Kafka-Spark integration. The environment for this section uses: Apache Spark 2.1.0 and Apache Kafka 0.10.1.0 (Download file: `kafka_2.11-0.10.1.0.tgz`).

First, we start a single-node ZooKeeper using the script provided with Apache Kafka distribution, as shown:

```
bin/zookeeper-server-start.sh config/zookeeper.properties
```

After the Zookeeper node is up and running, we start the Kafka server using the script available in the Apache Kafka distribution, as follows:

```
bin/kafka-server-start.sh config/server.properties
```

Next, we create a topic called `test`, to which we will send messages for Spark streaming to consume. For our simple example, we specify both the replication factor and the number of partitions as `1`. We can use the utility script available for this purpose, as shown:

```
bin/kafka-topics.sh --create --zookeeper localhost:2181 --replication-
factor 1 --partitions 1 --topic test
```

We can see the list of topics (including "test") using this script:

```
bin/kafka-topics.sh --list --zookeeper localhost:2181
```

Next, we start a command line-based producer to send messages to Kafka, as follows. Here, each line is sent as a separate message. You should see each line appear in your Spark streaming query (running in a different window) as you type it and hit enter (as illustrated):

```
bin/kafka-console-producer.sh --broker-list localhost:9092 --topic test
This is the first message.
This is another message.
```

In a separate window, start Spark shell with the appropriate Kafka packages specified in the command line, as shown:

```
Aurobindos-MacBook-Pro-2:spark-2.1.0-bin-hadoop2.7 aurobindosarkar$
./bin/spark-shell --packages org.apache.spark:spark-streaming-
kafka-0-10_2.11:2.1.0,org.apache.spark:spark-sql-kafka-0-10_2.11:2.1.0
```

After Spark shell starts up, we will create a streaming Dataset with the format specified as "kafka". In addition, we will also specify the Kafka server and the port it's running on, and explicitly subscribe to the topic we created earlier, as follows. The key and value fields are cast to String type to make the output human-readable:

```
scala> val ds1 =
spark.readStream.format("kafka").option("kafka.bootstrap.servers",
"localhost:9092").option("subscribe", "test").load().selectExpr("CAST(key
AS STRING)", "CAST(value AS STRING)").as[(String, String)]
```

Next, we will start a streaming query that outputs the streaming Dataset to the standard output, as shown:

```
scala> val query =
ds1.writeStream.outputMode("append").format("console").start()
```

You should see the following output as you type sentences in the Kafka producer window:

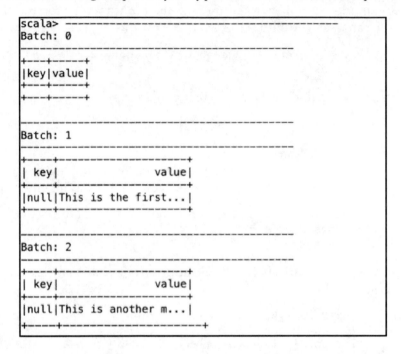

Introducing Kafka-Spark Structured Streaming

Then, we will provide another example of Kafka-Spark Structured Streaming, where we direct the contents of a iPinYou bids file to a producer, as demonstrated:

```
Aurobindos-MacBook-Pro-2:kafka_2.11-0.10.1.0 aurobindosarkar$ bin/kafka-
console-producer.sh --broker-list localhost:9092 --topic connect-test <
/Users/aurobindosarkar/Downloads/make-ipinyou-data-master/original-
data/ipinyou.contest.dataset/bidfiles/bid.20130311.txt
```

We will also create a new topic, called `connect-test`, a new streaming Dataset that contains the records from the file, and a new streaming query that lists them on the screen, as shown:

```scala
scala> val ds2 =
spark.readStream.format("kafka").option("kafka.bootstrap.servers",
"localhost:9092").option("subscribe", "connect-
test").load().selectExpr("CAST(key AS STRING)", "CAST(value AS
STRING)").as[(String, String)]

scala> val query =
ds2.writeStream.outputMode("append").format("console").start()
```

The truncated output is given here. The records are spread across multiple batches as they stream in:

```
scala> -------------------------------------------
Batch: 0
-------------------------------------------
+---+-----+
|key|value|
+---+-----+
+---+-----+


-------------------------------------------
Batch: 1
-------------------------------------------
+----+--------------------+
| key|               value|
+----+--------------------+
|null|e3d962536ef3ac709...|
|null|f2ce7b51f499eae08...|
|null|dabbf5f389089c39d...|
|null|55cc617434cd07963...|
|null|68859f0ea7e3578ed...|
|null|de10b3396b222f60f...|
|null|bceaf9e7a3d7fa5d2...|
|null|375afd6a39e551874...|
|null|67f35f322a4936370...|
|null|1dbfbeafe74bbd9e0...|
|null|6d1f7c8008fd440b9...|
|null|c682cd3427d24bce3...|
|null|be35239ec494563fd...|
|null|c3872ff374277ad36...|
|null|5530617cd63368116...|
|null|8927586d9cbdd83a2...|
|null|bec9fd1c23f5f3908...|
|null|a35a52d81f0f78ed7...|
|null|661d603c23219d0fa...|
|null|184bf096e7fa66a12...|
+----+--------------------+
only showing top 20 rows
```

In the next section, we will create a receiver for accessing an arbitrary streaming data source.

Writing a receiver for a custom data source

So far, we have worked with data sources that have built-in support available in Spark. However, Spark Streaming can receive data from any arbitrary source, but we will need to implement a receiver for receiving data from the custom data source.

In this section, we will define a custom data source for public APIs available from the **Transport for London** (TfL) site. This site makes a unified API available for each mode of transportation in London. These APIs provide access to real-time data, for instance, rail arrivals. The output is available in the XML and JSON formats. We will use the APIs for current arrival predictions of London underground on a specific line.

 The reference site for TfL is `https://tfl.gov.uk`; register on this site to generate an application key for accessing the APIs.

We will start by extending the abstract class `Receiver` and implementing the `onStart()` and `onStop()` methods. In the `onStart()` method, we start the threads responsible for receiving the data and in `onStop()`, we stop these threads. The `receive` method receives the stream of data using a HTTP client, as shown:

```
import org.apache.spark.storage.StorageLevel
import org.apache.spark.streaming.receiver.Receiver
import org.jfarcand.wcs.{TextListener, WebSocket}
import scala.util.parsing.json.JSON
import scalaj.http.Http
import java.io.BufferedReader;
import java.io.IOException;
import java.io.InputStreamReader;
import org.apache.http.HttpResponse;
import org.apache.http.client.ClientProtocolException;
import org.apache.http.client.methods.HttpGet;
import org.apache.http.impl.client.DefaultHttpClient;
/**
* Spark Streaming Example TfL Receiver
*/
class TFLArrivalPredictionsByLine() extends
Receiver[String](StorageLevel.MEMORY_ONLY) with Runnable {
//Replace the app_key parameter with your own key
private val tflUrl =
"https://api.tfl.gov.uk/Line/circle/Arrivals?stopPointId=940GZZLUERC&app_id
=a73727f3&app_key=xxx"
@transient
private var thread: Thread = _
```

```
override def onStart(): Unit = {
   thread = new Thread(this)
   thread.start()
}
override def onStop(): Unit = {
   thread.interrupt()
}
override def run(): Unit = {
   while (true){
     receive();
     Thread.sleep(60*1000);
   }
}
private def receive(): Unit = {
   val httpClient = new DefaultHttpClient();
   val getRequest = new HttpGet(tflUrl);
   getRequest.addHeader("accept", "application/json");
   val response = httpClient.execute(getRequest);
   if (response.getStatusLine().getStatusCode() != 200) {
      throw new RuntimeException("Failed : HTTP error code : "
          + response.getStatusLine().getStatusCode());
   }
   val br = new BufferedReader(
      new InputStreamReader((response.getEntity().getContent())));
   var output=br.readLine();
   while(output!=null){
      println(output)
      output=br.readLine()
   }
}
}
}
```

The following object creates the StreamingContext and starts the application. The awaitTermination() method ensures that the application runs continuously.

You can terminate the application using *Ctrl + C* :

```
import org.apache.spark.SparkConf
import org.apache.spark.streaming.{Seconds, StreamingContext}
/**
 * Spark Streaming Example App
 */
object TFLStreamingApp {
def main(args: Array[String]) {
   val conf = new SparkConf().setAppName("TFLStreaming")
   val ssc = new StreamingContext(conf, Seconds(300))
   val stream = ssc.receiverStream(new TFLArrivalPredictionsByLine())
   stream.print()
   if (args.length > 2) {
      stream.saveAsTextFiles(args(2))
   }
   ssc.start()
   ssc.awaitTermination()
   }
}
```

The `sbt` file used for compiling and packing the application is listed here:

```
name := "spark-streaming-example"
version := "1.0"
scalaVersion := "2.11.7"
resolvers += "jitpack" at "https://jitpack.io"
libraryDependencies ++= Seq("org.apache.spark" %% "spark-core" % "2.0.0",
"org.apache.spark" %% "spark-streaming" % "2.0.0",
"org.apache.httpcomponents" % "httpclient" % "4.5.2",
"org.scalaj" %% "scalaj-http" % "2.2.1",
"org.jfarcand" % "wcs" % "1.5")
```

We use the `spark-submit` command to execute our application, as follows:

```
Aurobindos-MacBook-Pro-2:scala-2.11 aurobindosarkar$
/Users/aurobindosarkar/Downloads/spark-2.2.0-bin-hadoop2.7/bin/spark-submit
--class TFLStreamingApp --master local[*] spark-streaming-
example_2.11-1.0.jar
```

The output from the streaming program is as follows:

[{"$type":"Tfl.Api.Presentation.Entities.Prediction,
Tfl.Api.Presentation.Entities","id":"-
403982650","operationType":1,"vehicleId":"201","naptanId":"940GZZLUER
C","stationName":"Edgware Road (Circle Line) Underground
Station","lineId":"circle","lineName":"Circle","platformName":"Eastbo
und - Platform
1","bearing":"","destinationNaptanId":"940GZZLUERC","destinationName"
:"Edgware Road (Circle Line) Underground Station","timestamp":"2017-
08-25T18:02:52Z","timeToStation":693,"currentLocation":"Between
Sloane Square and South Kensington","towards":"Edgware Road
(Circle)","expectedArrival":"2017-08-
25T18:14:25Z","timeToLive":"2017-08-
25T18:14:25Z","modeName":"tube","timing":{"$type":"Tfl.Api.Presentati
on.Entities.PredictionTiming,
Tfl.Api.Presentation.Entities","countdownServerAdjustment":"00:00:00"
,"source":"0001-01-01T00:00:00","insert":"0001-01-
01T00:00:00","read":"2017-08-25T18:02:31.585Z","sent":"2017-08-
25T18:02:52Z","received":"0001-01-
01T00:00:00"}},{"$type":"Tfl.Api.Presentation.Entities.Prediction,
Tfl.Api.Presentation.Entities","id":"1116945755","operationType":1,"v
ehicleId":"202","naptanId":"940GZZLUERC","stationName":"Edgware Road
(Circle Line) Underground
Station","lineId":"circle","lineName":"Circle","platformName":"Eastbo
und - Platform
1","bearing":"","destinationNaptanId":"940GZZLUERC","destinationName"
:"Edgware Road (Circle Line) Underground Station","timestamp":"2017-
08-25T18:02:52Z","timeToStation":1053,"currentLocation":"At St.
James's Park Platform 1","towards":"Edgware Road
(Circle)","expectedArrival":"2017-08-
25T18:20:25Z","timeToLive":"2017-08-
25T18:20:25Z","modeName":"tube","timing":{"$type":"Tfl.Api.Presentati
on.Entities.PredictionTiming,
Tfl.Api.Presentation.Entities","countdownServerAdjustment":"00:00:00"
,"source":"0001-01-01T00:00:00","insert":"0001-01-
01T00:00:00","read":"2017-08-25T18:02:31.6Z","sent":"2017-08-
25T18:02:52Z","received":"0001-01-
01T00:00:00"}},{"$type":"Tfl.Api.Presentation.Entities.Prediction,
Tfl.Api.Presentation.Entities","id":"557369852","operationType":1,"ve
hicleId":"203","naptanId":"940GZZLUERC","stationName":"Edgware Road
(Circle Line) Underground
Station","lineId":"circle","lineName":"Circle","platformName":"Eastbo
und - Platform
1","bearing":"","destinationNaptanId":"940GZZLUERC","destinationName"
:"Edgware Road (Circle Line) Underground Station","timestamp":"2017-
08-25T18:02:52Z","timeToStation":1713,"currentLocation":"At Monument
Platform 1","towards":"Edgware Road
(Circle)","expectedArrival":"2017-08-
25T18:31:25Z","timeToLive":"2017-08-
25T18:31:25Z","modeName":"tube","timing":{"$type":"Tfl.Api.Presentati
on.Entities.PredictionTiming,
Tfl.Api.Presentation.Entities","countdownServerAdjustment":"00:00:00"
,"source":"0001-01-01T00:00:00","insert":"0001-01-
01T00:00:00","read":"2017-08-25T18:02:31.632Z","sent":"2017-08-
25T18:02:52Z","received":"0001-01-01T00:00:00"}}]

Summary

In this chapter, we introduced streaming data applications. We provided a few examples of using Spark SQL DataFrame/Dataset APIs to build streaming applications. Additionally, we showed the use of Kafka in structured streaming applications. Finally, we presented an example of creating a receiver for a custom data source.

In the next chapter, we will shift our focus to using Spark SQL in machine learning applications. Specifically, we will explore key concepts of feature engineering and machine learning pipelines.

6

Using Spark SQL in Machine Learning Applications

n this chapter, we will present typical use cases for using Spark SQL in machine learning applications. We will focus on the Spark machine learning API called `spark.ml`, which is the recommended solution for implementing ML workflows. The `spark.ml` API is built on DataFrames and provides many ready-to-use packages, including feature extractors, Transformers, selectors, and machine learning algorithms, such as classification, regression, and clustering algorithms. We will also use Apache Spark to perform **exploratory data analysis (EDA)**, data pre-processing, feature engineering, and developing machine learning pipelines using `spark.ml` APIs and algorithms.

More specifically, in this chapter, you will learn the following topics:

- Machine learning applications
- Key components of Spark ML pipelines
- Understand Feature engineering
- Implementing machine learning pipelines/applications
- Code examples using Spark MLlib

Introducing machine learning applications

Machine learning, predictive analytics, and related data science topics are becoming increasingly popular for solving real-world problems across varied business domains.

Today, machine learning applications are driving mission-critical business decision-making in many organizations. These applications include recommendation engines, targeted advertising, speech recognition, fraud detection, image recognition and categorization, and so on.

In the next section, we will introduce the key components of the Spark ML pipeline API.

Understanding Spark ML pipelines and their components

The machine learning pipeline API was introduced in Apache Spark 1.2. Spark MLlib provides an API for developers to create and execute complex ML workflows. The Pipeline API lets developers quickly assemble distributed machine learning pipelines as the API has been standardized for applying different machine learning algorithms. Additionally, we can also combine multiple machine learning algorithms into a single pipeline. These pipelines consist of several key components that ease the implementation of data analytics and machine learning applications.

The main components of an ML pipeline are listed here:

- **Datasets**: Spark SQL DataFrames/Datasets are used for storing and processing data in an ML pipeline. The DataFrames/Datasets API provides a standard API and a common way of dealing with both static data (typically, for batch processing) as well as streaming data (typically, for online stream processing). As we will see in the following sections, these Datasets will be used for storing and processing input data, transformed input data, feature vectors, labels, predictions, and so on.
- **Pipelines**: ML workflows are implemented as pipelines consisting of a sequence of stages. For example, you could have a text preprocessing pipeline for the "Complete Submission Text File" of a `10-K` filing on the Edgar website. Such a pipeline would take the lines from the document as input at one end and produce a list of words as output, after passing through a series of Transformers (that apply regexes and other filters to the data in a particular sequence). Several examples of data and ML pipelines are presented in this chapter, as well as in `Chapter 9`, *Developing Applications with Spark SQL*.

- **Pipeline stages**: Each pipeline stage comprises of a Transformer or an Estimator that is executed in a specified sequence.
    - **Transformer**: This is an algorithm that transforms an input DataFrame into another DataFrame with one or more features added to it. There are several Transformers such as RegexTokenizer, Binarizer, OneHotEncoder, various indexers (for example, `StringIndexer` and `VectorIndexer`) and others available as a part of the library. You can also define your own custom Transformers like we do in `Chapter 9`, *Developing Applications with Spark SQL.*
    - **Estimator**: This is a machine learning algorithm that learns from the input data provided. The input to an estimator is a DataFrame and the output is a Transformer. There are several Estimators available in the MLlib libraries such as `LogisticRegression`, `RandomForest`, and so on. The output Transformers from these Estimators are the corresponding models, such as the LogisticRegressionModel, RandomForestModel, and so on.

Understanding the steps in a pipeline application development process

A machine learning pipeline application development process typically includes the following steps:

- **Data ingestion**: The input data ingested by a typical machine learning pipeline comes from multiple data sources, often in several different formats (as described in `Chapter 2`, *Using Spark SQL for Processing Structured and SemiStructured Data*). These sources can include files, databases (RDBMSs, NoSQL, Graph, and so on), Web Services (for example, REST end-points), Kafka and Amazon Kinesis streams, and others.
- **Data cleansing and preprocessing**: Data cleansing is a critical step in the overall data analytics pipeline. This preprocessing step fixes data quality issues and makes it suitable for consumption by the machine learning models. For example, we may need to remove HTML tags and replace special characters (such as ` ` and others) from the source HTML documents. We might have to rename columns (or specify them) as per the required standardized formats for Spark MLlib pipelines. Most importantly, we will also need to combine various columns in the DataFrame into a single column containing the feature vector.

- **Feature engineering**: In this step, we extract and generate specific features from the input data using various techniques. These are then combined into a feature vector and passed to the next step in the process. Typically, a `VectorAssembler` is used to create the feature vector from the specified DataFrame columns.
- **Model training**: Machine learning model training involves specifying an algorithm and some training data (which the model can learn from). Typically, we split our input Dataset into training and test Datasets, by randomly selecting a certain proportion of the input records for each of these Datasets. The model is trained by calling the `fit()` method on the training Dataset.
- **Model validation**: This step involves evaluating and tuning the ML model to assess how good the predictions are. In this step, the model is applied to the test Dataset, using the `transform()` method, and appropriate performance measures for the model are computed, for example, accuracy, error, and so on.
- **Model selection**: In this step, we choose the parameters for the Transformers and Estimators that produce the best ML model. Typically, we create a parameter grid and execute a grid-search for the most suitable set of parameters for a given model using a process called cross-validation. The best model returned by the cross validator can be saved and later loaded into the production environment.
- **Model Deployment**: Finally, we deploy the best model for production. For some models, it may be easier to convert the model parameters (such as coefficients, intercepts, or decision trees with branching logic) to other formats (such as JSON) for simpler and more efficient deployments in complex production environments. More details on such deployments can be got from Chapter 12, *Spark SQL in Large-Scale Application Architectures*.

The deployed models will need to be continuously maintained, upgraded, optimized, and so on, in the production environment.

Introducing feature engineering

Feature engineering is the process of using domain knowledge of the data to create features that are key to applying machine learning algorithms. Any attribute can be a feature, and choosing a good set of features that helps solve the problem and produce acceptable results is key to the whole process. This step is often the most challenging aspect of machine learning applications. Both the quality and quantity/number of features greatly influences the overall quality of the model.

Better features also means more flexibility because they can result in good results even when less than optimal models are used. Most ML models can pick up on the structure and patterns in the underlying data, reasonably well. The flexibility of good features allows us to use less complex models that are faster and easier to understand and maintain. Better features also typically result in simpler models. Such features make it easier to select the right models and the most optimized parameters.

 For a good blog on feature engineering, refer: Discover Feature Engineering, How to Engineer Features and How to Get Good at It, Jason Brownlee, at: `https://machinelearningmastery.com/discover-feature-engineering-how-to-engineer-features-and-how-to-get-good-at-it/`

Producing a feature vector for every piece of information in a real-world Dataset is impractical from a processing and computing costs perspective. Typically, feature transformations, such as indexing and binning, are used to reduce the dimensionality of predictor variables. Additionally, irrelevant and low-frequency values are generally removed from the model, and continuous variables are grouped into a reasonable number of bins. Some of the original features may be highly correlated, or redundant, and can, therefore, be dropped from further consideration as well. Additionally, multiple features can be combined to yield new features (thereby reducing the overall dimensionality as well). Depending on the model, we may also have to normalize the values of some variables to avoid skewed results from using absolute values. We apply transformations on the training Dataset to obtain a feature vector that will be fed into a machine learning algorithm.

Thus, feature engineering is an iterative process comprising of multiple cycles of data selection and model evaluation. If the problem is well defined then the iterative process can be stopped at an appropriate point, and other configurations, or models, attempted.

Creating new features from raw data

Selecting features from raw data could lead to many different feature sets however we need to keep the ones that are most relevant to the problem to be solved.

Feature selection can reveal the importance of various features, but those features have to be identified first. The number of features can be limited by our ability to collect the data but once collected it is entirely dependent on our selection process. Usually, they need to be created manually, and this requires time, patience, creativity, and familiarity with the raw input data.

Transformations of the raw input data depends on the nature of the data. For example, with textual data, it could mean generating document vectors while with image data, it could mean applying various filters to extract the contours from an image. Hence, the process is largely manual, slow, iterative, and requires lots of domain expertise.

Estimating the importance of a feature

We have to choose a subset from among hundreds and thousands of potential features to include in the modeling process. Making these choices requires deeper insights about the features that may have the greatest impact upon model performance. Typically, the features under consideration are scored and then ranked as per their scores. Generally, the features with the highest scores are selected for inclusion in the training Dataset, while others are ignored. Additionally, we may generate new features from the raw data features, as well. How do we know whether these generated features are helpful to the task at hand?

Different approaches can be used for estimating the importance of features. For example, we can group sets of related features and compare the performance of the model without those features to the complete model (with the dropped features included). We can also execute a k-fold cross-validation for both, the complete and dropped models, and compare them on various statistical measures. However, this approach can be too expensive to run continuously in production as it requires building every model k-times (for a k-fold cross-validation) for every feature group, which can be many (depending on the level of grouping). So, in practice, this exercise is performed periodically on a representative sample of models.

Other effective techniques for feature engineering include visualization and applying specific methods known to work well on certain types of data. Visualization can be a powerful tool to quickly analyze relationships between features and evaluate the impact of generated features. Using well-known approaches and methods in various domains can help accelerate the feature engineering process. For example, for textual data, using n-grams, TF-IDF, feature hashing, and others, are well known and widely applied feature engineering methods.

Understanding dimensionality reduction

Primarily, dimensionality reduction deals with achieving a suitable reduction in the number of predictor variables in the model. It helps by selecting features that become part of the training Dataset after limiting the number of resulting columns in the feature matrix using various transformations. The attributes that are evaluated to be largely irrelevant to the problem need to be removed.

There will be some features that will be more important to the model's accuracy than others. There will also be some features that become redundant in the presence of other features.

Feature selection addresses these challenges by selecting a subset of features that is most useful in solving the problem. Feature selection algorithms may compute correlation coefficients, covariances, and other statistics for choosing a good set of features. A feature is generally included, if it is highly correlated with the dependent variable (the thing being predicted). We can also use **Principal Component Analysis** (**PCA**) and unsupervised clustering methods for feature selection. More advanced methods may search through various feature sets creating and evaluating models automatically in order to derive the best predictive subgroup of features.

Deriving good features

In this section, we will provide additional tips for deriving good features and measures for assessing them. These features can be handcrafted by a domain expert or automated using methods such as PCA or deep learning (see `Chapter 10`, *Using Spark SQL in Deep Learning Applications*). Each of these approaches can be used independently, or jointly, to arrive at the best set of features.

When working on machine learning projects, tasks such as data preparation and cleansing are key, in addition to the actual learning models and algorithms used to solve the business problems. In the absence of data pre-processing steps in machine learning applications, the resulting patterns will not be accurate or useful and/or the prediction results will have a lower accuracy.

Here, we present a few general tips to derive a good set of pre-processed features and cleansed data:

- Explore grouping for categorical values and/or limiting the number of categorical values that become predictor variables in the feature matrix to only the most common ones.
    - Evaluate and add new features by computing polynomial features from the provided features. However, be careful to avoid overfitting, which can occur when the model closely fits the data containing excessive number of features. This results in a model that memorizes the data, rather than learns from it, which in turn reduces its ability to predict new data accurately.

- Evaluating each feature to test its correlation with the classes independently by using a ranking metric, such as Pearson's correlation. We can then select a subset of features, such as the top 10%, or the top 20%, of the ranked features.
- Evaluating how good each feature is using criteria, such as Gini index and entropy.
- Exploring the covariance between features; for example, if two features are changing the same way, it will probably not serve the overall purpose to select both of them as features.
- A model may also underfit the training Dataset, which will result in lower model accuracy. When your model is underfitting a Dataset, you should consider introducing new features.
- A date-time field contains a lot of information that can be difficult for a model to take advantage of in its original format. Decompose date-time fields into separate fields for month, day, year, and so on, to allow models to leverage these relationships.
- Apply linear Transformers to numerical fields, such as weights and distances, for use in regression and other algorithms.
- Explore storing a quantity measure (such weights or distances) as a rate or an aggregate quantity over a time interval to expose structures, such as seasonality.

In the next section, we will present a detailed code example of a Spark ML pipeline.

Implementing a Spark ML classification model

The first step in implementing a machine learning model is to perform EDA on input data. This analysis would typically involve data visualization using tools such as Zeppelin, assessing feature types (numeric/categorical), computing basic statistics, computing covariances, and correlation coefficients, creating pivot tables, and so on (for more details on EDA, see Chapter 3, *Using Spark SQL for Data Exploration*).

The next step involves executing data pre-processing and/or data munging operations. In almost all cases, the real-world input data will not be high quality data ready for use in a model. There will be several transformations required to convert the features from the source format to final variables; for example, categorical features may need to be transformed to a binary variable for each categorical value using one-hot encoding technique (for more details on data munging, see Chapter 4, *Using Spark SQL for Data Munging*).

Next is the feature engineering step. In this step, we will derive new features to include, along with other existing features, in the training data. Use the tips provided earlier in this chapter to derive a good set of features to be ultimately used in training the model.

Finally, we will train the model using the selected features and test it using the test Dataset.

 For a good blog containing a detailed step-by-step example of a classification model applied to the Kaggle knowledge challenge--Titanic: Machine Learning from Disaster, refer: *Building Classification model using Apache Spark* by Vishnu Viswanath at: http://vishnuviswanath.com/ spark_lr.html.

These steps, along with the operations and input/output at each stage, are shown in the following figure:

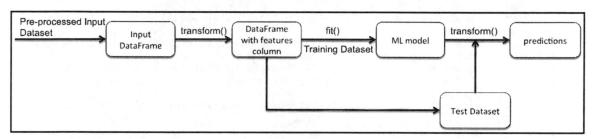

We will use the publicly available diabetes Dataset that consists of 101,766 rows, representing ten years of clinical care records from 130 US hospitals and integrated delivery networks. It includes over 50 features (attributes) representing patient and hospital outcomes.

 The Dataset can be downloaded from the UCI website at https:// archive.ics.uci.edu/ml/datasets/Diabetes+130- US+hospitals+for+years+1999-2008.

The source ZIP file contains two CSV files. The first file, diabetic_data.csv, is the main input Dataset, and the second file, IDs_mapping.csv, is the master data for admission_type_id, discharge_disposition_id, and admission_source_id. The second file is small enough to manually split into three parts, one for each set of ID mappings.

The example in this section closely follows the approach and analysis presented in: Impact of HbA1c measurement on hospital readmission rates: analysis of 70,000 clinical database patient records, by Beata Strack, Jonathan P. DeShazo, Chris Gennings, Juan L. Olmo, Sebastian Ventura, Krzysztof J. Cios and John N. Clore, Biomed Res Int. 2014; 2014: 781670, available at: http://europepmc.org/articles/PMC3996476.

First, we will import all the packages required for this coding exercise:

```scala
scala> import spark.implicits._
scala> import org.apache.spark.sql.types._
scala> import org.apache.spark.sql.{DataFrameNaFunctions, Row}
scala> import org.apache.spark.ml.feature.{StringIndexer, VectorAssembler,
IndexToString, VectorIndexer, OneHotEncoder, PCA, Binarizer, VectorSlicer,
StandardScaler, Bucketizer, ChiSqSelector, Normalizer }
scala> import org.apache.spark.ml.Pipeline
scala> import org.apache.spark.ml.evaluation.{MulticlassClassificationEvaluator,
BinaryClassificationEvaluator}
scala> import org.apache.spark.sql.functions.{ sum,when , row_number, max, broadcast}
scala> import org.apache.spark.sql.expressions.Window
scala> import org.apache.spark.ml.classification.{RandomForestClassificationModel,
RandomForestClassifier, LogisticRegression, DecisionTreeClassificationModel,
DecisionTreeClassifier, GBTClassificationModel, GBTClassifier}
scala> import org.apache.spark.ml.tuning.{CrossValidator, ParamGridBuilder}

scala> import org.apache.spark.ml.linalg.{Vector, Vectors}
```

Exploring the diabetes Dataset

The Dataset contains attributes/features originally selected by clinical experts based on their potential connection to the diabetic condition or management.

A full list of the features and their description is available at https://www. hindawi.com/journals/bmri/2014/781670/tab1/.

We load the input data into a Spark DataFrame, as follows:

```scala
scala> val inDiaDataDF = spark.read.option("header",
true).csv("file:///Users/aurobindosarkar/Downloads/dataset_diabetes/diabeti
c_data.csv").cache()
```

We can display the schema of the DataFrame created in the previous step to list the columns or fields in the DataFrame, as shown:

```scala
scala> inDiaDataDF.printSchema()
```

```
root
 |-- encounter_id: string (nullable = true)
 |-- patient_nbr: string (nullable = true)
 |-- race: string (nullable = true)
 |-- gender: string (nullable = true)
 |-- age: string (nullable = true)
 |-- weight: string (nullable = true)
 |-- admission_type_id: string (nullable = true)
 |-- discharge_disposition_id: string (nullable = true)
 |-- admission_source_id: string (nullable = true)
 |-- time_in_hospital: string (nullable = true)
 |-- payer_code: string (nullable = true)
 |-- medical_specialty: string (nullable = true)
 |-- num_lab_procedures: string (nullable = true)
 |-- num_procedures: string (nullable = true)
 |-- num_medications: string (nullable = true)
 |-- number_outpatient: string (nullable = true)
 |-- number_emergency: string (nullable = true)
 |-- number_inpatient: string (nullable = true)
 |-- diag_1: string (nullable = true)
 |-- diag_2: string (nullable = true)
 |-- diag_3: string (nullable = true)
 |-- number_diagnoses: string (nullable = true)
 |-- max_glu_serum: string (nullable = true)
 |-- A1Cresult: string (nullable = true)
 |-- metformin: string (nullable = true)
 |-- repaglinide: string (nullable = true)
 |-- nateglinide: string (nullable = true)
 |-- chlorpropamide: string (nullable = true)
 |-- glimepiride: string (nullable = true)
 |-- acetohexamide: string (nullable = true)
 |-- glipizide: string (nullable = true)
 |-- glyburide: string (nullable = true)
 |-- tolbutamide: string (nullable = true)
 |-- pioglitazone: string (nullable = true)
 |-- rosiglitazone: string (nullable = true)
 |-- acarbose: string (nullable = true)
 |-- miglitol: string (nullable = true)
 |-- troglitazone: string (nullable = true)
 |-- tolazamide: string (nullable = true)
 |-- examide: string (nullable = true)
 |-- citoglipton: string (nullable = true)
 |-- insulin: string (nullable = true)
 |-- glyburide-metformin: string (nullable = true)
 |-- glipizide-metformin: string (nullable = true)
 |-- glimepiride-pioglitazone: string (nullable = true)
 |-- metformin-rosiglitazone: string (nullable = true)
 |-- metformin-pioglitazone: string (nullable = true)
 |-- change: string (nullable = true)
 |-- diabetesMed: string (nullable = true)
 |-- readmitted: string (nullable = true)
```

Next, we print out a few sample records to get a high-level sense of the values contained in the fields of the Dataset:

```scala
scala> inDiaDataDF.take(5).foreach(println)
```

```
[2278392,8222157,Caucasian,Female,[0-10),?,6,25,1,1,?,Pediatrics-
Endocrinology,41,0,1,0,0,0,250.83,?,?,1,None,None,No,No,No,No,No,No,No,No,No,No,No,
No,No,No,No,No,No,No,No,No,No,No,No,NO]
[149190,55629189,Caucasian,Female,[10-
20),?,1,1,7,3,?,?,59,0,18,0,0,0,276,250.01,255,9,None,None,No,No,No,No,No,No,No,No,
No,No,No,No,No,No,No,No,Up,No,No,No,No,No,Ch,Yes,>30]
[64410,86047875,AfricanAmerican,Female,[20-
30),?,1,1,7,2,?,?,11,5,13,2,0,1,648,250,V27,6,None,None,No,No,No,No,No,No,Steady,No,No
,No,No,No,No,No,No,No,No,No,No,No,No,No,Yes,NO]
[500364,82442376,Caucasian,Male,[30-
40),?,1,1,7,2,?,?,44,1,16,0,0,0,8,250.43,403,7,None,None,No,No,No,No,No,No,No,No,No,No
,No,No,No,No,No,No,No,Up,No,No,No,No,No,Ch,Yes,NO]
[16680,42519267,Caucasian,Male,[40-
50),?,1,1,7,1,?,?,51,0,8,0,0,0,197,157,250,5,None,None,No,No,No,No,No,No,Steady,No,No,
No,No,No,No,No,No,No,No,Steady,No,No,No,No,No,Ch,Yes,NO]
```

We can also compute the basic statistics for numerical columns using `dataFrame.describe("column")`. For example, we display the count, mean, standard deviation, and min and max values of a few numeric data columns:

```scala
scala> inDiaDataDF.select("num_lab_procedures", "num_procedures",
"num_medications", "number_diagnoses").describe().show()
```

```
+-------+------------------+------------------+------------------+---------
---------+
|summary|num_lab_procedures|    num_procedures|   num_medications|
number_diagnoses|
+-------+------------------+------------------+------------------+---------
---------+
|  count|            101766|            101766|            101766|
101766|
|   mean| 43.09564098028811| 1.339730361810428|16.021844230882614|
7.422606764538254|
| stddev| 19.67436224914214|1.7058069791211583|
8.127566209167293|1.9336001449974298|
|    min|                 1|                 0|                 1|
1|
|    max|                99|                 6|                 9|
9|
+-------+------------------+------------------+------------------+---------
---------+
```

The original input Dataset contains incomplete, redundant, and noisy information, as expected in any real-world Dataset. There are several fields that have a high percentage of missing values.

We compute the number of records that have specific fields missing, as follows:

```scala
scala>
inDiaDataDF.select($"weight").groupBy($"weight").count().select($"weight",
(($"count" / inDiaDataDF.count())*100).alias("percent_recs")).where("weight
= '?'").show()
+------+-----------------+
|weight|     percent_recs|
+------+-----------------+
|     ?|96.85847925633315|
+------+-----------------+

scala>
inDiaDataDF.select($"payer_code").groupBy($"payer_code").count().select($"p
ayer_code", (($"count" /
inDiaDataDF.count())*100).alias("percent_recs")).where("payer_code =
'?'").show()

+----------+-----------------+
|payer_code|     percent_recs|
+----------+-----------------+
|         ?|39.5574160328597|
+----------+-----------------+

scala>
inDiaDataDF.select($"medical_specialty").groupBy($"medical_specialty").coun
t().select($"medical_specialty", (($"count" /
inDiaDataDF.count())*100).alias("percent_recs")).where("medical_specialty =
'?'").show()

+-----------------+-----------------+
|medical_specialty|     percent_recs|
+-----------------+-----------------+
|                ?|49.08220820313268|
+-----------------+-----------------+
```

As computed precedingly, the features with many missing values are identified to be weight, payer code, and medical specialty. We drop the weight and payer code columns, however, the medical specialty attribute (potentially, a very relevant feature) is retained:

```scala
scala> val diaDataDrpDF = inDiaDataDF.drop("weight", "payer_code")
```

The Dataset also contains records of multiple inpatient visits by some of the patients. Here, we extract a set of patients with multiple inpatient visits.

We observe that the overall number of such patients is significant:

```
scala>
diaDataDrpDF.select($"patient_nbr").groupBy($"patient_nbr").count().where("
count > 1").show(5)

+-----------+-----+
|patient_nbr|count|
+-----------+-----+
|    4311585|    2|
|    4624767|    2|
|   24962301|    3|
|   11889666|    2|
|    2585367|    2|
+-----------+-----+
only showing top 5 rows

scala>
diaDataDrpDF.select($"patient_nbr").groupBy($"patient_nbr").count().where("
count > 1").count()
res67: Long = 16773
```

As mentioned in the reference study/paper, such observations cannot be considered as statistically independent, hence, we include only the first encounter for each patient. After these operations are completed, we verify that there are no patient records remaining in the DataFrame corresponding to multiple visit records:

```
scala> val w =
Window.partitionBy($"patient_nbr").orderBy($"encounter_id".desc)

scala> val diaDataSlctFirstDF = diaDataDrpDF.withColumn("rn",
row_number.over(w)).where($"rn" === 1).drop("rn")

scala>
diaDataSlctFirstDF.select($"patient_nbr").groupBy($"patient_nbr").count().w
here("count > 1").show()
+-----------+-----+
|patient_nbr|count|
+-----------+-----+
+-----------+-----+

scala> diaDataSlctFirstDF.count()
res35: Long = 71518
```

As in the reference study/paper, we also remove records of encounters that resulted in a patient's death to avoid bias:

```
scala> val diaDataAdmttedDF =
diaDataSlctFirstDF.filter($"discharge_disposition_id" =!= "11")

scala> diaDataAdmttedDF.count()
res16: Long = 69934
```

After performing the mentioned operations, we were left with 69,934 encounters that constitute the final Dataset used for further analysis.

Next, we execute a set of JOIN operations to understand the data better in terms of top categories of discharge disposition, admission types, and admission sources:

```
scala> val joinDF = diaDataAdmttedDF.join(dchrgDispDF,
diaDataAdmttedDF("discharge_disposition_id") ===
dchrgDispDF("dchrgDispId")).withColumnRenamed("description",
"discharge_disposition").drop(dchrgDispDF("dchrgDispId")).join(admTypeDF,
diaDataAdmttedDF("admission_type_id") ===
admTypeDF("admTypeId")).withColumnRenamed("description",
"admission_type").drop(admTypeDF("admTypeId")).join(admSrcDF,
diaDataAdmttedDF("admission_source_id") ===
admSrcDF("admission_source_id")).withColumnRenamed("description",
"admission_source").drop(admSrcDF("admission_source_id"))
```

```
scala> joinDF.select("encounter_id", "dchrgDisp", "admType",
"admission_source").show()
```

```
+------------+-----------------+---------+-------------------+
|encounter_id|        dchrgDisp|  admType|   admission_source|
+------------+-----------------+---------+-------------------+
|   392013782| Discharged to home| Elective|  Physician Referral|
|    46598346|             NULL| Elective|Transfer from a h...|
|   138229974| Discharged to home|Emergency|     Emergency Room|
|     7269804|Discharged/transf...|   Urgent|  Physician Referral|
|   311887940| Discharged to home|   Urgent|     Emergency Room|
|   201558258|Discharged/transf...|Emergency|     Emergency Room|
|   230227854| Discharged to home|   Urgent|  Physician Referral|
|    59322732|             NULL| Elective|  Physician Referral|
|   128185728| Discharged to home|   Urgent|     Emergency Room|
|   180128832|Discharged/transf...|Emergency|     Emergency Room|
|   119373450|Discharged/transf...| Elective|  Physician Referral|
|    82723956| Discharged to home|Emergency|     Emergency Room|
|   259028538| Discharged to home|Emergency|  Physician Referral|
|   361461086| Discharged to home|   Urgent|  Physician Referral|
|    59154006| Discharged to home| Elective|  Physician Referral|
|   233433594|Discharged/transf...|Emergency|     Emergency Room|
|   423739748| Discharged to home|   Urgent|  Physician Referral|
|   190090386| Discharged to home|   Urgent|     Emergency Room|
|   147463902|Discharged/transf...|Emergency|     Emergency Room|
|   366137420|Discharged/transf...| Elective|  Physician Referral|
+------------+-----------------+---------+-------------------+
only showing top 20 rows
```

```
scala> joinDF.select("encounter_id",
"dchrgDisp").groupBy("dchrgDisp").count().orderBy($"count".desc).take(10).f
oreach(println)
```

```
[Discharged to home,43473]
[Discharged/transferred to SNF,9167]
[Discharged/transferred to home with home health service,8442]
[NULL,2397]
[Discharged/transferred to another short term hospital,1463]
[Discharged/transferred to another rehab fac including rehab units of a hospital
.,1274]
[Discharged/transferred to another type of inpatient care institution,844]
[Not Mapped,675]
[Discharged/transferred to ICF,554]
[Left AMA,411]
```

```
scala> joinDF.select("encounter_id",
"admType").groupBy("admType").count().orderBy($"count".desc).take(5).foreac
h(println)
[Emergency,35988]
[Elective,13698]
[Urgent,12799]
[NULL,4373]
[Not Available,2752]
```

```
scala> joinDF.select("encounter_id",
"admission_source").groupBy("admission_source").count().orderBy($"count".de
sc).take(5).foreach(println)

[ Emergency Room,37649]
[ Physician Referral,21196]
[NULL,4801]
[Transfer from a hospital,2622]
[ Transfer from another health care facility,1797]
```

In the next section, we will execute a series of data munging or data pre-processing steps to improve the overall data quality.

Pre-processing the data

There are several data munging steps required to preprocess the data. We will start by addressing the missing field, values. We have several options when dealing with null or missing values. We can drop them using `df.na.drop()`, or fill them with default values using `df.na.fill()`. Such fields can be replaced with the most commonly occurring values for that column, and in the case of numeric fields they can also be replaced with average values. Additionally, you can also train a regression model on the column and use it to predict the field values for rows where values are missing.

Here, we have the missing fields represented with a ? value in the Dataset, so we use the `df.na.replace()` function to replace them with the "Missing" string.

This operation is illustrated for the `medical_specialty` field, as shown:

```
scala>
diaDataAdmttedDF.select("medical_specialty").where("medical_specialty =
'?'").groupBy("medical_specialty").count().show()

+-----------------+-----+
|medical_specialty|count|
+-----------------+-----+
|                ?|33733|
+-----------------+-----+

scala> val diaDataRplcMedSplDF =
diaDataAdmttedDF.na.replace("medical_specialty", Map("?" -> "Missing"))
```

The `medical_specialty` field can have values, such as cardiology, internal medicine, family/general practice, surgeon, or Missing. To a model, the Missing value appears like any other choice for `medical_specialty`. We could have created a new binary feature called `has_ medical_specialty` and assigned it a value of 1 when a row contained the value and 0 when it was unknown or missing. Alternatively, we could also have created a binary feature for each value of `medical_specialty`, such as `Is_Cardiology`, `Is_Surgeon`, and `Is_Missing`. These additional features can then be used instead of, or in addition to, the `medical_specialty` feature in different models.

Next, guided by the analysis contained in the original paper, we drop a set of columns from further analysis in this chapter, to keep the size of the problem reasonable, as shown:

```
scala> val diaDataDrpColsDF = diaDataRplcMedSplDF.drop("encounter_id", "patient_nbr",
"diag_2", "diag_3", "max_glu_serum", "metformin", "repaglinide", "nateglinide",
"chlorpropamide", "glimepiride", "acetohexamide", "glipizide", "glyburide",
"tolbutamide", "pioglitazone", "rosiglitazone", "acarbose", "miglitol",
"troglitazone", "tolazamide", "examide", "citoglipton", "insulin", "glyburide-
metformin", "glipizide-metformin", "glimepiride-pioglitazone", "metformin-
rosiglitazone", "metformin-pioglitazone")
```

As in the referenced study/paper, we also consider four groups of encounters: no HbA1c test performed, HbA1c performed and in normal range, HbA1c performed and the result is greater than 8 percent, and HbA1c performed and the result is greater than 8 percent.

These steps to accomplish this grouping are executed as follows:

```
scala> diaDataDrpColsDF.groupBy($"A1Cresult").count().show()
```

```
+---------+-----+
|A1Cresult|count|
+---------+-----+
|     None|57645|
|       >8| 5866|
|     Norm| 3691|
|       >7| 2732|
+---------+-----+
```

```
scala> def udfA1CGrps() = udf[Double, String] { a => val x = a match { case
"None" => 1.0; case ">8" => 2.0; case ">7" => 3.0; case "Norm" => 4.0;};
x; }
```

```
scala> val diaDataA1CResultsDF = diaDataDrpColsDF.withColumn("A1CResGrp",
udfA1CGrps()($"A1Cresult"))
```

```
scala>
diaDataA1CResultsDF.groupBy("A1CResGrp").count().withColumn("Percent_of_Pop
ulation", ($"count" /
diaDataA1CResultsDF.count())*100).withColumnRenamed("count",
"Num_of_Encounters").show()
+--------------------+-----------------+--------------------+
|           A1CResGrp|Num_of_Encounters|Percent_of_Population|
+--------------------+-----------------+--------------------+
|No test was perfo...|            57645|    82.42771756227299|
|Result was high a...|             5866|    8.387908599536706|
|Normal result of ...|             3691|     5.27783338576372|
|Result was high b...|             2732|    3.906540452426573|
+--------------------+-----------------+--------------------+
```

Since our primary objective focuses on factors that lead to early readmission, the readmission attribute (or the outcome) has two values: Readmitted, if the patient was readmitted within 30 days of discharge or Not Readmitted, which covers both readmission after 30 days and no readmission at all.

We create a new ordinal feature, called Readmitted, with two values: Readmitted and Not Readmitted. You can use similar approaches for age categories as well:

```
scala> def udfReAdmBins() = udf[String, String] { a => val x = a match {
case "<30" => "Readmitted"; case "NO" => "Not Readmitted"; case ">30" =>
"Not Readmitted";}; x; }
```

```
scala> val diaDataReadmtdDF = diaDataA1CResultsDF.withColumn("Readmitted",
udfReAdmBins()($"readmitted"))
```

We display the numbers of several features versus the values of the target variable, as follows. This will help identify skews in the number of records based on various attributes in the input Dataset:

```scala
scala>
diaDataReadmtdDF.groupBy("race").pivot("Readmitted").agg(count("Readmitted"
)).show()
+---------------+--------------+----------+
|           race|Not Readmitted|Readmitted|
+---------------+--------------+----------+
|      Caucasian|         49710|      2613|
|          Other|          1095|        51|
|AfricanAmerican|         12185|       423|
|       Hispanic|          1424|        70|
|          Asian|           478|        25|
|              ?|          1795|        65|
+---------------+--------------+----------+

scala>
diaDataReadmtdDF.groupBy("A1CResGrp").pivot("Readmitted").agg(count("Readmi
tted")).orderBy("A1CResGrp").show()
+-------------------+--------------+----------+
|          A1CResGrp|Not Readmitted|Readmitted|
+-------------------+--------------+----------+
|No test was perfo...|         54927|      2718|
|Normal result of ...|          3545|       146|
|Result was high a...|          5618|       248|
|Result was high b...|          2597|       135|
+-------------------+--------------+----------+

scala>
diaDataReadmtdDF.groupBy("gender").pivot("Readmitted").agg(count("Readmitte
d")).show()
+---------------+--------------+----------+
|         gender|Not Readmitted|Readmitted|
+---------------+--------------+----------+
|         Female|         35510|      1701|
|Unknown/Invalid|             3|      null|
|           Male|         31174|      1546|
+---------------+--------------+----------+
```

Next, we group the various age ranges into various categories and adds it as a column to obtain our final version of the Dataset, as illustrated. Additionally, we remove the three rows where the gender is Unknown/Invalid:

```scala
scala> def udfAgeBins() = udf[String, String] { a => val x = a match { case
"[0-10)" => "Young"; case "[10-20)" => "Young"; case "[20-30)" => "Young";
```

```
case "[30-40)" => "Middle"; case "[40-50)" => "Middle"; case "[50-60)" =>
"Middle"; case "[60-70)" => "Elder";  case "[70-80)" => "Elder"; case
"[80-90)" => "Elder"; case "[90-100)" => "Elder";}; x;}

scala> val diaDataAgeBinsDF = diaDataReadmtdDF.withColumn("age_category",
udfAgeBins()($"age"))

scala> val diaDataRmvGndrDF = diaDataAgeBinsDF.filter($"gender" =!=
"Unknown/Invalid")
```

```
scala>  val diaDataFinalDF = diaDataRmvGndrDF.select($"race", $"gender",
$"age_category", $"admission_type_id".cast(IntegerType),
$"discharge_disposition_id".cast(IntegerType),
$"admission_source_id".cast(IntegerType), $"time_in_hospital".cast(IntegerType),
$"num_lab_procedures".cast(DoubleType), $"num_procedures".cast(IntegerType),
$"num_medications".cast(IntegerType), $"number_outpatient".cast(IntegerType),
$"number_emergency".cast(IntegerType), $"number_inpatient".cast(IntegerType),
$"diag_1", $"number_diagnoses".cast(IntegerType), $"A1CResGrp", $"change",
$"diabetesMed", $"Readmitted").withColumnRenamed("age_category", "age")
```

The schema for the final DataFrame after the pre-processing steps is, as shown:

```
scala> diaDataFinalDF.printSchema()
```

```
root
 |-- race: string (nullable = true)
 |-- gender: string (nullable = true)
 |-- age: string (nullable = true)
 |-- admission_type_id: integer (nullable = true)
 |-- discharge_disposition_id: integer (nullable = true)
 |-- admission_source_id: integer (nullable = true)
 |-- time_in_hospital: integer (nullable = true)
 |-- num_lab_procedures: double (nullable = true)
 |-- num_procedures: integer (nullable = true)
 |-- num_medications: integer (nullable = true)
 |-- number_outpatient: integer (nullable = true)
 |-- number_emergency: integer (nullable = true)
 |-- number_inpatient: integer (nullable = true)
 |-- diag_1: string (nullable = true)
 |-- number_diagnoses: integer (nullable = true)
 |-- A1CResGrp: double (nullable = true)
 |-- change: string (nullable = true)
 |-- diabetesMed: string (nullable = true)
 |-- Readmitted: string (nullable = true)
```

We display a few sample records from the final DataFrame, as shown:

```scala
scala> diaDataFinalDF.take(5).foreach(println)
```

```
[Other,Male,Elder,3,1,1,3,33,2,10,1,0,1,428,9,No test was performed,No,Yes,Not
Readmitted]
[Caucasian,Female,Middle,3,18,4,13,44,0,11,0,0,2,V57,5,No test was
performed,No,Yes,Not Readmitted]
[Hispanic,Female,Elder,1,1,7,3,73,4,14,0,0,0,401,9,No test was performed,No,Yes,Not
Readmitted]
[Caucasian,Male,Elder,2,2,1,4,48,3,11,0,0,0,562,9,No test was performed,No,Yes,Not
Readmitted]
[Other,Female,Middle,2,1,7,1,13,1,6,0,0,0,427,6,No test was performed,No,No,Not
Readmitted]
```

After completing the data preprocessing phase, we now shift our focus to building the machine learning pipeline.

Building the Spark ML pipeline

In our example ML pipeline, we will have a sequence of pipeline components, which are detailed in the following sections.

Using StringIndexer for indexing categorical features and labels

In this exercise, we will be training a random forest classifier. First, we will index the categorical features and labels as required by `spark.ml`. Next, we will assemble the feature columns into a vector column because every `spark.ml` machine learning algorithm expects it. Finally, we can train our random forest on a training Dataset. Optionally, we can also unindex the labels to make them more readable.

There are several ready-to-use Transformers available to index categorical features. We can assemble all the features into one vector (using `VectorAssembler`) and then use a `VectorIndexer` to index it. The drawback of `VectorIndexer` is that it will index every feature that has less than `maxCategories` number of different values. It does not differentiate whether a given feature is categorical or not. Alternatively, we can index every categorical feature one by one using a `StringIndexer`, as follows.

We use a `StringIndexer` to transform String features to `Double` values. For example, the `raceIndexer` is an estimator that transforms the race column, that is, it generates indices for the different races in the input column, and creates a new output column called `raceCat`.

The `fit()` method then converts the column into a `StringType` and counts the numbers of each race. These steps are shown here:

```scala
scala> val raceIndexer = new
StringIndexer().setInputCol("race").setOutputCol("raceCat").fit(diaDataFina
lDF)

scala> raceIndexer.transform(diaDataFinalDF).select("race",
"raceCat").show()
```

```
+----------------+-------+
|            race|raceCat|
+----------------+-------+
|           Other|    4.0|
|       Caucasian|    0.0|
|        Hispanic|    3.0|
|       Caucasian|    0.0|
|           Other|    4.0|
|       Caucasian|    0.0|
|       Caucasian|    0.0|
|       Caucasian|    0.0|
|       Caucasian|    0.0|
|       Caucasian|    0.0|
|       Caucasian|    0.0|
|       Caucasian|    0.0|
|AfricanAmerican |    1.0|
|       Caucasian|    0.0|
|       Caucasian|    0.0|
|       Caucasian|    0.0|
|       Caucasian|    0.0|
|       Caucasian|    0.0|
|       Caucasian|    0.0|
|       Caucasian|    0.0|
+----------------+-------+
only showing top 20 rows
```

`raceIndexer.transform()` assigns the generated index to each value of the race in the column. For example, `AfricanAmerican` is assigned `1.0`, `Caucasian` is assigned `0.0`, and so on, as shown.

```scala
scala> raceIndexer.transform(diaDataFinalDF).select("race",
"raceCat").groupBy("raceCat").count().show()
+-------+-----+
|raceCat|count|
+-------+-----+
|    0.0|52323|
|    1.0|12608|
|    4.0| 1145|
|    3.0| 1494|
```

```
|     2.0|  1858|
|     5.0|   503|
+-------+-----+

scala> val raceIndexer = new
StringIndexer().setInputCol("race").setOutputCol("raceCat").fit(diaDataFina
lDF)

scala> val rDF = raceIndexer.transform(diaDataFinalDF)
```

Similarly, we create indexers for the gender, age groups, HbA1c test results, change of medications, and diabetes medications prescribed, and fit them to the resulting DataFrames at each step:

```
scala> val genderIndexer = new
StringIndexer().setInputCol("gender").setOutputCol("genderCat").fit(rDF)

scala> val gDF = genderIndexer.transform(rDF)

scala>  val ageCategoryIndexer  = new
StringIndexer().setInputCol("age").setOutputCol("ageCat").fit(gDF)

scala> val acDF = ageCategoryIndexer.transform(gDF)

scala>  val A1CresultIndexer  = new
StringIndexer().setInputCol("A1CResGrp").setOutputCol("A1CResGrpCat").fit(a
cDF)

scala> val a1crDF = A1CresultIndexer.transform(acDF)

scala> val changeIndexer  = new
StringIndexer().setInputCol("change").setOutputCol("changeCat").fit(a1crDF)

scala> val cDF = changeIndexer.transform(a1crDF)

scala> val diabetesMedIndexer  = new
StringIndexer().setInputCol("diabetesMed").setOutputCol("diabetesMedCat").f
it(cDF)

scala> val dmDF = diabetesMedIndexer.transform(cDF)
```

We print the schema of the resulting DataFrame containing the columns for various indexers:

```scala
scala>  dmDF.printSchema()
```

```
root
 |-- race: string (nullable = true)
 |-- gender: string (nullable = true)
 |-- age: string (nullable = true)
 |-- admission_type_id: integer (nullable = true)
 |-- discharge_disposition_id: integer (nullable = true)
 |-- admission_source_id: integer (nullable = true)
 |-- time_in_hospital: integer (nullable = true)
 |-- num_lab_procedures: double (nullable = true)
 |-- num_procedures: integer (nullable = true)
 |-- num_medications: integer (nullable = true)
 |-- number_outpatient: integer (nullable = true)
 |-- number_emergency: integer (nullable = true)
 |-- number_inpatient: integer (nullable = true)
 |-- diag_1: string (nullable = true)
 |-- number_diagnoses: integer (nullable = true)
 |-- A1CResGrp: double (nullable = true)
 |-- change: string (nullable = true)
 |-- diabetesMed: string (nullable = true)
 |-- Readmitted: string (nullable = true)
 |-- raceCat: double (nullable = true)
 |-- genderCat: double (nullable = true)
 |-- ageCat: double (nullable = true)
 |-- A1CResGrpCat: double (nullable = true)
 |-- changeCat: double (nullable = true)
 |-- diabetesMedCat: double (nullable = true)
```

We can also index the labels using `StringIndexer`, as follows:

```scala
scala> val labelIndexer = new
StringIndexer().setInputCol("Readmitted").setOutputCol("indexedLabel")
```

Alternatively, we can also define our feature indexers, succinctly, as illustrated. The sequence of `StringIndexers` can then be concatenated with the numeric features to derive the features vector using a `VectorAssembler`:

```scala
scala> val stringIndexers = catFeatColNames.map { colName =>
     |    new StringIndexer()
     |       .setInputCol(colName)
     |       .setOutputCol(colName + "Cat")
     |       .fit(diaDataFinalDF)
     |  }
```

We need not have explicitly called the `fit()` and `transform()` methods for each indexer, that can be handled by the pipeline, automatically.

The behavior of the pipeline can be summarized are listed as follows:

- It will execute each stage and pass the result of the current stage to the next
- If the stage is a Transformer, then the pipeline calls `transform()` on it
- If the stage is an Estimator, then the pipeline first calls `fit()` followed by `transform()`
- If it is the last stage in the pipeline, then the Estimator will not call `transform()` (after `fit()`)

Using VectorAssembler for assembling features into one column

Now that our indexing is done, we need to assemble all our feature columns into a single column containing a vector that groups all our features. To do that, we'll use the `VectorAssembler` Transformer, as in the following steps. However, first, due to the significant skew in the number of records for each label, we sample the records in appropriate proportions to have nearly equal numbers of records for each label:

```scala
scala> val dataDF = dmDF.stat.sampleBy("Readmitted", Map("Readmitted" ->
1.0, "Not Readmitted" -> .030), 0)

scala> val assembler = new
VectorAssembler().setInputCols(Array("num_lab_procedures",
"num_procedures", "num_medications", "number_outpatient",
"number_emergency", "number_inpatient", "number_diagnoses",
"admission_type_id", "discharge_disposition_id", "admission_source_id",
"time_in_hospital", "raceCat", "genderCat", "ageCat", "A1CresultCat",
"changeCat", "diabetesMedCat")).setOutputCol("features")
```

Alternatively, we can also achieve the same by following the steps listed here:

```scala
scala> val numFeatNames = Seq("num_lab_procedures", "num_procedures",
"num_medications", "number_outpatient", "number_emergency",
"number_inpatient", "number_diagnoses", "admission_type_id",
"discharge_disposition_id", "admission_source_id", "time_in_hospital")

scala> val catFeatNames = catFeatColNames.map(_ + "Cat")

scala> val allFeatNames = numFeatNames ++ catFeatNames

scala> val assembler = new
VectorAssembler().setInputCols(Array(allFeatNames:
_*)).setOutputCol("features")
```

We apply the `transform()` operation and print a few sample records of the resulting DataFrame, as shown:

```
scala> val df2 = assembler.transform(dataDF)

scala> df2.select("Readmitted", "features").take(5).foreach(println)
```

```
[Readmitted,(17,[0,2,6,7,8,9,10,12,15],[50.0,20.0,6.0,3.0,1.0,1.0,6.0,1.0,1.0])]
[Not Readmitted,[17.0,5.0,4.0,0.0,1.0,0.0,5.0,3.0,1.0,7.0,2.0,0.0,1.0,0.0,0.0,1.0,0.0]]
[Not Readmitted,(17,[0,2,3,6,7,8,9,10],[41.0,13.0,1.0,6.0,1.0,6.0,7.0,1.0])]
[Not Readmitted,(17,[0,2,5,6,7,8,9,10,12,15],[35.0,12.0,1.0,2.0,1.0,1.0,7.0,3.0,1.0,1.0])]
[Not Readmitted,[50.0,0.0,9.0,0.0,0.0,0.0,5.0,1.0,1.0,7.0,4.0,1.0,1.0,1.0,0.0,1.0,0.0]]
```

`VectorIndexer` is used for indexing the features. We will pass all the feature columns that are used for the prediction to create a new vector column called `indexedFeatures`, as shown:

```
scala> val featureIndexer = new
VectorIndexer().setInputCol("features").setOutputCol("indexedFeatures").set
MaxCategories(4).fit(df2)
```

In the next section, we will train a random forest classifier.

Using a Spark ML classifier

Now that that data is in the proper format expected by `spark.ml` machine learning algorithms, we will create a `RandomForestClassifier` component, as follows:

```
scala> val rf = new
RandomForestClassifier().setLabelCol("indexedLabel").setFeaturesCol("indexe
dFeatures").setNumTrees(10)
```

The standardized DataFrame format, allows easy replacement of the `RandomForestClassifier` with other `spark.ml` classifiers, such as `DecisionTreeClassifier` and `GBTClassifier`, as shown:

```
scala> val dt = new
DecisionTreeClassifier().setLabelCol("indexedLabel").setFeaturesCol("indexe
dFeatures")

scala> val gbt = new
GBTClassifier().setLabelCol("indexedLabel").setFeaturesCol("indexedFeatures
").setMaxIter(10)
```

In the following section, we will create our pipeline by assembling the label and feature indexers, and the random forest classifier as stages in the pipeline.

Creating a Spark ML pipeline

Next, we will create a pipeline object using all the components we have defined till now. Since all the different steps have been implemented, we can assemble our pipeline, as shown:

```scala
scala> val pipeline = new Pipeline().setStages(Array(labelIndexer,
featureIndexer, rf))
```

In the next section, we will create training and test Datasets from the input Dataset.

Creating the training and test Datasets

To train and evaluate the model, we split the input data, randomly, between two DataFrames: a training set (containing 80 percent of the records) and a test set(containing 20 percent of the records). We will train the model using the training set and then evaluate it using the test set. The following can be used to split input data:

```scala
scala> val Array(trainingData, testData) = df2.randomSplit(Array(0.8, 0.2),
11L)
```

We will now use the pipeline to fit the training data. A `PipelineModel` object is returned as a result of fitting the pipeline to the training data:

```scala
scala> val model = pipeline.fit(trainingData)
```

In the next section, we will make predictions on our test Dataset.

Making predictions using the PipelineModel

The `PipelineModel` object from the previous step is used for making predictions on the test Dataset, as follows:

```scala
scala> val predictions = model.transform(testData)

scala> predictions.select("prediction", "indexedLabel",
"features").show(25)
```

```
+----------+------------+--------------------+
|prediction|indexedLabel|            features|
+----------+------------+--------------------+
|       0.0|         0.0|(17,[0,1,2,6,7,8,...|
|       0.0|         0.0|(17,[0,2,3,5,6,7,...|
|       0.0|         0.0|(17,[0,2,6,7,8,9,...|
|       0.0|         0.0|[66.0,2.0,30.0,2....|
|       0.0|         1.0|[17.0,5.0,4.0,0.0...|
|       0.0|         0.0|[35.0,0.0,16.0,1....|
|       1.0|         0.0|[1.0,0.0,8.0,0.0,...|
|       0.0|         0.0|(17,[0,1,2,5,6,7,...|
|       0.0|         1.0|(17,[0,2,6,7,8,9,...|
|       0.0|         0.0|[48.0,2.0,22.0,12...|
|       0.0|         1.0|[32.0,2.0,13.0,0....|
|       0.0|         1.0|(17,[0,2,6,7,8,9,...|
|       0.0|         1.0|(17,[0,1,2,6,7,8,...|
|       0.0|         0.0|(17,[0,2,6,7,8,9,...|
|       0.0|         1.0|(17,[0,2,3,6,7,8,...|
|       0.0|         0.0|(17,[0,2,5,6,7,8,...|
|       0.0|         0.0|(17,[0,2,6,7,8,9,...|
|       0.0|         0.0|(17,[0,1,2,6,7,8,...|
|       0.0|         0.0|[50.0,2.0,43.0,0....|
|       0.0|         0.0|(17,[0,1,2,6,7,8,...|
|       0.0|         1.0|[44.0,1.0,14.0,0....|
|       1.0|         0.0|(17,[0,2,4,6,7,8,...|
|       0.0|         0.0|(17,[0,2,5,6,7,8,...|
|       0.0|         0.0|[70.0,1.0,15.0,1....|
|       0.0|         0.0|[43.0,2.0,17.0,0....|
+----------+------------+--------------------+
only showing top 25 rows
```

Next, we will evaluate our model by measuring the accuracy of the predictions, as shown in the following steps:

```scala
scala> val evaluator = new
MulticlassClassificationEvaluator().setLabelCol("indexedLabel").setPredicti
onCol("prediction").setMetricName("accuracy")

scala> val accuracy = evaluator.evaluate(predictions)
accuracy: Double = 0.6483412322274882
```

```
scala> println("Test Error = " + (1.0 - accuracy))
Test Error = 0.3516587677725118
```

Finally, we can also print our random forest model to understand the logic being used in the ten trees created in our model, as illustrated:

```
scala> val rfModel =
model.stages(2).asInstanceOf[RandomForestClassificationModel]

scala> println("Learned classification forest model:\n" +
rfModel.toDebugString)
```

```
Learned classification forest model:
RandomForestClassificationModel (uid=rfc_d921395cbedc) with 10 trees
  Tree 0 (weight 1.0):
    If (feature 6 <= 5.0)
     If (feature 5 <= 2.0)
      If (feature 2 <= 12.0)
       If (feature 11 in {1.0,2.0,3.0,4.0,5.0})
        If (feature 1 <= 1.0)
         Predict: 1.0
        Else (feature 1 > 1.0)
         Predict: 0.0
       Else (feature 11 not in {1.0,2.0,3.0,4.0,5.0})
        If (feature 1 <= 3.0)
         Predict: 1.0
        Else (feature 1 > 3.0)
         Predict: 1.0
  .
  .
  .
Else (feature 5 > 2.0)
        If (feature 10 <= 2.0)
         If (feature 14 in {2.0})
          Predict: 0.0
         Else (feature 14 not in {2.0})
          Predict: 1.0
        Else (feature 10 > 2.0)
         If (feature 5 <= 3.0)
          Predict: 0.0
         Else (feature 5 > 3.0)
          Predict: 0.0
```

In the next section, we will show the process of cross-validation to pick the best predictive model from a set of parameters.

Selecting the best model

In order to select the best model, we will perform a grid search over a set of parameters. For each combination of parameters, we will perform cross-validation and retain the best model according to some performance indicator. This process can be tedious, but `spark.ml` simplifies it with an easy-to-use API.

For cross-validation, we choose a value k for the number of folds, for example, a value of 3 will split the Dataset into three parts. From those three parts, three different training and test data pairs will be generated (two-thirds of the data for training and one-third for test). The model is evaluated on the average of the chosen performance indicator over the three pairs.

There is a set of values assigned to each of the parameters. The parameters used in our example are maxBins (the maximum number of bins used for discretizing continuous features and for splitting features at each node), maxDepth (the maximum depth of a tree), and impurity (the criterion used for information gain calculations).

First, we create a grid of parameters, as illustrated:

```scala
scala> val paramGrid = new ParamGridBuilder().addGrid(rf.maxBins, Array(25,
28, 31)).addGrid(rf.maxDepth, Array(4, 6, 8)).addGrid(rf.impurity,
Array("entropy", "gini")).build()
```

```
paramGrid: Array[org.apache.spark.ml.param.ParamMap] =
Array({
        rfc_63209c8eb2c9-impurity: entropy,
        rfc_63209c8eb2c9-maxBins: 25,
        rfc_63209c8eb2c9-maxDepth: 4
}, {
        rfc_63209c8eb2c9-impurity: entropy,
        rfc_63209c8eb2c9-maxBins: 28,
        rfc_63209c8eb2c9-maxDepth: 4
}, {
        rfc_63209c8eb2c9-impurity: entropy,
        rfc_63209c8eb2c9-maxBins: 31,
        rfc_63209c8eb2c9-maxDepth: 4
}, {
        rfc_63209c8eb2c9-impurity: gini,
        rfc_63209c8eb2c9-maxBins: 25,
        rfc_63209c8eb2c9-maxDepth: 4
}, {
        rfc_63209c8eb2c9-impurity: gini,
        rfc_63209c8eb2c9-maxBins: 28,
        rfc_63209c8eb2c9-maxDepth: 4
}, {
        rfc_63209c8eb2c9-impurity: gini,
        rfc_63209c8eb2c9-maxBins: 31,
        rfc_63209c8eb2c9-maxDepth: 4
}, {
        rfc_63209c8eb2c9-impurity: entropy,
        rfc_63209c8eb2c9-maxBins: 25,
        rfc_63209c8eb2c9-maxDepth: 6
}, {
        rfc_63209c8eb2c9-impu...
```

Next, we will define an Evaluator which, as its name implies, will evaluate our model according to some metric. There are built-in Evaluators available for regression, and binary and multi-class classification models.

```scala
scala> val evaluator = new
BinaryClassificationEvaluator().setLabelCol("indexedLabel")
```

Finally, after choosing k=2 (set to a higher number for real-world models), the number of folds the data will be split into during cross-validation, we can create a CrossValidator object, as follows:

```scala
scala> val cv = new
CrossValidator().setEstimator(pipeline).setEvaluator(evaluator).setEstimato
rParamMaps(paramGrid).setNumFolds(2)
```

You have to be careful when running cross-validation, especially on bigger Datasets, as it will train **k x p models**, where *p* is the product of the number of values for each param in your grid. So, for a *p* of 18, the cross-validation will train 36 different models.

Since our CrossValidator is an Estimator, we can obtain the best model for our data by calling the fit() method on it:

```scala
scala> val crossValidatorModel = cv.fit(df2)
```

We can now make predictions on testData, as illustrated here. Note a slight improvement in the accuracy value as compared to the values before cross-validation:

```scala
scala> val predictions = crossValidatorModel.transform(testData)

scala> predictions.select("prediction", "indexedLabel",
"features").show(25)
```

```
+----------+------------+--------------------+
|prediction|indexedLabel|            features|
+----------+------------+--------------------+
|       0.0|         0.0|(17,[0,1,2,6,7,8,...|
|       0.0|         0.0|(17,[0,2,3,5,6,7,...|
|       0.0|         0.0|(17,[0,2,6,7,8,9,...|
|       0.0|         0.0|[66.0,2.0,30.0,2....|
|       1.0|         1.0|[17.0,5.0,4.0,0.0...|
|       0.0|         0.0|[35.0,0.0,16.0,1....|
|       0.0|         0.0|[1.0,0.0,8.0,0.0,...|
|       0.0|         0.0|(17,[0,1,2,5,6,7,...|
|       0.0|         1.0|(17,[0,2,6,7,8,9,...|
|       0.0|         0.0|[48.0,2.0,22.0,12...|
|       0.0|         1.0|[32.0,2.0,13.0,0....|
|       0.0|         1.0|(17,[0,2,6,7,8,9,...|
|       0.0|         1.0|(17,[0,1,2,6,7,8,...|
|       0.0|         0.0|(17,[0,2,6,7,8,9,...|
|       0.0|         1.0|(17,[0,2,3,6,7,8,...|
|       0.0|         0.0|(17,[0,2,5,6,7,8,...|
|       0.0|         0.0|(17,[0,2,6,7,8,9,...|
|       0.0|         0.0|(17,[0,1,2,6,7,8,...|
|       0.0|         0.0|[50.0,2.0,43.0,0....|
|       0.0|         0.0|(17,[0,1,2,6,7,8,...|
|       0.0|         1.0|[44.0,1.0,14.0,0....|
|       0.0|         0.0|(17,[0,2,4,6,7,8,...|
|       0.0|         0.0|(17,[0,2,5,6,7,8,...|
|       0.0|         0.0|[70.0,1.0,15.0,1....|
|       0.0|         0.0|[43.0,2.0,17.0,0....|
+----------+------------+--------------------+
only showing top 25 rows
```

```scala
scala>  val accuracy = evaluator.evaluate(predictions)
accuracy: Double = 0.6823964115630783
```

```
scala>  println("Test Error = " + (1.0 - accuracy))
Test Error = 0.3176035884369217
```

In the next section, we will show you the power of common interfaces that Spark ML exposes to ease the development and testing of ML pipelines.

Changing the ML algorithm in the pipeline

In an earlier section, we showed how easy it is replace the RandomForestClassifier with other classifiers, such as, the DecisionTreeClassifier or the GBTClassifer. In this section, we will replace the random forest classifier with a logistic regression model. Logistic regression explains the relationship between a binary-valued dependent variable based on other variables called independent variables. The binary values, 0 or 1, can represent prediction values such as pass/fail, yes/no, dead/alive, and so on. Based on the values of the independent variables, it predicts the probability that the dependent variable takes one of the categorical values, such as a 0 or a 1.

First, we will create a LogtisticRegression component, as shown:

```
scala> val lr = new
LogisticRegression().setMaxIter(10).setRegParam(0.3).setElasticNetParam(0.8
).setLabelCol("indexedLabel").setFeaturesCol("indexedFeatures")
```

We can use the label and feature indexers from before and combine them with the logistic regression component to create a new pipeline, as follows. Furthermore, we use the fit() and transform() methods to train and then make predictions on the test Dataset. Note that the code looks very similar to the approach used earlier for the random forest pipeline:

```
scala> val pipeline = new Pipeline().setStages(Array(labelIndexer,
featureIndexer, lr))

scala> val Array(trainingData, testData) = df2.randomSplit(Array(0.8, 0.2),
11L)

scala> val model = pipeline.fit(trainingData)

scala> val predictions = model.transform(testData)

scala> predictions.select("A1CResGrpCat", "indexedLabel",
"prediction").show()
+------------+------------+----------+
|A1CResGrpCat|indexedLabel|prediction|
+------------+------------+----------+
|         0.0|         0.0|       0.0|
|         0.0|         0.0|       0.0|
```

```
|          3.0|        0.0|       0.0|
|          3.0|        0.0|       0.0|
|          0.0|        1.0|       0.0|
|          0.0|        0.0|       0.0|
|          0.0|        0.0|       0.0|
|          0.0|        0.0|       0.0|
|          0.0|        1.0|       0.0|
|          0.0|        0.0|       0.0|
|          0.0|        1.0|       0.0|
|          0.0|        1.0|       0.0|
|          0.0|        1.0|       0.0|
|          0.0|        0.0|       0.0|
|          0.0|        1.0|       0.0|
|          0.0|        0.0|       0.0|
|          0.0|        0.0|       0.0|
|          0.0|        0.0|       0.0|
|          1.0|        0.0|       0.0|
|          0.0|        0.0|       0.0|
+------------+------------+----------+
only showing top 20 rows

scala> predictions.select($"indexedLabel",
$"prediction").where("indexedLabel != prediction").count()
res104: Long = 407
```

Over the next several sections, we will introduce a series of tools and utilities available in Spark, that can be used to achieve better ML models.

Introducing Spark ML tools and utilities

In the following sections, we will explore various tools and utilities that Spark ML offers to select features and create superior ML models easily and efficiently.

Using Principal Component Analysis to select features

As mentioned earlier, we can derive new features using **Principal Component Analysis (PCA)** on the data. This approach depends on the problem, so it is imperative to have a good understanding about the domain.

This exercise typically requires creativity and common sense to choose a set of features that may be relevant to the problem. A more extensive exploratory data analysis is typically required to help understand the data better and/or to identify patterns that lead to a good set of features.

PCA is a statistical procedure that converts a set of potentially correlated variables into a, typically, reduced set of linearly uncorrelated variables. The resulting set of uncorrelated variables are called principal components. A PCA class trains a model to project vectors to a lower dimensional space. The following example shows how to project our multi-dimensional feature vector into three-dimensional principal components.

 According to Wikipedia, https://en.wikipedia.org/wiki/Principal_component_analysis, "This transformation is defined in such a way that the first principal component has the largest possible variance (that is, it accounts for as much of the variability in the data as possible), and each succeeding component, in turn, has the highest variance possible under the constraint that it is orthogonal to the preceding components."

We will be building our model using the Dataset used to fit in the random forest algorithm used for classification earlier in this chapter:

```scala
scala> val pca = new
PCA().setInputCol("features").setOutputCol("pcaFeatures").setK(3).fit(df2)

scala> val result = pca.transform(df2).select("pcaFeatures")

scala> result.take(5).foreach(println)
[[-52.49989457347012,-13.91558303051395,-0.9577895037038642]]
[[-17.787698281398306,-2.3653156500575743,0.67773733633875]]
[[-42.61350777796136,-8.019782413210889,4.744540532872854]]
[[-36.62417236331611,-7.161756365322481,-0.06153645411567934]]
[[-51.157132286686824,-2.6029561027003685,0.8995320464587268]]
```

Using encoders

In this section, we use one-hot encoding to map a column of label indices to a column of binary vectors with, at most, a single one-value. This encoding allows algorithms that expect continuous features, such as LogisticRegression, to use categorical features:

```scala
scala> val indexer = new
StringIndexer().setInputCol("race").setOutputCol("raceIndex").fit(df2)

scala> val indexed = indexer.transform(df2)
```

```
scala> val encoder = new
OneHotEncoder().setInputCol("raceIndex").setOutputCol("raceVec")

scala> val encoded = encoder.transform(indexed)

scala> encoded.select("raceVec").show()
```

```
+--------------+
|       raceVec|
+--------------+
|(5,[0],[1.0])|
|(5,[0],[1.0])|
|(5,[0],[1.0])|
|(5,[0],[1.0])|
|(5,[1],[1.0])|
|(5,[1],[1.0])|
|(5,[0],[1.0])|
|(5,[0],[1.0])|
|(5,[1],[1.0])|
|(5,[0],[1.0])|
|(5,[0],[1.0])|
|(5,[0],[1.0])|
|(5,[0],[1.0])|
|(5,[0],[1.0])|
|(5,[1],[1.0])|
|(5,[0],[1.0])|
|(5,[0],[1.0])|
|(5,[0],[1.0])|
|(5,[0],[1.0])|
|(5,[0],[1.0])|
+--------------+
only showing top 20 rows
```

Using Bucketizer

Bucketizer is used to transform a column of continuous features to a column of feature buckets. We specify the n+1 splits parameter for mapping continuous features into n buckets. The splits should be in a strictly increasing order.

Typically, we add `Double.NegativeInfinity` and `Double.PositiveInfinity` as the outer bounds of the splits to prevent potential out of Bucketizer bounds exceptions. In the following example, we specify six splits, and then define a `bucketizer` for the `num_lab_procedures` feature (with values varying from 1 to 126 in our Dataset), as follows:

```
scala> val splits = Array(Double.NegativeInfinity, 20.0, 40.0, 60.0, 80.0,
100.0, Double.PositiveInfinity)

scala> val bucketizer = new
```

```
Bucketizer().setInputCol("num_lab_procedures").setOutputCol("bucketedLabPro
cs").setSplits(splits)

scala> // Transform original data into its bucket index.

scala> val bucketedData = bucketizer.transform(df2)

scala> println(s"Bucketizer output with ${bucketizer.getSplits.length-1}
buckets")
Bucketizer output with 6 buckets
```

```
scala> bucketedData.select("num_lab_procedures", "bucketedLabProcs").show()
+------------------+----------------+
|num_lab_procedures|bucketedLabProcs|
+------------------+----------------+
|              50.0|             2.0|
|              17.0|             0.0|
|              41.0|             2.0|
|              35.0|             1.0|
|              50.0|             2.0|
|              31.0|             1.0|
|              55.0|             2.0|
|              63.0|             3.0|
|              29.0|             1.0|
|              38.0|             1.0|
|               2.0|             0.0|
|              66.0|             3.0|
|              35.0|             1.0|
|              59.0|             2.0|
|              60.0|             3.0|
|              41.0|             2.0|
|              41.0|             2.0|
|              66.0|             3.0|
|              41.0|             2.0|
|               6.0|             0.0|
+------------------+----------------+
only showing top 20 rows
```

Using VectorSlicer

A `VectorSlicer` is a Transformer that takes a feature vector and returns a new feature vector that is a subset of the original features. It is useful for extracting features from a vector column. We can use a `VectorSlicer` to test our model with different numbers and combinations of features.

In the following example, we use four features initially, and then drop one of them. These slices of features can be used to test the importance of including/excluding features from the set of features:

```scala
scala> val slicer = new
VectorSlicer().setInputCol("features").setOutputCol("slicedfeatures").setNa
mes(Array("raceCat", "genderCat", "ageCat", "A1CResGrpCat"))

scala> val output = slicer.transform(df2)

scala> output.select("slicedFeatures").take(5).foreach(println)
[(4,[1],[1.0])]
[[0.0,1.0,0.0,0.0]]
[(4,[],[])]
[(4,[1],[1.0])]
[[1.0,1.0,1.0,0.0]]

scala> val slicer = new
VectorSlicer().setInputCol("features").setOutputCol("slicedfeatures").setNa
mes(Array("raceCat", "genderCat", "ageCat"))

scala> val output = slicer.transform(df2)

scala> output.select("slicedFeatures").take(5).foreach(println)
[(3,[1],[1.0])]
[[0.0,1.0,0.0]]
[(3,[],[])]
[(3,[1],[1.0])]
[[1.0,1.0,1.0]]
```

Using Chi-squared selector

`ChiSqSelector` enables chi-squared feature selection. It operates on labeled data with categorical features. `ChiSqSelector` uses the chi-squared test of independence to choose the features. In our example, we use the `numTopFeatures` to choose a fixed number of top features that yield features with the most predictive power:

```scala
scala> def udfReAdmLabels() = udf[Double, String] { a => val x = a match {
case "Readmitted" => 0.0; case "Not Readmitted" => 0.0; }; x; }

scala> val df3 = df2.withColumn("reAdmLabel",
udfReAdmLabels()($"Readmitted"))

scala> val selector = new
ChiSqSelector().setNumTopFeatures(1).setFeaturesCol("features").setLabelCol
```

```
("reAdmLabel").setOutputCol("selectedFeatures")

scala> val result = selector.fit(df3).transform(df3)

scala> println(s"ChiSqSelector output with top
${selector.getNumTopFeatures} features selected")
ChiSqSelector output with top 1 features selected

scala> result.select("selectedFeatures").show()
```

```
+----------------+
|selectedFeatures|
+----------------+
|  (1,[0],[50.0])|
|          [17.0]|
|  (1,[0],[41.0])|
|  (1,[0],[35.0])|
|          [50.0]|
|  (1,[0],[31.0])|
|  (1,[0],[55.0])|
|  (1,[0],[63.0])|
|          [29.0]|
|  (1,[0],[38.0])|
|   (1,[0],[2.0])|
|          [66.0]|
|          [35.0]|
|  (1,[0],[59.0])|
|  (1,[0],[60.0])|
|  (1,[0],[41.0])|
|  (1,[0],[41.0])|
|  (1,[0],[66.0])|
|          [41.0]|
|           [6.0]|
+----------------+
only showing top 20 rows
```

Using a Normalizer

We can normalize the data using a Normalizer object (a Transformer). The input to a Normalizer is a column created by the `VectorAssembler`. It normalizes the values in the column to produce a new column containing the normalized values.a new feature vector with a subarray of the original features. It is useful for extracting features from a vector column This normalization can help standardize input data and improve the behavior of learning algorithms:

```
val normalizer = new Normalizer().setInputCol("raw_features
").setOutputCol("features")
```

Retrieving our original labels

`IndexToString` is the reverse operation of `StringIndexer` that converts the indices back to their original labels. The random forests transform method of the model produced by the `RandomForestClassifier` produces a prediction column that contains indexed labels that we need unindexed to retrieve the original label values, as shown:

```scala
scala> val labelIndexer = new
StringIndexer().setInputCol("Readmitted").setOutputCol("indexedLabel").fit(
df2)

scala> val featureIndexer = new
VectorIndexer().setInputCol("features").setOutputCol("indexedFeatures").set
MaxCategories(4).fit(df2)

scala> val Array(trainingData, testData) = df2.randomSplit(Array(0.7, 0.3))

scala> val gbt = new
GBTClassifier().setLabelCol("indexedLabel").setFeaturesCol("indexedFeatures
").setMaxIter(10)

scala> val labelConverter = new
IndexToString().setInputCol("prediction").setOutputCol("predictedLabel").se
tLabels(labelIndexer.labels)

scala> val pipeline = new Pipeline().setStages(Array(labelIndexer,
featureIndexer, gbt, labelConverter))

scala> val model = pipeline.fit(trainingData)

scala> val predictions = model.transform(testData)

scala> predictions.select("predictedLabel", "indexedLabel",
"features").show(5)
+--------------+------------+--------------------+
|predictedLabel|indexedLabel|            features|
+--------------+------------+--------------------+
|     Readmitted|         0.0|(17,[0,2,5,6,7,8,...|
|Not Readmitted|         1.0|[43.0,1.0,7.0,0.0...|
|     Readmitted|         1.0|(17,[0,2,5,6,7,8,...|
|     Readmitted|         0.0|(17,[0,1,2,6,7,8,...|
|     Readmitted|         0.0|(17,[0,2,6,7,8,9,...|
+--------------+------------+--------------------+
only showing top 5 rows
```

In the next section, we will switch focus to presenting an example of Spark ML clustering using the k-means algorithm.

Implementing a Spark ML clustering model

In this section, we will explain clustering with Spark ML. We will use a publicly available Dataset about the student's knowledge status about a subject.

 The Dataset is available for download from the UCI website at `https://archive.ics.uci.edu/ml/datasets/User+Knowledge+Modeling`.

The attributes of the records contained in the Dataset have reproduced here from the UCI website mentioned previously for reference:

- **STG**: The degree of study time for goal object materials (input value)
- **SCG**: The degree of repetition number of users for goal object materials (input value)
- **STR**: The degree of study time of users for related objects with the goal object (input value)
- **LPR**: The exam performance of a user for related objects with the goal object (input value)
- **PEG**: The exam performance of a user for goal objects (input value)
- **UNS**: The knowledge level of the user (target value)

First, we will write a UDF to create two levels representing the two categories of the students--beneath average and beyond average from the five contained in the original Dataset. We combine the training and test CSV files to obtain a sufficient number of input records:

```scala
scala> def udfLabels() = udf[Integer, String] { a => val x = a match { case
"very_low" => 0; case "Very Low" => 0; case "Low" => 0; case "Middle" => 1;
case "High" => 1; }; x; }
```

We will read the input Dataset and create a column called `label` that is populated by the UDF. This allows us to have nearly equal numbers of records for each category:

```scala
scala> val inDataDF = spark.read.option("header",
true).csv("file:///Users/aurobindosarkar/Downloads/Data_User_Modeling.csv")
.withColumn("label", udfLabels()($"UNS"))

scala> inDataDF.select("label").groupBy("label").count().show()
+-----+-----+
|label|count|
+-----+-----+
|    1|  224|
```

```
|    0|  179|
+-----+-----+

scala> inDataDF.cache()
```

Next, we cast the numeric fields to `Double` values, verify the number of records in the DataFrame, display a few sample records, and print the schema, as shown:

```
scala> val inDataFinalDF = inDataDF.select($"STG".cast(DoubleType),
$"SCG".cast(DoubleType), $"STR".cast(DoubleType), $"LPR".cast(DoubleType),
$"PEG".cast(DoubleType), $"UNS", $"label")

scala> inDataFinalDF.count()
res2: Long = 403

scala> inDataFinalDF.take(5).foreach(println)
[0.0,0.0,0.0,0.0,0.0,very_low,0]
[0.08,0.08,0.1,0.24,0.9,High,1]
[0.06,0.06,0.05,0.25,0.33,Low,0]
[0.1,0.1,0.15,0.65,0.3,Middle,1]
[0.08,0.08,0.08,0.98,0.24,Low,0]

scala> inDataFinalDF.printSchema()
root
 |-- STG: double (nullable = true)
 |-- SCG: double (nullable = true)
 |-- STR: double (nullable = true)
 |-- LPR: double (nullable = true)
 |-- PEG: double (nullable = true)
 |-- UNS: string (nullable = true)
 |-- label: integer (nullable = true)
```

Next, we will use `VectorAssembler` to create the features column, as shown:

```
scala> val allFeatNames = Seq("STG", "SCG", "STR", "LPR", "PEG")

scala> val assembler = new
VectorAssembler().setInputCols(Array(allFeatNames:
_*)).setOutputCol("features")

scala> val df2 = assembler.transform(inDataFinalDF)

scala> df2.cache()

scala> import org.apache.spark.ml.clustering.KMeans

Below, we create the k-means component with 2 clusters.
```

```
scala> val kmeans = new KMeans().setK(2).setSeed(1L)

scala> val model = kmeans.fit(df2)
```

You can use `explainParams` to list the details of the k-means model, as follows:

```
scala> println(kmeans.explainParams)
featuresCol: features column name (default: features)
initMode: The initialization algorithm. Supported options: 'random' and 'k-
means||'. (default: k-means||)
initSteps: The number of steps for k-means|| initialization mode. Must be >
0. (default: 2)
k: The number of clusters to create. Must be > 1. (default: 2, current: 2)
maxIter: maximum number of iterations (>= 0) (default: 20)
predictionCol: prediction column name (default: prediction)
seed: random seed (default: -1689246527, current: 1)
tol: the convergence tolerance for iterative algorithms (>= 0) (default:
1.0E-4)
```

Evaluate the quality of clustering by computing the **Within Set Sum of Squared Errors (WSSSE)**. The standard k-means algorithm aims at minimizing the sum of squares of the distance between the centroid to the points in each cluster. Increasing the value of k can reduce this error. The optimal k is usually one where there is an "elbow" in the WSSSE graph:

```
scala> val WSSSE = model.computeCost(df2)
WSSSE: Double = 91.41199908476494

scala> println(s"Within Set Sum of Squared Errors = $WSSSE")
Within Set Sum of Squared Errors = 91.41199908476494

scala> model.clusterCenters.foreach(println)
[0.310042654028436,0.31230331753554513,0.41459715639810407,0.45081042654028
43,0.2313886255924172]
[0.4005052083333334,0.40389583333333334,0.5049739583333334,0.40994791666666
65,0.7035937499999997]

scala> val transformed =  model.transform(df2)

scala> transformed.take(5).foreach(println)
[0.0,0.0,0.0,0.0,0.0,very_low,0,(5,[],[]),0]
[0.08,0.08,0.1,0.24,0.9,High,1,[0.08,0.08,0.1,0.24,0.9],1]
[0.06,0.06,0.05,0.25,0.33,Low,0,[0.06,0.06,0.05,0.25,0.33],0]
[0.1,0.1,0.15,0.65,0.3,Middle,1,[0.1,0.1,0.15,0.65,0.3],0]
[0.08,0.08,0.08,0.98,0.24,Low,0,[0.08,0.08,0.08,0.98,0.24],0]
```

Here, we will compute the number of differences between the labels and the predicted values in our Dataset:

```scala
scala>
transformed.select("prediction").groupBy("prediction").count().orderBy("pre
diction").show()
+----------+-----+
|prediction|count|
+----------+-----+
|         0|  211|
|         1|  192|
+----------+-----+

scala> val y1DF = transformed.select($"label", $"prediction").where("label
!= prediction")

scala> y1DF.count()
res14: Long = 34
```

Now, we will separate the DataFrames containing the prediction values of 0 and 1 to display sample records:

```scala
scala> transformed.filter("prediction = 0").show()
```

```
+----+-----+----+----+----+--------+-----+---------------+----------+
| STG|  SCG| STR| LPR| PEG|     UNS|label|       features|prediction|
+----+-----+----+----+----+--------+-----+---------------+----------+
| 0.0|  0.0| 0.0| 0.0| 0.0|very_low|    0|      (5,[],[])|         0|
|0.06| 0.06|0.05|0.25|0.33|     Low|    0|[0.06,0.06,0.05,0...|      0|
| 0.1|  0.1|0.15|0.65| 0.3|  Middle|    1|[0.1,0.1,0.15,0.6...|      0|
|0.08| 0.08|0.08|0.98|0.24|     Low|    0|[0.08,0.08,0.08,0...|      0|
| 0.1|  0.1|0.43|0.29|0.56|  Middle|    1|[0.1,0.1,0.43,0.2...|      0|
|0.15| 0.02|0.34| 0.4|0.01|very_low|    0|[0.15,0.02,0.34,0...|      0|
| 0.2| 0.14|0.35|0.72|0.25|     Low|    0|[0.2,0.14,0.35,0....|      0|
|0.06| 0.06|0.51|0.41| 0.3|     Low|    0|[0.06,0.06,0.51,0...|      0|
| 0.1|  0.1|0.52|0.78|0.34|  Middle|    1|[0.1,0.1,0.52,0.7...|      0|
|0.05| 0.07| 0.7|0.01|0.05|very_low|    0|[0.05,0.07,0.7,0....|      0|
| 0.1| 0.25| 0.1|0.08|0.33|     Low|    0|[0.1,0.25,0.1,0.0...|      0|
|0.15| 0.32|0.05|0.27|0.29|     Low|    0|[0.15,0.32,0.05,0...|      0|
|0.12| 0.28| 0.2|0.78| 0.2|     Low|    0|[0.12,0.28,0.2,0....|      0|
|0.18| 0.31|0.32|0.42|0.28|     Low|    0|[0.18,0.31,0.32,0...|      0|
|0.06| 0.29|0.35|0.76|0.25|     Low|    0|[0.06,0.29,0.35,0...|      0|
|0.04| 0.28|0.55|0.25| 0.1|very_low|    0|[0.04,0.28,0.55,0...|      0|
|0.09|0.255| 0.6|0.45|0.25|     Low|    0|[0.09,0.255,0.6,0...|      0|
|0.15|0.295|0.75|0.65|0.24|     Low|    0|[0.15,0.295,0.75,...|      0|
| 0.1|0.256| 0.7|0.76|0.16|     Low|    0|[0.1,0.256,0.7,0....|      0|
|0.06| 0.35|0.12|0.43|0.29|     Low|    0|[0.06,0.35,0.12,0...|      0|
+----+-----+----+----+----+--------+-----+---------------+----------+
only showing top 20 rows
```

```
scala> transformed.filter("prediction = 1").show()
```

```
+----+-----+----+----+----+------+-----+-----------------+----------+
| STG| SCG| STR| LPR| PEG|   UNS|label|         features|prediction|
+----+-----+----+----+----+------+-----+-----------------+----------+
|0.08| 0.08| 0.1|0.24| 0.9|  High|    1|[0.08,0.08,0.1,0....|        1|
|0.09| 0.15| 0.4| 0.1|0.66|Middle|    1|[0.09,0.15,0.4,0....|        1|
| 0.0|  0.0| 0.5| 0.2|0.85|  High|    1|[0.0,0.0,0.5,0.2,...|        1|
|0.18| 0.18|0.55| 0.3|0.81|  High|    1|[0.18,0.18,0.55,0...|        1|
| 0.1|  0.1| 0.7|0.15| 0.9|  High|    1|[0.1,0.1,0.7,0.15...|        1|
| 0.2|  0.2| 0.7| 0.3| 0.6|Middle|    1|[0.2,0.2,0.7,0.3,...|        1|
|0.12| 0.12|0.75|0.35| 0.8|  High|    1|[0.12,0.12,0.75,0...|        1|
| 0.2| 0.29|0.25|0.49|0.56|Middle|    1|[0.2,0.29,0.25,0....|        1|
|0.18|  0.3|0.37|0.12|0.66|Middle|    1|[0.18,0.3,0.37,0....|        1|
| 0.1| 0.27|0.31|0.29|0.65|Middle|    1|[0.1,0.27,0.31,0....|        1|
|0.09|  0.3|0.68|0.18|0.85|  High|    1|[0.09,0.3,0.68,0....|        1|
|0.08|0.325|0.62|0.94|0.56|  High|    1|[0.08,0.325,0.62,...|        1|
|0.15|0.275| 0.8|0.21|0.81|  High|    1|[0.15,0.275,0.8,0...|        1|
|0.12|0.245|0.75|0.31|0.59|Middle|    1|[0.12,0.245,0.75,...|        1|
|0.18| 0.32|0.04|0.19|0.82|  High|    1|[0.18,0.32,0.04,0...|        1|
| 0.2| 0.45|0.28|0.31|0.78|  High|    1|[0.2,0.45,0.28,0....|        1|
| 0.2| 0.49| 0.6| 0.2|0.78|  High|    1|[0.2,0.49,0.6,0.2...|        1|
|0.14| 0.49|0.55|0.29| 0.6|Middle|    1|[0.14,0.49,0.55,0...|        1|
|0.17| 0.36| 0.8|0.14|0.66|Middle|    1|[0.17,0.36,0.8,0....|        1|
| 0.1| 0.39|0.75|0.31|0.62|Middle|    1|[0.1,0.39,0.75,0....|        1|
+----+-----+----+----+----+------+-----+-----------------+----------+
only showing top 20 rows
```

We can also use `describe` to see the summary statistics for each of the predicted labels, as illustrated:

```
scala> transformed.filter("prediction = 0").select("STG", "SCG", "STR",
"LPR", "PEG").describe().show()
```

```
+-------+-------------------+-------------------+-------------------+-------------------+-------------------+
|summary|                STG|                SCG|                STR|                LPR|                PEG|
+-------+-------------------+-------------------+-------------------+-------------------+-------------------+
|  count|                211|                211|                211|                211|                211|
|   mean|0.310042654028436| 0.3123033175355451| 0.414597156398104|0.45081042654028425|0.23138862559241719|
| stddev|0.18270580849465212|0.19447554121739496|0.24365901973174997|0.25108964835256975|0.11058937632395373|
|    min|                0.0|                0.0|                0.0|                0.0|                0.0|
|    max|               0.77|               0.85|               0.88|               0.99|               0.56|
+-------+-------------------+-------------------+-------------------+-------------------+-------------------+
```

```
scala> transformed.filter("prediction = 1").select("STG", "SCG", "STR",
"LPR", "PEG").describe().show()
```

```
+-------+------------------+------------------+------------------+------------------+-------------------+
|summary|               STG|               SCG|               STR|               LPR|                PEG|
+-------+------------------+------------------+------------------+------------------+-------------------+
|  count|               192|               192|               192|               192|                192|
|   mean|0.4005052083333334|0.40389583333333334|0.5049739583333334|0.4099479166666666|0.7035937499999997|
| stddev|0.2315183888390661|0.2275363375463664|0.2418739543429287|0.2634536974048102|0.13779528621524523|
|    min|               0.0|               0.0|              0.02|              0.01|               0.32|
|    max|              0.99|               0.9|              0.95|              0.99|               0.99|
+-------+------------------+------------------+------------------+------------------+-------------------+
```

```
scala> println("No. of mis-matches between predictions and labels =" +
y1DF.count()+"\nTotal no. of records=  "+ transformed.count()+"\nCorrect
predictions =  "+ (1-(y1DF.count()).toDouble/transformed.count())+"\nMis-
match = "+ (y1DF.count()).toDouble/transformed.count())

No. of mis-matches between predictions and labels =34
Total no. of records= 403
Correct predictions = 0.9156327543424317
Mis-match = 0.08436724565756824
```

Next, we will feed in a couple of test input records, and the model will predict the cluster for them:

```
scala> val testDF = spark.createDataFrame(Seq((0.08,0.08,0.1,0.24,0.9,
Vectors.dense(0.08,0.08,0.1,0.24,0.9)))).toDF("STG", "SCG", "STR", "LPR",
"PEG", "features")

scala> model.transform(testDF).show()
+----+----+---+----+---+--------------------+----------+
| STG| SCG|STR| LPR|PEG|            features|prediction|
+----+----+---+----+---+--------------------+----------+
|0.08|0.08|0.1|0.24|0.9|[0.08,0.08,0.1,0....|         1|
+----+----+---+----+---+--------------------+----------+

scala> val testDF = spark.createDataFrame(Seq((0.06,0.06,0.05,0.25,0.33,
Vectors.dense(0.06,0.06,0.05,0.25,0.33)))).toDF("STG", "SCG", "STR", "LPR",
"PEG", "features")

scala> model.transform(testDF).show()
+----+----+----+----+----+--------------------+----------+
| STG| SCG| STR| LPR| PEG|            features|prediction|
+----+----+----+----+----+--------------------+----------+
|0.06|0.06|0.05|0.25|0.33|[0.06,0.06,0.05,0...|         0|
+----+----+----+----+----+--------------------+----------+
```

Topics, such as streaming ML applications and architectures for large-scale processing, will be covered in detail in Chapter 12, *Spark SQL in Large-Scale Application Architectures.*

Summary

In this chapter, we introduced machine learning applications. We covered one of the most important topics in machine learning, called feature engineering. Additionally, we provided code examples using Spark ML APIs to build a classification pipeline and a clustering application. Additionally, we also introduced a few tools and utilities that can help select features and build models more easily and efficiently.

In the next chapter, we will introduce GraphFrame applications and provide examples of using Spark SQL DataFrame/Dataset APIs to build graph applications. We will also apply various graph algorithms to graph applications.

7
Using Spark SQL in Graph Applications

In this chapter, we will present typical use cases for using Spark SQL in graph applications. Graphs are common in many different domains. Typically, graphs are analyzed using special graph processing engines. GraphX is the Spark component for graph computations. It is based on RDDs and supports graph abstractions and operations, such as subgraphs, aggregateMessages, and so on. In addition, it also exposes a variant of the Pregel API. However, our focus will be on the GraphFrame API implemented on top of Spark SQL Dataset/DataFrame APIs. GraphFrames is an integrated system that combines graph algorithms, pattern matching, and queries. GraphFrame API is still in beta (as of Spark 2.2) but is definitely the future graph processing API for Spark applications.

More specifically, in this chapter, you will learn the following topics:

- Using GraphFrames for creating large-scale graphs
- Executing some basic graph operations
- Motif analysis using GraphFrames
- Processing subgraphs using GraphFrames
- Executing graph algorithms
- Processing graphs containing multiple types of relationships
- Partitioning in GraphFrames

Introducing large-scale graph applications

Analysis of graphs based on large Datasets is becoming increasingly important in various areas, such as social networks, communication networks, citation networks, web graphs, transport networks, product co-purchasing networks, and so on. Typically, graphs are created from source data in a tabular or relational format, and then applications, such as search and graph algorithms, are run on them to derive key insights.

GraphFrames provide a declarative API that can be used for both interactive queries and standalone programs on large-scale graphs. As GraphFrames are implemented on top of Spark SQL, it enables parallel processing and optimization across the computation:

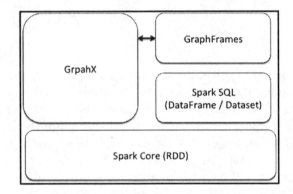

The main programming abstraction in GraphFrame's API is a GraphFrame. Conceptually, it consists of two DataFrames representing the vertices and edges of the graph. The vertices and edges may have multiple attributes, which can also be used in queries. For example, in a social network, the vertices can contain the name, age, location, and other attributes, while the edges can represent the relationships between the nodes (people in the network). As the GraphFrame model can support user-defined attributes with each vertex and edge, it is equivalent to the property graph model. Additionally, views can be defined using patterns to match various shapes of subgraphs in the network.

In the following sections, we will build graphs from several public Datasets that are available in a relational format, and then run various graph operations and algorithms on them. GraphFrames optimize the execution across the relational and graph portions of the computation. These computations can be specified using relational operators, patterns, and calls to algorithms.

In the following sections, we will use the Spark shell for defining graphs, querying them, and running algorithms on them interactively.

Exploring graphs using GraphFrames

In this section, we explore data, modeled as a graph, using Spark GraphFrames. The vertices and edges of the graph are stored as DataFrames, and Spark SQL and DataFrame-based queries are supported to operate on them. As DataFrames can support a variety of data sources, we can read our input vertices and edges information from relational tables, files (JSON, Parquet, Avro, and CSV), and so on.

The vertex DataFrame must contain a column called id which specifies unique IDs for each vertex. Similarly, the edges DataFrame must contain two columns named src (source vertex ID) and dst (destination vertex ID). Both the vertices and edges DataFrames can contain additional columns for the attributes.

GraphFrames exposes a concise language-integrated API that unifies graph analytics and relational queries. The system optimizes across the steps based on join plans and performing algebraic optimizations. Machine learning code, external data sources, and UDFs can be integrated with GraphFrames to build more complex applications.

We will start our coding exercises with a simple example in which we read in the vertices and edges from a file containing Amazon co-purchase data. The nodes represent the various items and the edges between the source and destination vertices define an **alsopurchased** relationship. The Dataset for these exercises can be downloaded from https://snap.stanford.edu/data/amazon0601.html.

Start the Spark shell as shown to include the GraphFrame library in the Spark shell environment:

```
./bin/spark-shell --packages graphframes:graphframes:0.3.0-spark2.0-s_2.11
--driver-memory 12g
```

First, we import all the packages we need in our examples, as listed here:

```
scala> import org.apache.spark.sql.types._
scala> import org.apache.spark.sql.functions._
scala> import spark.implicits._
scala> import org.apache.spark.sql.Row
scala> import org.graphframes._
```

Constructing a GraphFrame

A GraphFrame can be constructed using two DataFrames: a vertex DataFrame and an edge DataFrame. Here, we create the GraphFrame from a single DataFrame containing edge information.

We will derive the vertex DataFrame from the source and destination vertices specified for the edges contained in our input file.

Read in the input file to create an RDD for the edges, as shown:

```
scala> val edgesRDD =
spark.sparkContext.textFile("file:///Users/aurobindosarkar/Downloads/amznco
purchase/amazon0601.txt")
```

Next, define a schema for the edges and convert the edges RDD into a DataFrame, as shown in the next few steps:

```
scala> val schemaString = "src dst"
scala> val fields = schemaString.split(" ").map(fieldName =>
StructField(fieldName, StringType, nullable = false))

scala> val edgesSchema = new StructType(fields)

scala> val rowRDD = edgesRDD.map(_.split("\t")).map(attributes =>
Row(attributes(0).trim, attributes(1).trim))

scala> val edgesDF = spark.createDataFrame(rowRDD, edgesSchema)
```

Next, we create a DataFrame for the vertices by selecting distinct source and destination vertices from the edges DataFrame. A union of the resulting two DataFrames, with distinct vertices selected, gives us the final vertices DataFrame:

```
scala> val srcVerticesDF = edgesDF.select($"src").distinct
scala> val destVerticesDF = edgesDF.select($"dst").distinct
scala> val verticesDF =
srcVerticesDF.union(destVerticesDF).distinct.select($"src".alias("id"))
```

We can verify the number of nodes and vertices in these DataFrames by matching them with the numbers reported at the source site (for our input Dataset):

```
scala> edgesDF.count()
res0: Long = 3387388
scala> verticesDF.count()
res1: Long = 403394
```

Next, we create a GraphFrame for the Amazon co-purchase data from the vertices and edges DataFrames:

```
scala> val g = GraphFrame(verticesDF, edgesDF)
```

In the next section, we will explore a few properties of the graph we just created.

Basic graph queries and operations

In this section, we will cover simple graph queries and operations on the structure of our graph. These include displays of the vertices, edges, and the in- and out-degrees of the vertices, as shown:

```
scala> g.vertices.show(5)
+---+
| id|
+---+
|296|
|467|
|675|
|691|
|829|
+---+
only showing top 5 rows
scala> g.edges.show(5)
+---+---+
|src|dst|
+---+---+
|  0|  1|
|  0|  2|
|  0|  3|
|  0|  4|
|  0|  5|
+---+---+
only showing top 5 rows
scala> g.inDegrees.show(5)
+----+--------+
|  id|inDegree|
+----+--------+
| 467|      28|
|1090|       9|
| 296|       5|
|3959|       7|
|6240|      44|
+----+--------+
only showing top 5 rows
scala> g.outDegrees.show(5)
+---+---------+
| id|outDegree|
+---+---------+
|296|       10|
|467|       10|
|675|       10|
|691|       10|
```

```
|829|        10|
+---+---------+
only showing top 5 rows
```

We can also apply filters to the edges and vertices and their properties, as shown:

```
scala> g.edges.filter("src == 2").show()
+---+---+
|src|dst|
+---+---+
|  2|  0|
|  2|  1|
|  2|  3|
|  2|  4|
|  2|  6|
|  2| 10|
|  2| 47|
|  2| 54|
|  2|118|
|  2|355|
+---+---+
scala> g.edges.filter("src == 2").count()
res6: Long = 10
scala> g.edges.filter("dst == 2").show()
+---+---+
|src|dst|
+---+---+
|  0|  2|
|  1|  2|
|  3|  2|
+---+---+
scala> g.inDegrees.filter("inDegree >= 10").show(5)
+----+--------+
| id|inDegree|
+----+--------+
| 467|      28|
|6240|      44|
|1159|      12|
|1512|     110|
| 675|      13|
+----+--------+
only showing top 5 rows
```

Additionally, we can also use `groupBy` and `sort` operations, as shown in the following examples:

```
scala>
g.inDegrees.groupBy("inDegree").count().sort(desc("inDegree")).show(5)
+--------+-----+
|inDegree|count|
+--------+-----+
|    2751|    1|
|    2487|    1|
|    2281|    1|
|    1512|    1|
|    1174|    1|
+--------+-----+
only showing top 5 rows
scala>
g.outDegrees.groupBy("outDegree").count().sort(desc("outDegree")).show(5)
+---------+------+
|outDegree| count|
+---------+------+
|       10|279108|
|        9| 13297|
|        8| 11370|
|        7| 11906|
|        6| 12827|
+---------+------+
only showing top 5 rows
```

In the next section, we explore structural patterns present in our graph.

Motif analysis using GraphFrames

Finding motifs helps us execute queries to discover structural patterns in our graphs. Network motifs are subgraphs or patterns that occur repeatedly in the graph and represent the interactions or relationships between the vertices. Motifs can be used in our product co-purchasing graph to gain insights into user behavior based on structural properties of the graph representing the products, and their attributes and the relationships between them. Such information can be used in recommendation and/or advertising engines.

For example, the following motif represents a use case where a customer who bought product **(a)** also purchased the other two products, **(b)**, and **(c)**, as well:

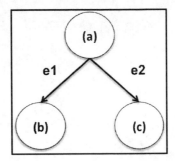

 Refer to *Motif Analysis* in the *Amazon Product Co-Purchasing Network*, by *Abhishek Srivastava* for a detailed coverage of motif analysis.

In this section, we will use GraphFrames to primarily model 3- and 4-node motifs that represent various relationships in the co-purchasing network Dataset. GraphFrame motif finding uses a declarative **Domain-Specific Language** (DSL) for expressing structural queries. Within a pattern, names are assigned to vertices and edges. The basic unit of a pattern is an edge. For example, (a) - [e] -> (b) expresses an edge e from vertex a to vertex b. The vertices are denoted by parentheses (a), while edges are denoted by square brackets [e]. A pattern is expressed as a union of edges and the edge patterns can be joined with semicolons.

We will start our coding exercises with a simple query in which we search for sets of products where purchases of product a also meant purchases of product b or vice versa. The find operation here will search for pairs of vertices connected by edges in both directions:

```scala
scala> val motifs = g.find("(a)-[e]->(b); (b)-[e2]->(a)")
scala> motifs.show(5)
+--------+---------------+--------+---------------+
|       a|              e|       b|             e2|
+--------+---------------+--------+---------------+
| [85609]| [85609,100018]|[100018]| [100018,85609]|
| [86839]| [86839,100042]|[100042]| [100042,86839]|
| [55528]| [55528,100087]|[100087]| [100087,55528]|
|[178970]|[178970,100124]|[100124]|[100124,178970]|
|[100124]|[100124,100125]|[100125]|[100125,100124]|
+--------+---------------+--------+---------------+
only showing top 5 rows
```

We can also apply filters to the result; for example, we have specified the value of the vertex b as 2 in the following filter:

```
scala> motifs.filter("b.id == 2").show()
+---+-----+---+-----+
|  a|   e|  b|   e2|
+---+-----+---+-----+
|[3]|[3,2]|[2]|[2,3]|
|[0]|[0,2]|[2]|[2,0]|
|[1]|[1,2]|[2]|[2,1]|
+---+-----+---+-----+
```

The following example specifies two separate edges from a (to b and c). This pattern typically represents a case in which when a customer buy a product **(a)** then she also buys either of, or both, **(b)** and **(c)**:

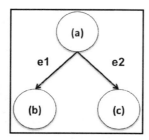

Additionally, the pattern also specifies that the same vertex a is the common source for edges e1 and e2:

```
scala> val motifs3 = g.find("(a)-[e1]->(b); (a)-[e2]->(c)").filter("(b !=
c)")

scala> motifs3.show(5)
+--------+----------------+--------+----------------+--------+
|       a|              e1|       b|              e2|       c|
+--------+----------------+--------+----------------+--------+
|[109254]|   [109254,8742]|  [8742]|[109254,100010]|[100010]|
|[109254]|   [109254,8741]|  [8741]|[109254,100010]|[100010]|
|[109254]|  [109254,59782]| [59782]|[109254,100010]|[100010]|
|[109254]|[109254,115349]|[115349]|[109254,100010]|[100010]|
|[109254]|  [109254,53996]| [53996]|[109254,100010]|[100010]|
+--------+----------------+--------+----------------+--------+
only showing top 5 rows
```

As the edges columns contain redundant information, we can omit names for vertices or edges in motifs when they are not required; for example, in the pattern `(a)-[]->(b)`, `[]` represents an arbitrary edge between vertices a and b.

There is no column for the edge in the result. Similarly, `(a)-[e]->()` indicates an outgoing edge of vertex a but does not name the destination vertex:

```
scala> val motifs3 = g.find("(a)-[]->(b); (a)-[]->(c)").filter("(b != c)")
scala> motifs3.show()
+--------+--------+--------+
|       a|       b|       c|
+--------+--------+--------+
|[109254]|  [8742]|[100010]|
|[109254]|  [8741]|[100010]|
|[109254]| [59782]|[100010]|
|[109254]|[115349]|[100010]|
|[109254]| [53996]|[100010]|
|[109254]|[109257]|[100010]|
|[109254]| [62046]|[100010]|
|[109254]| [94411]|[100010]|
|[109254]|[115348]|[100010]|
|[117041]| [73722]|[100010]|
|[117041]|[193912]|[100010]|
|[117041]| [52568]|[100010]|
|[117041]| [57835]|[100010]|
|[117041]|[164019]|[100010]|
|[117041]| [63821]|[100010]|
|[117041]|[162691]|[100010]|
|[117041]| [69365]|[100010]|
|[117041]|  [4849]|[100010]|
|[148522]|  [8742]|[100010]|
|[148522]|[100008]|[100010]|
+--------+--------+--------+
only showing top 20 rows
scala> motifs3.count()
res20: Long = 28196586
```

In the following example, we specify two separate edges from a (to b and c), and another edge from b to a. This pattern typically represents the case in which there is a reciprocating relationship between a and b (a strongly connected component indicative of a close similarity between the products):

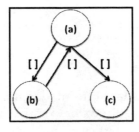

```
scala> val motifs3 = g.find("(a)-[]->(b); (a)-[]->(c); (b)-
[]->(a)").filter("(b != c)")
scala> motifs3.show()
+-------+--------+--------+
|      a|       b|       c|
+-------+--------+--------+
|[85609]|[100018]| [85611]|
|[85609]|[100018]| [85610]|
|[85609]|[100018]| [85752]|
|[85609]|[100018]| [28286]|
|[85609]|[100018]| [93910]|
|[85609]|[100018]| [85753]|
|[85609]|[100018]| [60945]|
|[85609]|[100018]| [47246]|
|[85609]|[100018]| [85614]|
|[86839]|[100042]|[100040]|
|[86839]|[100042]| [46600]|
|[86839]|[100042]|[100039]|
|[86839]|[100042]|[100041]|
|[86839]|[100042]| [27186]|
|[86839]|[100042]|[100044]|
|[86839]|[100042]|[100043]|
|[86839]|[100042]| [86841]|
|[86839]|[100042]| [86838]|
|[55528]|[100087]| [55531]|
|[55528]|[100087]| [40067]|
+-------+--------+--------+
only showing top 20 rows
scala> motifs3.count()
res17: Long = 15657738
```

In the following example, we specify two separate edges from a and c (to b). This pattern typically represents the case in which when customers buys largely unrelated products (a and c), then they also buy b. This is a converging motif and the business can use this information to, for example, stock this subset of products together:

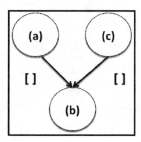

```
scala> val motifs3 = g.find("(a)-[]->(b); (c)-[]->(b)").filter("(a != c)")
scala> motifs3.show(5)
+--------+------+--------+
|       a|     b|       c|
+--------+------+--------+
|[365079]|[8742]|[100010]|
|[241393]|[8742]|[100010]|
| [33284]|[8742]|[100010]|
|[198072]|[8742]|[100010]|
|[203728]|[8742]|[100010]|
+--------+------+--------+
only showing top 5 rows
scala> motifs3.count()
res24: Long = 119218310
```

In the following example, we specify edges from a to b and b to c, and another one from c to b. This pattern typically represents the case in which when a customer buys a product **(a)**, she may also buy **(b)** and then go on to buy **(c)**. This can be indicative of some prioritization on the items being purchased. Additionally, the strongly connected component in the motif indicates a close relationship between **(b)** and **(c)**:

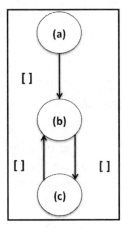

```
scala> val motifs3 = g.find("(a)-[]->(b); (b)-[]->(c); (c)-[]->(b)")
scala> motifs3.show(5)
+--------+-------+--------+
|       a|      b|       c|
+--------+-------+--------+
|[188454]|[85609]|[100018]|
| [85611]|[85609]|[100018]|
| [98017]|[85609]|[100018]|
|[142029]|[85609]|[100018]|
| [64516]|[85609]|[100018]|
```

```
+--------+-------+--------+
only showing top 5 rows
scala> motifs3.count()
res26: Long = 23373805.
```

 The 4-node motifs example is very resource intensive requiring over 100 GB disk space and over 14 GB RAM. Alternatively, you can refer to the next section to create a smaller subgraph to run this example.

In the next example, we present a `4-node` motif. This pattern typically represents the case in which there is a higher probability of a customer buying **(b)**:

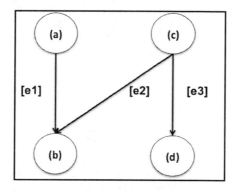

```
scala> val motifs4 = g.find("(a)-[e1]->(b); (c)-[e2]->(b); (c)-
[e3]->(d)").filter("(a != c) AND (d != b) AND (d != a)")
scala> motifs4.show(5)
```

a	e1	b	c	e2	e3	d
[365079]	[365079,8742]	[8742]	[109254]	[109254,8742]	[109254,100010]	[100010]
[241393]	[241393,8742]	[8742]	[109254]	[109254,8742]	[109254,100010]	[100010]
[33284]	[33284,8742]	[8742]	[109254]	[109254,8742]	[109254,100010]	[100010]
[198072]	[198072,8742]	[8742]	[109254]	[109254,8742]	[109254,100010]	[100010]
[203728]	[203728,8742]	[8742]	[109254]	[109254,8742]	[109254,100010]	[100010]

only showing top 5 rows

```
scala> motifs4.count()
res2: Long = 945551688
```

In the next section, we shift our focus to creating and processing subgraphs.

Processing subgraphs

GraphFrames provide a powerful way to select subgraphs based on a combination of motif finding and DataFrame filters. The following examples show how to select a subgraph based on vertex and edge filters:

```scala
scala> val v2 = g.vertices.filter("src < 10")
scala> val e2 = g.edges.filter("src < 10")
scala> val g2 = GraphFrame(v2, e2)
scala> g2.edges.groupBy("src").count().show()
+---+-----+
|src|count|
+---+-----+
|  7|   10|
|  3|   10|
|  8|   10|
|  0|   10|
|  5|   10|
|  6|   10|
|  9|   10|
|  1|   10|
|  4|   10|
|  2|   10|
+---+-----+
scala> val paths = g.find("(a)-[e]->(b)").filter("e.src < e.dst")
scala> val e2 = paths.select("e.*")
scala> e2.show(5)
+------+------+
|   src|   dst|
+------+------+
|100008|100010|
|100226|100227|
|100225|100227|
|100224|100227|
|100223|100227|
+------+------+
only showing top 5 rows
```

In the next section, we will apply a series of graph algorithms to our graph.

Applying graph algorithms

GraphFrames provide a suite of standard graph algorithms. We provide brief descriptions of the graph algorithms and code snippets for applying them.

First, we compute the **strongly connected component (SCC)** of each vertex and return a graph with each vertex assigned to the SCC containing that vertex. We display the count of nodes in the SCC, as shown:

```
val result = g.stronglyConnectedComponents.maxIter(10).run()
result.select("id",
"component").groupBy("component").count().sort($"count".desc).show()
+---------+------+
|component| count|
+---------+------+
|        0|395234|
|   312598|   111|
|   379229|   105|
|   107295|    81|
|   359845|    70|
|    40836|    64|
|   357970|    64|
|   189338|    61|
|   369081|    59|
|   152634|    58|
|   167178|    55|
|    35086|    50|
|    81674|    48|
|   376845|    48|
|   177702|    47|
|   319708|    44|
|   130664|    43|
|   279703|    41|
|   273764|    41|
|   324355|    40|
+---------+------+
only showing top 20 rows
```

Next, we compute the number of triangles passing through each vertex. The number of triangles is a measure of the density of the vertex neighborhood. There are many practical applications of triangle counting in networks, for example, community detection, roles behavior, spam detection, detecting subsets of web pages with a common topic, and so on:

```
val results = g.triangleCount.run()
results.select("id", "count").show()
+------+-----+
|    id|count|
+------+-----+
|100010|   73|
|100140|   15|
|100227|  332|
|100263|    9|
```

```
|100320|    8|
|100553|   41|
|100704|    3|
|100735|   13|
|100768|   37|
| 10096|   58|
|100964|   87|
|101021|   30|
|101122|   52|
|101205|  152|
|101261|   31|
|101272|   19|
|102113|   38|
|102521|   23|
|102536|    2|
|102539|   37|
+------+-----+
only showing top 20 rows
```

In the following example, we will apply the PageRank algorithm to determine an estimate of how important the product is. The underlying assumption is that more popular products are likely to receive more links from other product nodes:

```
val results = g.pageRank.resetProbability(0.15).tol(0.01).run()
val prank = results.vertices.sort(desc("pagerank"))
prank.show(5)
+-----+------------------+
|   id|          pagerank|
+-----+------------------+
|   45| 586.2075242838272|
| 1036| 512.2355738350872|
| 1037|  506.900472599229|
|   50| 485.4457370914238|
| 1039|438.64149165397276|
+----+------------------+
only showing top 5 rows
```

In the next example, we apply the Label Propagation algorithm to find communities of products in our graph:

```
val results = g.labelPropagation.maxIter(10).run()
results.select("id", "label").show()
+-----+-----+
|label|count|
+-----+-----+
| 1677|    2|
| 5385|   23|
| 7279|   11|
```

```
|  9233|     7|
|  9458|    10|
|  9978|    80|
| 10422|     8|
| 11945|    13|
| 13098|     6|
| 13452|    12|
| 14117|    49|
| 21899|    20|
| 23019|    12|
| 27651|    80|
| 29824|    17|
| 30421|     9|
| 32571|     4|
| 37310|     1|
| 41424|    48|
| 45726|     4|
+-----+-----+
only showing top 20 rows
results.select("id",
"label").groupBy("label").count().sort(desc("count")).show(5)
+-----+-----+
|label|count|
+-----+-----+
| 1110| 2830|
|  352| 2266|
| 9965| 1413|
| 9982|  828|
|11224|  761|
+-----+-----+
only showing top 5 rows
```

In the following example, we apply the Shortest Paths algorithm to find a path between two vertices in the graph so that the number of its constituent edges is minimized:

```
val results = g.shortestPaths.landmarks(Seq("1110", "352")).run()
results.select("id", "distances").take(5).foreach(println)
[8,Map(352 -> 3, 1110 -> 9)]
[22,Map(352 -> 4, 1110 -> 4)]
[290,Map(352 -> 4, 1110 -> 6)]
[752,Map()]
[2453,Map(352 -> 8, 1110 -> 11)]
```

In the following section, we show how to save GraphFrames to persistent storage and then retrieve the same to recreate the original GraphFrame.

Saving and loading GraphFrames

As GraphFrames are built on the DataFrames API, they support saving and loading to and from various data sources. In the following code, we show saving the vertices and edges to Parquet files on HDFS:

```
g.vertices.write.parquet("hdfs://localhost:9000/gf/vertices")
g.edges.write.parquet("hdfs://localhost:9000/gf/edges")
```

We can recreate the vertex and edge DataFrames from persistent storage, and then the graph, as shown:

```
val v = spark.read.parquet("hdfs://localhost:9000/gf/vertices")
val e = spark.read.parquet("hdfs://localhost:9000/gf/edges")
val g = GraphFrame(v, e)
```

In the next section, we use a richer Dataset to demonstrate the use of vertex and edge attributes in GraphFrames-based applications.

Analyzing JSON input modeled as a graph

In this section, we will analyze a JSON Dataset modeled as a graph. We will apply GraphFrame functions from the previous sections and introduce some new ones.

For hands-on exercises in this section, we use a Dataset containing Amazon product metadata; product information and reviews on around 548,552 products. This Dataset can be downloaded from `https://snap.stanford.edu/data/amazon-meta.html`.

For processing simplicity, the original Dataset was converted to a JSON format file with each line representing a complete record. Use the Java program (`Preprocess.java`) provided with this chapter for the conversion.

First, we create a DataFrame from the input file, and print out the schema and a few sample records. It is a complex schema with nested elements:

```
scala> val df1 =
spark.read.json("file:///Users/aurobindosarkar/Downloads/input.json")
scala> df1.printSchema()
root
|-- ASIN: string (nullable = true)
|-- Id: long (nullable = true)
|-- ReviewMetaData: struct (nullable = true)
|    |-- avg_rating: double (nullable = true)
|    |-- downloaded: long (nullable = true)
|    |-- total: long (nullable = true)
|-- categories: long (nullable = true)
|-- categoryLines: array (nullable = true)
|    |-- element: struct (containsNull = true)
|    |    |-- category: string (nullable = true)
|-- group: string (nullable = true)
|-- reviewLines: array (nullable = true)
|    |-- element: struct (containsNull = true)
|    |    |-- review: struct (nullable = true)
|    |    |    |-- customerId: string (nullable = true)
|    |    |    |-- date: string (nullable = true)
|    |    |    |-- helpful: long (nullable = true)
|    |    |    |-- rating: long (nullable = true)
|    |    |    |-- votes: long (nullable = true)
|-- salerank: long (nullable = true)
|-- similarLines: array (nullable = true)
|    |-- element: struct (containsNull = true)
|    |    |-- similar: string (nullable = true)
|-- similars: long (nullable = true)
|-- title: string (nullable = true)
scala> df1.take(5).foreach(println)
```

```
[0771044445,0,null,null,null,null,null,null,null,null,null]

[0827229534,1,[5.0,2,2],2,WrappedArray([|Books[283155]|Subjects[1000]|Religion &
Spirituality[22]|Christianity[12290]|Clergy[12360]|Preaching[12368]],
[|Books[283155]|Subjects[1000]|Religion &
Spirituality[22]|Christianity[12290]|Clergy[12360]|Sermons[12370]]),Book,WrappedArray(
[[A2JW67OY8U6HHK,2000-7-28,9,5,10]], [[A2VE83MZF98ITY,2003-12-
14,5,5,6]]),396585,WrappedArray([0804215715], [156101074X], [0687023955],
[0687074231], [082721619X]),5,Patterns of Preaching: A Sermon Sampler]

[0738700797,2,[4.5,12,12],2,WrappedArray([|Books[283155]|Subjects[1000]|Religion &
Spirituality[22]|Earth-Based Religions[12472]|Wicca[12484]],
[|Books[283155]|Subjects[1000]|Religion & Spirituality[22]|Earth-Based
Religions[12472]|Witchcraft[12486]]),Book,WrappedArray([[A11NCO6YTE4BTJ,2001-12-
16,4,5,5]], [[A9CQ3PLRNIR83,2002-1-7,5,4,5]], [[A13SG9ACZ905IM,2002-1-24,8,5,8]],
[[A1BDAI6VEYMAZA,2002-1-28,4,5,4]], [[A2P6KAWXJ16234,2002-2-6,16,4,16]],
[[AMACWC3M7PQFR,2002-2-14,5,4,5]], [[A3G07UV9XX14D8,2002-3-23,6,4,6]],
[[A1GIL64QK68WKL,2002-5-23,8,5,8]], [[AEOBOF2ONQJWV,2003-2-25,5,5,8]],
[[A3IGHTES8ME05L,2003-11-25,5,5,5]], [[A1CP26N8RHYVVO,2004-2-11,9,1,13]],
[[ANEIANHOWAT9D,2005-2-7,1,5,1]]),168596,WrappedArray([0738700827], [1567184960],
[1567182836], [0738700525], [0738700940]),5,Candlemas: Feast of Flames]

[0486287785,3,[5.0,1,1],1,WrappedArray([|Books[283155]|Subjects[1000]|Home &
Garden[48]|Crafts &
Hobbies[5126]|General[5144]]),Book,WrappedArray([[A3IDGASRQAW8B2,2003-7-
10,2,5,2]]),1270652,null,0,World War II Allied Fighter Planes Trading Cards]

[0842328327,4,[4.0,1,1],5,WrappedArray([|Books[283155]|Subjects[1000]|Religion &
Spirituality[22]|Christianity[12290]|Reference[172810]|Commentaries[12155]|New
Testament[12159]], [|Books[283155]|Subjects[1000]|Religion &
Spirituality[22]|Christianity[12290]|Christian Living[12333]|Discipleship[12335]],
[|Books[283155]|Subjects[1000]|Religion &
Spirituality[22]|Christianity[12290]|Bibles[12059]|Translations[764432]|Life
Application[572080]], [|Books[283155]|Subjects[1000]|Religion & Spirituality[22]|Bible
& Other Sacred Texts[12056]|Bible[764430]|New Testament[572082]],
[|Books[283155]|Subjects[1000]|Religion &
Spirituality[22]|Christianity[12290]|Bibles[12059]|Study Guides, History &
Reference[764438]|General[572094]]),Book,WrappedArray([[A2591BUPXCS705,2004-8-
19,1,4,1]]),631289,WrappedArray([0842328130], [0830818138], [0842330313],
[0842328610], [0842328572]),5,Life Application Bible Commentary: 1 and 2 Timothy and
Titus]
```

We can print out an array of struct elements in the data. More specifically, we print out the list of similar products (that get co-purchased with the current product):

```scala
scala> val x1=df1.select(df1.col("similarLines"))
scala> df1.select(df1.col("similarLines.similar")).take(5).foreach(println)
```

We can also flatten the nested structure of the reviews element by using explode and access specific elements within it:

```scala
scala> val flattened = df1.select($"ASIN",
explode($"reviewLines.review").as("review_flat"))
scala> flattened.show()
+----------+--------------------+
|      ASIN|         review_flat|
+----------+--------------------+
|0827229534|[A2JW67OY8U6HHK,2...|
|0827229534|[A2VE83MZF98ITY,2...|
|0738700797|[A11NCO6YTE4BTJ,2...|
|0738700797|[A9CQ3PLRNIR83,20...|
|0738700797|[A13SG9ACZ9O5IM,2...|
|0738700797|[A1BDAI6VEYMAZA,2...|
|0738700797|[A2P6KAWXJ16234,2...|
|0738700797|[AMACWC3M7PQFR,20...|
|0738700797|[A3GO7UV9XX14D8,2...|
|0738700797|[A1GIL64QK68WKL,2...|
|0738700797|[AEOBOF2ONQJWV,20...|
|0738700797|[A3IGHTES8ME05L,2...|
|0738700797|[A1CP26N8RHYVVO,2...|
|0738700797|[ANEIANH0WAT9D,20...|
|0486287785|[A3IDGASRQAW8B2,2...|
|0842328327|[A2591BUPXCS705,2...|
|0486220125|[ATVPDKIKX0DER,19...|
|0486220125|[AUEZ7NVOEHYRY,19...|
|0486220125|[ATVPDKIKX0DER,19...|
|0486220125|[AJYG6ZJUQPZ9M,20...|
+----------+--------------------+
only showing top 20 rows
scala> val flatReview = flattened.select("ASIN", "review_flat.customerId")
```

Next, we create the nodes and edges DataFrames, as shown:

```scala
scala> val nodesDF = df1.select($"ASIN".alias("id"),
$"Id".alias("productId"), $"title", $"ReviewMetaData", $"categories",
$"categoryLines", $"group", $"reviewLines", $"salerank", $"similarLines",
$"similars")
```

For the edges DataFrame, we use explode on similar or also purchased products column called `similarLines` to create new rows for each element in the array:

```scala
scala> val edgesDF = df1.select($"ASIN".alias("src"),
explode($"similarLines.similar").as("dst"))
scala> val g = GraphFrame(nodesDF, edgesDF)
```

Next, we show some basic operations using the node attributes:

```
scala> g.edges.filter("salerank < 100").count()
res97: Long = 750
scala> g.vertices.groupBy("group").count().show()
+------------+------+
|       group| count|
+------------+------+
|       Video| 26131|
|         Toy|     8|
|         DVD| 19828|
|      Sports|     1|
|        null|  5868|
|Baby Product|     1|
| Video Games|     1|
|        Book|393561|
|       Music|103144|
|    Software|     5|
|          CE|     4|
+------------+------+
```

Next, we create a subgraph for Book group products only:

```
scala> val v2 = g.vertices.filter("group = 'Book'")
scala> val g2 = GraphFrame(v2, e2)
scala> g2.vertices.count()
res6: Long = 393561
```

It is important to note that the number of edges is equal to the edges in the original graph. GraphFrame does not automatically remove the edges that are not related to Book group products:

```
scala> g2.edges.count()
res7: Long = 1788725
```

In the following steps, we join the vertices and edges DataFrames, temporarily, to get rid of the extra edges in our DataFrame and create a GraphFrame with nodes and edges related to Book products only:

```
scala> val v2t = v2.select("id")
scala> val e2t = v2t.join(e2, v2t("id") === e2("src"))
scala> e2t.count()
res8: Long = 1316257
scala> val e2t1 = v2t.join(e2, v2t("id") === e2("src")).drop("id")
scala> val e2t2 = v2t.join(e2t1, v2t("id") === e2t1("dst")).drop("id")
scala> e2t2.count()
res9: Long = 911960
scala> val g2f = GraphFrame(v2, e2t2)
```

```
scala> g2f.vertices.count()
res10: Long = 393561
scala> g2f.edges.count()
res11: Long = 911960
```

We can combine the motif finding with filters containing the attributes of the vertices:

```
scala> g2.edges.take(5).foreach(println)
[B00008MNUJ,0822959046]
[0786632550,0793529395]
[0942272463,0942272692]
[0942272463,1567183298]
[0060537612,0689820305]
scala> val es = g.edges.filter("salerank < 100")
scala> val e3 = es.select("src", "dst")
scala> val g3 = GraphFrame(g.vertices, e3)
scala> val motifs = g3.find("(a)-[e]->(b); (b)-[e2]->(a)")
scala> motifs.show()
```

a	e	b	e2
[6301798643,93678...	[6301798643,63017...	[6301797973,51638...	[6301797973,63017...
[B00000J2I0,38585...	[B00000J2I0,63052...	[6305242143,34489...	[6305242143,B0000...
[0451524934,44922...	[0451524934,03167...	[0316769487,98756...	[0316769487,04515...
[6300185788,11281...	[6300185788,15588...	[1558807225,20377...	[1558807225,63001...
[0156027321,62424...	[0156027321,01420...	[0142001740,33797...	[0142001740,01560...
[6303182135,46688...	[6303182135,63031...	[6303182232,34106...	[6303182232,63031...
[6304424841,53266...	[6304424841,63034...	[6303499988,66050...	[6303499988,63044...
[6302728657,24467...	[6302728657,63016...	[6301627024,28339...	[6301627024,63027...
[0316769487,98756...	[0316769487,04515...	[0451524934,44922...	[0451524934,03167...
[6304401744,46640...	[6304401744,63044...	[6304424841,53266...	[6304424841,63044...
[0345342968,29543...	[0345342968,04515...	[0451524934,44922...	[0451524934,03453...
[6303182232,34106...	[6303182232,63031...	[6303182135,46688...	[6303182135,63031...
[B00004S36U,37060...	[B00004S36U,B0000...	[B00004S36S,37060...	[B00004S36S,B0000...
[0385504209,296,T...	[0385504209,06710...	[0671027360,37685...	[0671027360,03855...
[0385504209,296,T...	[0385504209,06710...	[0671027387,42470...	[0671027387,03855...
[1880685000,47585...	[1880685000,15804...	[1580420826,45175...	[1580420826,18806...
[0671027387,42470...	[0671027387,03855...	[0385504209,296,T...	[0385504209,06710...
[6301627024,28339...	[6301627024,63027...	[6302728657,24467...	[6302728657,63016...
[6304424841,53266...	[6304424841,63044...	[6304401744,46640...	[6304401744,63044...
[0142001740,33797...	[0142001740,01560...	[0156027321,62424...	[0156027321,01420...

```
only showing top 20 rows
```

```
scala> motifs.filter("b.ReviewMetaData.avg_rating > 4.0").show()
```

```
+--------------------+--------------------+--------------------+--------------------+
|                   a|                   e|                   b|                  e2|
+--------------------+--------------------+--------------------+--------------------+
|[6301798643,93678...|[6301798643,63017...|[6301797973,51638...|[6301797973,63017...|
|[B00000J2I0,38585...|[B00000J2I0,63052...|[6305242143,34489...|[6305242143,B0000...|
|[6300185788,11281...|[6300185788,15588...|[1558807225,20377...|[1558807225,63001...|
|[6303182135,46688...|[6303182135,63031...|[6303182232,34106...|[6303182232,63031...|
|[6304424841,53266...|[6304424841,63034...|[6303499988,66050...|[6303499988,63044...|
|[6302728657,24467...|[6302728657,63016...|[6301627024,28339...|[6301627024,63027...|
|[0316769487,98756...|[0316769487,04515...|[0451524934,44922...|[0451524934,03167...|
|[0345342968,29543...|[0345342968,04515...|[0451524934,44922...|[0451524934,03453...|
|[6303182232,34106...|[6303182232,63031...|[6303182135,46688...|[6303182135,63031...|
|[B00004S36U,37060...|[B00004S36U,B0000...|[B00004S36S,37060...|[B00004S36S,B0000...|
|[6301627024,28339...|[6301627024,63027...|[6302728657,24467...|[6302728657,63016...|
|[6304424841,53266...|[6304424841,63044...|[6304401744,46640...|[6304401744,63044...|
|[B00004S36S,37060...|[B00004S36S,B0000...|[B00004S36U,37060...|[B00004S36U,B0000...|
|[1580420826,45175...|[1580420826,18806...|[1880685000,47585...|[1880685000,15804...|
|[6305242143,34489...|[6305242143,B0000...|[B00000J2I0,38585...|[B00000J2I0,63052...|
|[B0000508U6,50505...|[B0000508U6,B0000...|[B000069AUI,53688...|[B000069AUI,B0000...|
|[B00008NG5V,27054...|[B00008NG5V,B0000...|[B00005V8PZ,14861...|[B00005V8PZ,B0000...|
|[0316346624,89000...|[0316346624,00666...|[0066620996,15485...|[0066620996,03163...|
|[B00005V8PZ,14861...|[B00005V8PZ,B0000...|[B00008NG5V,27054...|[B00008NG5V,B0000...|
|[B000069AUI,53688...|[B000069AUI,B0000...|[B0000508U6,50505...|[B0000508U6,B0000...|
+--------------------+--------------------+--------------------+--------------------+
```

```
scala> val paths = g3.find("(a)-[e]->(b)").filter("a.group = 'Book' AND
b.group = 'Book'").filter("a.salerank < b.salerank")
scala> val e2 = paths.select("e.src", "e.dst")
scala> val g2 = GraphFrame(g.vertices, e2)
scala> g2.vertices.take(5).foreach(println)
```

```
[0771044445,0,null,null,null,null,null,null,null,null,null]

[0827229534,1,Patterns of Preaching: A Sermon
Sampler,[5.0,2,2],2,WrappedArray([|Books[283155]|Subjects[1000]|Religion &
Spirituality[22]|Christianity[12290]|Clergy[12360]|Preaching[12368]],
[|Books[283155]|Subjects[1000]|Religion &
Spirituality[22]|Christianity[12290]|Clergy[12360]|Sermons[12370]]),Book,WrappedArray(
[[A2JW67OY8U6HHK,2000-7-28,9,5,10]], [[A2VE83MZF98ITY,2003-12-
14,5,5,6]]),396585,WrappedArray([0804215715], [156101074X], [0687023955],
[0687074231], [082721619X]),5]

[0738700797,2,Candlemas: Feast of
Flames,[4.5,12,12],2,WrappedArray([|Books[283155]|Subjects[1000]|Religion &
Spirituality[22]|Earth-Based Religions[12472]|Wicca[12484]],
[|Books[283155]|Subjects[1000]|Religion & Spirituality[22]|Earth-Based
Religions[12472]|Witchcraft[12486]]),Book,WrappedArray([[A11NCO6YTE4BTJ,2001-12-
16,4,5,5]], [[A9CQ3PLRNIR83,2002-1-7,5,4,5]], [[A13SG9ACZ905IM,2002-1-24,8,5,8]],
[[A1BDAI6VEYMAZA,2002-1-28,4,5,4]], [[A2P6KAWXJ16234,2002-2-6,16,4,16]],
[[AMACWC3M7PQFR,2002-2-14,5,4,5]], [[A3GO7UV9XX14D8,2002-3-23,6,4,6]],
[[A1GIL64QK68WKL,2002-5-23,8,5,8]], [[AEOBOF2ONQJWV,2003-2-25,5,5,8]],
[[A3IGHTES8ME05L,2003-11-25,5,5,5]], [[A1CP26N8RHYVVO,2004-2-11,9,1,13]],
[[ANEIANH0WAT9D,2005-2-7,1,5,1]]),168596,WrappedArray([0738700827], [1567184960],
[1567182836], [0738700525], [0738700940]),5]

[0486287785,3,World War II Allied Fighter Planes Trading
Cards,[5.0,1,1],1,WrappedArray([|Books[283155]|Subjects[1000]|Home & Garden[48]|Crafts
& Hobbies[5126]|General[5144]]),Book,WrappedArray([[A3IDGASRQAW8B2,2003-7-
10,2,5,2]]),1270652,null,0]

[0842328327,4,Life Application Bible Commentary: 1 and 2 Timothy and
Titus,[4.0,1,1],5,WrappedArray([|Books[283155]|Subjects[1000]|Religion &
Spirituality[22]|Christianity[12290]|Reference[172810]|Commentaries[12155]|New
Testament[12159]], [|Books[283155]|Subjects[1000]|Religion &
Spirituality[22]|Christianity[12290]|Christian Living[12333]|Discipleship[12335]],
[|Books[283155]|Subjects[1000]|Religion &
Spirituality[22]|Christianity[12290]|Bibles[12059]|Translations[764432]|Life
Application[572080]], [|Books[283155]|Subjects[1000]|Religion & Spirituality[22]|Bible
& Other Sacred Texts[12056]|Bible[764430]|New Testament[572082]],
[|Books[283155]|Subjects[1000]|Religion &
Spirituality[22]|Christianity[12290]|Bibles[12059]|Study Guides, History &
Reference[764438]|General[572094]]),Book,WrappedArray([[A2591BUPXCS705,2004-8-
19,1,4,1]]),631289,WrappedArray([0842328130], [0830818138], [0842330313],
[0842328610], [0842328572]),5]
```

GraphFrames provides the `AggregateMessages` primitive for developing graph algorithms. This component can be used for sending messages between vertices, and also for aggregating the messages for each vertex.

In the following example, we compute the sum of the number of purchased products of adjacent products:

```scala
scala> import org.graphframes.lib.AggregateMessages
```

```
scala> val AM = AggregateMessages
scala> val msgToSrc = AM.dst("similars")
scala> val msgToDst = AM.src("similars")
scala> val agg =
g.aggregateMessages.sendToSrc(msgToSrc).sendToDst(msgToDst).agg(sum(AM.msg)
.as("SummedSimilars"))
scala> agg.show()
+----------+--------------+
|        id| SummedSimilars|
+----------+--------------+
|0004708237|             5|
|0023605103|            35|
|0027861317|            30|
|0028624599|            30|
|0028633784|            40|
|0028642074|            45|
|0030259282|            10|
|0060082135|            20|
|0060279257|            20|
|0060298804|            25|
|0060392436|            25|
|0060540745|           125|
|0060611561|           100|
|0060921005|            15|
|0060925175|            48|
|0060929081|            54|
|0060959126|            10|
|0060960388|            29|
|006097060X|            50|
|0060988940|            25|
+----------+--------------+
only showing top 20 rows
```

In the next section, we explore GraphFrames with edges representing multiple types of relationships.

Processing graphs containing multiple types of relationships

For the next few examples, we use an augmented edges DataFrame containing a relationship column. We insert two types of relationships in the column based on the number of similar purchases and the number of categories that a product belongs to.

For this, we join the nodes and edges DataFrames, and subsequently drop the node-related columns after the relationship computation is completed to obtain our final edges DataFrame (with the relationship column suitably populated):

```
scala> val joinDF = nodesDF.join(edgesDF).where(nodesDF("id") ===
edgesDF("src")).withColumn("relationship", when(($"similars" > 4) and
($"categories" <= 3), "highSimilars").otherwise("alsoPurchased"))
scala> val edgesDFR = joinDF.select("src", "dst", "relationship")
scala> val gDFR = GraphFrame(nodesDF, edgesDFR)
```

Next, we count the number of records for each type of relationship and list a few edges along with the relationship values:

```
scala> gDFR.edges.groupBy("relationship").count().show()
+-------------+-------+
| relationship|  count|
+-------------+-------+
|alsoPurchased|1034375|
| highSimilars| 754350|
+-------------+-------+
scala> gDFR.edges.show()
+----------+----------+-------------+
|       src|       dst| relationship|
+----------+----------+-------------+
|0004708237|4770027508|alsoPurchased|
|0023605103|0830812717| highSimilars|
|0023605103|0830812865| highSimilars|
|0023605103|0800611365| highSimilars|
|0023605103|0801063914| highSimilars|
|0023605103|0802819478| highSimilars|
|0027861317|0803706197| highSimilars|
|0027861317|0525452710| highSimilars|
|0027861317|0152014829| highSimilars|
|0027861317|068980718X| highSimilars|
|0027861317|0761317910| highSimilars|
|0028624599|1889392138|alsoPurchased|
|0028624599|0934081239|alsoPurchased|
|0028624599|0761528245|alsoPurchased|
|0028624599|0761518045|alsoPurchased|
|0028624599|0811836878|alsoPurchased|
|0028633784|0812046943| highSimilars|
|0028633784|0812046005| highSimilars|
|0028633784|0028629051| highSimilars|
|0028633784|0140144358| highSimilars|
+----------+----------+-------------+
only showing top 20 rows
```

In the following example, we filter on product vertices with a sales rank of following 2,000,000 and edges having the `highSimilars` relationship:

```scala
scala> val v2 = gDFR.vertices.filter("salerank < 2000000")
scala> val e2 = gDFR.edges.filter("relationship = 'highSimilars'")
scala> val g2 = GraphFrame(v2, e2)
```

In the following example, we create a subgraph from selected columns and filter on a specific group of products. We also select a subset of edges based on the `highSimilars` relationship. Furthermore, we find the motifs and apply further filters on them to obtain the final results:

```scala
scala> val v2 = gDFR.vertices.select("id", "group",
"similars").filter("group = 'Book'")
scala> val e2 = gDFR.edges.filter("relationship = 'highSimilars'")
scala> val g2 = GraphFrame(v2, e2)
scala> val result1 = g2.find("(a)-[]->(b); (b)-[]->(c); !(a)-
[]->(c)").filter("(a.group = c.group) and (a.similars = c.similars)")
scala> val result2 = result1.filter("a.id != c.id").select("a.id",
"a.group", "a.similars", "c.id", "c.group", "c.similars")
scala> result2.show(5)
+----------+-----+--------+----------+-----+--------+
|        id|group|similars|        id|group|similars|
+----------+-----+--------+----------+-----+--------+
|0002551489| Book|       5|0002154129| Book|       5|
|0006388515| Book|       5|0679738711| Book|       5|
|0020438001| Book|       5|0395169615| Book|       5|
|0023078251| Book|       5|0394704371| Book|       5|
|0023237309| Book|       5|0874415098| Book|       5|
+----------+-----+--------+----------+-----+--------+
only showing top 5 rows
```

Next, we apply a few graph algorithms to the subgraphs that are based on node and edge relationship attributes. In the following example, we first find the motifs matching the pattern in our graph, and then filter on a combination of node and edge attributes. We run the BFS algorithm on the final subgraph:

```scala
scala> val paths = gDFR.find("(a)-[e]->(b)").filter("e.relationship =
'highSimilars'").filter("a.group = b.group")
scala> val e2 = paths.select("e.src", "e.dst", "e.relationship")
scala> val g2 = GraphFrame(gDFR.vertices, e2)
scala> val numEHS = g2.edges.count()
numEHS: Long = 511524
scala> val bfsDF = gDFR.bfs.fromExpr("group = 'Book'").toExpr("categories <
3").edgeFilter("relationship != 'alsoPurchased'").maxPathLength(3).run()
scala> bfsDF.take(2).foreach(println)
```

```
[[[0827229534,1,Patterns of Preaching: A Sermon
Sampler,[5.0,2,2],2,WrappedArray([|Books[283155]|Subjects[1000]|Religion &
Spirituality[22]|Christianity[12290]|Clergy[12360]|Preaching[12368]],
[|Books[283155]|Subjects[1000]|Religion &
Spirituality[22]|Christianity[12290]|Clergy[12360]|Sermons[12370]]),Book,WrappedArray(
[[A2JW670Y8U6HHK,2000-7-28,9,5,10]], [[A2VE83MZF98ITY,2003-12-
14,5,5,6]]),396585,WrappedArray([0804215715], [156101074X], [0687023955],
[0687074231], [082721619X]),5],[0827229534,1,Patterns of Preaching: A Sermon
Sampler,[5.0,2,2],2,WrappedArray([|Books[283155]|Subjects[1000]|Religion &
Spirituality[22]|Christianity[12290]|Clergy[12360]|Preaching[12368]],
[|Books[283155]|Subjects[1000]|Religion &
Spirituality[22]|Christianity[12290]|Clergy[12360]|Sermons[12370]]),Book,WrappedArray(
[[A2JW670Y8U6HHK,2000-7-28,9,5,10]], [[A2VE83MZF98ITY,2003-12-
14,5,5,6]]),396585,WrappedArray([0804215715], [156101074X], [0687023955],
[0687074231], [082721619X]),5]]


[[[0738700797,2,Candlemas: Feast of
Flames,[4.5,12,12],2,WrappedArray([|Books[283155]|Subjects[1000]|Religion &
Spirituality[22]|Earth-Based Religions[12472]|Wicca[12484]],
[|Books[283155]|Subjects[1000]|Religion & Spirituality[22]|Earth-Based
Religions[12472]|Witchcraft[12486]]),Book,WrappedArray([[A11NCO6YTE4BTJ,2001-12-
16,4,5,5]], [[A9CQ3PLRNIR83,2002-1-7,5,4,5]], [[A13SG9ACZ905IM,2002-1-24,8,5,8]],
[[A1BDAI6VEYMAZA,2002-1-28,4,5,4]], [[A2P6KAWXJ16234,2002-2-6,16,4,16]],
[[AMACWC3M7PQFR,2002-2-14,5,4,5]], [[A3GO7UV9XX14D8,2002-3-23,6,4,6]],
[[A1GIL64QK68WKL,2002-5-23,8,5,8]], [[AEOBOF2ONQJWV,2003-2-25,5,5,8]],
[[A3IGHTES8ME05L,2003-11-25,5,5,5]], [[A1CP26N8RHYVVO,2004-2-11,9,1,13]],
[[ANEIANH0WAT9D,2005-2-7,1,5,1]]),168596,WrappedArray([0738700827], [1567184960],
[1567182836], [0738700525], [0738700940]),5],[0738700797,2,Candlemas: Feast of
Flames,[4.5,12,12],2,WrappedArray([|Books[283155]|Subjects[1000]|Religion &
Spirituality[22]|Earth-Based Religions[12472]|Wicca[12484]],
[|Books[283155]|Subjects[1000]|Religion & Spirituality[22]|Earth-Based
Religions[12472]|Witchcraft[12486]]),Book,WrappedArray([[A11NCO6YTE4BTJ,2001-12-
16,4,5,5]], [[A9CQ3PLRNIR83,2002-1-7,5,4,5]], [[A13SG9ACZ905IM,2002-1-24,8,5,8]],
[[A1BDAI6VEYMAZA,2002-1-28,4,5,4]], [[A2P6KAWXJ16234,2002-2-6,16,4,16]],
[[AMACWC3M7PQFR,2002-2-14,5,4,5]], [[A3GO7UV9XX14D8,2002-3-23,6,4,6]],
[[A1GIL64QK68WKL,2002-5-23,8,5,8]], [[AEOBOF2ONQJWV,2003-2-25,5,5,8]],
[[A3IGHTES8ME05L,2003-11-25,5,5,5]], [[A1CP26N8RHYVVO,2004-2-11,9,1,13]],
[[ANEIANH0WAT9D,2005-2-7,1,5,1]]),168596,WrappedArray([0738700827], [1567184960],
[1567182836], [0738700525], [0738700940]),5]]
```

In the following example, we run the PageRank algorithm on the Books subgraph to find the top ten book titles:

```scala
scala> val v2 = gDFR.vertices.select("id", "group", "title").filter("group
= 'Book'")
scala> val e2 = gDFR.edges.filter("relationship = 'highSimilars'")
scala> val g2 = GraphFrame(v2, e2)
scala> val results = g2.pageRank.resetProbability(0.15).tol(0.01).run()
scala> val prank = results.vertices.sort(desc("pagerank"))
scala> prank.take(10).foreach(println)
```

```
[1857444000,Book,Art of Attack in Chess,19.15963251427946]
[1880673851,Book,My System: 21st Century Edition,18.07328127614439]
[0812917561,Book,Ideas Behind the Chess Openings : Algebraic Edition
(Chess),17.77792169452039]
[096290497X,Book,Discerning of Spirits,17.64175373421938]
[0345457684,Book,Altered Carbon,16.11861824590565]
[0793521610,Book,Building a Jazz Vocabulary,14.999654656171334]
[0812579844,Book,The Golden Age (The Golden Age, Book 1),14.91395417693351]
[0553382136,Book,Spin State,14.641071672237276]
[0684135051,Book,Knitting Without Tears : Basic Techniques and Easy-to-Follow
Directions for Garments to Fit All Sizes (Knitting Without Tears SL
466),14.397031132425692]
[0884893723,Book,Understanding Catholic Christianity,13.957694196742478]
```

Understanding GraphFrame internals

In the following sections, we briefly present GraphFrame internals with respect to its
execution plan and partitioning.

Viewing GraphFrame physical execution plan

As the GraphFrames are built on Spark SQL DataFrames, we can view the physical plan to
understand the execution of the graph operations, as shown:

```
scala> g.edges.filter("salerank < 100").explain()
```

```
== Physical Plan ==
*Project [ASIN#0 AS src#37, dst#40]
+- Generate explode(similarLines#8.similar), true, false, [dst#40]
   +- *Project [ASIN#0, similarLines#8]
      +- *Filter (isnotnull(salerank#7L) && (salerank#7L < 100))
         +- *FileScan json [ASIN#0,salerank#7L,similarLines#8] Batched: false, Format:
JSON, Location: InMemoryFileIndex[file:/Users/aurobindosarkar/Downloads/input.json],
PartitionFilters: [], PushedFilters: [IsNotNull(salerank), LessThan(salerank,100)],
ReadSchema:
struct<ASIN:string,salerank:bigint,similarLines:array<struct<similar:string>>>
```

We will explore this in more detail in `Chapter 11`, *Tuning Spark SQL Components for
Performance*.

Understanding partitioning in GraphFrames

Spark splits data into partitions and executes computations on the partitions in parallel. You can adjust the level of partitioning to improve the efficiency of Spark computations.

In the following example, we examine the results of repartitioning a GraphFrame. We can partition our GraphFrame based on the column values of the vertices DataFrame. Here, we use the values in the group column to partition by group or product type. Here, we will present the results of repartitioning by comparing the before and after distribution of the records.

First, we create the two GraphFrames as shown. As there are nulls in the group column, we replace them with a value of unknown:

```scala
scala> val v1 = g.vertices.select("id", "group").na.fill("unknown")
scala> val g1 = GraphFrame(v1, g.edges)
```

Next, we create the second GraphFrame after repartitioning the original GraphFrame. Here, we use the number of groups as our initial number of partitions:

```scala
scala> val v2 = g.vertices.select("id", "group").na.fill("unknown")
scala> val g2t1 = GraphFrame(v2, g.edges)
scala> val g2t2 = g2t1.vertices.repartition(11, $"group")
scala> val g2 = GraphFrame(g2t2, g.edges)
```

Displaying the vertices in the following two graphs shows that the records are bunched together by groups in the second graph:

```scala
scala> g1.vertices.show()
+----------+-------+
|        id|  group|
+----------+-------+
|0771044445|unknown|
|0827229534|   Book|
|0738700797|   Book|
|0486287785|   Book|
|0842328327|   Book|
|1577943082|   Book|
|0486220125|   Book|
|B00000AU3R|  Music|
|0231118597|   Book|
|1859677800|   Book|
|0375709363|   Book|
|0871318237|   Book|
|1590770218|   Book|
|0313230269|   Book|
|B00004W1W1|  Music|
```

```
|1559362022|    Book|
|0195110382|    Book|
|0849311012|    Book|
|B000007R0T|   Music|
|078510870X|    Book|
+----------+------+
only showing top 20 rows
scala> g2.vertices.show()
+----------+-----+
|        id| group|
+----------+-----+
|6303360041|Video|
|B0000060T5|Video|
|6304286961|Video|
|B000063W82|Video|
|B0000060TP|Video|
|0970911300|Video|
|B00000IBNZ|Video|
|B00000IC8N|Video|
|6303454488|Video|
|B00005LAF3|Video|
|6304733542|Video|
|6301045734|Video|
|6301967917|Video|
|6304702329|Video|
|0792296176|Video|
|6301966422|Video|
|B00000I9PH|Video|
|6303864120|Video|
|6304972857|Video|
|6301701720|Video|
+----------+-----+
only showing top 20 rows
```

The default number of partitions in the first graph is 9 and in the second, as specified, there are 11:

```
scala> g1.vertices.rdd.partitions.size
res85: Int = 9
scala> g2.vertices.rdd.partitions.size
res86: Int = 11
```

We can also write out the contents of the partitions to files to explore their contents, as shown:

```scala
scala>
g1.vertices.write.csv("file:///Users/aurobindosarkar/Downloads/g1/partition
s")
scala>
g2.vertices.write.csv("file:///Users/aurobindosarkar/Downloads/g2/partition
s")
```

The sample contents of a partition from one of the output files are listed here for the first graph showing a mix of records:

```
0771044445,unknown
0827229534,Book
0738700797,Book
0486287785,Book
0842328327,Book
1577943082,Book
0486220125,Book
B00000AU3R,Music
0231118597,Book
1859677800,Book
0375709363,Book
0871318237,Book
1590770218,Book
0313230269,Book
B00004W1W1,Music
.


.
B000053SPI,Music
1552126463,Book
1885588437,Book
1898323496,Book
0764224115,Book
0451409221,Book
1585674338,Book
B00004YR7L,Music
087793486X,Book
0793554098,Book
B00004YR7I,Music
0253214882,Book
```

The sample contents of a partition from one of the output files are listed here for the second graph showing records belonging to the same group:

```
0827229534,Book
0738700797,Book
0486287785,Book
0842328327,Book
1577943082,Book
0486220125,Book
0231118597,Book
1859677800,Book
0375709363,Book
0871318237,Book
1590770218,Book
0313230269,Book
1559362022,Book
0195110382,Book
0849311012,Book
078510870X,Book
3895780812,Book
0393049388,Book
0553525476,Book
.
.
.
0310208084,Book
0006176909,Book
0786632550,Book
0752808990,Book
4770023286,Book
0838409342,Book
0552139432,Book
B00006RGI2,Book
B000067JZT,Book
B00008MNUJ,Book
0060537612,Book
9700507734,Book
9627762644,Book
0970020503,Book
1930519206,Book
0879736836,Book
```

We notice that most of our records are in five main product groups and we may want to reduce the total number of partitions. We use the coalesce operation to achieve that, as shown:

```
scala> val g2c = g2.vertices.coalesce(5)
scala> g2c.rdd.partitions.size
res90: Int = 5
```

Summary

In this chapter, we introduced GraphFrame applications. We provided examples of using Spark SQL DataFrame/Dataset APIs to build graph applications. Additionally, we also applied various graph algorithms to graph applications.

In the next chapter, we will shift our focus to using Spark SQL with SparkR. Additionally, we will explore typical use cases and data visualization using Spark SQL and SparkR.

8
Using Spark SQL with SparkR

Many data scientists use R to perform exploratory data analysis, data visualization, data munging, data processing, and machine learning tasks. SparkR is an R package that enables practitioners to work with data by leveraging the Apache Spark's distributed processing capabilities. In this chapter, we will cover SparkR (an R frontend package) that leverages Spark's engine to perform data analysis at scale. We will also describe the key elements of SparkR's design and implementation.

More specifically, in this chapter, you will learn the following topics:

- What is SparkR?
- Understanding the SparkR architecture
- Understanding SparkR DataFrames
- Using SparkR for **Exploratory Data Analysis** (**EDA**) and data munging tasks
- Using SparkR for data visualization
- Using SparkR for machine learning

Introducing SparkR

R is a language and environment for statistical computing and data visualization. It is one of the most popular tools used by statisticians and data scientists. R is open source and provides a dynamic interactive environment with a rich set of packages and powerful visualization features. It is an interpreted language that includes extensive support for numerical computing, with data types for vectors, matrices, arrays, and libraries for performing numerical operations.

R provides support for structured data processing using DataFrames. R DataFrames make data manipulation simpler and more convenient. However, R's dynamic design limits the extent of possible optimizations. Additionally, interactive data analysis capabilities and overall scalability are also limited, as the R runtime is single threaded and can only process Datasets that fit in a single machine's memory.

 For more details on R, refer to the *R project website* at https://www.r-project.org/about.html.

SparkR addresses these shortcomings to enable data scientists to work with data at scale in a distributed environment. SparkR is an R package that provides a light-weight frontend so you can use Apache Spark from R. It combines Spark's distributed processing features, easy connectivity to varied data sources, and off-memory data structures with R's dynamic environment, interactivity, packages, and visualization features.

Traditionally, data scientists have been using R with other frameworks, such as Hadoop MapReduce, Hive, Pig, and so on. However, with SparkR, they can avoid using multiple big data tools and platforms, and working in multiple different languages to accomplish their objectives. SparkR allows them to do their work in R and use Spark's distributed computation model.

SparkR interfaces are similar to R and R packages rather than the Python/Scala/Java interfaces we have encountered thus far. SparkR implements a distributed dataframe that supports operations, such as statistical computations, selection of columns, SQL execution, filtering rows, performs aggregations, and so on, on large Datasets.

SparkR supports conversion to/from local R DataFrames. The tight integration of SparkR with the Spark project enables SparkR to reuse other Spark modules, including Spark SQL, MLlib, and so on. Additionally, the Spark SQL data sources API enables reading input from a variety of sources, such as HDFS, HBase, Cassandra, and file formats, such as CSV, JSON, Parquet, Avro, and so on.

In the next section, we present a brief overview of the SparkR architecture.

Understanding the SparkR architecture

SparkR's distributed DataFrame enables programming syntax that is familiar to R users. The high-level DataFrame API integrates the R API with the optimized SQL execution engine in Spark.

SparkR's architecture primarily consists of two components: an R to JVM binding on the driver that enables R programs to submit jobs to a Spark cluster and support for running R on the Spark executors.

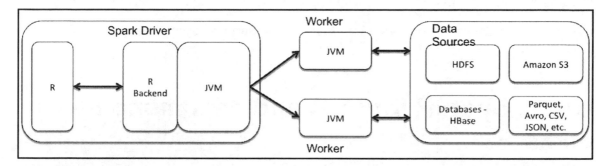

SparkR's design consists of support for launching **R** processes on Spark executor machines. However, there is an overhead associated with serializing the query and deserializing the results after they have been computed. As the amount of data transferred between **R** and the **JVM** increases, these overheads can become more significant as well. However, caching can enable efficient interactive query processing in SparkR.

 For a detailed description of SparkR design and implementation, refer: "SparkR: Scaling R Programs with Spark" by Shivaram Venkataraman1, Zongheng Yang, *et al*, available at: `https://cs.stanford.edu/~matei/papers/2016/sigmod_sparkr.pdf`.

In the next section, we next present an overview of the distributed DataFrame component of SparkR - the Spark DataFrames.

Understanding SparkR DataFrames

The main component of SparkR is a distributed DataFrame called **SparkR DataFrames**. The Spark DataFrame API is similar to local R DataFrames but scales to large Datasets using Spark's execution engine and the relational query optimizer. It is a distributed collection of data organized into columns similar to a relational database table or an R DataFrame.

Spark DataFrames can be created from many different data sources, such as data files, databases, R DataFrames, and so on. After the data is loaded, developers can use familiar R syntax for performing various operations, such as filtering, aggregations, and merges. SparkR performs a lazy evaluation on DataFrame operations.

Furthermore, SparkR supports many functions on DataFrames, including statistical functions. We can also use libraries such as magrittr to chain commands. Developers can execute SQL queries on SparkR DataFrames using the SQL commands. Finally, SparkR DataFrames can be converted into a local R DataFrame by using the collect operator.

In the next section, we introduce typical SparkR programming operations used in EDA and data munging tasks.

Using SparkR for EDA and data munging tasks

In this section, we will use Spark SQL and SparkR for preliminary exploration of our Datasets. The examples in this chapter use several publically available Datasets to illustrate the operations and can be run in the SparkR shell.

The entry point into SparkR is the SparkSession. It connects the R program to a Spark cluster. If you are working in the SparkR shell, the SparkSession is already created for you.

At this time, start SparkR shell, as shown:

```
Aurobindos-MacBook-Pro-2:spark-2.2.0-bin-hadoop2.7
aurobindosarkar$./bin/SparkR
```

You can install the required libraries, such as ggplot2, in your SparkR shell, as shown:

```
> install.packages('ggplot2', dep = TRUE)
```

Reading and writing Spark DataFrames

SparkR supports operating on a variety of data sources through the Spark DataFrames interface. SparkR's DataFrames supports a number of methods to read input, perform structured data analysis, and write DataFrames to the distributed storage.

The `read.df` method can be used for creating Spark DataFrames from a variety of data sources. We will need to specify the path to the input data file and the type of data source. The data sources API natively supports formats, such as CSV, JSON, and Parquet.

A complete list of functions can be found in the API docs available at: `http://spark.apache.org/docs/latest/api/R/`. For the initial set of code examples, we will use the Dataset from `Chapter 3`, *Using Spark SQL for Data Exploration*, that contains data related to the direct marketing campaigns (phone calls) of a Portuguese banking institution.

The input file is in **Comma-Separated values (CSV)** format contains a header and the fields are delimited by a semicolon. The input file can be any of the Spark data sources; for example, if it is JSON or Parquet format, then we just need to change the source parameter to `json` or `parquet`, respectively.

We can create a `SparkDataFrame` by loading our input CSV file using `read.df`, as shown:

```
> csvPath <- "file:///Users/aurobindosarkar/Downloads/bank-additional/bank-
additional-full.csv"

> df <- read.df(csvPath, "csv", header = "true", inferSchema = "true",
na.strings = "NA", delimiter= ";")
```

Similarly, we can write the DataFrame to the distributed storage using `write.df`. We specify the output DataFrame name and format in the source parameter (as in the `read.df` function).

The data sources API can be used to save the Spark DataFrames into multiple different file formats. For example, we can save the Spark DataFrame created in the previous step to a Parquet file using `write.df`:

```
write.df(df, path =
"hdfs://localhost:9000/Users/aurobindosarkar/Downloads/df.parquet", source
= "parquet", mode = "overwrite")
```

The `read.df` and `write.df` functions are used to bring data from the storage to the workers and write data from the workers to the storage, respectively. It does not bring this data into the R process.

Exploring structure and contents of Spark DataFrames

In this section, we explore the dimensions, schema, and data contained in the Spark DataFrames.

First, we cache the Spark DataFrame for performance using either the cache or the persist function. We can also specify storage level options, such as DISK_ONLY, MEMORY_ONLY, MEMORY_AND_DISK, and so on, as shown here:

```
> persist(df, "MEMORY_ONLY")
```

We can list the columns and associated data types of the Spark DataFrames by typing the name of the DataFrame, as shown here:

```
> df
```

Spark DataFrames[**age**:int, **job**:string, **marital**:string, **education**:string, **default**:string, **housing**:string, **loan**:string, **contact**:string, **month**:string, **day_of_week**:string, **duration**:int, **campaign**:int, **pdays**:int, **previous**:int, **poutcome**:string, **emp.var.rate**:double, **cons.price.idx**:double, **cons.conf.idx:double**, **euribor3m**:double, **nr.employed**:double, **y**:string]

SparkR can automatically infer the schema from the input file's header row. We can print the DataFrame schema, as shown here:

```
> printSchema(df)
```

```
root
 |-- age: integer (nullable = true)
 |-- job: string (nullable = true)
 |-- marital: string (nullable = true)
 |-- education: string (nullable = true)
 |-- default: string (nullable = true)
 |-- housing: string (nullable = true)
 |-- loan: string (nullable = true)
 |-- contact: string (nullable = true)
 |-- month: string (nullable = true)
 |-- day_of_week: string (nullable = true)
 |-- duration: integer (nullable = true)
 |-- campaign: integer (nullable = true)
 |-- pdays: integer (nullable = true)
 |-- previous: integer (nullable = true)
 |-- poutcome: string (nullable = true)
 |-- emp.var.rate: double (nullable = true)
 |-- cons.price.idx: double (nullable = true)
 |-- cons.conf.idx: double (nullable = true)
 |-- euribor3m: double (nullable = true)
 |-- nr.employed: double (nullable = true)
 |-- y: string (nullable = true)
```

We can also display the names of the columns in our DataFrame using the `names` function, as shown here:

```
> names(df)
```

```
 [1] "age"            "job"            "marital"     "education"
 [5] "default"        "housing"        "loan"        "contact"
 [9] "month"          "day_of_week"    "duration"    "campaign"
[13] "pdays"          "previous"       "poutcome"    "emp.var.rate"
[17] "cons.price.idx" "cons.conf.idx"  "euribor3m"   "nr.employed"
[21] "y"              "durationMins"
```

Next, we display a few sample values (from each of the columns) and records from the Spark DataFrame, as shown here:

```
> str(df)
```

```
'SparkDataFrame': 21 variables:
 $ age            : int 56 57 37 40 56 45
 $ job            : chr "housemaid" "services" "services" "admin." "services" "services"
 $ marital        : chr "married" "married" "married" "married" "married" "married"
 $ education      : chr "basic.4y" "high.school" "high.school" "basic.6y" "high.school" "basic.9y"
 $ default        : chr "no" "unknown" "no" "no" "no" "unknown"
 $ housing        : chr "no" "no" "yes" "no" "no" "no"
 $ loan           : chr "no" "no" "no" "no" "yes" "no"
 $ contact        : chr "telephone" "telephone" "telephone" "telephone" "telephone" "telephone"
 $ month          : chr "may" "may" "may" "may" "may" "may"
 $ day_of_week    : chr "mon" "mon" "mon" "mon" "mon" "mon"
 $ duration       : int 261 149 226 151 307 198
 $ campaign       : int 1 1 1 1 1 1
 $ pdays          : int 999 999 999 999 999 999
 $ previous       : int 0 0 0 0 0 0
 $ poutcome       : chr "nonexistent" "nonexistent" "nonexistent" "nonexistent" "nonexistent"
"nonexistent"
 $ emp.var.rate   : num 1.1 1.1 1.1 1.1 1.1 1.1
 $ cons.price.idx : num 93.994 93.994 93.994 93.994 93.994 93.994
 $ cons.conf.idx  : num −36.4 −36.4 −36.4 −36.4 −36.4 −36.4
 $ euribor3m      : num 4.857 4.857 4.857 4.857 4.857 4.857
 $ nr.employed    : num 5191 5191 5191 5191 5191 5191
 $ y              : chr "no" "no" "no" "no" "no" "no"
```

```
> head(df, 2)
```

```
age         job marital   education default housing loan    contact month
1  56 housemaid married    basic.4y      no      no   no telephone   may
2  57  services married high.school unknown      no   no telephone   may
  day_of_week duration campaign pdays previous    poutcome emp.var.rate
1         mon      261        1   999        0 nonexistent          1.1
2         mon      149        1   999        0 nonexistent          1.1
  cons.price.idx cons.conf.idx euribor3m nr.employed  y
1         93.994         −36.4     4.857        5191 no
2         93.994         −36.4     4.857        5191 no
```

We can display the dimensions of the DataFrame, as shown. Executing dim after the cache or persist function with the MEMORY_ONLY option is a good way to ensure the DataFrame is loaded and kept in memory for faster operations:

```
> dim(df)
[1] 41188 21
```

We can also use the count or the nrow function to compute the number of rows in our DataFrame:

```
> count(df)
[1] 41188
```

```
> nrow(df)
[1] 41188
```

Additionally, we can use the `distinct` function to get the number of distinct values contained in the specified column:

```
> count(distinct(select(df, df$age)))
[1] 78
```

Running basic operations on Spark DataFrames

In this section, we use SparkR to execute some basic operations on Spark DataFrames, including aggregations, splits, and sampling. For example, we can select columns of interest from the DataFrame. Here, we select only the `education` column from the DataFrame:

```
> head(select(df, df$education))
education
1 basic.4y
2 high.school
3 high.school
4 basic.6y
5 high.school
6 basic.9y
```

Alternatively, we can also specify the column name, as follows:

```
> head(select(df, "education"))
```

We can use the subset function to select rows meeting certain conditions, for example, rows with `marital` status `married`, as shown here:

```
> subsetMarried <- subset(df, df$marital == "married")

> head(subsetMarried, 2)
```

age	job	marital	education	default	housing	loan	contact	month
1 56	housemaid	married	basic.4y	no	no	no	telephone	may
2 57	services	married	high.school	unknown	no	no	telephone	may

	day_of_week	duration	campaign	pdays	previous	poutcome	emp.var.rate
1	mon	261	1	999	0	nonexistent	1.1
2	mon	149	1	999	0	nonexistent	1.1

	cons.price.idx	cons.conf.idx	euribor3m	nr.employed	y
1	93.994	−36.4	4.857	5191	no
2	93.994	−36.4	4.857	5191	no

We can use the filter function to only retain rows with education level basic.4y, as shown here:

```
> head(filter(df, df$education == "basic.4y"), 2)
```

```
age        job  marital education default housing loan   contact month
1  56 housemaid  married  basic.4y      no      no   no telephone   may
2  57 housemaid divorced  basic.4y      no     yes   no telephone   may
  day_of_week duration campaign pdays previous     poutcome emp.var.rate
1         mon      261        1   999        0 nonexistent          1.1
2         mon      293        1   999        0 nonexistent          1.1
  cons.price.idx cons.conf.idx euribor3m nr.employed   y
1         93.994         -36.4     4.857        5191  no
2         93.994         -36.4     4.857        5191  no
```

SparkR DataFrames support a number of common aggregations on the data after grouping. For example, we can compute a histogram of the marital status values in the Dataset, as follows. Here, we use the n operator to count the number of times each marital status appears:

```
> maritaldf <- agg(groupBy(df, df$marital), count = n(df$marital))

> head(maritaldf)
marital count
1 unknown 80
2 divorced 4612
3 married 24928
4 single 11568
```

We can also sort the output from the aggregation to get the most common set of marital statuses, as shown here:

```
> maritalCounts <- summarize(groupBy(df, df$marital), count =
n(df$marital))

> nMarriedCategories <- count(maritalCounts)

> head(arrange(maritalCounts, desc(maritalCounts$count)), num =
nMarriedCategories)
marital count
1 married 24928
2 single 11568
3 divorced 4612
4 unknown 80
```

Next, we use the magrittr package to pipeline functions instead of nesting them, as follows.

First, install the `magrittr` package using the `install.packages` command, if the package is not installed already:

```
> install.packages("magrittr")
```

Note that when loading and attaching a new package in R, it is possible to have a name conflict, where a function is masking another function. Depending on the load order of the two packages, some functions from the package loaded first are masked by those in the package loaded after. In such cases, we need to prefix such calls with the package name:

```
> library(magrittr)
```

We pipeline the `filter`, `groupBy`, and the `summarize` functions, as shown in the following example:

```
> educationdf <- filter(df, df$education == "basic.4y") %>%
groupBy(df$marital) %>% summarize(count = n(df$marital))

> head(educationdf)
```

```
  marital count
1  unknown     6
2 divorced   489
3  married  3228
4   single   453
```

Next, we create a local DataFrame from the distributed Spark version we have been working with so far. We use the `collect` function to move Spark DataFrame to a local/R DataFrame on the Spark driver, as shown. Typically, you would summarize or take a sample of your data before moving it to a local DataFrame:

```
> collect(summarize(df,avg_age = mean(df$age)))
avg_age
1 40.02406
```

We can create a `sample` from our DataFrame and move it to a local DataFrame, as shown. Here, we take 10% of the input records and create a local DataFrame from it:

```
> ls1df <- collect(sample(df, FALSE, 0.1, 11L))
> nrow(df)
[1] 41188
> nrow(ls1df)
[1] 4157
```

SparkR also provides a number of functions that can directly be applied to the columns for data processing and aggregations.

For example, we can add a new column to our DataFrame containing a new column with the call duration converted from seconds to minutes, as shown here:

```
> df$durationMins <- round(df$duration / 60)

> head(df, 2)
```

The following is the output obtained:

```
age        job marital    education default housing loan   contact month
1  56 housemaid married     basic.4y      no      no   no telephone   may
2  57  services married high.school unknown      no   no telephone   may
  day_of_week duration campaign pdays previous    poutcome emp.var.rate
1         mon      261        1   999        0 nonexistent         1.1
2         mon      149        1   999        0 nonexistent         1.1
  cons.price.idx cons.conf.idx euribor3m nr.employed y durationMins
1         93.994         -36.4     4.857        5191 no            4
2         93.994         -36.4     4.857        5191 no            2
```

Executing SQL statements on Spark DataFrames

A Spark DataFrames can also be registered as a temporary view in Spark SQL that allows us to run SQL queries over its data. The `sql` function enables applications to run SQL queries programmatically and return the result as a Spark DataFrame.

First, we register the Spark DataFrame as a temporary view:

```
> createOrReplaceTempView(df, "customer")
```

Next, we execute the SQL statements using the `sql` function. For example, we select the `education`, `age`, `marital`, `housing`, and `loan` columns for customers aged between 13 and 19 years, as shown here:

```
> sqldf <- sql("SELECT education, age, marital, housing, loan FROM customer
WHERE age >= 13 AND age <= 19")

> head(sqldf)
```

```
  education age marital housing loan
1   basic.9y  19  single     yes   no
2 high.school  18  single      no   no
3 high.school  18  single     yes  yes
4   basic.9y  19  single     yes   no
5   basic.6y  19  single      no   no
6   basic.9y  19  single      no   no
```

Merging SparkR DataFrames

We can explicitly specify the columns that SparkR should merge the DataFrames on using the operation parameters by and by.x/by.y. The merge operation determines how SparkR should merge DataFrames based on the values, all.x and all.y, which indicate which rows in x and y should be included in the join, respectively. For example, we can specify an inner join (default) by explicitly specifying all.x = FALSE, all.y = FALSE, or a left outer join with all.x = TRUE, all.y = FALSE.

For more details on join and merge operations, refer to https://github. com/UrbanInstitute/sparkr-tutorials/blob/master/merging.md.

Alternatively, we can also use the join operation to merge the DataFrames by row.

For the following example, we use the crimes Dataset available at: https://archive.ics. uci.edu/ml/Datasets/Communities+and+Crime+Unnormalized.

As before, we read in the input Dataset, as shown here:

```
> library(magrittr)
> csvPath <-
"file:///Users/aurobindosarkar/Downloads/CommViolPredUnnormalizedData.csv"
> df <- read.df(csvPath, "csv", header = "false", inferSchema = "false",
na.strings = "NA", delimiter= ",")
```

Next, we select specific columns related to the type of crime and rename the default column names to more meaningful names, as shown here:

```
> crimesStatesSubset = subset(df, select = c(1,2, 130, 132, 134, 136, 138,
140, 142, 144))
```

```
> crimesStatesdf <- withColumnRenamed(crimesStatesSubset, "_c0", "comm") %>%
withColumnRenamed("_c1", "code") %>% withColumnRenamed("_c1", "st")  %>%
withColumnRenamed("_c129", "nmurders")  %>% withColumnRenamed("_c131", "nrapes")  %>%
withColumnRenamed("_c133", "nrobberies")  %>% withColumnRenamed("_c135", "nassaults")
%>% withColumnRenamed("_c137", "nburglaries")  %>% withColumnRenamed("_c139",
"nlarcenies")  %>% withColumnRenamed("_c141", "nautothefts")  %>%
withColumnRenamed("_c143", "narsons")
```

```
> head(crimesStatesdf, 2)
```

```
                     comm code nmurders nrapes nrobberies nassaults nburglaries
1 BerkeleyHeightstownship   NJ        0      0          1         4          14
2         Marpletownship   PA        0      1          5        24          57
  nlarcenies nautothefts narsons
1        138          16       2
2        376          26       1
```

Next, we read in a Dataset containing the names of US states, as shown here:

```
> state_names <-
read.df("file:///Users/aurobindosarkar/downloads/csv_hus/states.csv",
"csv", header = "true", inferSchema = "true", na.strings = "NA", delimiter=
",")
```

We list out the columns of the two DataFrames using the names function. The common column between the two DataFrames is the "code" column (containing state codes):

```
> names(crimesStatesdf)
[1] "comm" "code" "nmurders" "nrapes" "nrobberies"
[6] "nassaults" "nburglaries" "nlarcenies" "nautothefts" "narsons"

> names(state_names)
[1] "st" "name" "code"
```

Next, we perform an inner join using the common column:

```
> m1df <- merge(crimesStatesdf, state_names)
> head(m1df, 2)
```

```
            comm code_x nmurders nrapes nrobberies nassaults nburglaries
1 Anchoragecity     AK       23    212        568      1410        1880
2    Juneaucity     AK        0     12          3        18         128
  nlarcenies nautothefts narsons st   name code_y
1      10660        1387     105  2 Alaska     AK
2        857          59       7  2 Alaska     AK
```

Here, we perform an inner join based on specifying the expression explicitly:

```
> m2df <- merge(crimesStatesdf, state_names, by = "code")
> head(m2df, 2)
```

```
            comm code_x nmurders nrapes nrobberies nassaults nburglaries
1 Anchoragecity     AK       23    212        568      1410        1880
2    Juneaucity     AK        0     12          3        18         128
  nlarcenies nautothefts narsons st   name code_y
1      10660        1387     105  2 Alaska     AK
2        857          59       7  2 Alaska     AK
```

For the following example, we use the tennis tournament match statistics Dataset available at: `http://archive.ics.uci.edu/ml/Datasets/ Tennis+Major+Tournament+Match+Statistics`.

The following is the output obtained:

```
> library(magrittr)
> usPath <- "file:///Users/aurobindosarkar/Downloads/Tennis-Major-Tournaments-Match-Statistics/USOpen-women-2013.csv"
> usdf <- read.df(usPath, "csv", header = "true", inferSchema = "true", na.strings = "NA", delimiter= ",")
> ussubdf <- select(usdf, "Player 1", "Player 2", "ROUND", "Result")%>% withColumnRenamed("Player 1", "p1") %>%
withColumnRenamed("Player 2", "p2")
> showDF(ussubdf, 2)
+----------+----------+-----+------+
|       p1|        p2|ROUND|Result|
+----------+----------+-----+------+
|S Williams|V Azarenka|    7|     1|
|F Pennetta|V Azarenka|    6|     0|
+----------+----------+-----+------+
only showing top 2 rows
> wimPath <- "file:///Users/aurobindosarkar/Downloads/Tennis-Major-Tournaments-Match-Statistics/Wimbledon-women-2013.csv"
> wimdf <- read.df(wimPath, "csv", header = "true", inferSchema = "true", na.strings = "NA", delimiter= ",")
> wimsubdf <- select(usdf, "Player 1", "Player 2", "ROUND", "Result")%>% withColumnRenamed("Player 1", "p1") %>%
withColumnRenamed("Player 2", "p2")
> showDF(wimsubdf, 2)
+----------+----------+-----+------+
|       p1|        p2|ROUND|Result|
+----------+----------+-----+------+
|S Williams|V Azarenka|    7|     1|
|F Pennetta|V Azarenka|    6|     0|
+----------+----------+-----+------+
only showing top 2 rows

We can append the rows of wimsubdf to ussubdf using the rbind operation as shown below.

> df1 <- rbind(ussubdf, wimsubdf)
> showDF(df1, 2)
+----------+----------+-----+------+
|       p1|        p2|ROUND|Result|
+----------+----------+-----+------+
|S Williams|V Azarenka|    7|     1|
|F Pennetta|V Azarenka|    6|     0|
+----------+----------+-----+------+
only showing top 2 rows
```

Using User Defined Functions (UDFs)

In SparkR, several types of **User Defined Functions (UFDs)** are supported. For example, we can run a given function on a large Dataset using `dapply` or `dapplyCollect`. The `dapply` function applies a function to each partition of a Spark DataFrame. The output of the function should be a data.frame.

The schema specifies the row format of the resulting a Spark DataFrame:

```
> df1 <- select(df, df$duration)

> schema <- structType(structField("duration", "integer"),
+ structField("durMins", "double"))

> df2 <- dapply(df1, function(x) { x <- cbind(x, x$duration / 60) },
schema)
> head(collect(df2))
```

```
  duration  durMins
1      261 4.350000
2      149 2.483333
3      226 3.766667
4      151 2.516667
5      307 5.116667
6      198 3.300000
```

Similar to dapply, the `dapplyCollect` function applies the function to each partition of a Spark DataFrames and collects the result back. The output of the function should be a `data.frame` and the schema parameter is not required. Note that `dapplyCollect` can fail if the output of UDF cannot be transferred to the driver or fit in the driver's memory.

We can use `gapply` or `gapplyCollect` to run a given function on a large Dataset grouping by input columns. In the following example, we determine a set of top duration values:

```
> df1 <- select(df, df$duration, df$age)

> schema <- structType(structField("age", "integer"),
structField("maxDuration", "integer"))

> result <- gapply(
+ df1,
+ "age",
+ function(key, x) {
+ y <- data.frame(key, max(x$duration))
+ },
+ schema)
> head(collect(arrange(result, "maxDuration", decreasing = TRUE)))
```

```
  age maxDuration
1  33        4918
2  52        4199
3  27        3785
4  31        3643
5  37        3631
6  28        3509
```

The `gapplyCollect` similarly applies a function to each partition of a Spark DataFrames but also collects the result back to an R `data.frame`.

In the next section, we introduce SparkR functions to compute summary statistics for our example Datasets.

Using SparkR for computing summary statistics

The describe (or summary) operation creates a new DataFrame that contains count, mean, max, mean, and standard deviation values for a specified DataFrame or a list of numerical columns:

```
> sumstatsdf <- describe(df, "duration", "campaign", "previous", "age")

> showDF(sumstatsdf)
```

```
+-------+------------------+-----------------+-------------------+------------------+
|summary|          duration|         campaign|           previous|               age|
+-------+------------------+-----------------+-------------------+------------------+
|  count|             41188|            41188|              41188|             41188|
|   mean|258.2850101971448 |2.567592502670681|0.17296299893172767| 40.02406040594348|
| stddev|259.27924883646455|2.770013542902331|0.49490107983928927|10.421249980934057|
|    min|                 0|                1|                  0|                17|
|    max|              4918|               56|                  7|                98|
+-------+------------------+-----------------+-------------------+------------------+
```

Computing these values on a large Dataset can be computationally expensive. Hence, we present the individual computation of these statistical measures here:

```
> avgagedf <- agg(df, mean = mean(df$age))

> showDF(avgagedf) # Print this DF
+-----------------+
| mean            |
+-----------------+
|40.02406040594348|
+-----------------+
```

Next, we create a DataFrame that lists the minimum and maximum values and the range width:

```
> agerangedf <- agg(df, minimum = min(df$age), maximum = max(df$age),
range_width = abs(max(df$age) - min(df$age)))

> showDF(agerangedf)
```

Next, we compute the sample variance and standard deviation as shown here:

```
> agevardf <- agg(df, variance = var(df$age))

> showDF(agevardf)
+------------------+
| variance         |
+------------------+
|108.60245116511807|
+------------------+

> agesddf <- agg(df, std_dev = sd(df$age))

> showDF(agesddf)
+------------------+
| std_dev          |
+------------------+
|10.421249980934057|
+------------------+
```

The operation `approxQuantile` returns approximate quantiles for a DataFrame column. We specify the quantiles to be approximated using the probabilities parameter and the acceptable error by the `relativeError` parameter. We define a new DataFrame, `df1`, that drops missing values for `age` and then computes the approximate Q1, Q2, and Q3 values, as shown here:

```
> df1 <- dropna(df, cols = "age")

> quartilesdf <- approxQuantile(x = df1, col = "age", probabilities =
c(0.25, 0.5, 0.75), relativeError = 0.001)

> quartilesdf
[[1]]
[1] 32
[[2]]
[1] 38
[[3]]
[1] 47
```

We can measure the magnitude and the direction of the skew in the distribution of a column by using the `skewness` operation. In the following example, we measure the skewness for the `age` column:

```
> ageskdf <- agg(df, skewness = skewness(df$age))

> showDF(ageskdf)
+------------------+
| skewness         |
+------------------+
|0.7846682380932389|
+------------------+
```

Similarly, we can measure the kurtosis of a column. Here, we measure the kurtosis for the `age` column:

```
> agekrdf <- agg(df, kurtosis = kurtosis(df$age))

> showDF(agekrdf)
+------------------+
| kurtosis         |
+------------------+
|0.7910698035274022|
+------------------+
```

Next, we compute the sample covariance and correlation between two DataFrame columns. Here, we compute the covariance and correlation between the `age` and `duration` columns:

```
> covagedurdf <- cov(df, "age", "duration")

> corragedurdf <- corr(df, "age", "duration", method = "pearson")

> covagedurdf
[1] -2.339147

> corragedurdf
[1] -0.000865705
```

Next, we create a relative frequency table for the job column. The relative frequency for each distinct job category value is shown in the Percentage column:

```
> n <- nrow(df)

> jobrelfreqdf <- agg(groupBy(df, df$job), Count = n(df$job), Percentage = n(df$job) * (100/n))

> showDF(jobrelfreqdf)
```

```
+-------------+-----+------------------+
|         job|Count|        Percentage|
+-------------+-----+------------------+
|   management| 2924| 7.099155093716616|
|      retired| 1720| 4.175973584539186|
|      unknown|  330|0.8012042342429834|
|self-employed| 1421|3.4500339904826647|
|      student|  875|2.1244051665533648|
|  blue-collar| 9254| 22.46770904146839|
| entrepreneur| 1456|3.5350101971447994|
|       admin.|10422|25.303486452364766|
|   technician| 6743| 16.37127318636496|
|     services| 3969| 9.636301835486064|
|     housemaid| 1060|2.5735651160532194|
|   unemployed| 1014|2.4618821015829853|
+-------------+-----+------------------+
```

Finally, we create a contingency table between two categorical columns with the operation `crosstab`. In the following example, we create a contingency table for the job and marital columns:

```
> contabdf <- crosstab(df, "job", "marital")

> contabdf
```

```
   job_marital divorced married single unknown
1     housemaid      161     777    119       3
2      services      532    2294   1137       6
3 self-employed      133     904    379       5
4       student        9      41    824       1
5       retired      348    1274     93       5
6       unknown       13     234     74       9
7        admin.     1280    5253   3875      14
8   blue-collar      728    6687   1825      14
9    technician      774    3670   2287      12
10  entrepreneur      179    1071    203       3
11   management      331    2089    501       3
12   unemployed      124     634    251       5
```

In the next section, we use SparkR to execute various data visualization tasks.

Using SparkR for data visualization

The SparkR extension of the ggplot2 package, `ggplot2.SparkR`, allows SparkR users to build powerful visualizations.

In this section, we use various plots to visualize our data. Additionally, we also present examples of plotting of data on maps and visualizing graphs:

```
> csvPath <- "file:///Users/aurobindosarkar/Downloads/bank-additional/bank-additional-full.csv"

> df <- read.df(csvPath, "csv", header = "true", inferSchema = "true", na.strings = "NA", delimiter= ";")

> persist(df, "MEMORY_ONLY")

> require(ggplot2)
```

 Refer to the ggplot website for different options available to improve the displays of each of your plots at `http://docs.ggplot2.org`.

In the next step, we plot a basic bar graph that gives frequency counts for the different marital statuses in the data:

```
> ldf <- collect(select(df, df$age, df$duration, df$education, df$marital, df$job))

> g1 <- ggplot(ldf, aes(x = marital))

> g1 + geom_bar()
```

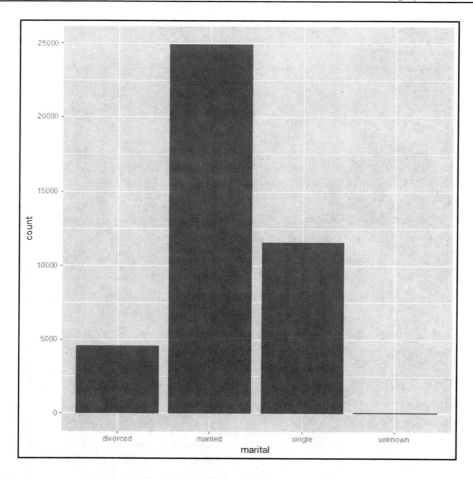

In the following example, we plot a histogram for the **age** column and several bar graphs that give frequency counts for the education, marital status, and job values:

```
> library(MASS)

> par(mfrow=c(2,2))

> truehist(ldf$"age", h = 5, col="slategray3", xlab="Age Groups(5 years)")

> barplot((table(ldf$education)), names.arg=c("1", "2", "3", "4", "5", "6",
"7", "8"), col=c("slateblue", "slateblue2", "slateblue3", "slateblue4",
"slategray", "slategray2", "slategray3", "slategray4"), main="Education")

> barplot((table(ldf$marital)), names.arg=c("Divorce", "Married", "Single",
"Unknown"), col=c("slategray", "slategray1", "slategray2", "slategray3"),
main="Marital Status")
```

```
> barplot((table(ldf$job)), , names.arg=c("1", "2", "3", "4", "5", "6",
"7", "8", "9", "a", "b", "c"), main="Job")
```

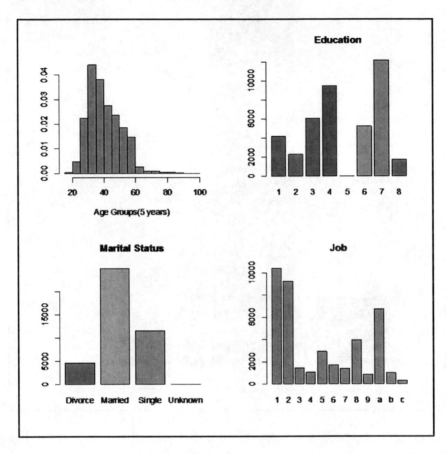

The following expression creates a bar graph that describes the proportional frequency of education levels grouped over marital types:

```
> g2 <- ggplot(ldf, aes(x = marital, fill = education))

> g2 + geom_bar(position = "fill")
```

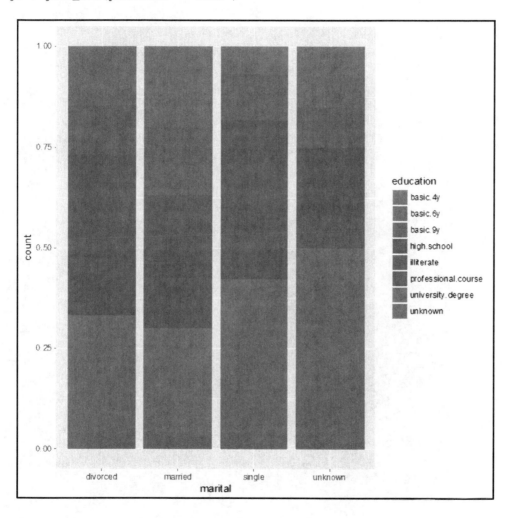

The following expression plots a histogram that gives frequency counts across binned **age** values in the data:

```
> g3 <- ggplot(ldf, aes(age))
```

```
> g3 + geom_histogram(binwidth=5)
```

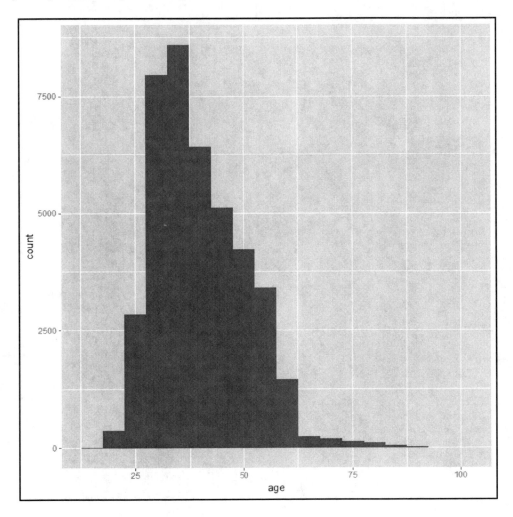

The following expression returns a frequency polygon equivalent to the histogram plotted previously:

```
> g3 + geom_freqpoly(binwidth=5)
```

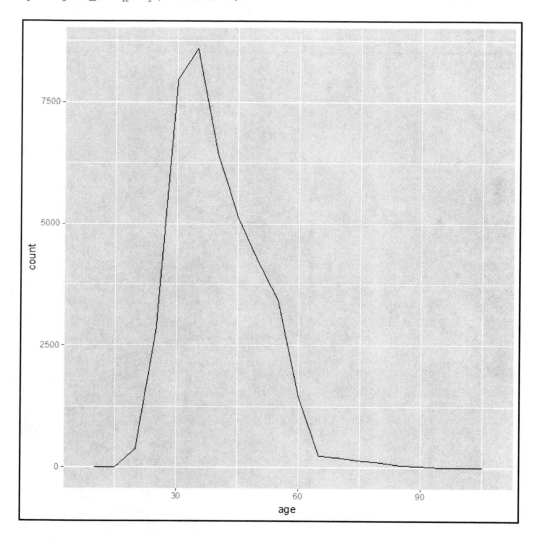

The following expression gives a boxplot of call duration values across types of **marital** statuses:

```
> g4 <- ggplot(ldf, aes(x = marital, y = duration))

> g4 + geom_boxplot()
```

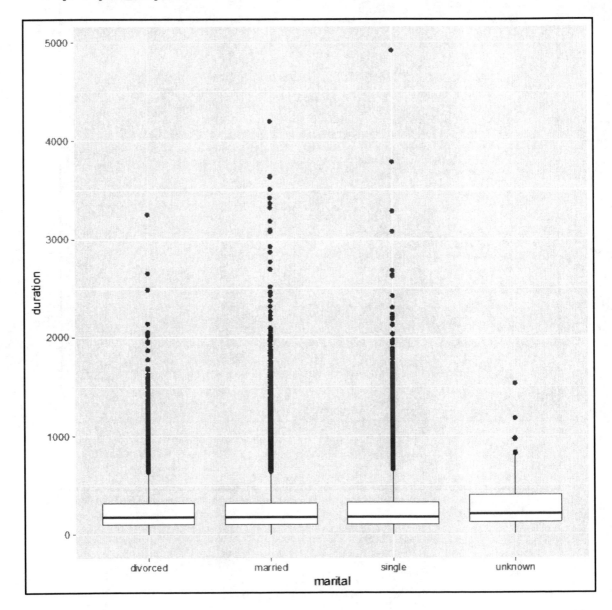

The following expression facets age histograms across different levels of education:

```
> g3 + geom_histogram() + facet_wrap(~education)
```

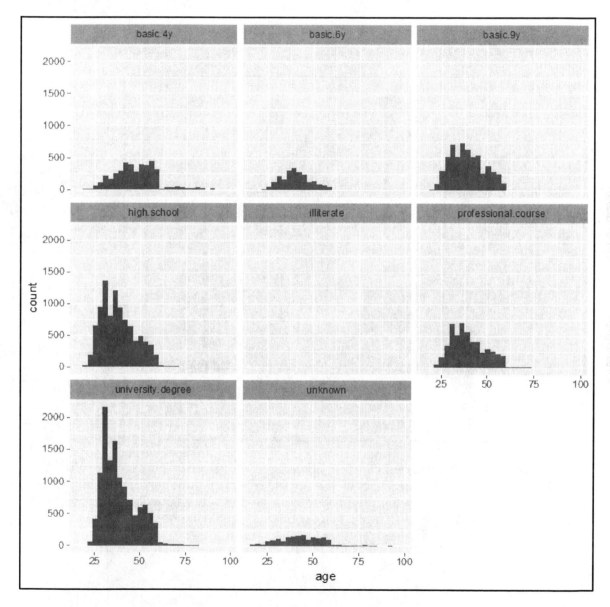

In the following example, we show several box plots simultaneously for different columns:

```
> par(mfrow=c(1,2))

> boxplot(ldf$age, col="slategray2", pch=19, main="Age")

> boxplot(ldf$duration, col="slategray2", pch=19, main="Duration")
```

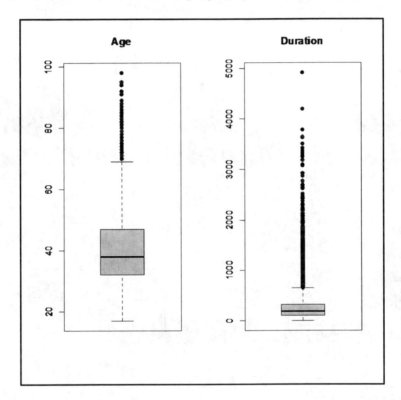

When building expressions or functions in SparkR, we should avoid computationally expensive operations. For example, even though the collect operation in SparkR allows us to leverage ggplot2 features, we should collect data as sparingly as possible, since we need to ensure the operation results fit into a single node's available memory.

The problem with the following scatterplot is overplotting. The points are plotted on top of one another, distorting the visual appearance of the plot. We can adjust the value of the alpha parameter to use transparent points:

```
> ggplot(ldf, aes(age, duration)) + geom_point(alpha = 0.3) +
stat_smooth() I
```

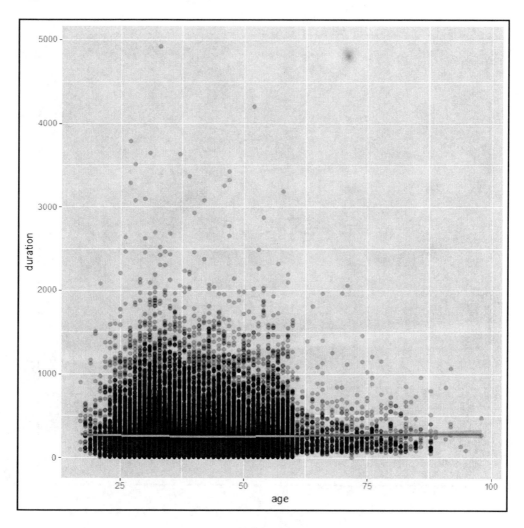

To display as a two-dimensional set of panels or to wrap the panels into multiple rows, we use `facet_wrap`:

```
> ageAndDurationValuesByMarital <- ggplot(ldf, aes(age, duration)) +
geom_point(alpha = "0.2") + facet_wrap(~marital)

> ageAndDurationValuesByMarital
```

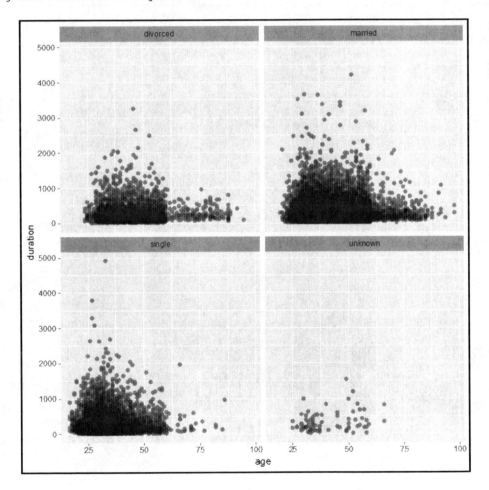

The adjusted alpha-value improves the visualization of scatterplots; however, we can summarize the points to average values and plot them to get a much clearer visualization, as shown in the following example:

```
> createOrReplaceTempView(df, "customer")

> localAvgDurationEducationAgeDF <- collect(sql("select education, avg(age)
as avgAge, avg(duration) as avgDuration from customer group by education"))

> avgAgeAndDurationValuesByEducation <-
ggplot(localAvgDurationEducationAgeDF, aes(group=education, x=avgAge,
y=avgDuration)) + geom_point() +
geom_text(data=localAvgDurationEducationAgeDF, mapping=aes(x=avgAge,
y=avgDuration, label=education), size=2, vjust=2, hjust=0.75)

> avgAgeAndDurationValuesByEducation
```

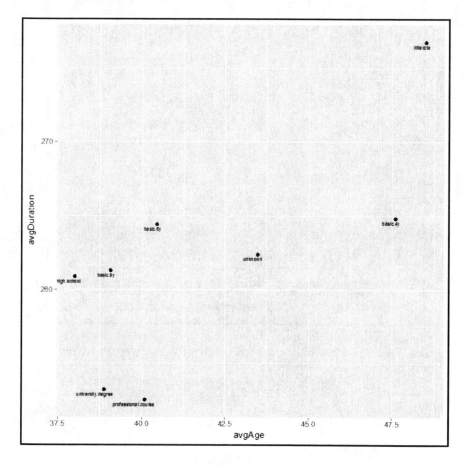

In the next example, we create a **Density plot** and overlay a line passing through the mean. Density plots are a good way to view the distribution of a variable; for example, in our example, we plot the call duration values:

```
> plot(density(ldf$duration), main = "Density Plot", xlab = "Duration",
yaxt = 'n')

> abline(v = mean(ldf$duration), col = 'green', lwd = 2)

> legend('topright', legend = c("Actual Data", "Mean"), fill = c('black',
'green'))
```

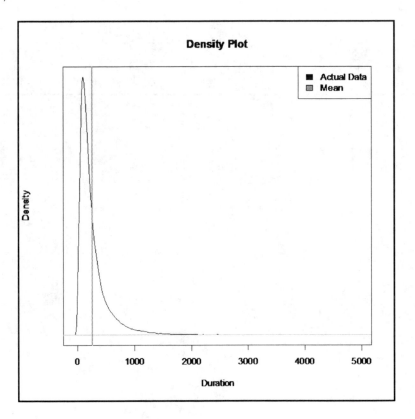

In the next section, we will present an example of plotting values on a map.

Visualizing data on a map

In this section, we describe how to merge two data sets and plot the results on a map:

```
> csvPath <-
"file:///Users/aurobindosarkar/Downloads/CommViolPredUnnormalizedData.csv"

> df <- read.df(csvPath, "csv", header = "false", inferSchema = "false",
na.strings = "NA", delimiter= ",")

> persist(df, "MEMORY_ONLY")

> xdf = select(df, "_c1","_c143")

> newDF <- withColumnRenamed(xdf, "_c1", "state")

> arsonsstatesdf <- withColumnRenamed(newDF, "_c143", "narsons")
```

The Dataset we want to visualize is the average number of arsons by state, as computed here:

```
> avgArsons <- collect(agg(groupBy(arsonsstatesdf, "state"),
AVG_ARSONS=avg(arsonsstatesdf$narsons)))
```

Next, we read `states.csv` Dataset into an R DataFrame:

```
> state_names <-
read.csv("file:///Users/aurobindosarkar/downloads/csv_hus/states.csv")
```

Next, we replace the state code with the state name using a `factor` variable:

```
> avgArsons$region <- factor(avgArsons$state, levels=state_names$code,
labels=tolower(state_names$name))
```

To create a map of the United States with the states colored according to the average number of arsons per state, we can use the `ggplot2`'s `map_data` function:

```
> states_map <- map_data("state")
```

Finally, we merge the Dataset with the map and use `ggplot` to display the map, as shown here:

```
> merged_data <- merge(states_map, avgArsons, by="region")

> ggplot(merged_data, aes(x = long, y = lat, group = group, fill =
AVG_ARSONS)) + geom_polygon(color = "white") + theme_bw()
```

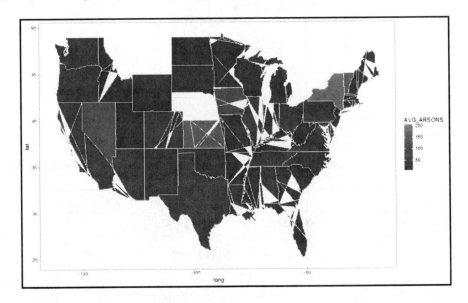

 For more on plotting on geographical maps, refer to the *Exploring geographical data using SparkR and ggplot2* by Jose A. Dianes at `https://www.codementor.io/spark/tutorial/exploratory-geographical-data-using-sparkr-and-ggplot2`.

In the next section, we present an example of graph visualization.

Visualizing graph nodes and edges

It is key to visualize graphs to get a sense of the overall structural properties. In this section, we will plot several graphs in the SparkR shell.

 For more details, refer to *Static and dynamic network visualization with R* by Katherine Ognynova at `http://kateto.net/network-visualization`.

For the following example, we use a Dataset containing the network of interactions on the stack exchange website Ask Ubuntu available at: `https://snap.stanford.edu/data/sx-askubuntu.html`.

We create a local DataFrame from ten percent sample of the data and create a plot of the graph, as shown here:

```
> library(igraph)

> library(magrittr)

> inDF <- read.df("file:///Users/aurobindosarkar/Downloads/sx-
askubuntu.txt", "csv", header="false", delimiter=" ")

> linksDF <- subset(inDF, select = c(1, 2)) %>% withColumnRenamed("_c0",
"src") %>% withColumnRenamed("_c1", "dst")

> llinksDF <- collect(sample(linksDF, FALSE, 0.01, 1L))

> g1 <- graph_from_data_frame(llinksDF, directed = TRUE, vertices = NULL)

> plot(g1, edge.arrow.size=.001, vertex.label=NA, vertex.size=0.1)
```

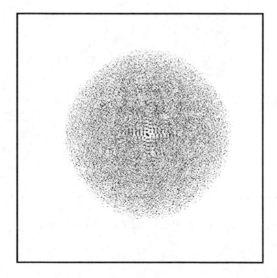

We can obtain a clearer visualization in this example by reducing the sample size further and removing certain edges, such as loops, as shown here:

```
> inDF <- read.df("file:///Users/aurobindosarkar/Downloads/sx-
askubuntu.txt", "csv", header="false", delimiter=" ")

> linksDF <- subset(inDF, select = c(1, 2)) %>% withColumnRenamed("_c0",
"src") %>% withColumnRenamed("_c1", "dst")

> llinksDF <- collect(sample(linksDF, FALSE, 0.0005, 1L))

> g1 <- graph_from_data_frame(llinksDF, directed = FALSE)

> g1 <- simplify(g1, remove.multiple = F, remove.loops = T)

> plot(g1, edge.color="black", vertex.color="red", vertex.label=NA,
vertex.size=2)
```

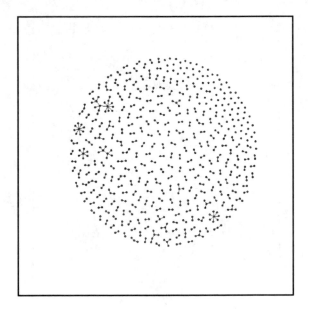

In the next section, we explore using SparkR for machine learning tasks.

Using SparkR for machine learning

SparkR supports a growing list of machine learning algorithms, such as **Generalized Linear Model (glm)**, Naive Bayes Model, K-Means Model, Logistic Regression Model, **Latent Dirichlet Allocation (LDA)** Model, Multilayer Perceptron Classification Model, Gradient Boosted Tree Model for Regression and Classification, Random Forest Model for Regression and Classification, **Alternating Least Squares (ALS)** matrix factorization Model, and so on.

SparkR uses Spark MLlib to train the model. The summary and predict functions are used to print a summary of the fitted model and make predictions on new data, respectively. The `write.ml`/`read.ml` operations can be used to save/load the fitted models. SparkR also supports a subset of the available R formula operators for model fitting, such as ~, ., :, +, and −.

For the following examples, we use a wine quality Dataset available at `https://archive.ics.uci.edu/ml/Datasets/Wine+Quality`:

```
> library(magrittr)

> csvPath <-
"file:///Users/aurobindosarkar/Downloads/winequality/winequality-white.csv"
```

```
> indf <- read.df(csvPath, "csv", header = "true", inferSchema = "true", na.strings =
"NA", delimiter= ";") %>% withColumnRenamed("fixed acidity", "fixed_acidity") %>%
withColumnRenamed("volatile acidity", "volatile_acidity") %>%
withColumnRenamed("citric acid", "citric_acid") %>% withColumnRenamed("residual
sugar", "residual_sugar") %>% withColumnRenamed("free sulfur dioxide",
"free_sulfur_dioxide") %>% withColumnRenamed("total sulfur dioxide",
"total_sulfur_dioxide")
```

```
> winedf <- mutate(indf, label = ifelse(indf$quality >= 6, 1, 0))

> winedf <- drop(winedf, "quality")

> seed <- 12345
```

We create the training and test DataFrames using the sample function, as shown here:

```
> trainingdf <- sample(winedf, withReplacement=FALSE, fraction=0.9,
seed=seed)

> testdf <- except(winedf, trainingdf)
```

Next, we fit a logistic regression model against a SparkDataFrame, as shown here:

```
> model <- spark.logit(trainingdf, label ~ ., maxIter = 10, regParam = 0.1,
elasticNetParam = 0.8)
```

Following, we use the summary function to print a summary of the fitted model:

```
> summary(model)
```

```
$coefficients
                     Estimate
(Intercept)          -0.6862963
fixed_acidity        0
volatile_acidity     0.3257158
citric_acid          0
residual_sugar       0
chlorides            0.3837135
free_sulfur_dioxide  0
total_sulfur_dioxide 3.210866e-08
density              0.5516459
pH                   0
sulphates            0
alcohol              -0.05705867
```

Next, we use the predict function to make predictions on the test DataFrame:

```
> predictions <- predict(model, testdf)
```

```
> showDF(select(predictions, "label", "rawPrediction", "probability",
"prediction"), 5)
```

```
+-----+--------------------+--------------------+----------+
|label|       rawPrediction|         probability|prediction|
+-----+--------------------+--------------------+----------+
|  0.0|[0.54081405225716...|[0.63200176671046...|       1.0|
|  1.0|[0.63103229228006...|[0.65272349447245...|       1.0|
|  1.0|[0.60251318150008...|[0.64623107184477...|       1.0|
|  1.0|[0.68397029023517...|[0.66462424819744...|       1.0|
|  1.0|[0.66050917673984...|[0.65937475866608...|       1.0|
+-----+--------------------+--------------------+----------+
```

only showing top 5 rows

Next, we count the number of mismatches between the labels and the predicted values:

```
> nrow(filter(predictions, predictions$label != predictions$prediction))
[1] 111
```

In the following example, we fit a Random Forest Classification model on a Spark DataFrames. We then use the `summary` function to get a summary of the fitted Random Forest model and the `predict` function to make predictions on the test data, as shown here:

```
> model <- spark.randomForest(trainingdf, label ~ ., type="classification",
maxDepth = 5, numTrees = 10)
```

```
> summary(model)
```

```
Formula:  label ~ .
Number of features:  11
Features:  fixed_acidity volatile_acidity citric_acid residual_sugar chlorides
free_sulfur_dioxide total_sulfur_dioxide density pH sulphates alcohol
Feature importances:
(11,[0,1,2,3,4,5,6,7,8,9,10],[0.016116203679387833,0.2000841279602036,0.06203377364164
843,0.04659246031382119,0.053967074218643885,0.09524761178321549,0.019576446849627522,
0.1974904528512302,0.02585073108815522,0.014956220347921618,0.26808489726614504])
Number of trees:  10
Tree weights:  1 1 1 1 1 1 1 1 1 1
 RandomForestClassificationModel (uid=rfc_caed094ec80d) with 10 trees
  Tree 0 (weight 1.0):
    If (feature 10 <= 10.5666666666667)
     If (feature 5 <= 14.0)
      If (feature 1 <= 0.305)
       If (feature 2 <= 0.26)
        If (feature 8 <= 2.96)
         Predict: 0.0
        Else (feature 8 > 2.96)
         Predict: 1.0
             .
             .
             .
Else (feature 5 > 16.0)
        If (feature 2 <= 0.25)
         If (feature 4 <= 0.049)
          Predict: 0.0
         Else (feature 4 > 0.049)
          Predict: 1.0
        Else (feature 2 > 0.25)
         If (feature 1 <= 0.2)
          Predict: 0.0
         Else (feature 1 > 0.2)
          Predict: 1.0
```

```
> predictions <- predict(model, testdf)
```

```
> showDF(select(predictions, "label", "rawPrediction", "probability",
"prediction"), 5)
```

```
+-----+--------------------+--------------------+----------+
|label|       rawPrediction|         probability|prediction|
+-----+--------------------+--------------------+----------+
|  0.0|[5.20659697980061...|[0.52065969798006...|       1.0|
|  1.0|[6.75105122414708...|[0.67510512241470...|       1.0|
|  1.0|[7.69196575734326...|[0.76919657573432...|       1.0|
|  1.0|[7.86345675093300...|[0.78634567509330...|       1.0|
|  1.0|[8.95741684971412...|[0.89574168497141...|       1.0|
+-----+--------------------+--------------------+----------+
only showing top 5 rows
```

```
> nrow(filter(predictions, predictions$label != predictions$prediction))
[1] 79
```

Similar to the previous examples, we fit a generalized linear model in the following example:

```
> csvPath <-
"file:///Users/aurobindosarkar/Downloads/winequality/winequality-white.csv"
```

```
> indf <- read.df(csvPath, "csv", header = "true", inferSchema = "true", na.strings =
"NA", delimiter= ";") %>% withColumnRenamed("fixed acidity", "fixed_acidity") %>%
withColumnRenamed("volatile acidity", "volatile_acidity") %>%
withColumnRenamed("citric acid", "citric_acid") %>% withColumnRenamed("residual
sugar", "residual_sugar") %>% withColumnRenamed("free sulfur dioxide",
"free_sulfur_dioxide") %>% withColumnRenamed("total sulfur dioxide",
"total_sulfur_dioxide")
```

```
> trainingdf <- sample(indf, withReplacement=FALSE, fraction=0.9,
seed=seed)
```

```
> testdf <- except(indf, trainingdf)
```

```
> model <- spark.glm(indf, quality ~ ., family = gaussian, tol = 1e-06,
maxIter = 25, weightCol = NULL, regParam = 0.1)
```

```
> summary(model)
```

```
Deviance Residuals:
(Note: These are approximate quantiles with relative error <= 0.01)
    Min      1Q   Median      3Q      Max
-3.8070  -0.5037  -0.0498   0.4456   3.1916

Coefficients:
                       Estimate     Std. Error    t value    Pr(>|t|)
(Intercept)            48.828       7.6391        6.3919     1.7914e-10
fixed_acidity          -0.021401    0.014567      -1.4691    0.14186
volatile_acidity       -1.6505      0.10606       -15.562    0
citric_acid            0.043129     0.089881      0.47984    0.63136
residual_sugar         0.033293     0.0034613     9.6187     0
chlorides              -1.5754      0.50526       -3.118     0.0018317
free_sulfur_dioxide    0.0041696    0.00074331    5.6095     2.1407e-08
total_sulfur_dioxide   -0.00075066  0.00032633    -2.3004    0.02147
density                -46.604      7.7231        -6.0344    1.7133e-09
pH                     0.27827      0.078437      3.5477     0.00039231
sulphates              0.43647      0.092228      4.7325     2.2805e-06
alcohol                0.2551       0.012896      19.781     0

(Dispersion parameter for gaussian family taken to be 0.571833)

    Null deviance: 3841  on 4897   degrees of freedom
Residual deviance: 2794  on 4886   degrees of freedom
AIC: 11176

Number of Fisher Scoring iterations: 1
```

```
> predictions <- predict(model, testdf)

> showDF(select(predictions, "quality", "prediction"), 5)
```

```
+-------+------------------+
|quality|        prediction|
+-------+------------------+
|      7| 6.555843712558648|
|      8|6.2422874502179795|
|      6| 5.664827458475145|
|      5| 5.263011944877043|
|      6| 6.050373346784674|
+-------+------------------+
only showing top 5 rows
```

Next, we present an example of clustering, where we fit a multivariate Gaussian mixture model against a Spark DataFrames:

```
> winedf <- mutate(indf, label = ifelse(indf$quality >= 6, 1, 0))

> winedf <- drop(winedf, "quality")

> trainingdf <- sample(winedf, withReplacement=FALSE, fraction=0.9,
seed=seed)

> testdf <- except(winedf, trainingdf)

> testdf <- except(winedf, trainingdf)

> model <- spark.gaussianMixture(trainingdf, ~ sulphates + citric_acid +
fixed_acidity + total_sulfur_dioxide + chlorides + free_sulfur_dioxide +
density + volatile_acidity + alcohol + pH + residual_sugar, k = 2)

> summary(model)

> predictions <- predict(model, testdf)

> showDF(select(predictions, "label", "prediction"), 5)
```

```
+-----+----------+
|label|prediction|
+-----+----------+
|  0.0|         0|
|  1.0|         1|
|  1.0|         1|
|  1.0|         1|
|  1.0|         1|
+-----+----------+
only showing top 5 rows
```

Next, we perform a two-sided **Kolmogorov-Smirnov (KS)** test for data sampled from a continuous distribution. We compare the largest difference between the empirical cumulative distribution of the data and the theoretical distribution to test the null hypothesis that the sample data comes from that theoretical distribution. In the following example, we illustrate the test on the `fixed_acidity` column against the normal distribution:

```
> test <- spark.kstest(indf, "fixed_acidity", "norm", c(0, 1))

> testSummary <- summary(test)

> testSummary
```

Kolmogorov-Smirnov test summary:

```
degrees of freedom = 0

statistic = 0.9999276519560749

pValue = 0.0
#Very strong presumption against null hypothesis: Sample follows
theoretical distribution.
```

Finally, in the following example, we perform distributed training of multiple models using `spark.lapply`. The results of all the computations must fit in a single machine's memory:

```
> library(magrittr)

> csvPath <-
"file:///Users/aurobindosarkar/Downloads/winequality/winequality-white.csv"

> indf <- read.df(csvPath, "csv", header = "true", inferSchema = "true",
na.strings = "NA", delimiter= ";") %>% withColumnRenamed("fixed acidity",
"fixed_acidity") %>% withColumnRenamed("volatile acidity",
"volatile_acidity") %>% withColumnRenamed("citric acid", "citric_acid") %>%
withColumnRenamed("residual sugar", "residual_sugar") %>%
withColumnRenamed("free sulfur dioxide", "free_sulfur_dioxide") %>%
withColumnRenamed("total sulfur dioxide", "total_sulfur_dioxide")

> lindf <- collect(indf)
```

We pass a read-only list of arguments for the family parameter of the generalized linear model, as shown here:

```
> families <- c("gaussian", "poisson")

> train <- function(family) {
```

```
+ model <- glm(quality ~ ., lindf, family = family)
+ summary(model)
+ }
```

The following statement returns a list of the model summaries:

```
> model.summaries <- spark.lapply(families, train)
```

Finally, we can print the summary of both the models, as shown here:

```
> print(model.summaries)
```

The summary of model 1 is:

```
[[1]]

Call:
glm(formula = quality ~ ., family = family, data = lindf)

Deviance Residuals:
    Min      1Q   Median      3Q      Max
-3.8348  -0.4934  -0.0379   0.4637   3.1143

Coefficients:
                      Estimate Std. Error t value Pr(>|t|)
(Intercept)          1.502e+02  1.880e+01   7.987 1.71e-15 ***
fixed_acidity        6.552e-02  2.087e-02   3.139  0.00171 **
volatile_acidity    -1.863e+00  1.138e-01 -16.373  < 2e-16 ***
citric_acid          2.209e-02  9.577e-02   0.231  0.81759
residual_sugar       8.148e-02  7.527e-03  10.825  < 2e-16 ***
chlorides           -2.473e-01  5.465e-01  -0.452  0.65097
free_sulfur_dioxide  3.733e-03  8.441e-04   4.422 9.99e-06 ***
total_sulfur_dioxide -2.857e-04 3.781e-04  -0.756  0.44979
density             -1.503e+02  1.907e+01  -7.879 4.04e-15 ***
pH                   6.863e-01  1.054e-01   6.513 8.10e-11 ***
sulphates            6.315e-01  1.004e-01   6.291 3.44e-10 ***
alcohol              1.935e-01  2.422e-02   7.988 1.70e-15 ***
---
Signif. codes:  0 '***' 0.001 '**' 0.01 '*' 0.05 '.' 0.1 ' ' 1

(Dispersion parameter for gaussian family taken to be 0.5645372)

    Null deviance: 3841.0  on 4897  degrees of freedom
Residual deviance: 2758.3  on 4886  degrees of freedom
AIC: 11113

Number of Fisher Scoring iterations: 2
```

The summary of model 2 is:

```
[[2]]

Call:
glm(formula = quality ~ ., family = family, data = lindf)

Deviance Residuals:
     Min        1Q    Median        3Q       Max
 -1.67362  -0.20825  -0.01416   0.18914   1.21919

Coefficients:
                       Estimate Std. Error z value Pr(>|z|)
(Intercept)           2.809e+01  1.114e+01   2.521 0.011698 *
fixed_acidity         1.281e-02  1.188e-02   1.078 0.281003
volatile_acidity     -3.346e-01  6.423e-02  -5.208 1.9e-07 ***
citric_acid           2.529e-03  5.328e-02   0.047 0.962138
residual_sugar        1.456e-02  4.365e-03   3.335 0.000854 ***
chlorides            -6.267e-02  3.128e-01  -0.200 0.841191
free_sulfur_dioxide   6.224e-04  4.631e-04   1.344 0.178939
total_sulfur_dioxide -3.694e-05  2.104e-04  -0.176 0.860626
density              -2.736e+01  1.130e+01  -2.421 0.015457 *
pH                    1.235e-01  5.903e-02   2.092 0.036417 *
sulphates             1.087e-01  5.450e-02   1.995 0.046011 *
alcohol               3.036e-02  1.421e-02   2.137 0.032594 *
---
Signif. codes:  0 '***' 0.001 '**' 0.01 '*' 0.05 '.' 0.1 ' ' 1

(Dispersion parameter for poisson family taken to be 1)

    Null deviance: 656.56  on 4897  degrees of freedom
Residual deviance: 471.74  on 4886  degrees of freedom
AIC: 18258

Number of Fisher Scoring iterations: 4
```

Summary

In this chapter, we introduced SparkR. We covered SparkR architecture and SparkR DataFrames API. Additionally, we provided code examples for using SparkR for EDA and data munging tasks, data visualization, and machine learning.

In the next chapter, we will build Spark applications using a mix of Spark modules. We will present examples of applications that combine Spark SQL with Spark Streaming, Spark Machine Learning, and so on.

9
Developing Applications with Spark SQL

In this chapter, we will present several examples of developing applications using Spark SQL. We will primarily focus on text analysis-based applications, including preprocessing pipelines, bag-of-words techniques, computing readability metrics for financial documents, identifying themes in document corpuses, and using Naive Bayes classifiers. Additionally, we will describe the implementation of a machine learning example.

More specifically, you will learn about the following in this chapter:

- Spark SQL-based application's development
- Preprocessing textual data
- Building preprocessing data pipelines
- Identifying themes in document corpuses
- Using Naive Bayes classifiers
- Developing a machine learning application

Introducing Spark SQL applications

Machine learning, predictive analytics, and related data science topics are becoming increasingly popular for solving real-world problems across business domains. These applications are driving mission-critical business decision making in many organizations. Examples of such applications include recommendation engines, targeted advertising, speech recognition, fraud detection, image recognition and categorization, and so on. Spark (and Spark SQL) is increasingly becoming the platform of choice for these large-scale distributed applications.

With the availability of online data sources for financial news, earning conference calls, regulatory filings, social media, and so on, interest in the automated and intelligent analysis of textual and other unstructured data available in various formats, including text, audio, and video, has proliferated. These applications include sentiment analysis from regulatory filings, large-scale automated analysis of news articles and stories, twitter analysis, stock price prediction applications, and so on.

In this chapter, we will present some approaches and techniques for dealing with textual data. Additionally, we will present some examples of applying machine learning models on textual data to classify documents, derive insights from document corpuses, and process textual information for sentiment analysis.

In the next section, we start our coverage with a few methods that help in converting regulatory filings into collections of words. This step allows the use of domain-specific dictionaries to classify the tone of the documents, train algorithms to identify document characteristics or identify hidden structures as common topics across a collection of documents.

 For a more detailed survey of textual analysis methods in accounting and finance, refer to *Textual Analysis in Accounting and Finance: A Survey* by Tim Loughran and Bill McDonald, at `https://papers.ssrn.com/sol3/papers.cfm?abstract_id=2504147`.

We will also examine typical issues, challenges, and limitations present in implementing textual analysis applications, for example, converting tokens to words, disambiguating sentences, and cleansing embedded tags, documents, and other noisy elements present in financial disclosure documents. Also, note that the use of HTML formatting is a leading source of errors while parsing documents. Such parsing depends on the consistency in the structure of the text and the related markup language, often resulting in significant errors. Additionally, it is important to understand that we are often interested in both the intended and the unintended information conveyed by text.

Understanding text analysis applications

The inherent nature of language and writing leads to problems of high dimensionality while analyzing documents. Hence, some of the most widely used textual methods rely on the critical assumption of independence, where the order and direct context of a word are not important. Methods, where word sequence is ignored, are typically labeled as "bag-of-words" techniques.

Textual analysis is a lot more imprecise compared to quantitative analysis. Textual data requires an additional step of translating the text into quantitative measures, which are then used as inputs for various text-based analytics or ML methods. Many of these methods are based on deconstructing a document into a term-document matrix consisting of rows of words and columns of word counts.

In applications using a bag of words, the approach to normalizing the word counts is important as the raw counts directly dependent on the document length. A simple use of proportions can solve this problem, however, we might also want to adjust a word's weight. Typically, these approaches are based on the rarity of a given term in the document, for example, **term frequency-inverse document frequency (tf-idf)**.

In the next section, we will explore using Spark SQL for the textual analysis of financial documents.

Using Spark SQL for textual analysis

In this section, we will present a detailed example of typical preprocessing required for preparing data for textual analysis (from the accounting and finance domain). We will also compute a few metrics for readability (a measure of whether the receiver of information can accurately reconstruct the intended message).

Preprocessing textual data

In this section, we will develop a set of functions for preprocessing a 10-K statement. We will be using the "complete submission text file" for a 10-K filing on the EDGAR website as the input text in our example.

 For more details on the Regex expressions used to preprocess 10-K filings refer to *The Annual Report Algorithm: Retrieval of Financial Statements and Extraction of Textual Information,* by Jorg Hering at http://airccj.org/ CSCP/vol7/csit76615.pdf.

First, we import all the packages required in this chapter:

```scala
scala> import spark.implicits._
scala> import org.apache.spark.sql._
scala> import org.apache.spark.sql.types._
scala> import scala.util.matching.Regex
scala> import org.apache.spark.ml.{Pipeline, PipelineModel}
scala> import org.apache.spark.rdd.RDD
scala> import scala.math
```

```
scala> import org.apache.spark.ml.feature.{HashingTF, IDF, RegexTokenizer,
Tokenizer, NGram, StopWordsRemover, CountVectorizer}
scala> import org.apache.spark.sql.{Row, DataFrame}
scala> import org.apache.spark.ml.feature.{VectorAssembler, StringIndexer,
IndexToString} scala> import
org.apache.spark.ml.classification.{RandomForestClassificationModel,
RandomForestClassifier, LogisticRegression, NaiveBayes, NaiveBayesModel}
scala> import org.apache.spark.ml.Pipeline
scala> import org.apache.spark.ml.evaluation.{RegressionEvaluator,
MulticlassClassificationEvaluator}
scala> import org.apache.spark.ml.linalg.Vector
scala> import org.apache.spark.ml.tuning.{CrossValidator, ParamGridBuilder,
TrainValidationSplit}
scala> import org.apache.spark.ml.clustering.{LDA}
scala> import scala.collection.mutable.WrappedArray
scala> import org.apache.spark.ml._

//The following package will be created later in this Chapter.
scala> import org.chap9.edgar10k._
```

Next, we read the input file and convert the input rows into a single string for our processing. You can download the input file for the following example from https://www.sec.gov/Archives/edgar/data/320193/000119312514383437/0001193125-14-383437-index.html:

```
scala> val inputLines =
sc.textFile("file:///Users/aurobindosarkar/Downloads/edgardata/0001193125-1
4-383437.txt")

scala> val linesToString = inputLines.toLocalIterator.mkString
```

As the pre-processing functions are executed, the length of the input string progressively reduces as a lot of extraneous or unrelated text/tags are removed at each step. We compute the starting length of the original string to track the impact of applying specific functions in each of the processing steps:

```
scala> linesToString.length
res0: Int = 11917240
```

Typically, as the first step, we eliminate the abbreviations, headings, and numbers (with decimals) from the input text. The next code snippet presents a function used to remove abbreviations. Other rules dealing with headings and decimal numbers can also be included here. You can uncomment the `println` statements to display the input and output string lengths (representing pre- and post-processing lengths):

```
scala> def deleteAbbrev(instr: String): String = {
     |        //println("Input string length="+ instr.length())
```

```
    |        val pattern = new Regex("[A-Z]\\.([A-Z]\\.)+")
    |        val str = pattern.replaceAllIn(instr, " ")
    |        //println("Output string length ="+ str.length())
    |        //println("String length reduced by="+ (instr.length -
str.length()))
    |        str
    | }

scala> val lineRemAbbrev = deleteAbbrev(linesToString)
```

In addition, `10-K` files are composed of several exhibits--XBRL, graphics, and other documents (file) types embedded in the financial statements; these include Microsoft Excel files (file extension `*.xlsx`), ZIP files (file extension `*.zip`), and encoded PDF files (file extension `*.pdf`).

In the following step, we apply additional rules for deleting these embedded documents:

```
scala> def deleteDocTypes(instr: String): String = {
    |        //println("Input string length="+ instr.length())
    |        val pattern = new
Regex("(?s)<TYPE>(GRAPHIC|EXCEL|PDF|ZIP|COVER|CORRESP|EX-10[01].INS|EX-99.S
DR [KL].INS|EX-10[01].SCH|EX-99.SDR [KL].SCH|EX-10[01].CAL|EX-99.SDR
[KL].CAL|EX-10[01].DEF|EX-99.SDR [KL].LAB|EX-10[01].LAB|EX-99.SDR
[KL].LAB|EX-10[01].PRE|EX-99.SDR [KL].PRE|EX-10[01].PRE|EX-99.SDR
[KL].PRE).*?</TEXT>")
    |        val str = pattern.replaceAllIn(instr, " ")
    |        //println("Output string length ="+ str.length())
    |        //println("String length reduced by="+ (instr.length -
str.length()))
    |        str
    | }

scala> val lineRemDocTypes = deleteDocTypes(lineRemAbbrev)
```

Next, we delete all the metadata included in the core document and the exhibits, as follows:

```
scala> def deleteMetaData(instr: String): String = {
    |        val pattern1 = new Regex("<HEAD>.*?</HEAD>")
    |        val str1 = pattern1.replaceAllIn(instr, " ")
    |        val pattern2 = new
Regex("(?s)<TYPE>.*?<SEQUENCE>.*?<FILENAME>.*?<DESCRIPTION>.*?")
    |        val str2 = pattern2.replaceAllIn(str1, " ")
    |        str2
    | }

scala> val lineRemMetaData = deleteMetaData(lineRemDocTypes)
```

Before deleting all the HTML elements and their corresponding attributes, we delete the tables in the document since they normally contain non-textual (quantitative) information.

The following function uses a set of regular expressions applied to delete tables and HTML elements embedded in the financial statement:

```scala
scala> def deleteTablesNHTMLElem(instr: String): String = {
     |         val pattern1 = new Regex("(?s)(?i)<Table.*?</Table>")
     |         val str1 = pattern1.replaceAllIn(instr, " ")
     |         val pattern2 = new Regex("(?s)<[^>]*>")
     |         val str2 = pattern2.replaceAllIn(str1, " ")
     |         str2
     | }

scala> val lineRemTabNHTML = deleteTablesNHTMLElem(lineRemMetaData)
```

Next, we extract the text in the body section of each of the HTML-formatted documents. As the EDGAR system accepts submissions with extended character sets, such as , &, ®, and so on--they will need to be decoded and/or appropriately replaced for textual analysis.

We show a few examples of these in this function:

```scala
scala> def deleteExtCharset(instr: String): String = {
     |         val pattern1 = new Regex("(?s)( | |&#x(A|a)0;)")
     |         val str1 = pattern1.replaceAllIn(instr, " ")
     |         val pattern2 = new Regex("('|')")
     |         val str2 = pattern2.replaceAllIn(str1, "'")
     |         val pattern3 = new Regex("x")
     |         val str3 = pattern3.replaceAllIn(str2, " ")
     |         val pattern4 = new Regex("(¨|§|&reg;|™|&copy;)")
     |         val str4 = pattern4.replaceAllIn(str3, " ")
     |         val pattern5 = new Regex("("|"|")")
     |         val str5 = pattern5.replaceAllIn(str4, "\"")
     |         val pattern6 = new Regex("&amp;")
     |         val str6 = pattern6.replaceAllIn(str5, "&")
     |         val pattern7 = new Regex("(–|—|-)")
     |         val str7 = pattern7.replaceAllIn(str6, "-")
     |         val pattern8 = new Regex("/")
     |         val str8 = pattern8.replaceAllIn(str7, "/")
     |         str8
     | }

scala> val lineRemExtChrst = deleteExtCharset(lineRemTabNHTML)
```

Next, we define a function that cleans up excess blanks, line feed, and carriage returns:

```scala
scala> def deleteExcessLFCRWS(instr: String): String = {
     |         val pattern1 = new Regex("[\n\r]+")
     |         val str1 = pattern1.replaceAllIn(instr, "\n")
     |         val pattern2 = new Regex("[\t]+")
     |         val str2 = pattern2.replaceAllIn(str1, " ")
     |         val pattern3 = new Regex("\\s+")
     |         val str3 = pattern3.replaceAllIn(str2, " ")
     |         str3
     | }

scala> val lineRemExcessLFCRWS = deleteExcessLFCRWS(lineRemExtChrst)
```

In the next code block, we define a function to illustrate the removal of a user-specified set of strings. These strings can be read from an input file or a database. This step is not required if you can implement Regex for extraneous text that are, typically, present throughout the document (and vary from document to document), but do not have any additional value in textual analysis:

```scala
scala> def deleteStrings(str: String): String = {
     |         val strings = Array("IDEA: XBRL DOCUMENT", "\\/\\* Do Not
Remove This Comment \\*\\/", "v2.4.0.8")
     |         //println("str="+ str.length())
     |         var str1 = str
     |         for(myString <- strings) {
     |           var pattern1 = new Regex(myString)
     |           str1 = pattern1.replaceAllIn(str1, " ")
     |         }
     |         str1
     | }

scala> val lineRemStrings = deleteStrings(lineRemExcessLFCRWS)
```

In the next step, we remove all the URLs, filenames, digits, and punctuation (except the periods) from the document string. The periods are retained at this stage for computing the number of periods (representing the number of sentences) in the text (as shown in the following section):

```scala
scala> def deleteAllURLsFileNamesDigitsPunctuationExceptPeriod(instr:
String): String = {
     |         val pattern1 = new Regex("\\b(https?|ftp|file)://[-a-zA-
Z0-9+&@#/%?=~_|!:,.;]*[-a-zA-Z0-9+&@#/%=~_|]")
     |         val str1 = pattern1.replaceAllIn(instr, "")
     |         val pattern2 = new Regex("[_a-zA-Z0-9\\-
\\.]+.(txt|sgml|xml|xsd|htm|html)")
     |         val str2 = pattern2.replaceAllIn(str1, " ")
```

```
|            val pattern3 = new Regex("[^a-zA-Z|^.]")
|            val str3 = pattern3.replaceAllIn(str2, " ")
|            str3
| }

scala> val lineRemAllUrlsFileNamesDigitsPuncXPeriod =
deleteAllURLsFileNamesDigitsPunctuationExceptPeriod(lineRemStrings)
```

In the next section, we will discuss some metrics typically used to measure readability, that is, whether the textual information contained in a `10-K` filing is accessible to the user.

Computing readability

The Fog Index and the number of words contained in the annual report have been widely used as measures of readability for annual reports (that is, `Form 10-Ks`). The Fog Index is a function of two variables: average sentence length (in words) and complex words (defined as the percentage of words with more than two syllables):

Fog Index = 0.4 * (average number of words per sentence + percentage of complex words)

The Fog Index equation estimates the number of years of education needed to understand the text on a first reading. Thus, a Fog Index value of `16` implies that the reader needs sixteen years of education--essentially a college degree--to comprehend the text on a first reading. Generally, documents with a Fog Index of above eighteen are considered unreadable since more than a master's degree is needed to understand the text.

Parsing the `10-K` for computing the average number of words per sentence is typically a difficult and error-prone process because these documents contain a variety of abbreviations, and use periods to delineate section identifiers or as spacers. Additionally, real-world systems will also need to identify the many lists contained in such filings (based on punctuation and line spacing). For example, such an application will need to avoid counting the periods in section headers, ellipses, or other cases where a period is likely not terminating a sentence, and then assume that the remaining periods are sentence terminations.

The average words-per-sentence metric is determined by the number of words divided by the number of sentence terminations. This is typically done by removing abbreviations and other spurious sources of periods and then counting the number of sentence terminators and the number of words.

We compute the number of periods left in the text, as follows:

```scala
scala> val countPeriods = lineRemAllUrlsFileNamesDigitsPuncXPeriod.count(_
== '.')
countPeriods: Int = 2538
```

Next, we remove all the periods (and any other non-alphabetic characters remaining in our text) to arrive at an initial set of words contained in our original document. Note that all of these words may still not be legitimate words:

```scala
scala> def keepOnlyAlphas(instr: String): String = {
     |          val pattern1 = new Regex("[^a-zA-Z|]")
     |          val str1 = pattern1.replaceAllIn(instr, " ")
     |          val str2 = str1.replaceAll("[\\s]+", " ")
     |          str2
     | }

scala> val lineWords =
keepOnlyAlphas(lineRemAllUrlsFileNamesDigitsPuncXPeriod)
```

```
lineWords: String = " ACCESSION NUMBER CONFORMED SUBMISSION TYPE KPUBLIC DOCUMENT
COUNT CONFORMED PERIOD OF REPORT FILED AS OF DATE DATE AS OF CHANGE FILER COMPANY DATA
COMPANY CONFORMED NAME APPLE INC CENTRAL INDEX KEY STANDARD INDUSTRIAL CLASSIFICATION
ELECTRONIC COMPUTERS IRS NUMBER STATE OF INCORPORATION CA FISCAL YEAR END FILING
VALUES FORM TYPE K SEC ACT Act SEC FILE NUMBER FILM NUMBER BUSINESS ADDRESS STREET ONE
INFINITE LOOP CITY CUPERTINO STATE CA ZIP BUSINESS PHONE MAIL ADDRESS STREET ONE
INFINITE LOOP CITY CUPERTINO STATE CA ZIP FORMER COMPANY FORMER CONFORMED NAME APPLE
COMPUTER INC DATE OF NAME CHANGE K Table of Contents UNITED STATES SECURITIES AND
EXCHANGE COMMISSION Washington Form K Mark One For the fiscal year ended September or
For the transition period from to Commis...
```

In the following step, we convert the string of words into a DataFrame and use the `explode()` function to create a row for each of the words:

```scala
scala> val wordsStringDF = sc.parallelize(List(lineWords)).toDF()

scala> val wordsDF = wordsStringDF.withColumn("words10k",
explode(split($"value", "[\\s]"))).drop("value")
```

Next, we read in a dictionary (preferably a domain-specific dictionary). We will match our list of words against this dictionary to arrive at our final list of words (they should all be legitimate words after this stage).

```scala
scala> val dictDF = spark.read.format("csv").option("header",
"true").load("file:///Users/aurobindosarkar/Downloads/edgardata/LoughranMcD
onald_MasterDictionary_2014.csv")
```

For our purposes, we have used the Loughran & McDonold's Master Dictionary as it contains words typically found in 10-K statements. You can download the `LoughranMcDonald_MasterDictionary_2014.csv` file and the associated documentation from `https://www3.nd.edu/~mcdonald/Word_Lists.html`.

In the next step, we join our word list DataFrame with the dictionary, and compute the number of words in our final list:

```
scala> val joinWordsDict = wordsDF.join(dictDF, lower(wordsDF("words10k"))
=== lower(dictDF("Word")))

scala> val numWords = joinWordsDict.count()
numWords: Long = 54701
```

The average words per sentence are computed by dividing the number of words by the number of periods computed earlier:

```
scala> val avgWordsPerSentence = numWords / countPeriods
avgWordsPerSentence: Long = 21
```

We use the `Syllables` column in the dictionary to compute the number of words in our word list that have more than two syllables, as follows:

```
scala> val numPolySylb = joinWordsDict.select("words10k",
"Syllables").where(joinWordsDict("Syllables") > 2)

scala> val polySCount = numPolySylb.count()
polySCount: Long = 14093
```

Finally, we plug in the parameters into our equation to compute the Fog Index, as illustrated:

```
scala> val fogIndex = 0.4*(avgWordsPerSentence+((polySCount/numWords)*100))
fogIndex: Double = 8.4
```

The argument against the use of readability measures, such as the Fog Index, in financial documents is the observation that a majority of these documents are not distinguishable based on the writing style used. Additionally, even though the percentage of complex words in these documents may be high, such words, or industry jargon, are easily understood by the audience for such documents (for example, the investor community).

As a simple proxy for readability of annual reports, Loughran and McDonald suggest using the natural log of gross 10-K file size (complete submission text file). Compared to the Fog Index, this measure is a lot easier to obtain and does not involve complicated parsing of 10-K documents.

In the following step, we present a function to compute the file (or, more specifically, the RDD) size:

```scala
scala> def calcFileSize(rdd: RDD[String]): Long = {
     |    rdd.map(_.getBytes("UTF-8").length.toLong)
     |        .reduce(_+_) //add the sizes together
     | }
```

```scala
scala> val lines =
sc.textFile("file:///Users/aurobindosarkar/Downloads/edgardata/0001193125-1
4-383437.txt")
```

The file size (in MB) and the log of the file sizes can be calculated as follows:

```scala
scala> val fileSize = calcFileSize(lines)/1000000.0
fileSize: Double = 11.91724
```

```scala
scala> math.log(fileSize)
res1: Double = 2.477986091202679
```

Although file size is a good proxy for the readability of documents such as the 10-K filings, it may be less suitable for text from press releases, newswire stories, and earnings conference calls. In such cases, as the length of the text does not vary significantly, other approaches that focus more on the content may be more suitable.

In the next section, we will discuss using word lists in textual analysis.

Using word lists

In measuring the tone or sentiment of a financial document, practitioners typically count the number of words associated with a particular sentiment scaled by the total number of words in the document. Thus, for example, higher proportions of negative words in a document indicate a more pessimistic tone.

The use of dictionaries to measure tone has several important advantages. Apart from the convenience in computing sentiment at scale, the use of such dictionaries promotes standardization by eliminating individual subjectivity. An important component of classifying words is identifying the most frequently occurring words within each classification.

In the following step, we use the word-sentiment indicators contained in the dictionary to get a sense of the sentiment or tone of the 10-K filing. This can be computed relative to the past filings by the same organization, or against other organizations in the same or different sector(s):

```scala
scala> val negWordCount = joinWordsDict.select("words10k",
"negative").where(joinWordsDict("negative") > 0).count()
negWordCount: Long = 1004

scala> val sentiment = negWordCount / (numWords.toDouble)
sentiment: Double = 0.01835432624632091
```

Typically, the use of modal words is also important in such analyses. For example, the use of weaker modal words (for example, may, could, and might) could possibly signal issues at the firm:

```scala
scala> val modalWordCount = joinWordsDict.select("words10k",
"modal").where(joinWordsDict("modal") > 0).groupBy("modal").count()
```

In the following code, we count the number of words for each category of modal words. As per the reference documentation of the dictionary used here, a 1 indicates "strong modal" (for example, words such as "always", "definitely", and "never"), a 2 indicates "moderate modal" (for example, words such as "can", "generally", and "usually"), and a 3 indicates "weak modal" (for example, words such as "almost", "could", "might", and "suggests"):

```scala
scala> modalWordCount.show()
+-----+-----+
|modal|count|
+-----+-----+
|    3|  386|
|    1|  115|
|    2|  221|
+-----+-----+
```

In the next section, we will use some of the functions defined in this section to create a data preprocessing pipeline for 10-K filings.

Creating data preprocessing pipelines

In this section, we will convert some of the data processing functions from the previous sections into custom Transformers. These Transformer objects map an input DataFrame to an output DataFrame and are typically used to prepare DataFrames for machine learning applications.

We create the following classes as `UnaryTransformer` objects that apply transformations to one input DataFrame column and produce another by appending a new column (containing the processing results of the applied function) to it. These custom Transformer objects can then be a part of a processing pipeline.

First, we create the four custom `UnaryTransformer` classes that we will use in our example, as follows:

TablesNHTMLElemCleaner.scala

```scala
package org.chap9.edgar10k
import org.apache.spark.ml.UnaryTransformer
import org.apache.spark.sql.types.{DataType, DataTypes, StringType}
import scala.util.matching.Regex
import org.apache.spark.ml.util.Identifiable

class TablesNHTMLElemCleaner(override val uid: String) extends
UnaryTransformer[String, String, TablesNHTMLElemCleaner] {
    def this() = this(Identifiable.randomUID("cleaner"))
    def deleteTablesNHTMLElem(instr: String): String = {
        val pattern1 = new Regex("(?s)(?i)<Table.*?</Table>")
        val str1 = pattern1.replaceAllIn(instr, " ")
        val pattern2 = new Regex("(?s)<[^>]*>")
        val str2 = pattern2.replaceAllIn(str1, " ")
        str2
    }

override protected def createTransformFunc: String => String = {
    deleteTablesNHTMLElem _
}

override protected def validateInputType(inputType: DataType): Unit = {
    require(inputType == StringType)
}

override protected def outputDataType: DataType = DataTypes.StringType
}
```

AllURLsFileNamesDigitsPunctuationExceptPeriodCleaner.scala

```scala
package org.chap9.edgar10k
import org.apache.spark.ml.UnaryTransformer
import org.apache.spark.sql.types.{DataType, DataTypes, StringType}
import scala.util.matching.Regex
import org.apache.spark.ml.util.Identifiable

class AllURLsFileNamesDigitsPunctuationExceptPeriodCleaner(override val
```

```
uid: String) extends UnaryTransformer[String, String,
AllURLsFileNamesDigitsPunctuationExceptPeriodCleaner] {
    def this() = this(Identifiable.randomUID("cleaner"))
    def deleteAllURLsFileNamesDigitsPunctuationExceptPeriod(instr: String):
String = {
        val pattern1 = new Regex("\\b(https?|ftp|file)://[-a-zA-
Z0-9+&@#/%?=~_|!:,.;]*[-a-zA-Z0-9+&@#/%=~_|]")
        val str1 = pattern1.replaceAllIn(instr, "")
        val pattern2 = new Regex("[_a-zA-Z0-9\\-
\\.]+.(txt|sgml|xml|xsd|htm|html)")
        val str2 = pattern2.replaceAllIn(str1, " ")
        val pattern3 = new Regex("[^a-zA-Z|^.]")
        val str3 = pattern3.replaceAllIn(str2, " ")
        str3
}

override protected def createTransformFunc: String => String = {
    deleteAllURLsFileNamesDigitsPunctuationExceptPeriod _
}

override protected def validateInputType(inputType: DataType): Unit = {
    require(inputType == StringType)
}

override protected def outputDataType: DataType = DataTypes.StringType
}
```

OnlyAlphasCleaner.scala

```
package org.chap9.edgar10k
import org.apache.spark.ml.UnaryTransformer
import org.apache.spark.sql.types.{DataType, DataTypes, StringType}
import scala.util.matching.Regex
import org.apache.spark.ml.util.Identifiable
class OnlyAlphasCleaner(override val uid: String) extends
UnaryTransformer[String, String, OnlyAlphasCleaner] {
    def this() = this(Identifiable.randomUID("cleaner"))
    def keepOnlyAlphas(instr: String): String = {
       val pattern1 = new Regex("[^a-zA-Z|]")
       val str1 = pattern1.replaceAllIn(instr, " ")
       val str2 = str1.replaceAll("[\\s]+", " ")
       str2
    }
override protected def createTransformFunc: String => String = {
   keepOnlyAlphas _
}

override protected def validateInputType(inputType: DataType): Unit = {
```

```
require(inputType == StringType)
}

override protected def outputDataType: DataType = DataTypes.StringType
}
```

ExcessLFCRWSCleaner.scala

```
package org.chap9.edgar10k
import org.apache.spark.ml.UnaryTransformer
import org.apache.spark.sql.types.{DataType, DataTypes, StringType}
import scala.util.matching.Regex
import org.apache.spark.ml.util.Identifiable

class ExcessLFCRWSCleaner(override val uid: String) extends
UnaryTransformer[String, String, ExcessLFCRWSCleaner] {
    def this() = this(Identifiable.randomUID("cleaner"))
    def deleteExcessLFCRWS(instr: String): String = {
    val pattern1 = new Regex("[\n\r]+")
    val str1 = pattern1.replaceAllIn(instr, "\n")
    val pattern2 = new Regex("[\t]+")
    val str2 = pattern2.replaceAllIn(str1, " ")
    val pattern3 = new Regex("\\s+")
    val str3 = pattern3.replaceAllIn(str2, " ")
    str3
}

override protected def createTransformFunc: String => String = {
    deleteExcessLFCRWS _
}

override protected def validateInputType(inputType: DataType): Unit = {
    require(inputType == StringType)
}

override protected def outputDataType: DataType = DataTypes.StringType
}
```

Create the following `build.sbt` file for compiling and packaging the target classes:

```
name := "Chapter9"
version := "2.0"
scalaVersion := "2.11.8"
libraryDependencies ++= Seq(
("org.apache.spark" % "spark-core_2.11" % "2.2.0" % "provided"),
("org.apache.spark" % "spark-sql_2.11" % "2.2.0" % "provided"),
("org.apache.spark" % "spark-mllib_2.11" % "2.2.0" % "provided")
)
```

```
libraryDependencies += "com.github.scopt" %% "scopt" % "3.4.0"
libraryDependencies += "com.typesafe" % "config" % "1.3.0"
libraryDependencies += "com.typesafe.scala-logging" %% "scala-logging-api"
% "2.1.2"
libraryDependencies += "com.typesafe.scala-logging" %% "scala-logging-
slf4j" % "2.1.2"
libraryDependencies += "org.scalatest" % "scalatest_2.11" % "3.0.1" %
"test"
```

Use the following SBT command to compile and package the classes into a JAR file:

```
Aurobindos-MacBook-Pro-2:Chapter9 aurobindosarkar$ sbt package
```

Finally, restart Spark shell with the preceding JAR file included in the session:

```
Aurobindos-MacBook-Pro-2:spark-2.2.1-SNAPSHOT-bin-hadoop2.7
aurobindosarkar$ bin/spark-shell --driver-memory 12g --conf
spark.driver.maxResultSize=12g --conf spark.sql.shuffle.partitions=800 --
jars
/Users/aurobindosarkar/Downloads/Chapter9/target/scala-2.11/chapter9_2.11-2
.0.jar
```

The Dataset for the following example, Reuters-21578, Distribution 1.0, can be downloaded from https://archive.ics.uci.edu/ml/datasets/reuters-21578+text+categorization+collection.

Here, we will take one of the entries demarcated by <Reuters>...</Reuters> tags in the downloaded SGML files to create a new input file containing a single story. This roughly simulates a new story coming into our pipeline. More specifically, this story can be coming in via a Kafka queue, and we can create a continuous Spark SQL application to process the incoming story text.

First, we read in the newly created file into a DataFrame, as illustrated:

```
scala> val linesDF1 =
sc.textFile("file:///Users/aurobindosarkar/Downloads/reuters21578/reut2-020
-1.sgm").toDF()
```

Next, we create instances of Transformers using the classes we defined earlier in this section. The Transformers are chained together in the pipeline by specifying the output columns for each of the Transformer as the input column to the next Transformer in the chain:

```
scala> val tablesNHTMLElemCleaner = new
TablesNHTMLElemCleaner().setInputCol("value").setOutputCol("tablesNHTMLElem
Cleaned")
```

```
scala> val allURLsFileNamesDigitsPunctuationExceptPeriodCleaner = new
AllURLsFileNamesDigitsPunctuationExceptPeriodCleaner().setInputCol("tablesN
HTMLElemCleaned").setOutputCol("allURLsFileNamesDigitsPunctuationExceptPeri
odCleaned")

scala> val onlyAlphasCleaner = new
OnlyAlphasCleaner().setInputCol("allURLsFileNamesDigitsPunctuationExceptPer
iodCleaned").setOutputCol("text")

scala> val excessLFCRWSCleaner = new
ExcessLFCRWSCleaner().setInputCol("text").setOutputCol("cleaned")
```

After processing the text through our cleansing components, we add two more stages in order to tokenize and remove stop words from our text, as demonstrated. We use the generic stop words list file available at https://www3.nd.edu/~mcdonald/Word_Lists.html:

```
scala> val tokenizer = new
RegexTokenizer().setInputCol("cleaned").setOutputCol("words").setPattern("\
\W")

scala> val stopwords: Array[String] =
sc.textFile("file:///Users/aurobindosarkar/Downloads/StopWords_GenericLong.
txt").flatMap(_.stripMargin.split("\\s+")).collect
```

```
stopwords: Array[String] = Array(a, a's, able, about, above, according, accordingly,
across, actually, after, afterwards, again, against, ain't, all, allow, allows,
almost, alone, along, already, also, although, always, am, among, amongst, an, and,
another, any, anybody, anyhow, anyone, anything, anyway, anyways, anywhere, apart,
appear, appreciate, appropriate, are, aren't, around, as, aside, ask, asking,
associated, at, available, away, awfully, b, be, became, because, become, becomes,
becoming, been, before, beforehand, behind, being, believe, below, beside, besides,
best, better, between, beyond, both, brief, but, by, c, c'mon, c's, came, can, can't,
cannot, cant, cause, causes, certain, certainly, changes, clearly, co, com, come,
comes, concerning, consequently, consider, consideri...
```

```
scala> val remover = new
StopWordsRemover().setStopWords(stopwords).setCaseSensitive(false).setInput
Col("words").setOutputCol("filtered")
```

At this stage, the components for all our processing stages are ready to be assembled into a pipeline.

For more details on Spark pipelines, refer to https://spark.apache.org/docs/latest/ml-pipeline.html.

We create a pipeline and chain all the Transformers to specify the pipeline stages, as follows:

```scala
scala> val pipeline = new
Pipeline().setStages(Array(tablesNHTMLElemCleaner,
allURLsFileNamesDigitsPunctuationExceptPeriodCleaner, onlyAlphasCleaner,
excessLFCRWSCleaner, tokenizer, remover))
```

The `pipeline.fit()` method is called on the original DataFrame containing the raw text document:

```scala
scala> val model = pipeline.fit(linesDF1)
```

We can use the pipeline model from the preceding step to transform our original Dataset to the form required to feed other downstream textual applications. We also drop the columns from intermediate processing steps to clean up our DataFrame:

```scala
scala> val cleanedDF =
model.transform(linesDF1).drop("value").drop("tablesNHTMLElemCleaned").drop
("excessLFCRWSCleaned").drop("allURLsFileNamesDigitsPunctuationExceptPeriod
Cleaned").drop("text").drop("word")
```

Furthermore, we can clean up the final output column by removing any rows containing empty strings or spaces, as follows:

```scala
scala> val finalDF = cleanedDF.filter(($"cleaned" =!= "") && ($"cleaned"
=!= " "))
scala> cleanedDF.count()
res3: Long = 62
```

The rest of the processing is similar to what we presented earlier. The following steps explode the column containing our words into separate rows, join our final list of words with the dictionary, and then compute the sentiment and modal word's usage:

```scala
scala> val wordsInStoryDF = finalDF.withColumn("wordsInStory",
explode(split($"cleaned", "[\\s]"))).drop("cleaned")

scala> val joinWordsDict = wordsInStoryDF.join(dictDF,
lower(wordsInStoryDF("wordsInStory")) === lower(dictDF("Word")))

scala> wordsInStoryDF.count()
res4: Long = 457

scala> val numWords = joinWordsDict.count().toDouble
numWords: Double = 334.0

scala> joinWordsDict.select("wordsInStory").show()
```

```
+------------+
|wordsInStory|
+------------+
|       money|
|       japan|
|          IF|
|      DOLLAR|
|     FOLLOWS|
|          IF|
|      DOLLAR|
|     FOLLOWS|
|        WALL|
|      STREET|
|        WILL|
|      DIVEST|
|          By|
|          If|
|         the|
|      dollar|
|        goes|
|         the|
|         way|
|          of|
+------------+
only showing top 20 rows
```

```scala
scala> val negWordCount = joinWordsDict.select("wordsInStory",
"negative").where(joinWordsDict("negative") > 0).count()
negWordCount: Long = 8

scala> val sentiment = negWordCount / (numWords.toDouble)
sentiment: Double = 0.023952095808383235

scala> val modalWordCount = joinWordsDict.select("wordsInStory",
"modal").where(joinWordsDict("modal") > 0).groupBy("modal").count()

scala> modalWordCount.show()
+-----+-----+
|modal|count|
+-----+-----+
|    3|    2|
|    1|    5|
|    2|    4|
+-----+-----+
```

The next set of steps illustrates the use of the preceding pipeline for processing another story from our corpus. We can then compare these results to get a relative sense of pessimism (reflected by measures of negative sentiment) in the stories:

```scala
scala> val linesDF2 =
sc.textFile("file:///Users/aurobindosarkar/Downloads/reuters21578/reut2-008
-1.sgm").toDF()

scala> val cleanedDF =
model.transform(linesDF2).drop("value").drop("tablesNHTMLElemCleaned").drop
("excessLFCRWSCleaned").drop("allURLsFileNamesDigitsPunctuationExceptPeriod
Cleaned").drop("text").drop("word")
cleanedDF: org.apache.spark.sql.DataFrame = [cleaned: string,

scala> val finalDF = cleanedDF.filter(($"cleaned" =!= "") && ($"cleaned"
=!= " "))

scala> cleanedDF.count()
res7: Long = 84

scala> val wordsInStoryDF = finalDF.withColumn("wordsInStory",
explode(split($"cleaned", "[\\s]"))).drop("cleaned")

scala> val joinWordsDict = wordsInStoryDF.join(dictDF,
lower(wordsInStoryDF("wordsInStory")) === lower(dictDF("Word")))

scala> wordsInStoryDF.count()
res8: Long = 598

scala> val numWords = joinWordsDict.count().toDouble
numWords: Double = 483.0

scala> joinWordsDict.select("wordsInStory").show()
```

```
+------------+
|wordsInStory|
+------------+
|         MAR|
|       sugar|
|       grain|
|        corn|
|       SUGAR|
|     PROGRAM|
|       SUGAR|
|     PROGRAM|
|         CUT|
|        SENT|
|          TO|
|    CONGRESS|
|          BY|
|       MARCH|
|         The|
| Agriculture|
|  Department|
|     formally|
| transmitted|
|          to|
+------------+
only showing top 20 rows
```

```
scala> val negWordCount = joinWordsDict.select("wordsInStory",
"negative").where(joinWordsDict("negative") > 0).count()
negWordCount: Long = 15
```

Based on the following negative sentiment computation, we can conclude that this story
is, relatively, more pessimistic than the previous one analyzed:

```
scala> val sentiment = negWordCount / (numWords.toDouble)
sentiment: Double = 0.031055900621118012

scala> val modalWordCount = joinWordsDict.select("wordsInStory",
"modal").where(joinWordsDict("modal") > 0).groupBy("modal").count()

scala> modalWordCount.show()
+-----+-----+
|modal|count|
+-----+-----+
|    3|    1|
|    1|    3|
|    2|    4|
+-----+-----+
```

In the next section, we will shift our focus to identifying the major themes within a corpus
of documents.

Understanding themes in document corpuses

Bag-of-words-based techniques can also be used to classify common themes in documents or to identify themes within a corpus of documents. Broadly, these techniques, like most, are attempting to reduce the dimensionality of the term-document matrix, based on each word's relation to latent variables in this case.

One of the earliest approaches to this type of classification was **Latent Semantic Analysis (LSA)**. LSA can avoid the limitations of count-based methods associated with synonyms and terms with multiple meanings. Over the years, the concept of LSA has evolved into another model called **Latent Dirichlet Allocation (LDA)**.

LDA allows us to identify latent thematic structure within a collection of documents. Both LSA and LDA use the term-document matrix for reducing the dimensionality of the term space and for producing the topic weights. A constraint of both the LSA and LDA techniques is that they work best when applied to large documents.

 For more detailed explanation of LDA, refer to *Latent Dirichlet Allocation,* by David M. Blei, Andrew Y. Ng, and Michael I. Jordan, at http://ai.stanford.edu/~ang/papers/jair03-lda.pdf.

Now, we present an example of using LDA over a corpus of XML documents.

Start the Spark shell with the package for reading XML documents as we will be reading an XML-based corpus in this section:

```
Aurobindos-MacBook-Pro-2:spark-2.2.1-SNAPSHOT-bin-hadoop2.7
aurobindosarkar$ bin/spark-shell --driver-memory 12g --conf
spark.driver.maxResultSize=12g --conf spark.sql.shuffle.partitions=800 --
packages com.databricks:spark-xml_2.11:0.4.1
```

Next, we define a few constants for the number of topics, maximum number of iterations, and the vocabulary size, as shown:

```
scala> val numTopics: Int = 10
scala> val maxIterations: Int = 100
scala> val vocabSize: Int = 10000
```

The PERMISSIVE mode, used as follows, allows us to continue creating a DataFrame even while encountering corrupt records during parsing. The rowTag parameter specifies the XML node to be read. Here, we are interested in the sentences present in the document for our topic's analysis using LDA.

The Dataset for this example contains 4,000 Australian legal cases from the **Federal Court of Australia (FCA)**, and can be downloaded from `https://archive.ics.uci.edu/ml/datasets/Legal+Case+Reports`.

We read in all the case files, as demonstrated:

```scala
scala> val df =
spark.read.format("com.databricks.spark.xml").option("rowTag",
"sentences").option("mode",
"PERMISSIVE").load("file:///Users/aurobindosarkar/Downloads/corpus/fulltext
/*.xml")
```

Next, we generate document IDs for each of the legal cases, as follows:

```scala
scala> val docDF = df.select("sentence._VALUE").withColumn("docId",
monotonically_increasing_id()).withColumn("sentences", concat_ws(",",
$"_VALUE")).drop("_VALUE")

scala> // Split each document into words
scala> val tokens = new
RegexTokenizer().setGaps(false).setPattern("\\p{L}+").setInputCol("sentence
s").setOutputCol("words").transform(docDF)

scala> //Remove stop words using the default stop word list provided with
the Spark distribution.
scala> val filteredTokens = new
StopWordsRemover().setCaseSensitive(false).setInputCol("words").setOutputCo
l("filtered").transform(tokens)
```

We use a `CountVectorizer` (and `CountVectorizerModel`) to convert our collection of legal documents into vectors of token counts. Here, we do not have a priori dictionary available, so the `CountVectorizer` is used as an Estimator to extract the vocabulary and generate a `CountVectorizerModel`. The model produces sparse representations for the documents over the vocabulary, which is then passed to the LDA algorithm. During the fitting process, the `CountVectorizer` will select the top `vocabSize` words ordered by term frequency across the corpus:

```scala
scala> val cvModel = new
CountVectorizer().setInputCol("filtered").setOutputCol("features").setVocab
Size(vocabSize).fit(filteredTokens)

scala> val termVectors = cvModel.transform(filteredTokens).select("docId",
"features")

scala> val lda = new LDA().setK(numTopics).setMaxIter(maxIterations)

scala> val ldaModel = lda.fit(termVectors)
```

```
scala> println("Model was fit using parameters: " +
ldaModel.parent.extractParamMap)

Model was fit using parameters: {
lda_8b00356ca964-checkpointInterval: 10,
lda_8b00356ca964-featuresCol: features,
lda_8b00356ca964-k: 10,
lda_8b00356ca964-keepLastCheckpoint: true,
lda_8b00356ca964-learningDecay: 0.51,
lda_8b00356ca964-learningOffset: 1024.0,
lda_8b00356ca964-maxIter: 100,
lda_8b00356ca964-optimizeDocConcentration: true,
lda_8b00356ca964-optimizer: online,
lda_8b00356ca964-seed: 1435876747,
lda_8b00356ca964-subsamplingRate: 0.05,
lda_8b00356ca964-topicDistributionCol: topicDistribution
}
```

We compute the log-likelihood and the log-perplexity of the LDA model, as shown. A model with higher likelihood implies a better model. Similarly, lower perplexity represents a better model:

```
scala> val ll = ldaModel.logLikelihood(termVectors)
ll: Double = -6.912755229181568E7

scala> val lp = ldaModel.logPerplexity(termVectors)
lp: Double = 7.558777992719632

scala> println(s"The lower bound on the log likelihood of the entire
corpus: $ll")
The lower bound on the log likelihood of the entire corpus:
-6.912755229181568E7

scala> println(s"The upper bound on perplexity: $lp")
The upper bound on perplexity: 7.558777992719632
```

Next, we use the `describeTopics()` function to display the topics described by their top-weighted terms, as illustrated:

```
scala> val topicsDF = ldaModel.describeTopics(3)

scala> println("The topics described by their top-weighted terms:")
The topics described by their top-weighted terms are the following:

scala> topicsDF.show(false)
```

```
+------+-----------------+----------------------------------------------------------------------+
|topic|termIndices      |termWeights                                                           |
+------+-----------------+----------------------------------------------------------------------+
|0    |[40, 168, 0]     |[0.013479828514522157, 0.007988498264811112, 0.0078345569720004216]|
|1    |[3, 231, 292]    |[0.011157720765464901, 0.010950386549468765, 0.009933881657369987]|
|2    |[0, 32, 3]       |[0.016998033029244405, 0.00897362312135043, 0.005552939490101682] |
|3    |[3, 44, 211]     |[0.010640383419263965, 0.009589519391260229, 0.008719954776309678]|
|4    |[559, 130, 678]  |[0.014699094408320094, 0.013142729264265737, 0.006943073670536392]|
|5    |[4, 12, 1]       |[0.034504142560020877, 0.02081996234868235, 0.0165535310091123631]|
|6    |[0, 6, 13]       |[0.1008048266175278, 0.012606198050741528, 0.012490689284082269]  |
|7    |[124, 198, 218]  |[0.024444393452602815, 0.02039110399678152, 0.0199516758774353071]|
|8    |[197, 6, 447]    |[0.008833939029528915, 0.007881170922130781, 0.0060909595819592994]|
|9    |[2, 1, 9]        |[0.017878616381976048, 0.012342706034341355, 0.009959389216233391]|
+------+-----------------+----------------------------------------------------------------------+
```

```
scala> val transformed = ldaModel.transform(termVectors)

scala> transformed.select("docId",
"topicDistribution").take(3).foreach(println)

[0, [0.0,0.0,0.0,0.0,0.0,0.0,0.0,0.0,0.0,0.0]]
[8589934592, [8.963966883240337E-5,7.477786237947913E-5,1.16952147240077773E-
4,7.651092413869693E-5,5.878144972523343E-5,1.533289774455994E-4,8.25079403
4920294E-5,6.472049126896475E-5,7.008103300313653E-5,0.9992126995056172]]
[17179869184, [9.665344356333612E-6,8.06287932260242E-6,0.13933607311582796,
8.249745717562721E-6,6.338075472527743E-6,1.6528598250017008E-5,8.896370685
87104E-6,6.978449157294409E-6,0.029630980885952427,0.8309682265352574]]

scala> val vocab = cvModel.vocabulary
```

```
vocab: Array[String] = Array(mr, applicant, court, act, tribunal, made, evidence, may,
application, respondent, v, decision, appellant, said, case, claim, order, also,
whether, first, time, j, one, ltd, b, person, reasons, australia, costs, relevant,
notice, upon, agreement, relation, appeal, proceedings, federal, hearing, pty,
information, company, part, matter, judgment, conduct, respect, circumstances,
question, however, ms, section, respondents, date, must, given, make, second,
minister, issue, review, within, law, applicants, counsel, fact, proceeding, parties,
orders, two, documents, c, provided, terms, particular, basis, see, referred,
statement, view, letter, claims, effect, australian, business, party, set, fca,
following, period, cth, group, subject, present, matters, reason, ...
```

We can display the results containing the actual terms corresponding to the term indices, as follows. It is quite evident from the words displayed here that we are dealing with a legal corpus:

```
scala> for ((row) <- topicsDF) {
| var i = 0
| var termsString = ""
| var topicTermIndicesString = ""
| val topicNumber = row.get(0)
| val topicTerms:WrappedArray[Int] =
```

```
row.get(1).asInstanceOf[WrappedArray[Int]]
|
| for (i <- 0 to topicTerms.length-1){
| topicTermIndicesString += topicTerms(i) +", "
| termsString += vocab(topicTerms(i)) +", "
| }
|
| println ("Topic: "+ topicNumber+ "|["+topicTermIndicesString + "]|[" +
termsString +"]")
| }

Topic: 1|[3, 231, 292, ]|[act, title, native, ]
Topic: 5|[4, 12, 1, ]|[tribunal, appellant, applicant, ]
Topic: 6|[0, 6, 13, ]|[mr, evidence, said, ]
Topic: 0|[40, 168, 0, ]|[company, scheme, mr, ]
Topic: 2|[0, 32, 3, ]|[mr, agreement, act, ]
Topic: 7|[124, 198, 218, ]|[commissioner, income, tax, ]
Topic: 3|[3, 44, 211, ]|[act, conduct, price, ]
Topic: 8|[197, 6, 447, ]|[trade, evidence, mark, ]
Topic: 4|[559, 130, 678, ]|[patent, dr, university, ]
Topic: 9|[2, 1, 9, ]|[court, applicant, respondent, ]Using
```

The next main topic in textual analysis is collocated words. For some words, much of their meaning is derived from their collocation with other words. Predicting word meaning based on collocation is generally one of the most common extensions beyond the simple bag-of-words approach.

In the next section, we will examine the use of Naive Bayes classifier on n-gram.

Using Naive Bayes classifiers

Naive Bayes classifiers are a family of probabilistic classifiers based on applying the Bayes' conditional probability theorem. These classifiers assume independence between the features. Naive Bayes is often the baseline method for text categorization with word frequencies as the feature set. Despite the strong independence assumptions, the Naive Bayes classifiers are fast and easy to implement; hence, they are used very commonly in practice.

While Naive Bayes is very popular, it also suffers from errors that can lead to favoring of one class over the other(s). For example, skewed data can cause the classifier to favor one class over another. Similarly, the independence assumption can lead to erroneous classification weights that favor one class over another.

For specific heuristics for dealing with problems associated with Naive Bayes classifers, refer to *Tackling the Poor Assumptions of Naive Bayes Text Classifiers*, by Rennie, Shih, et al at `https://people.csail.mit.edu/jrennie/papers/icml03-nb.pdf`.

One of the main advantages of the Naive Bayes approach is that it does not require a large training Dataset to estimate the parameters necessary for classification. Among the various approaches for word classification using supervised machine learning, the Naive Bayes method is extremely popular; for example, which sentences in an annual report can be classified as being "negative," "positive," or "neutral". Naive Bayes method is also most commonly used with n-grams and **Support Vector Machines (SVMs)**.

N-grams are used for a variety of different tasks. For example, n-grams can be used for developing features for supervised machine learning models such as SVMs, Maximum Entropy models, and Naive Bayes. When the value of N is 1, the n-grams are referred to as unigrams (essentially, the individual words in a sentence; when the value of N is 2, they are called bigrams, when N is 3, they are called trigrams, and so on. The main idea here is to use tokens such as bigrams in the feature space instead of individual words or unigrams.

The Dataset for this example contains approximately 1.69 million Amazon reviews for the electronics category, and can be downloaded from `http://jmcauley.ucsd.edu/data/amazon/`.

For a more detailed explanation of steps used in this example, check out Natural Language Processing with Apache Spark ML and Amazon Reviews (Parts 1 & 2), Mike Seddon, at `http://mike.seddon.ca/natural-language-processing-with-apache-spark-ml-and-amazon-reviews-part-1/`.

First, we read the input JSON file to create our input DataFrame:

```
scala> val inDF =
spark.read.json("file:///Users/aurobindosarkar/Downloads/reviews_Electronic
s_5.json")

scala> inDF.show()
```

```
+----------+---------+-------+--------------------+-----------+--------------+--------------------+--------------------+--------------+
|      asin|  helpful|overall|          reviewText| reviewTime|    reviewerID|        reviewerName|             summary|unixReviewTime|
+----------+---------+-------+--------------------+-----------+--------------+--------------------+--------------------+--------------+
|0528881469|   [0, 0]|    5.0|We got this GPS f...|  06 2, 2013|A094DHGC771SJ|              amazdnu|       Gotta have GPS!|    1370131200|
|0528881469| [12, 15]|    1.0|I'm a professiona...| 11 25, 2010|AMO214LNFCEI4|      Amazon Customer|     Very Disappointed|    1290643200|
|0528881469| [43, 45]|    3.0|Well, what can I ...|  09 9, 2010|A3N7T0DYB3Y4IG|         C. A. Freeman|        1st impression|    1283990400|
|0528881469|  [9, 10]|    2.0|Not going to writ...| 11 24, 2010|A1H8PY3QHMQQA0|Dave M. Shaw "mac...|     Great grafics, PO...|    1290556800|
|0528881469|   [0, 0]|    1.0|I've had mine for...| 09 29, 2011|A24EV6RXELQZ63|          Wayne Smith|     Major issues, onl...|    1317254400|
|0594451647|   [3, 3]|    5.0|I am using this w...|  01 3, 2014|A2JXAZZI9PHK9Z|Billy G. Noland "...|     HDMI Nook adapter...|    1388707200|
|0594451647|   [0, 0]|    2.0|The cable is very...| 04 27, 2014|A2P5U7BDKKT7FW|           Christian|     Cheap proprietary...|    1398556800|
|0594451647|   [0, 0]|    5.0|This adaptor is r...|  05 4, 2014|AAZ084UMH8VZ2|D. L. Brown "A Kn...|     A Perfdect Nook H...|    1399161600|
|0594451647|   [0, 0]|    4.0|This adapter easi...| 07 11, 2014|AEZ3CR6BKIROJ|         Mark Dietter|     A nice easy to us...|    1405036800|
|0594451647|   [3, 3]|    5.0|This product real...| 01 20, 2014|A3BY5KCNQZXV5U|             Matenai|     This works great ...|    1390176000|
|0594481813|   [2, 2]|    4.0|This item is just...| 04 16, 2014|A7S2B0I67WNWB|              AllyMG|           As expected|    1397606400|
|0594481813|   [0, 0]|    5.0|bought for a spar...|  05 5, 2014|A3HICVLF4PFFMN|      Amazon Customer|            great fit|    1399248000|
|0594481813|   [1, 1]|    5.0|My son crewed my ...| 06 24, 2013|ANSKSPEEAKY7S|                Gena|          Works Great|    1372032000|
|0594481813|   [0, 1]|    3.0|This is a good be...| 05 25, 2013|A2QBZA4S1ROX9Q|                Jake|            It Works|    1369440000|
|0594481813|   [2, 2]|    5.0|I lost my B&N ori...|  03 9, 2014|ANY6JUFM0GH8U|          J. Clement|     Great replacement...|    1394323200|
|0594481813|   [0, 0]|    3.0|It does 2A and ch...| 08 31, 2013|AT09WGFUM934H|                John|     This is the oem c...|    1377907200|
|0594481813|   [3, 5]|    3.0|Go to Target or B...| 09 18, 2013|AGAKHE014LQFU|           Nicodimus|     $45 for a power c...|    1379462400|
|0594481813|   [2, 2]|    4.0|Works well, a lit...| 06 27, 2013|A1S6B5QFWGVL5U|          T. Vaughan|      Good replacement|    1372291200|
|0972683275|   [0, 0]|    5.0|This is a great b...| 07 12, 2014|A20XXTXXF2TCPY|                null|     Excelant mount fo...|    1405123200|
|0972683275|   [1, 1]|    5.0|This mount is jus...| 04 30, 2013|A2IDCSC6NVONIZ|             2Cents!|              Perfect|    1367280000|
+----------+---------+-------+--------------------+-----------+--------------+--------------------+--------------------+--------------+
only showing top 20 rows
```

You can print the schema, as shown:

```
scala> inDF.printSchema()
root
 |-- asin: string (nullable = true)
 |-- helpful: array (nullable = true)
 |    |-- element: long (containsNull = true)
 |-- overall: double (nullable = true)
 |-- reviewText: string (nullable = true)
 |-- reviewTime: string (nullable = true)
 |-- reviewerID: string (nullable = true)
 |-- reviewerName: string (nullable = true)
 |-- summary: string (nullable = true)
 |-- unixReviewTime: long (nullable = true)
```

Next, we print out the count of records for each of the rating values, as follows. Note that the number of records is highly skewed in favor of rating five. This skew can impact our results in favor of rating five versus the other ratings:

```
scala> inDF.groupBy("overall").count().orderBy("overall").show()
+-------+-------+
|overall|  count|
+-------+-------+
|    1.0| 108725|
```

```
|      2.0|   82139|
|      3.0|  142257|
|      4.0|  347041|
|      5.0|1009026|
+-------+-------+
```

We create a view from the DataFrame, as follows. This step can conveniently help us create a more balanced training DataFrame containing an equal number of records from each of the rating categories:

```
scala> inDF.createOrReplaceTempView("reviewsTable")

scala> val reviewsDF = spark.sql(
| """
| SELECT text, label, rowNumber FROM (
| SELECT
| overall AS label, reviewText AS text, row_number() OVER (PARTITION BY
overall ORDER BY rand()) AS rowNumber FROM reviewsTable
| ) reviewsTable
| WHERE rowNumber <= 60000
| """
| )

scala> reviewsDF.groupBy("label").count().orderBy("label").show()
+-----+-----+
|label|count|
+-----+-----+
|  1.0|60000|
|  2.0|60000|
|  3.0|60000|
|  4.0|60000|
| 5.0|60000|
+-----+-----+
```

Now, we create our training and test Datasets using the row numbers:

```
scala> val trainingData = reviewsDF.filter(reviewsDF("rowNumber") <=
50000).select("text","label")

scala> val testData = reviewsDF.filter(reviewsDF("rowNumber") >
10000).select("text","label")
```

In the given steps, we tokenize our text, remove stop words, and create bigrams and trigrams:

```scala
scala> val regexTokenizer = new RegexTokenizer().setPattern("[a-zA-
Z']+").setGaps(false).setInputCol("text")

scala> val remover = new
StopWordsRemover().setInputCol(regexTokenizer.getOutputCol)

scala> val bigrams = new NGram().setN(2).setInputCol(remover.getOutputCol)

scala> val trigrams = new NGram().setN(3).setInputCol(remover.getOutputCol)
```

In the next steps, we define `HashingTF` instances for the unigrams, the bigrams, and the trigrams:

```scala
scala> val removerHashingTF = new
HashingTF().setInputCol(remover.getOutputCol)

scala> val ngram2HashingTF = new
HashingTF().setInputCol(bigrams.getOutputCol)

scala> val ngram3HashingTF = new
HashingTF().setInputCol(trigrams.getOutputCol)

scala> val assembler = new
VectorAssembler().setInputCols(Array(removerHashingTF.getOutputCol,
ngram2HashingTF.getOutputCol, ngram3HashingTF.getOutputCol))

scala> val labelIndexer = new
StringIndexer().setInputCol("label").setOutputCol("indexedLabel").fit(revie
wsDF)

scala> val labelConverter = new
IndexToString().setInputCol("prediction").setOutputCol("predictedLabel").se
tLabels(labelIndexer.labels)
```

Then, we create an instance of the Naive Bayes classifier:

```scala
scala> val nb = new
NaiveBayes().setLabelCol(labelIndexer.getOutputCol).setFeaturesCol(assemble
r.getOutputCol).setPredictionCol("prediction").setModelType("multinomial")
```

We assemble our processing pipeline, as illustrated:

```scala
scala> val pipeline = new Pipeline().setStages(Array(regexTokenizer,
remover, bigrams, trigrams, removerHashingTF, ngram2HashingTF,
ngram3HashingTF, assembler, labelIndexer, nb, labelConverter))
```

We create a parameter grid to be used for cross-validation to arrive at the best set of parameters for our model, as follows:

```
scala> val paramGrid = new
ParamGridBuilder().addGrid(removerHashingTF.numFeatures,
Array(1000,10000)).addGrid(ngram2HashingTF.numFeatures,
Array(1000,10000)).addGrid(ngram3HashingTF.numFeatures,
Array(1000,10000)).build()

paramGrid: Array[org.apache.spark.ml.param.ParamMap] =
Array({
hashingTF_4b2023cfcec8-numFeatures: 1000,
hashingTF_7bd4dd537583-numFeatures: 1000,
hashingTF_7cd2d166ac2c-numFeatures: 1000
}, {
hashingTF_4b2023cfcec8-numFeatures: 10000,
hashingTF_7bd4dd537583-numFeatures: 1000,
hashingTF_7cd2d166ac2c-numFeatures: 1000
}, {
hashingTF_4b2023cfcec8-numFeatures: 1000,
hashingTF_7bd4dd537583-numFeatures: 10000,
hashingTF_7cd2d166ac2c-numFeatures: 1000
}, {
hashingTF_4b2023cfcec8-numFeatures: 10000,
hashingTF_7bd4dd537583-numFeatures: 10000,
hashingTF_7cd2d166ac2c-numFeatures: 1000
}, {
hashingTF_4b2023cfcec8-numFeatures: 1000,
hashingTF_7bd4dd537583-numFeatures: 1000,
hashingTF_7cd2d166ac2c-numFeatures: 10000
}, {
hashingTF_4b2023cfcec8-numFeatures: 10000,
hashingTF_7bd4dd537...
```

In the next step, note that a k-fold cross-validation performs model selection by splitting the Dataset into a set of non-overlapping, randomly partitioned folds that are used as separate training and test Datasets; for example, with k=3 folds, K-fold cross-validation will generate three (training, test) Dataset pairs, each of which uses 2/3 of the data for training and 1/3 for testing.

Each fold is used as the test set exactly once. To evaluate a particular ParamMap, CrossValidator computes the average evaluation metric for the three models produced by fitting the Estimator on the two different (training, test) Dataset pairs. After identifying the best ParamMap, CrossValidator finally refits the Estimator using the best ParamMap on the entire Dataset:

```
scala> val cv = new
CrossValidator().setEstimator(pipeline).setEvaluator(new
MulticlassClassificationEvaluator().setLabelCol("indexedLabel").setPredicti
onCol("prediction").setMetricName("accuracy")).setEstimatorParamMaps(paramG
rid).setNumFolds(5)

scala> val cvModel = cv.fit(trainingData)

scala> val predictions = cvModel.transform(testData)

scala> val evaluator = new
MulticlassClassificationEvaluator().setLabelCol("indexedLabel").setPredicti
onCol("prediction").setMetricName("accuracy")

scala> val accuracy = evaluator.evaluate(predictions)
accuracy: Double = 0.481472

scala> println("Test Error = " + (1.0 - accuracy))
Test Error = 0.518528
```

The prediction results obtained are not good after executing the previous set of steps. Let's check whether we can improve the results by reducing the number of review categories and increase the number of records in our training set, as illustrated:

```
scala> def udfReviewBins() = udf[Double, Double] { a => val x = a match {
case 1.0 => 1.0; case 2.0 => 1.0; case 3.0 => 2.0; case 4.0 => 3.0; case
5.0 => 3.0;}; x;}

scala> val modifiedInDF = inDF.withColumn("rating",
udfReviewBins()($"overall")).drop("overall")

scala> modifiedInDF.show()
```

```
+----------+-------+-----------------+-----------+-------------+-----------------+------------------+---------------+------+
|      asin|helpful|       reviewText| reviewTime|   reviewerID|     reviewerName|           summary|unixReviewTime|rating|
+----------+-------+-----------------+-----------+-------------+-----------------+------------------+---------------+------+
|0528881469| [0, 0]|We got this GPS f...| 06 2, 2013| A094DHGC771SJ|          amazdnu|    Gotta have GPS!|    1370131200|   3.0|
|0528881469|[12, 15]|I'm a professiona...|11 25, 2010| AM0214LNFCEI4|  Amazon Customer| Very Disappointed|    1290643200|   1.0|
|0528881469|[43, 45]|Well, what can I ...| 09 9, 2010| A3N7T0DY83Y4IG|    C. A. Freeman|     1st impression|    1283990400|   2.0|
|0528881469| [9, 10]|Not going to writ...|11 24, 2010| A1H8PY3QHMQQA0|Dave M. Shaw "mac...|Great grafics, PO...|    1290556800|   1.0|
|0528881469| [0, 0]|I've had mine for...| 09 29, 2011| A24EV6RXELQZ63|      Wayne Smith|Major issues, onl...|    1317254400|   1.0|
|0594451647| [3, 3]|I am using this w...| 01 3, 2014| A2JXAZZI9PHK9Z|Billy G. Noland "...|HDMI Nook adapter...|    1388707200|   3.0|
|0594451647| [0, 0]|The cable is very...| 04 27, 2014| A2P5U7BDKKT7FW|        Christian|Cheap proprietary...|    1398556800|   1.0|
|0594451647| [0, 0]|This adaptor is r...| 05 4, 2014| AAZ084UMH8VZ2|D. L. Brown "A Kn...|A Perfdect Nook H...|    1399161600|   3.0|
|0594451647| [0, 0]|This adapter easi...| 07 11, 2014| AEZ3CR6BKIR0J|    Mark Dietter|A nice easy to us...|    1405036800|   3.0|
|0594451647| [3, 3]|This product real...| 01 20, 2014| A3BY5KCNQZXV5U|          Matenai|This works great ...|    1390176000|   3.0|
|0594481813| [2, 2]|This item is just...| 04 16, 2014| A7S2B0I67WNWB|           AllyMG|       As expected|    1397606400|   3.0|
|0594481813| [0, 0]|bought for a spar...| 05 5, 2014| A3HICVLF4PFFMN|  Amazon Customer|         great fit|    1399248000|   3.0|
|0594481813| [1, 1]|My son crewed my ...| 06 24, 2013| ANSKSPEEAKY7S|             Gena|      Works Great!|    1372032000|   3.0|
|0594481813| [0, 0]|This is a good be...| 05 25, 2013| A2QBZA4S1R0X9Q|             Jake|         It Works|    1369440000|   2.0|
|0594481813| [2, 2]|I lost my B&N ori...| 03 9, 2014| ANY6JUFM0GH8U| J. Clement|Great replacement...|    1394323200|   3.0|
|0594481813| [0, 0]|It does 2A and ch...| 08 31, 2014| AT09WGFUM934H|             John|This is the oem c...|    1377907200|   2.0|
|0594481813| [3, 5]|Go to Target or B...| 09 18, 2013| AGAKHE014LQFU|         Nicodimus|$45 for a power c...|    1379462400|   2.0|
|0594481813| [2, 2]|Works well, a lit...| 06 27, 2013| A1S6B5QFWGVL5U|       T. Vaughan|  Good replacement|    1372291200|   3.0|
|0972683275| [0, 0]|This is a great b...| 07 12, 2014| A20XXTXWF2TCPY|             null|Excelant mount fo...|    1405123200|   3.0|
|0972683275| [1, 1]|This mount is jus...| 04 30, 2013| A2IDCSC6NV0NIZ|          2Cents!|           Perfect|    1367280000|   3.0|
+----------+-------+-----------------+-----------+-------------+-----------------+------------------+---------------+------+
only showing top 20 rows
```

```scala
scala> modifiedInDF.groupBy("rating").count().orderBy("rating").show()
+------+-------+
|rating|  count|
+------+-------+
|   1.0| 190864|
|   2.0| 142257|
|   3.0|1356067|
+------+-------+


scala> modifiedInDF.createOrReplaceTempView("modReviewsTable")

scala> val reviewsDF = spark.sql(
| """
| SELECT text, label, rowNumber FROM (
| SELECT
| rating AS label, reviewText AS text, row_number() OVER (PARTITION BY
rating ORDER BY rand()) AS rowNumber FROM modReviewsTable
| ) modReviewsTable
| WHERE rowNumber <= 120000
| """
| )
reviewsDF: org.apache.spark.sql.DataFrame = [text: string,

scala> reviewsDF.groupBy("label").count().orderBy("label").show()
+-----+------+
|label| count|
+-----+------+
|  1.0|120000|
|  2.0|120000|
|  3.0|120000|
+-----+------+
```

```
scala> val trainingData = reviewsDF.filter(reviewsDF("rowNumber") <=
100000).select("text","label")

scala> val testData = reviewsDF.filter(reviewsDF("rowNumber") >
20000).select("text","label")

scala> val regexTokenizer = new RegexTokenizer().setPattern("[a-zA-
Z']+").setGaps(false).setInputCol("text")

scala> val remover = new
StopWordsRemover().setInputCol(regexTokenizer.getOutputCol)

scala> val bigrams = new NGram().setN(2).setInputCol(remover.getOutputCol)

scala> val trigrams = new NGram().setN(3).setInputCol(remover.getOutputCol)

scala> val removerHashingTF = new
HashingTF().setInputCol(remover.getOutputCol)

scala> val ngram2HashingTF = new
HashingTF().setInputCol(bigrams.getOutputCol)

scala> val ngram3HashingTF = new
HashingTF().setInputCol(trigrams.getOutputCol)

scala> val assembler = new
VectorAssembler().setInputCols(Array(removerHashingTF.getOutputCol,
ngram2HashingTF.getOutputCol, ngram3HashingTF.getOutputCol))

scala> val labelIndexer = new
StringIndexer().setInputCol("label").setOutputCol("indexedLabel").fit(revie
wsDF)
```

The label converter can be used to recover the original labels' text for improved readability in case of textual labels:

```
scala> val labelConverter = new
IndexToString().setInputCol("prediction").setOutputCol("predictedLabel").se
tLabels(labelIndexer.labels)
```

Next, we create an instance of our Naive Bayes classifier:

```
scala> val nb = new
NaiveBayes().setLabelCol(labelIndexer.getOutputCol).setFeaturesCol(assemble
r.getOutputCol).setPredictionCol("prediction").setModelType("multinomial")
```

We assemble our pipeline with all the Transformers and the Naive Bayes estimator, as follows:

```scala
scala> val pipeline = new Pipeline().setStages(Array(regexTokenizer,
remover, bigrams, trigrams, removerHashingTF, ngram2HashingTF,
ngram3HashingTF, assembler, labelIndexer, nb, labelConverter))
```

We use cross-validation to select the best parameters for our model, as shown:

```scala
scala> val paramGrid = new
ParamGridBuilder().addGrid(removerHashingTF.numFeatures,
Array(1000,10000)).addGrid(ngram2HashingTF.numFeatures,
Array(1000,10000)).addGrid(ngram3HashingTF.numFeatures,
Array(1000,10000)).build()

paramGrid: Array[org.apache.spark.ml.param.ParamMap] =
Array({
hashingTF_2f3a479f07ef-numFeatures: 1000,
hashingTF_0dc7c74af716-numFeatures: 1000,
hashingTF_17632a08c82c-numFeatures: 1000
}, {
hashingTF_2f3a479f07ef-numFeatures: 10000,
hashingTF_0dc7c74af716-numFeatures: 1000,
hashingTF_17632a08c82c-numFeatures: 1000
}, {
hashingTF_2f3a479f07ef-numFeatures: 1000,
hashingTF_0dc7c74af716-numFeatures: 10000,
hashingTF_17632a08c82c-numFeatures: 1000
}, {
hashingTF_2f3a479f07ef-numFeatures: 10000,
hashingTF_0dc7c74af716-numFeatures: 10000,
hashingTF_17632a08c82c-numFeatures: 1000
}, {
hashingTF_2f3a479f07ef-numFeatures: 1000,
hashingTF_0dc7c74af716-numFeatures: 1000,
hashingTF_17632a08c82c-numFeatures: 10000
}, {
hashingTF_2f3a479f07ef-numFeatures: 10000,
hashingTF_0dc7c74af...

scala> val cv = new
CrossValidator().setEstimator(pipeline).setEvaluator(new
MulticlassClassificationEvaluator().setLabelCol("indexedLabel").setPredicti
onCol("prediction").setMetricName("accuracy")).setEstimatorParamMaps(paramG
rid).setNumFolds(5)

scala> val cvModel = cv.fit(trainingData)
```

```
scala> val predictions = cvModel.transform(testData)

scala> val evaluator = new
MulticlassClassificationEvaluator().setLabelCol("indexedLabel").setPredicti
onCol("prediction").setMetricName("accuracy")

scala> val accuracy = evaluator.evaluate(predictions)
accuracy: Double = 0.63663

scala> println("Test Error = " + (1.0 - accuracy))
Test Error = 0.36336999999999997
```

Note the significant improvement in our prediction results as a result of clubbing ratings into fewer categories and increasing the number of records for training our model.

In the next section, we will present an example of machine learning on textual data.

Developing a machine learning application

In this section, we will present a machine learning example for textual analysis. Refer to Chapter 6, *Using Spark SQL in Machine Learning Applications*, for more details about the machine learning code presented in this section.

The Dataset used in the following example contains 1,080 documents of free text business descriptions of Brazilian companies categorized into a subset of nine categories. You can download this Dataset from https://archive.ics.uci.edu/ml/datasets/CNAE-9.

```
scala> val inRDD =
spark.sparkContext.textFile("file:///Users/aurobindosarkar/Downloads/CNAE-9
.data")

scala> val rowRDD = inRDD.map(_.split(",")).map(attributes =>
Row(attributes(0).toDouble, attributes(1).toDouble, attributes(2).toDouble,
attributes(3).toDouble, attributes(4).toDouble, attributes(5).toDouble,
.
.
.
attributes(852).toDouble, attributes(853).toDouble,
attributes(854).toDouble, attributes(855).toDouble,
attributes(856).toDouble))
```

Next, we define a schema for the input records:

```
scala> val schemaString = "label _c715 _c195 _c480 _c856 _c136 _c53 _c429
_c732 _c271 _c742 _c172 _c45 _c374 _c233 _c720
.
.
.
_c408 _c604 _c766 _c676 _c52 _c755 _c728 _c693 _c119 _c160 _c141 _c516
_c419 _c69 _c621 _c423 _c137 _c549 _c636 _c772 _c799 _c336 _c841 _c82 _c123
_c474 _c470 _c286 _c555 _c36 _c299 _c829 _c361 _c263 _c522 _c495 _c135"

scala> val fields = schemaString.split(" ").map(fieldName =>
StructField(fieldName, DoubleType, nullable = false))

scala> val schema = StructType(fields)
```

We then use the schema to convert the RDD to a DataFrame, as illustrated:

```
scala> val inDF = spark.createDataFrame(rowRDD, schema)

scala> inDF.take(1).foreach(println)
```

```
[1.0,0.0,0.0,0.0,0.0,0.0,0.0,0.0,0.0,0.0,0.0,0.0,0.0,0.0,0.0,0.0,0.0,0.0,0.0,0.0,0.0,0.0,0.0,0.0,0.0,0.0,0.0,0.0,0.0,0.0,0.0,0.0,0.0,0.0,0.0,0.0,0.0,0.0,0.0,0.0,0.0,0.0,0.0,0.0,0.0,0.0,0.0,0.0,0.0,0.0,0.0,0.0,0.0,0.0,0.0,0.0,0.0,0.0,0.0,0.0,0.0,0.0,0.0,0.0,0.0,0.0,0.0,0.0,0.0,0.0,0.0,0.0,0.0,0.0,0.0,0.0,0.0,0.0,0.0,0.0,0.0,0.0,0.0,0.0,0.0,0.0,0.0,0.0,0.0,0.0,0.0,0.0,0.0,0.0,0.0,0.0,0.0,0.0,0.0,0.0,0.0,0.0,0.0,0.0,0.0,0.0,0.0,0.0,0.0,0.0,0.0,0.0,0.0,0.0,0.0,0.0,0.0,0.0,0.0,0.0,0.0,0.0,0.0,0.0,0.0,0.0,0.0,0.0,0.0,0.0,0.0,0.0,0.0,0.0,0.0,0.0,0.0,0.0,0.0,0.0,0.0,0.0,0.0,0.0,0.0,0.0,0.0,0.0,0.0,0.0,0.0,0.0,0.0,0.0,0.0,0.0,0.0,0.0,0.0,0.0,0.0,0.0,0.0,0.0,0.0,0.0,0.0,0.0,0.0,0.0,0.0,0.0,0.0,0.0,0.0,0.0,0.0,0.0,0.0,0.0,1.0,0.0,0.0,0.0,0.0,0.0,0.0,0.0,0.0,0.0,0.0,0.0,0.0,0.0,0.0,0.0,0.0,0.0,0.0,0.0,0.0,0.0,0.0,0.0,0.0,0.0,0.0,0.0,0.0,0.0,0.0,0.0,0.0,0.0,0.0,0.0,0.0,0.0,0.0,0.0,0.0,0.0,0.0,0.0,0.0,0.0,0.0,0.0,0.0,0.0,0.0,0.0,0.0,0.0,0.0,0.0,0.0,0.0,0.0,0.0,0.0,0.0,0.0,0.0,0.0,0.0,0.0,0.0,0.0,0.0,0.0,0.0,0.0,0.0,0.0,0.0,0.0,0.0,0.0,0.0,0.0,0.0,0.0,0.0,0.0,0.0,0.0,0.0,0.0,0.0,0.0,0.0,0.0,0.0,0.0,0.0,0.0,0.0,0.0,0.0,0.0,0.0,0.0,0.0,1.0,0.0,0.0,0.0,0.0,0.0,0.0,0.0,0.0,0.0,0.0,0.0,0.0,0.0,0.0,0.0,0.0,0.0,0.0,0.0,0.0,0.0,0.0,0.0,0.0,0.0,0.0,0.0,0.0,0.0,0.0,0.0,0.0,0.0,0.0,0.0,0.0,0.0,0.0,0.0,0.0,0.0,0.0,0.0,0.0,0.0,0.0,0.0,0.0,0.0,0.0,0.0,0.0,0.0,0.0,0.0,0.0,0.0,0.0,0.0,0.0,0.0,0.0,0.0,0.0,0.0,0.0,0.0,0.0,0.0,0.0,0.0,0.0,0.0,0.0,0.0,0.0,0.0,0.0,0.0,0.0,0.0,0.0,0.0,0.0,0.0,0.0,0.0,0.0,0.0,0.0,0.0,0.0,0.0,0.0,0.0,0.0,0.0,0.0,0.0,0.0,0.0,0.0,0.0,0.0,0.0,0.0,0.0,0.0,0.0,0.0,0.0,0.0,0.0,0.0,0.0,0.0,0.0,0.0,0.0,0.0,0.0,0.0,0.0,1.0,0.0,0.0,0.0,0.0,0.0,0.0,0.0,0.0,0.0,0.0,0.0,0.0,0.0,0.0,0.0,0.0,0.0,0.0,0.0,0.0,0.0,0.0,0.0,0.0,0.0,0.0,0.0]
```

Next, we add an index column to the DataFrame using the `monotonically_increasing_id()` function, as shown:

```scala
scala> val indexedDF= inDF.withColumn("id", monotonically_increasing_id())

scala> indexedDF.select("label", "id").show()
```

```
+-----+---+
|label| id|
+-----+---+
|  1.0|  0|
|  2.0|  1|
|  3.0|  2|
|  4.0|  3|
|  5.0|  4|
|  6.0|  5|
|  7.0|  6|
|  8.0|  7|
|  9.0|  8|
|  1.0|  9|
|  2.0| 10|
|  3.0| 11|
|  4.0| 12|
|  5.0| 13|
|  6.0| 14|
|  7.0| 15|
|  8.0| 16|
|  9.0| 17|
|  1.0| 18|
|  2.0| 19|
+-----+---+
only showing top 20 rows
```

In the following step, we assemble the feature vector:

```scala
scala> val columnNames =
Array("_c715","_c195","_c480","_c856","_c136","_c53","_c429","_c732","_c271
","_c742","_c172","_c45","_c374","_c233","_c720","_c294","_c461","_c87","_c
599","_c84","_c28","_c79","_c615","_c243","_c603","_c531","_c503","_c630","
_c33","_c428","_c385","_c751","_c664","_c540","_c626","_c730","_c9","_c699"
,"_c117","
.
.
.
c693","_c119","_c160","_c141","_c516","_c419","_c69","_c621","_c423","_c137
","_c549","_c636","_c772","_c799","_c336","_c841","_c82","_c123","id","_c47
4","_c470","_c286","_c555","_c36","_c299","_c829","_c361","_c263","_c522","
_c495","_c135")

scala> val assembler = new
```

```
VectorAssembler().setInputCols(columnNames).setOutputCol("features")

scala> val output = assembler.transform(indexedDF)

scala> output.select("id", "label", "features").take(5).foreach(println)
[0,1.0,(857,[333,606,829],[1.0,1.0,1.0])]
[1,2.0,(857,[725,730,740,844],[1.0,1.0,1.0,1.0])]
[2,3.0,(857,[72,277,844],[1.0,1.0,2.0])]
[3,4.0,(857,[72,606,813,822,844],[1.0,1.0,1.0,1.0,3.0])]
[4,5.0,(857,[215,275,339,386,475,489,630,844],[1.0,1.0,1.0,1.0,1.0,1.0,1.0,
4.0])]
```

We split the input Dataset into the training (90 percent of the records) and test (10 percent of the records) Datasets:

```
scala> val Array(trainingData, testData) = output.randomSplit(Array(0.9,
0.1), seed = 12345)

scala> val copyTestData = testData.drop("id").drop("features")
copyTestData: org.apache.spark.sql.DataFrame = [label: double, _c715:
double ... 855 more fields]

scala> copyTestData.coalesce(1).write.format("csv").option("header",
"false").mode("overwrite").save("file:///Users/aurobindosarkar/Downloads/CN
AE-9/input")
```

In the following step, we create and fit the logistic regression model on our training Dataset:

```
scala> val lr = new
LogisticRegression().setMaxIter(20).setRegParam(0.3).setElasticNetParam(0.8
)

scala> // Fit the model

scala> val lrModel = lr.fit(trainingData)
```

We can list the parameters of the model, as illustrated:

```
scala> println("Model was fit using parameters: " +
lrModel.parent.extractParamMap)

Model was fit using parameters: {
logreg_801d78ffc37d-aggregationDepth: 2,
logreg_801d78ffc37d-elasticNetParam: 0.8,
logreg_801d78ffc37d-family: auto,
logreg_801d78ffc37d-featuresCol: features,
logreg_801d78ffc37d-fitIntercept: true,
logreg_801d78ffc37d-labelCol: label,
```

```
logreg_801d78ffc37d-maxIter: 20,
logreg_801d78ffc37d-predictionCol: prediction,
logreg_801d78ffc37d-probabilityCol: probability,
logreg_801d78ffc37d-rawPredictionCol: rawPrediction,
logreg_801d78ffc37d-regParam: 0.3,
logreg_801d78ffc37d-standardization: true,
logreg_801d78ffc37d-threshold: 0.5,
logreg_801d78ffc37d-tol: 1.0E-6
}
```

Next, we display the coefficients and intercept values for our logistic regression model:

```
scala> println(s"Coefficients: \n${lrModel.coefficientMatrix}")
Coefficients:
10 x 857 CSCMatrix
(1,206) 0.33562831098750884
(5,386) 0.2803498729889301
(7,545) 0.525713129850472

scala> println(s"Intercepts: ${lrModel.interceptVector}")
Intercepts:
[-5.399655915806082,0.6130722758222028,0.6011509547631415,0.638133383665570
2,0.6011509547630515,0.5542027670693254,0.6325214445680327,0.53327033167331
28,0.6325214445681948,0.5936323589132501]
```

Next, we use the model to make predictions on the test Dataset, as demonstrated:

```
scala> val predictions = lrModel.transform(testData)
```

Select example rows to display the key columns in the predictions DataFrame, as shown:

```
scala> predictions.select("prediction", "label", "features").show(5)
```

```
+----------+-----+--------------------+
|prediction|label|            features|
+----------+-----+--------------------+
|       3.0|  1.0|(857,[331,493,704...|
|       1.0|  1.0|(857,[206,493,704...|
|       1.0|  1.0|(857,[70,206,510,...|
|       3.0|  2.0|(857,[402,707,844...|
|       3.0|  2.0|(857,[332,370,613...|
+----------+-----+--------------------+
only showing top 5 rows
```

We use an evaluator to compute the test error, as follows:

```scala
scala> val evaluator = new
MulticlassClassificationEvaluator().setLabelCol("label").setPredictionCol("
prediction").setMetricName("accuracy")
scala> val accuracy = evaluator.evaluate(predictions)
accuracy: Double = 0.2807017543859649
scala> println("Test Error = " + (1.0 - accuracy))
Test Error = 0.7192982456140351
```

The results of applying a logistic regression model to our Dataset are not particularly good.
Now, we define parameter grid to explore whether a better set of parameters can improve
the overall prediction results for our model:

```scala
scala> val lr = new LogisticRegression()
lr: org.apache.spark.ml.classification.LogisticRegression =
logreg_3fa32a4b5c6d

scala> val paramGrid = new ParamGridBuilder().addGrid(lr.regParam,
Array(0.1, 0.01)).addGrid(lr.elasticNetParam, Array(0.0, 0.5, 1.0)).build()

paramGrid: Array[org.apache.spark.ml.param.ParamMap] =
Array({
logreg_3fa32a4b5c6d-elasticNetParam: 0.0,
logreg_3fa32a4b5c6d-regParam: 0.1
}, {
logreg_3fa32a4b5c6d-elasticNetParam: 0.0,
logreg_3fa32a4b5c6d-regParam: 0.01
}, {
logreg_3fa32a4b5c6d-elasticNetParam: 0.5,
logreg_3fa32a4b5c6d-regParam: 0.1
}, {
logreg_3fa32a4b5c6d-elasticNetParam: 0.5,
logreg_3fa32a4b5c6d-regParam: 0.01
}, {
logreg_3fa32a4b5c6d-elasticNetParam: 1.0,
logreg_3fa32a4b5c6d-regParam: 0.1
}, {
logreg_3fa32a4b5c6d-elasticNetParam: 1.0,
logreg_3fa32a4b5c6d-regParam: 0.01
})
```

Here, we show the use of a `CrossValidator` to pick the better parameters for our model:

```scala
scala> val cv = new CrossValidator().setEstimator(lr).setEvaluator(new
MulticlassClassificationEvaluator).setEstimatorParamMaps(paramGrid).setNumF
olds(5)
```

Next, we run the cross-validation to choose the best set of parameters:

```scala
scala> val cvModel = cv.fit(trainingData)

scala> println("Model was fit using parameters: " +
cvModel.parent.extractParamMap)

Model was fit using parameters: {
    cv_00543dadc091-estimator: logreg_41377555b425,
    cv_00543dadc091-estimatorParamMaps:
    [Lorg.apache.spark.ml.param.ParamMap;@14ca1e23,
    cv_00543dadc091-evaluator: mcEval_0435b4f19e2a,
    cv_00543dadc091-numFolds: 5,
    cv_00543dadc091-seed: -1191137437
}
```

We make predictions on the test Dataset. Here, `cvModel` uses the best model found (`lrModel`):

```scala
scala> cvModel.transform(testData).select("id", "label", "probability",
"prediction").collect().foreach { case Row(id: Long, label: Double, prob:
Vector, prediction: Double) =>
| println(s"($id, $label) --> prob=$prob, prediction=$prediction")
| }
```

```
(99, 1.0) --> prob=[2.6027854456883833E-
7,0.9314238151102939,0.008305853987875035,0.009684546310917754,0.0086946549210834 97,0.
0079121061385523606,0.008594082752851902,0.008519690331111665,0.009154967029224 29,0.0077
100231395686196], prediction=1.0
(81, 1.0) --> prob=[7.498134657859313E-
7,0.7689461362309903,0.0276681467730525,0.03305074069318609,0.028689441789579495,0.026
109985274150933,0.02903619052527176,0.028159628722867137,0.03154087462238654,0.0267981
0555504927], prediction=1.0
.
.
.
(8589934797, 9.0) --> prob=[1.7113801070622645E-
6,0.05306638932278816,0.0587392018096767,0.04692529890827765,0.12399075223480296,0.074
38456473981786,0.12186164275694751,0.11653564109284925,0.10754704437383655,0.296947753
38089624], prediction=9.0
(8589934653, 9.0) --> prob=[1.2546665900143864E-
6,0.04134664431466302,0.04388117754243587,0.04929496870409657,0.08984018414356594,0.05
9337783485833365,0.06842089455713343,0.05013171592689752,0.04112335342906031,0.5566220
23229724], prediction=9.0
```

```scala
scala> val cvPredictions = cvModel.transform(testData)
cvPredictions: org.apache.spark.sql.DataFrame = [label: double, _c715:
double ... 860 more fields]

scala> cvPredictions.select("prediction", "label", "features").show(5)
```

```
+----------+-----+--------------------+
|prediction|label|            features|
+----------+-----+--------------------+
|       1.0|  1.0|(857,[331,493,704...|
|       1.0|  1.0|(857,[206,493,704...|
|       1.0|  1.0|(857,[70,206,510,...|
|       2.0|  2.0|(857,[402,707,844...|
|       2.0|  2.0|(857,[332,370,613...|
+----------+-----+--------------------+
```

```
scala> val evaluator = new
MulticlassClassificationEvaluator().setLabelCol("label").setPredictionCol("
prediction").setMetricName("accuracy")
```

Note the significant improvement in the prediction accuracy as a result of cross-validation:

```
scala> val accuracy = evaluator.evaluate(cvPredictions)
accuracy: Double = 0.9736842105263158

scala> println("Test Error = " + (1.0 - accuracy))
Test Error = 0.02631578947368418
```

Finally, save the model to the filesystem. We will retrieve it from the filesystem in the program later in this section:

```
scala>
cvModel.write.overwrite.save("file:///Users/aurobindosarkar/Downloads/CNAE-
9/model")
```

Next, we build an application, compile, package, and execute it using the code and the saved model and test data from our spark-shell session, as shown:

LRExample.scala

```
package org.chap9.ml
import scala.collection.mutable
import scopt.OptionParser
import org.apache.spark.sql._
import org.apache.spark.sql.types._
import org.apache.spark.ml._
import org.apache.spark.examples.mllib.AbstractParams
import org.apache.spark.ml.feature.{VectorAssembler}
import org.apache.spark.ml.classification.{LogisticRegression,
LogisticRegressionModel}
import org.apache.spark.ml.tuning.{CrossValidator, CrossValidatorModel}
import org.apache.spark.ml.evaluation.{MulticlassClassificationEvaluator}
import org.apache.spark.sql.{DataFrame, SparkSession}
```

```
object LRExample {
   case class Params(
   inputModelPath: String = null,
   testInput: String = ""
) extends AbstractParams[Params]

def main(args: Array[String]) {
   val defaultParams = Params()
   val parser = new OptionParser[Params]("LRExample") {
      head("LRExample: an example Logistic Regression.")
      arg[String]("inputModelPath")
      .text(s"input path to saved model.")
      .required()
      .action((x, c) => c.copy(inputModelPath = x))
      arg[String]("<testInput>")
      .text("test input path to new data")
      .required()
      .action((x, c) => c.copy(testInput = x))
   checkConfig { params =>
      if ((params.testInput == null) || (params.inputModelPath == null)) {
         failure(s"Both Test Input File && input model path values need to
be provided.")
      } else {
         success
      }
   }
}
parser.parse(args, defaultParams) match {
   case Some(params) => run(params)
   case _ => sys.exit(1)
   }
}
def run(params: Params): Unit = {
   val spark = SparkSession
      .builder
      .appName(s"LogisticRegressionExample with $params")
      .getOrCreate()
   println(s"LogisticRegressionExample with parameters:\n$params")
   val inRDD = spark.sparkContext.textFile("file://" + params.testInput)

   val rowRDD = inRDD.map(_.split(",")).map(attributes =>
Row(attributes(0).toDouble, attributes(1).toDouble, attributes(2).toDouble,
attributes(3).toDouble, attributes(4).toDouble, attributes(5).toDouble,
attributes(6).toDouble,
.
.
.
attributes(850).toDouble, attributes(851).toDouble,
```

```
attributes(852).toDouble, attributes(853).toDouble,
attributes(854).toDouble, attributes(855).toDouble,
attributes(856).toDouble))
val schemaString = "label _c715 _c195 _c480 _c856 _c136 _c53 _c429 _c732
_c271 _c742 _c172 _c45 _c374 _c233 _c720 _c294 _c461 _c87 _c599 _c84 _c28
_c79 _c615 _c243
.
.
.
_c336 _c841 _c82 _c123 _c474 _c470 _c286 _c555 _c36 _c299 _c829 _c361 _c263
_c522 _c495 _c135"
val fields = schemaString.split(" ").map(fieldName =>
StructField(fieldName, DoubleType, nullable = false))
val schema = StructType(fields)
val inDF = spark.createDataFrame(rowRDD, schema)
val indexedDF=
inDF.withColumn("id",org.apache.spark.sql.functions.monotonically_increasin
g_id())
val columnNames =
Array("_c715","_c195","_c480","_c856","_c136","_c53","_c429","_c732","_c271
","_c742","_c172","_c45","_c374","_c233","_c720","_c294","_c461","_c87","_c
599","_c84","_c28","_c
.
.
.
141","_c516","_c419","_c69","_c621","_c423","_c137","_c549","_c636","_c772"
,"_c799","_c336","_c841","_c82","_c123","id","_c474","_c470","_c286","_c555
","_c36","_c299","_c829","_c361","_c263","_c522","_c495","_c135")
    val assembler = new
VectorAssembler().setInputCols(columnNames).setOutputCol("features")
    val output = assembler.transform(indexedDF)
    val cvModel - CrossValidatorModel.load("file://"+ params.inputModelPath)
    val cvPredictions = cvModel.transform(output)
    val evaluator = new
MulticlassClassificationEvaluator().setLabelCol("label").setPredictionCol("
prediction").setMetricName("accuracy")
    val accuracy = evaluator.evaluate(cvPredictions)
    println("Test Error = " + (1.0 - accuracy))
    spark.stop()
  }
}
```

Create a lib folder inside your root SBT directory (the same as the directory containing the build.sbt file) and copy scopt_2.11-3.3.0.jar and spark-examples_2.11-2.2.1-SNAPSHOT.jar from spark distribution's examples directory into it.

Next, compile and package the source using the same `build.sbt` file used in an earlier section, as follows:

```
Aurobindos-MacBook-Pro-2:Chapter9 aurobindosarkar$ sbt package
```

Finally, execute your Spark Scala program using spark-submit, as shown:

```
Aurobindos-MacBook-Pro-2:scala-2.11 aurobindosarkar$
/Users/aurobindosarkar/Downloads/spark-2.2.1-SNAPSHOT-bin-
hadoop2.7/bin/spark-submit --jars
/Users/aurobindosarkar/Downloads/Chapter9/lib/spark-examples_2.11-2.2.1-
SNAPSHOT.jar,/Users/aurobindosarkar/Downloads/Chapter9/lib/scopt_2.11-3.3.0
.jar --class org.chap9.ml.LRExample --master local[*] chapter9_2.11-2.0.jar
/Users/aurobindosarkar/Downloads/CNAE-9/model
/Users/aurobindosarkar/Downloads/CNAE-9/input/part-00000-61f03111-53bb-4404
-bef7-0dd4ac1be950-c000.csv

LogisticRegressionExample with parameters:
{
inputModelPath: /Users/aurobindosarkar/Downloads/CNAE-9/model,
testInput:
/Users/aurobindosarkar/Downloads/CNAE-9/input/part-00000-61f03111-53bb-4404
-bef7-0dd4ac1be950-c000.csv
}
Test Error = 0.02631578947368418
```

Summary

In this chapter, we introduced a few Spark SQL applications in the textual analysis space. Additionally, we provided detailed code examples, including building a data preprocessing pipeline, implementing sentiment analysis, using Naive Bayes classifier with n-grams, and implementing an LDA application to identify themes in a document corpus. Additionally, we worked through the details of implementing an example of machine learning.

In the next chapter, we will focus on use cases for using Spark SQL in deep learning applications. We will explore a few of the emerging deep learning libraries and present examples of implementing deep learning related applications.

10
Using Spark SQL in Deep Learning Applications

Deep learning has emerged as a superior solution to several difficult problems in machine learning over the past decade. We hear about deep learning being deployed across many different areas, including computer vision, speech recognition, natural language processing, audio recognition, social media applications, machine translation, and biology. Often, the results produced using deep learning approaches have been comparable to or better than those produced by human experts.

There have been several different types of deep learning models that have been applied to different problems. We will review the basic concepts of these models and present some code. This is an emerging area in Spark, so even though there are several different libraries available, many are in their early releases or evolving on a daily basis. We will provide a brief overview of some of these libraries, including some code examples using Spark 2.1.0, Scala, and BigDL. We chose BigDL because it is one the few libraries that run directly on top of Spark Core (similar to other Spark packages) and works with Spark SQL DataFrame API and ML pipelines using a Scala API.

More specifically, in this chapter, you will learn the following:

- What is deep learning?
- Understanding the key concepts of various deep learning models
- Understanding deep learning in Spark
- Working with BigDL and Spark

Introducing neural networks

A neural network, or an **artificial neural network** (ANN), is a set of algorithms, or actual hardware, that is loosely modeled after the human brain. They are essentially an interconnected set of processing nodes that are designed to recognize patterns. They adapt to, or learn from, a set of training patterns such as images, sound, text, time series, and so on.

Neural networks are typically organized into layers that consist of interconnected nodes. These nodes communicate with each other by sending signals over the connections. Patterns are presented to the network via an input layer, which is then passed on to one or more hidden layers. Actual computations are executed in these hidden layers. The last hidden layer connects to an output layer that outputs the final answer.

The total input to a particular node is typically a function of the output from each of the connected nodes. The contribution from these inputs to a node can be excitatory or inhibitory, and ultimately helps determine whether and to what extent the signal progresses further through the network (via an activation function). Typically, sigmoid activation functions have been very popular. In some applications, a linear, semilinear, or the hyperbolic tan (`Tanh`) function have also been used. In cases where the output of a node is a stochastic function of the total input, the input determines the probability that a given node gets a high activation value.

The weights of the connections within the network are modified based on the learning rules; for example, when a neural network is initially presented with a pattern, it makes a guess as to what the weights might be. It then evaluates how far its answer is the actual one and makes appropriate adjustments to its connection weights.

 For good introduction to the basics of neural networks, refer: "*A Basic Introduction To Neural Networks*" by Bolo, available at: http://pages.cs. wisc.edu/~bolo/shipyard/neural/local.html.

We will present more specific details of various types of neural networks in the following sections.

Understanding deep learning

Deep learning is the application of ANNs to learn tasks. Deep learning methods are based on learning data representations, instead of task-specific algorithms. Though the learning can be supervised or unsupervised, the recent focus has been toward creating efficient systems that learn these representations from large-scale, unlabeled Datasets.

The following figure depicts a simple deep learning neural network with two hidden layers:

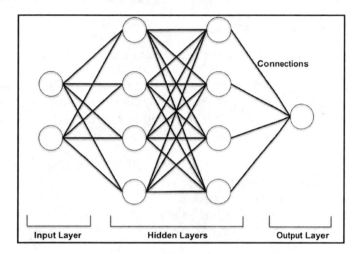

Deep learning typically comprises of multiple layers of processing units with the learning of feature representation occurring within each layer. These layers form a hierarchy of features and deep learning assumes that the hierarchy corresponds to the levels of abstraction. Hence, it exploits the idea of hierarchical explanatory factors, where the more abstract concepts at a higher level are learned from the lower-level ones. Varying the numbers of layers and layer sizes can provide different amounts of abstraction, as required by the use case.

Understanding representation learning

Deep learning methods are representation-learning methods with multiple levels of abstraction. Here, the non-linear modules transform the raw input into a representation at a higher, slightly more abstract level. Ultimately, very complex functions can be learned by composing sufficient numbers of such layers.

For a review paper on deep learning, refer to *Deep Learning*, by Yann LeCun, Yoshua Bengio, and Geoffrey Hinton, which is available at `http:/ /www.nature.com/nature/journal/v521/n7553/full/nature14539.html? foxtrotcallback=true`.

Now, we illustrate the process of learning representations and features in a traditional pattern recognition task:

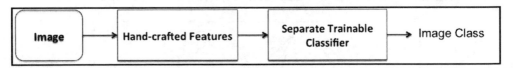

Traditional machine learning techniques were limited in their ability to process natural data in its original or raw form. Building such machine-learning systems required deep domain expertise and substantial effort to identify (and keep updated) the features from which the learning subsystem, often a classifier, can detect or classify patterns in the input.

Many of these conventional machine learning applications used linear classifiers on top of handcrafted features. Such classifiers typically required a good feature extractor that produced representations that were selective to the aspects of the image. However, all this effort is not required if good features could be learned, automatically, using a general-purpose learning procedure. This particular aspect of deep learning represents one of the key advantages of deep learning.

In contrast to the earlier machine learning techniques, the high-level process in deep learning is, typically, in which the end-to-end learning process involves features that are also learned from the data. This is illustrated here:

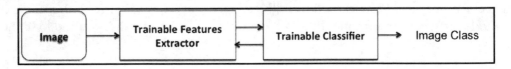

In the next section, we will briefly discuss one of most commonly used functions, stochastic gradient descent, for adjusting the weights in a network.

Understanding stochastic gradient descent

A deep learning system can consist of millions of adjustable weights, and millions of labeled examples are used to train the machine. In practice, **stochastic gradient descent (SGD)** optimization is used widely in many different situations. In SGD, the gradient describes the relationship between the network's error and a single weight, that is, how does the error vary as the weight is adjusted.

This optimization approach consists of:

- Presenting the input vector for a few examples
- Computing outputs and the errors
- Computing average gradient for the examples
- Adjusting weights, appropriately

This process is repeated for many small sets of training examples. The process stops when the average of the objective function stops decreasing.

This simple procedure usually produces a good set of weights very efficiently compared to the more sophisticated optimization techniques. Additionally, the training process takes a much shorter time as well. After the training process is complete, the performance of the system is measured by running the trained model on a test Dataset. The test set contains new inputs that have not been seen before (during the training phase) by the machine.

In deep learning neural networks, the activation function is typically set at the layer level and applies to all the neurons or nodes in a particular layer. Additionally, the output layer of a multilayered deep learning neural network plays a specific role; for example, in supervised learning (with labeled input), it applies the most likely label based on the signals received from the previous layer. Each node on the output layer represents one label, and that node produces one of the two possible outcomes, a 0 or a 1. While such neural networks produce a binary output, the input they receive is often continuous; for example, the input to a recommendation engine can include factors such as how much the customer spent in the previous month and the average number of customer visits per week over the past one month. The output layer has to process such signals into a probability measure for the given input.

Introducing deep learning in Spark

In this section, we will review some of the more popular deep learning libraries using Spark. These include CaffeOnSpark, DL4J, TensorFrames, and BigDL.

Introducing CaffeOnSpark

CaffeOnSpark was developed by Yahoo for large-scale distributed deep learning on Hadoop clusters. By combining the features from the deep learning framework Caffe with Apache Spark (and Apache Hadoop), CaffeOnSpark enables distributed deep learning on a cluster of GPU and CPU servers.

 For more details on CaffeOnSpark, refer to `https://github.com/yahoo/CaffeOnSpark`.

CaffeOnSpark supports neural network model training, testing, and feature extraction. It is complementary to non-deep learning libraries, Spark MLlib and Spark SQL. CaffeOnSpark's Scala API provides Spark applications with an easy mechanism to invoke deep learning algorithms over distributed Datasets. Here, deep learning is typically conducted in the same cluster as the existing data processing pipelines to support feature engineering and traditional machine learning applications. Hence, CaffeOnSpark allows deep learning training and testing processes to be embedded into Spark applications.

Introducing DL4J

DL4J supports training neural networks on a Spark cluster in order to accelerate network training. The current version of DL4J uses a process of parameter averaging on each cluster node in order to train the network. The training is complete when the master has a copy of the trained network.

 For more details on DL4J, refer to `https://deeplearning4j.org/spark`.

Introducing TensorFrames

Experimental TensorFlow binding for Scala and Apache Spark is currently available on GitHub. TensorFrames is essentially TensorFlow on Spark Dataframes that lets you manipulate Apache Spark's DataFrames with TensorFlow programs. The Scala support is currently more limited than Python--the Scala DSL features a subset of TensorFlow transforms.

 For more details on TensorFrames, visit `https://github.com/databricks/tensorframes`.

In Scala, the operations can be loaded from an existing graph defined in the `ProtocolBuffers` format or using a simple Scala DSL. However, given the overall popularity of TensorFlow, this library is gaining traction and is more popular with the Python community.

Working with BigDL

BigDL is an open source distributed deep learning library for Apache Spark. It was initially developed and open sourced by Intel. With BigDL, the developers can write deep learning applications as standard Spark programs. These programs directly run on top of the existing Spark or Hadoop clusters, as illustrated in this figure:

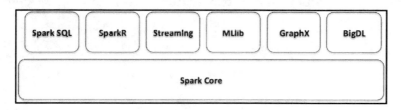

BigDL is modeled after Torch and it provides support for deep learning, including numeric computing (via Tensors) and `neural networks`. Additionally, the developers can load pretrained `Caffe` or `Torch` models into BigDL-Spark programs, as illustrated in the following figure:

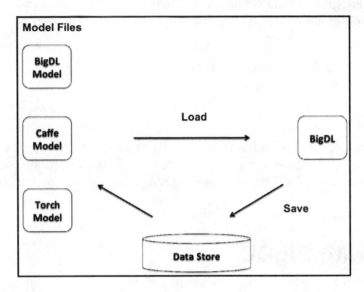

To achieve high performance, BigDL uses `Intel MKL` and multithreaded programming in each Spark task.

 For BigDL documentation, examples, and API guides, check out `https://bigdl-project.github.io/master/`.

The following figure shows how a BigDL program is executed at a high-level on a Spark cluster. With the help of a cluster manager and the driver program, Spark tasks are distributed across the Spark worker nodes or containers (executors):

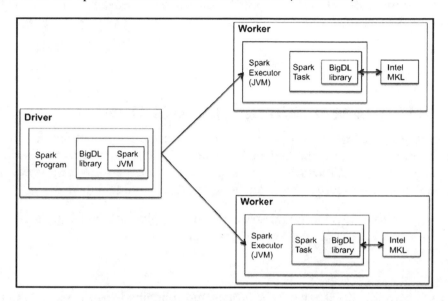

We will execute a few examples of deep neural networks available in the BigDL distribution in the later sections of this chapter. At this time, this is one of the few libraries that work with the Spark SQL DataFrame API and ML pipelines.

In the next section, we will highlight how Spark can be leveraged for tuning hyperparameters in parallel.

Tuning hyperparameters of deep learning models

When building a neural network, there are many important hyperparameters to choose carefully. Consider the given examples:

- Number of neurons in each layer: Very few neurons will reduce the expressive power of the network, but too many will substantially increase the running time and return noisy estimates
- Learning rate: If it is too high, the neural network will only focus on the last few samples seen and disregard all the experience accumulated before, and if it is too low, it will take too long to reach a good state

The hyperparameter tuning process is "embarrassingly parallel" and can be distributed using Spark.

For more details, refer to *Deep Learning with Apache Spark and TensorFlow*, by Tim Hunter, at https://databricks.com/blog/2016/01/25/deep-learning-with-apache-spark-and-tensorflow.html.

Introducing deep learning pipelines

There is an emerging library for supporting deep learning pipelines in Spark, which provides high-level APIs for scalable deep learning in Python with Apache Spark. Currently, TensorFlow and TensorFlow-backed Keras workflows are supported, with a focus on model inference/scoring and transfer learning on image data at scale.

To follow developments on deep learning pipelines in Spark, visit https://github.com/databricks/spark-deep-learning.

Furthermore, it provides tools for data scientists and machine learning experts to turn deep learning models into SQL UDFs that can be used by a much wider group of users. This is also a good way to produce a deep learning model.

In the next section, we will shift our focus to supervised learning.

Understanding Supervised learning

The most common form of machine learning is supervised learning; for example, if we are building a system to classify a specific set of images, we first collect a large Dataset of images from the same categories. During training, the machine is shown an image, and it produces an output in the form of a vector of scores, one for each category. As a result of the training, we expect the desired category to have the highest score out of all the categories.

A particular type of deep network--the **convolutional neural network (ConvNet/CNN)**--is much easier to train and generalizes much better than fully-connected networks. In supervised learning scenarios, deep convolutional networks have significantly improved the results of processing images, video, speech, and audio data. Similarly, recurrent nets have shone the light on sequential data, such as text and speech. We will explore these types of neural networks in the subsequent sections.

Understanding convolutional neural networks

Convolutional neural networks are a special kind of multilayered neural networks that are designed to recognize visual patterns directly from pixel images with minimal preprocessing. They can recognize patterns having wide variability and can effectively deal with distortions and simple geometric transformations. CNNs are also trained using a version of the backpropagation algorithm.

The architecture of a typical ConvNet is structured as a series of stages containing several stages of stacked convolution, and non-linearity and pooling layers, followed by additional convolutional and fully-connected layers. The non-linearity function is typically the **Rectified Linear Unit (ReLU)** function, and the role of the pooling layer is to semantically merge similar features into one. Thus, the pooling allows representations to vary very little when elements in the previous layer vary in position and appearance.

LeNet-5 is a convolutional network designed for handwritten and machine-printed character recognition. Here, we present an example of Lenet-5 available in the BigDL distribution.

 The full source code for the example is available at https://github.com/ intel-analytics/BigDL/tree/master/spark/dl/src/main/scala/com/ intel/analytics/bigdl/models/lenet.

Here, we will use Spark shell to execute the same code. Note that the values of the constants have all been taken from the source code available at the aforementioned site.

First, execute the `bigdl` shell script to set the environment:

```
source /Users/aurobindosarkar/Downloads/BigDL-master/scripts/bigdl.sh
```

We then start the Spark shell with the appropriate BigDL JAR specified, as follows:

```
bin/spark-shell --properties-file /Users/aurobindosarkar/Downloads/BigDL-
master/spark/dist/target/bigdl-0.2.0-SNAPSHOT-spark-2.0.0-scala-2.11.8-mac-
dist/conf/spark-bigdl.conf --jars /Users/aurobindosarkar/Downloads/BigDL-
master/spark/dist/target/bigdl-0.2.0-SNAPSHOT-spark-2.0.0-scala-2.11.8-mac-
dist/lib/bigdl-0.2.0-SNAPSHOT-jar-with-dependencies.jar
```

The Dataset for this example can be downloaded from http://yann.lecun.com/exdb/ mnist/.

The Spark shell session for this example is, as shown:

```
scala> import com.intel.analytics.bigdl._
scala> import com.intel.analytics.bigdl.dataset.DataSet
scala> import com.intel.analytics.bigdl.dataset.image.{BytesToGreyImg,
GreyImgNormalizer, GreyImgToBatch, GreyImgToSample}
scala> import com.intel.analytics.bigdl.nn.{ClassNLLCriterion, Module}
scala> import com.intel.analytics.bigdl.numeric.NumericFloat
scala> import com.intel.analytics.bigdl.optim._
scala> import com.intel.analytics.bigdl.utils.{Engine, T,
scala> import com.intel.analytics.bigdl.nn._
scala> import java.nio.ByteBuffer
scala> import java.nio.file.{Files, Path, Paths}
scala> import com.intel.analytics.bigdl.dataset.ByteRecord
scala> import com.intel.analytics.bigdl.utils.File

scala> val trainData = "/Users/aurobindosarkar/Downloads/mnist/train-
images-idx3-ubyte"
scala> val trainLabel = "/Users/aurobindosarkar/Downloads/mnist/train-
labels-idx1-ubyte"
scala> val validationData = "/Users/aurobindosarkar/Downloads/mnist/t10k-
images-idx3-ubyte"
scala> val validationLabel = "/Users/aurobindosarkar/Downloads/mnist/t10k-
labels-idx1-ubyte"

scala> val nodeNumber = 1 //Number of nodes
scala> val coreNumber = 2 //Number of cores

scala> Engine.init

scala> val model = Sequential[Float]()
model: com.intel.analytics.bigdl.nn.Sequential[Float] =
nn.Sequential {
[input -> -> output]
}

scala> val classNum = 10 //Number of classes (digits)
scala> val batchSize = 12
//The model uses the Tanh function for non-linearity.
//It has two sets layers comprising of Convolution-Non-Linearity-Pooling
//It uses a Softmax function to output the results

scala> model.add(Reshape(Array(1, 28, 28))).add(SpatialConvolution(1, 6, 5,
5)).add(Tanh()).add(SpatialMaxPooling(2, 2, 2,
2)).add(Tanh()).add(SpatialConvolution(6, 12, 5,
5)).add(SpatialMaxPooling(2, 2, 2, 2)).add(Reshape(Array(12 * 4 *
4))).add(Linear(12 * 4 * 4, 100)).add(Tanh()).add(Linear(100,
classNum)).add(LogSoftMax())
```

```
res1: model.type =
nn.Sequential {
[input -> (1) -> (2) -> (3) -> (4) -> (5) -> (6) -> (7) -> (8) -> (9) ->
(10) -> (11) -> (12) -> output]
(1): nn.Reshape(1x28x28)
(2): nn.SpatialConvolution(1 -> 6, 5 x 5, 1, 1, 0, 0)
(3): nn.Tanh
(4): nn.SpatialMaxPooling(2, 2, 2, 2, 0, 0)
(5): nn.Tanh
(6): nn.SpatialConvolution(6 -> 12, 5 x 5, 1, 1, 0, 0)
(7): nn.SpatialMaxPooling(2, 2, 2, 2, 0, 0)
(8): nn.Reshape(192)
(9): nn.Linear(192 -> 100)
(10): nn.Tanh
(11): nn.Linear(100 -> 10)
(12): nn.LogSoftMax
}

//The following is a private function in Utils.
scala> def load(featureFile: String, labelFile: String): Array[ByteRecord]
= {
|     val featureBuffer =
ByteBuffer.wrap(Files.readAllBytes(Paths.get(featureFile)))
|     val labelBuffer =
ByteBuffer.wrap(Files.readAllBytes(Paths.get(labelFile)));
|     val labelMagicNumber = labelBuffer.getInt();
|     require(labelMagicNumber == 2049);
|     val featureMagicNumber = featureBuffer.getInt();
|     require(featureMagicNumber == 2051);
|     val labelCount = labelBuffer.getInt();
|     val featureCount = featureBuffer.getInt();
|     require(labelCount == featureCount);
|     val rowNum = featureBuffer.getInt();
|     val colNum = featureBuffer.getInt();
|     val result = new Array[ByteRecord](featureCount);
|     var i = 0;
|     while (i < featureCount) {
|        val img = new Array[Byte]((rowNum * colNum));
|        var y = 0;
|        while (y < rowNum) {
|           var x = 0;
|           while (x < colNum) {
|               img(x + y * colNum) = featureBuffer.get();
|               x += 1;
|           }
|           y += 1;
|        }
|        result(i) = ByteRecord(img, labelBuffer.get().toFloat + 1.0f);
```

```
|        i += 1;
|     }
|     result;
| }

scala> val trainMean = 0.13066047740239506
scala> val trainStd = 0.3081078

scala> val trainSet = DataSet.array(load(trainData, trainLabel), sc) ->
BytesToGreyImg(28, 28) -> GreyImgNormalizer(trainMean, trainStd) ->
GreyImgToBatch(batchSize)

scala> val optimizer = Optimizer(model = model, dataset = trainSet,
criterion = ClassNLLCriterion[Float]())

scala> val testMean = 0.13251460696903547
scala> val testStd = 0.31048024
scala> val maxEpoch = 2

scala> val validationSet = DataSet.array(load(validationData,
validationLabel), sc) -> BytesToGreyImg(28, 28) ->
GreyImgNormalizer(testMean, testStd) -> GreyImgToBatch(batchSize)

scala> optimizer.setEndWhen(Trigger.maxEpoch(2))
scala> optimizer.setState(T("learningRate" -> 0.05, "learningRateDecay" ->
0.0))
scala>
optimizer.setCheckpoint("/Users/aurobindosarkar/Downloads/mnist/checkpoint"
, Trigger.severalIteration(500))
scala> optimizer.setValidation(trigger = Trigger.everyEpoch, dataset =
validationSet, vMethods = Array(new Top1Accuracy, new Top5Accuracy[Float],
new Loss[Float]))

scala> optimizer.optimize()

scala> model.save("/Users/aurobindosarkar/Downloads/mnist/model") //Save
the trained model to disk.
scala> val model =
Module.load[Float]("/Users/aurobindosarkar/Downloads/mnist/model")
//Retrieve the model from the disk
scala> val partitionNum = 2
scala> val rddData = sc.parallelize(load(validationData, validationLabel),
partitionNum)

scala> val transformer = BytesToGreyImg(28, 28) ->
GreyImgNormalizer(testMean, testStd) -> GreyImgToSample()

scala> val evaluationSet = transformer(rddData)
```

```
scala> val result = model.evaluate(evaluationSet, Array(new
Top1Accuracy[Float]), Some(batchSize))

scala> result.foreach(r => println(s"${r._2} is ${r._1}"))
Top1Accuracy is Accuracy(correct: 9831, count: 10000, accuracy: 0.9831)
```

In the next section, we will present an example of text classification.

Using neural networks for text classification

Other applications gaining importance involve natural language understanding and speech recognition.

The example in this section is available as a part of the BigDL distribution and the full source code is available at https://github.com/intel-analytics/BigDL/tree/master/spark/dl/src/main/scala/com/intel/analytics/bigdl/example/textclassification.

It uses a pretrained GloVe embedding to convert words to vectors, and then uses it to train the text classification model on a twenty Newsgroup Dataset with twenty different categories. This model can achieve over 90% accuracy after only two epochs of training.

The key portions the code defining the CNN model and optimizer are presented here:

```
val model = Sequential[Float]()

//The model has 3 sets of Convolution and Pooling layers.
model.add(Reshape(Array(param.embeddingDim, 1, param.maxSequenceLength)))
model.add(SpatialConvolution(param.embeddingDim, 128, 5, 1))
model.add(ReLU())
model.add(SpatialMaxPooling(5, 1, 5, 1))
model.add(SpatialConvolution(128, 128, 5, 1))
model.add(ReLU())
model.add(SpatialMaxPooling(5, 1, 5, 1))
model.add(SpatialConvolution(128, 128, 5, 1))
model.add(ReLU())
model.add(SpatialMaxPooling(35, 1, 35, 1))
model.add(Reshape(Array(128)))
model.add(Linear(128, 100))
model.add(Linear(100, classNum))
model.add(LogSoftMax())

//The optimizer uses the Adagrad method
val optimizer = Optimizer(
model = buildModel(classNum),
```

```
sampleRDD = trainingRDD,
criterion = new ClassNLLCriterion[Float](),
batchSize = param.batchSize
)

optimizer
.setOptimMethod(new Adagrad(learningRate = 0.01, learningRateDecay =
0.0002))
.setValidation(Trigger.everyEpoch, valRDD, Array(new Top1Accuracy[Float]),
param.batchSize)
.setEndWhen(Trigger.maxEpoch(20))
.optimize()
```

The input Datasets are described, as follows, along with their download URLs:

- **Embedding**: 100-dimensional pretrained GloVe embeddings of 400 k words trained on a 2014 dump of English Wikipedia. Download pretrained GloVe word embeddings from `http://nlp.stanford.edu/data/glove.6B.zip`.
- **Training data**: "20 Newsgroup dataset" containing 20 categories and with a total of 19,997 texts. Download 20 Newsgroup datasets as the training data from `http://www.cs.cmu.edu/afs/cs.cmu.edu/project/theo-20/www/data/news20.tar.gz`.

In our example, we have reduced the number of categories to eight to avoid `Out-of-Memory` exceptions on laptops with less than 16 GB RAM. Put these Datasets in `BASE_DIR`; the final directory structure should be as illustrated:

Use the following command to execute the text classifier:

```
Aurobindos-MacBook-Pro-2:BigDL aurobindosarkar$
/Users/aurobindosarkar/Downloads/BigDL-master/scripts/bigdl.sh --
/Users/aurobindosarkar/Downloads/spark-2.1.0-bin-hadoop2.7/bin/spark-submit
--master "local[2]" --driver-memory 14g --class
com.intel.analytics.bigdl.example.textclassification.TextClassifier
/Users/aurobindosarkar/Downloads/BigDL-
master/spark/dist/target/bigdl-0.2.0-SNAPSHOT-spark-2.0.0-scala-2.11.8-mac-
dist/lib/bigdl-0.2.0-SNAPSHOT-jar-with-dependencies.jar --batchSize 128 -b
/Users/aurobindosarkar/Downloads/textclassification -p 4
```

The sample output is given here for your reference:

```
17/08/16 14:50:07 INFO textclassification.TextClassifier$: Current
parameters:
TextClassificationParams(/Users/aurobindosarkar/Downloads/textclassificatio
n,1000,20000,0.8,128,100,4)
17/08/16 14:50:07 INFO utils.ThreadPool$: Set mkl threads to 1 on thread 1
17/08/16 14:50:09 INFO utils.Engine$: Auto detect executor number and
executor cores number
17/08/16 14:50:09 INFO utils.Engine$: Executor number is 1 and executor
cores number is 2
17/08/16 14:50:09 INFO utils.Engine$: Find existing spark context. Checking
the spark conf...
17/08/16 14:50:10 INFO utils.TextClassifier: Found 8000 texts.
17/08/16 14:50:10 INFO utils.TextClassifier: Found 8 classes
17/08/16 14:50:13 INFO utils.TextClassifier: Indexing word vectors.
17/08/16 14:50:16 INFO utils.TextClassifier: Found 17424 word vectors.
17/08/16 14:50:16 INFO optim.DistriOptimizer$: caching training rdd ...
17/08/16 14:50:37 INFO optim.DistriOptimizer$: Cache thread models...
17/08/16 14:50:37 INFO optim.DistriOptimizer$: model thread pool size is 1
17/08/16 14:50:37 INFO optim.DistriOptimizer$: Cache thread models... done
17/08/16 14:50:37 INFO optim.DistriOptimizer$: config {
learningRate: 0.01
maxDropPercentage: 0.0
computeThresholdbatchSize: 100
warmupIterationNum: 200
learningRateDecay: 2.0E-4
dropPercentage: 0.0
}
17/08/16 14:50:37 INFO optim.DistriOptimizer$: Shuffle data
17/08/16 14:50:37 INFO optim.DistriOptimizer$: Shuffle data complete. Takes
0.012679728s
17/08/16 14:50:38 INFO optim.DistriOptimizer$: [Epoch 1 0/6458][Iteration
1][Wall Clock 0.0s] Train 128 in 0.962042186seconds. Throughput is 133.0503
records/second. Loss is 2.0774076.
17/08/16 14:50:40 INFO optim.DistriOptimizer$: [Epoch 1 128/6458][Iteration
```

```
2][Wall Clock 0.962042186s] Train 128 in 1.320501728seconds. Throughput is
96.93285 records/second. Loss is 4.793501.
17/08/16 14:50:40 INFO optim.DistriOptimizer$: [Epoch 1 256/6458][Iteration
3][Wall Clock 2.282543914s] Train 128 in 0.610049842seconds. Throughput is
209.81892 records/second. Loss is 2.1110187.
17/08/16 14:50:41 INFO optim.DistriOptimizer$: [Epoch 1 384/6458][Iteration
4][Wall Clock 2.892593756s] Train 128 in 0.609548069seconds. Throughput is
209.99164 records/second. Loss is 2.0820618.
17/08/16 14:50:42 INFO optim.DistriOptimizer$: [Epoch 1 512/6458][Iteration
5][Wall Clock 3.502141825s] Train 128 in 0.607720212seconds. Throughput is
210.62325 records/second. Loss is 2.0860045.
17/08/16 14:50:42 INFO optim.DistriOptimizer$: [Epoch 1 640/6458][Iteration
6][Wall Clock 4.109862037s] Train 128 in 0.607034064seconds. Throughput is
210.86131 records/second. Loss is 2.086178.
   .
   .

   .
17/08/16 15:04:57 INFO optim.DistriOptimizer$: [Epoch 20
6144/6458][Iteration 1018][Wall Clock 855.715191033s] Train 128 in
0.771615991seconds. Throughput is 165.88562 records/second. Loss is
2.4244189E-4.
17/08/16 15:04:58 INFO optim.DistriOptimizer$: [Epoch 20
6272/6458][Iteration 1019][Wall Clock 856.486807024s] Train 128 in
0.770584628seconds. Throughput is 166.10765 records/second. Loss is
0.04117684.
17/08/16 15:04:59 INFO optim.DistriOptimizer$: [Epoch 20
6400/6458][Iteration 1020][Wall Clock 857.257391652s] Train 128 in
0.783425485seconds. Throughput is 163.38503 records/second. Loss is
3.2506883E-4.
17/08/16 15:04:59 INFO optim.DistriOptimizer$: [Epoch 20
6400/6458][Iteration 1020][Wall Clock 857.257391652s] Epoch finished. Wall
clock time is 861322.002763ms
17/08/16 15:04:59 INFO optim.DistriOptimizer$: [Wall Clock 861.322002763s]
Validate model...
17/08/16 15:05:02 INFO optim.DistriOptimizer$: Top1Accuracy is
Accuracy(correct: 1537, count: 1542, accuracy: 0.996757457846952)
```

In the next section, we will explore the use of deep neural networks for language processing.

Using deep neural networks for language processing

As discussed in `Chapter 9`, *Developing Applications with Spark SQL*, the standard approach to statistical modeling of language is typically based on counting the frequency of the occurrences of n-grams. This usually requires very large training corpora in most real-world use cases. Additionally, n-grams treat each word as an independent unit, so they cannot generalize across semantically related sequences of words. In contrast, neural language models associate each word with a vector of real-value features and therefore semantically-related words end up close to each other in that vector space. Learning word vectors also works very well when the word sequences come from a large corpus of real text. These word vectors are composed of learned features that are automatically discovered by the neural network.

Vector representations of words learned from text are now very widely used in natural-language applications. In the next section, we will explore Recurrent Neural Networks and their application to a text classification task.

Understanding Recurrent Neural Networks

Generally, for tasks involving sequential inputs, it is recommended to use **Recurrent Neural Networks (RNNs)**. Such input is processed one element at a time, while maintaining a "state vector" (in hidden units). The state implicitly contains information about all the past elements in the sequence.

Typically, in conventional RNNs, it is difficult to store information for a long time. In order to remember the input for a long time, the network can be augmented with explicit memory. Also, this is the approach used in the **Long Short-Term Memory (LSTM)** networks; they use hidden units that can remember the input. LSTM networks have proved to be more effective than conventional RNNs.

In this section, we will explore the Recurrent Neural Networks for modeling sequential data. The following figure illustrates a simple Recurrent Neural Network or an Elman network:

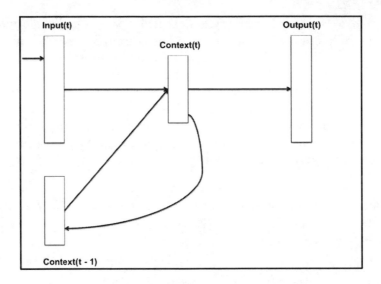

This is probably the simplest possible version of a Recurrent Neural Network that is easy to implement and train. The network has an input layer, a hidden layer (also called the context layer or state), and an output layer. The input to the network in time t is **Input(t)**, output is denoted as **Output(t)**, and **Context(t)** is state of the network (hidden layer). Input vector is formed by concatenating the vector representing the current word, and output from neurons in the context layer at time $t - 1$.

These networks are trained in several epochs, in which all the data from the training corpus is sequentially presented. To train the network, we can use the standard backpropagation algorithm with stochastic gradient descent. After each epoch, the network is tested on validation data. If the log-likelihood of validation data increases, the training continues in the new epoch. If no significant improvement is observed, the learning rate can be halved at the start of each new epoch. If there is no significant improvement as a result of changing the learning rate, the training is finished. Convergence of such networks is usually achieved after 10-20 epochs.

Here, the output layer represents a probability distribution of the next word when given the previous word and **Context(t − 1)**. Softmax ensures that the probability distribution is valid. At each training step, the error vector is computed, and the weights are updated with the standard backpropagation algorithm, as follows:

$error(t) = desired(t) - Output(t)$

Here, desired is a vector using 1-of-N coding, representing the word that should have been predicted in the particular context, and **Output(t)** is the actual output from the network.

To improve performance, we can merge all the words that occur less often than a given threshold value (in the training text) into a special rare token. Hence, all the rare words are thus treated equally, that is, the probability is distributed uniformly between them.

Now, we execute a simple RNN example provided in the BigDL library. The network is a fully-connected RNN where the output is fed back into the input. The example model supports sequence-to-sequence processing and is an implementation of a simple Recurrent Neural Network for language modeling.

For the full source code of this example, refer to https://github.com/ intel-analytics/BigDL/tree/master/spark/dl/src/main/scala/com/ intel/analytics/bigdl/models/rnn.

The input Dataset, Tiny Shakespeare Texts, can be downloaded from https://raw.githubusercontent.com/karpathy/char-rnn/master/data/ tinyshakespeare/input.txt.

After downloading the text, place it into an appropriate directory. We split the input Dataset into separate train.txt and val.txt files. In our example, we select 80% of the input to be the training Dataset, and the remaining 20 percent to be the validation Dataset.

Split the input Dataset by executing these commands:

```
head -n 8000 input.txt > val.txt
tail -n +8000 input.txt > train.txt
```

The SentenceSplitter and SentenceTokenizer classes use the Apache OpenNLP library. The trained model files--en-token.bin and en-sent.bin--can be downloaded from http://opennlp.sourceforge.net/models-1.5/.

The key parts of the code related to the model and the optimizer are listed here:

```
val model = Sequential[Float]()
//The RNN is created with the time-related parameter.
model.add(Recurrent[Float]()
.add(RnnCell[Float](inputSize, hiddenSize, Tanh[Float]())))
.add(TimeDistributed[Float](Linear[Float](hiddenSize, outputSize)))

//The optimization method used is SGD.
val optimMethod = if (param.stateSnapshot.isDefined) {
```

```
OptimMethod.load[Float](param.stateSnapshot.get)
} else {
    new SGD[Float](learningRate = param.learningRate, learningRateDecay =
0.0, weightDecay = param.weightDecay, momentum = param.momentum, dampening
= param.dampening)
}

val optimizer = Optimizer(
model = model,
dataset = trainSet,
criterion = TimeDistributedCriterion[Float](
    CrossEntropyCriterion[Float](), sizeAverage = true)
)

optimizer
.setValidation(Trigger.everyEpoch, validationSet, Array(new
Loss[Float](TimeDistributedCriterion[Float](CrossEntropyCriterion[Float](),
sizeAverage = true))))
.setOptimMethod(optimMethod)
.setEndWhen(Trigger.maxEpoch(param.nEpochs))
.setCheckpoint(param.checkpoint.get, Trigger.everyEpoch)
.optimize()
```

The following command executes the training program. Modify the parameters specific to your environment:

```
Aurobindos-MacBook-Pro-2:bigdl-rnn aurobindosarkar$
/Users/aurobindosarkar/Downloads/BigDL-master/scripts/bigdl.sh -- \
> /Users/aurobindosarkar/Downloads/spark-2.1.0-bin-hadoop2.7/bin/spark-
submit \
> --master local[2] \
> --executor-cores 2 \
> --total-executor-cores 2 \
> --class com.intel.analytics.bigdl.models.rnn.Train \
> /Users/aurobindosarkar/Downloads/dist-spark-2.1.1-scala-2.11.8-
mac-0.3.0-20170813.202825-21-dist/lib/bigdl-SPARK_2.1-0.3.0-SNAPSHOT-jar-
with-dependencies.jar \
> -f /Users/aurobindosarkar/Downloads/bigdl-rnn/inputdata/ -s
/Users/aurobindosarkar/Downloads/bigdl-rnn/saveDict/ --checkpoint
/Users/aurobindosarkar/Downloads/bigdl-rnn/model/ --batchSize 12 -e 2
```

The next extract is from the output generated during the training process:

```
17/08/16 21:32:38 INFO utils.ThreadPool$: Set mkl threads to 1 on thread 1
17/08/16 21:32:39 INFO utils.Engine$: Auto detect executor number and
executor cores number
17/08/16 21:32:39 INFO utils.Engine$: Executor number is 1 and executor
cores number is 2
```

```
17/08/16 21:32:39 INFO utils.Engine$: Find existing spark context. Checking
the spark conf...
17/08/16 21:32:41 INFO text.Dictionary: 272304 words and32885 sentences
processed
17/08/16 21:32:41 INFO text.Dictionary: save created dictionary.txt and
discard.txt to/Users/aurobindosarkar/Downloads/bigdl-rnn/saveDict
17/08/16 21:32:41 INFO rnn.Train$: maxTrain length = 25, maxVal = 22
17/08/16 21:32:42 INFO optim.DistriOptimizer$: caching training rdd ...
17/08/16 21:32:42 INFO optim.DistriOptimizer$: Cache thread models...
17/08/16 21:32:42 INFO optim.DistriOptimizer$: model thread pool size is 1
17/08/16 21:32:42 INFO optim.DistriOptimizer$: Cache thread models... done
17/08/16 21:32:42 INFO optim.DistriOptimizer$: config {
maxDropPercentage: 0.0
computeThresholdbatchSize: 100
warmupIterationNum: 200
isLayerwiseScaled: false
dropPercentage: 0.0
}
17/08/16 21:32:42 INFO optim.DistriOptimizer$: Shuffle data
17/08/16 21:32:42 INFO optim.DistriOptimizer$: Shuffle data complete.
Takes 0.011933988s
17/08/16 21:32:43 INFO optim.DistriOptimizer$: [Epoch 1 0/32885][Iteration
1][Wall Clock 0.0s] Train 12 in 0.642820037seconds. Throughput is 18.667744
records/second. Loss is 8.302014. Current learning rate is 0.1.
17/08/16 21:32:43 INFO optim.DistriOptimizer$: [Epoch 1 12/32885][Iteration
2][Wall Clock 0.642820037s] Train 12 in 0.211497603seconds. Throughput is
56.73823 records/second. Loss is 8.134232. Current learning rate is 0.1.
17/08/16 21:32:44 INFO optim.DistriOptimizer$: [Epoch 1 24/32885][Iteration
3][Wall Clock 0.85431764s] Train 12 in 0.337422962seconds. Throughput is
35.56367 records/second. Loss is 7.924248. Current learning rate is 0.1.
17/08/16 21:32:44 INFO optim.DistriOptimizer$: [Epoch 1 36/32885][Iteration
4][Wall Clock 1.191740602s] Train 12 in 0.189710956seconds. Throughput is
63.25412 records/second. Loss is 7.6132483. Current learning rate is 0.1.
17/08/16 21:32:44 INFO optim.DistriOptimizer$: [Epoch 1 48/32885][Iteration
5][Wall Clock 1.381451558s] Train 12 in 0.180944071seconds. Throughput is
66.31883 records/second. Loss is 7.095647. Current learning rate is 0.1.
17/08/16 21:32:44 INFO optim.DistriOptimizer$: [Epoch 1 60/32885][Iteration
6][Wall Clock 1.562395629s] Train 12 in 0.184258125seconds. Throughput is
65.12603 records/second. Loss is 6.3607793. Current learning rate is 0.1..
.
.
17/08/16 21:50:00 INFO optim.DistriOptimizer$: [Epoch 2
32856/32885][Iteration 5480][Wall Clock 989.905619531s] Train 12 in
0.19739412seconds. Throughput is 60.792084 records/second. Loss is
1.5389917. Current learning rate is 0.1.
17/08/16 21:50:00 INFO optim.DistriOptimizer$: [Epoch 2
32868/32885][Iteration 5481][Wall Clock 990.103013651s] Train 12 in
0.192780994seconds. Throughput is 62.2468 records/second. Loss is
```

```
1.3890615. Current learning rate is 0.1.
17/08/16 21:50:01 INFO optim.DistriOptimizer$: [Epoch 2
32880/32885][Iteration 5482][Wall Clock 990.295794645s] Train 12 in
0.197826032seconds. Throughput is 60.65936 records/second. Loss is
1.5320908. Current learning rate is 0.1.
17/08/16 21:50:01 INFO optim.DistriOptimizer$: [Epoch 2
32880/32885][Iteration 5482][Wall Clock 990.295794645s] Epoch finished.
Wall clock time is 1038274.610521ms
17/08/16 21:50:01 INFO optim.DistriOptimizer$: [Wall Clock 1038.274610521s]
Validate model...
17/08/16 21:50:52 INFO optim.DistriOptimizer$: Loss is (Loss: 1923.4493,
count: 1388, Average Loss: 1.3857704)
[Wall Clock 1038.274610521s] Save model to
/Users/aurobindosarkar/Downloads/bigdl-rnn/model//20170816_213242
```

Next, we use the saved model to run on the test Dataset, as shown:

```
Aurobindos-MacBook-Pro-2:bigdl-rnn aurobindosarkar$
/Users/aurobindosarkar/Downloads/BigDL-master/scripts/bigdl.sh -- \
> /Users/aurobindosarkar/Downloads/spark-2.1.0-bin-hadoop2.7/bin/spark-
submit \
> --master local[2] \
> --executor-cores 1 \
> --total-executor-cores 2 \
> --class com.intel.analytics.bigdl.models.rnn.Test \
> /Users/aurobindosarkar/Downloads/dist-spark-2.1.1-scala-2.11.8-
mac-0.3.0-20170813.202825-21-dist/lib/bigdl-SPARK_2.1-0.3.0-SNAPSHOT-jar-
with-dependencies.jar \
> -f /Users/aurobindosarkar/Downloads/bigdl-rnn/saveDict --model
/Users/aurobindosarkar/Downloads/bigdl-rnn/model/20170816_213242/model.5483
--words 20 --batchSize 12
17/08/16 21:53:21 INFO utils.ThreadPool$: Set mkl threads to 1 on thread 1
17/08/16 21:53:22 INFO utils.Engine$: Auto detect executor number and
executor cores number
17/08/16 21:53:22 INFO utils.Engine$: Executor number is 1 and executor
cores number is 2
17/08/16 21:53:22 INFO utils.Engine$: Find existing spark context. Checking
the spark conf...
17/08/16 21:53:24 WARN optim.Validator$: Validator(model, dataset) is
deprecated.
17/08/16 21:53:24 INFO optim.LocalValidator$: model thread pool size is 1
17/08/16 21:53:24 INFO optim.LocalValidator$: [Validation] 12/13 Throughput
is 84.44181986758397 record / sec
17/08/16 21:53:24 INFO optim.LocalValidator$: [Validation] 13/13 Throughput
is 115.81166197957567 record / sec
Loss is (Loss: 11.877369, count: 3, Average Loss: 3.959123)
```

Introducing autoencoders

An autoencoder neural network is an unsupervised learning algorithm that sets the target values to be equal to the input values. Hence, the autoencoder attempts to learn an approximation of an identity function.

Learning an identity function does not seem to be a worthwhile exercise; however, by placing constraints on the network, such as limiting the number of hidden units, we can discover interesting structures about the data. The key components of an autoencoder are depicted in this figure:

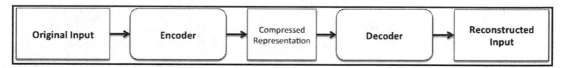

The original input, the compressed representation, and the output layers for an autoencoder are also illustrated in the following figure. More specifically, this figure represents a situation where, for example, an input image has pixel-intensity values from a 10×10 image (100 pixels), and there are 50 hidden units in layer two. Here, the network is forced to learn a "compressed" representation of the input, in which it must attempt to "reconstruct" the 100-pixel input using 50 hidden units:

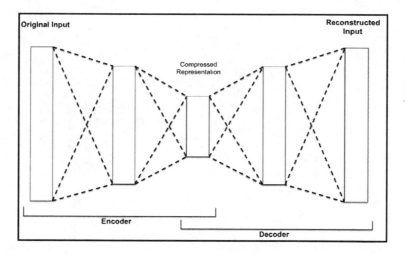

For more details on autoencoders, refer to *Reducing the Dimensionality of Data with Neural Networks* by G. E. Hinton and R. R. Salakhutdinov, available at https://www.cs.toronto.edu/~hinton/science.pdf.

Now, we present an example of an autoencoder from the BigDL distribution against the MNIST Dataset.

To train the autoencoder, you will need to download the MNIST Dataset from http:// yann.lecun.com/exdb/mnist/.

You will need to download the following:

```
train-images-idx3-ubyte.gz
train-labels-idx1-ubyte.gz (the labels file is not actually used in this
example)
```

Then, you have to unzip them to get the following files:

```
train-images-idx3-ubyte
train-labels-idx1-ubyte
```

For our implementation, ReLU is used as the activation function and the mean square error is used as the loss function. Key parts of the model and the optimizer code used in this example are listed here:

```
val rowN = 28
val colN = 28
val featureSize = rowN * colN
val classNum = 32
//The following model uses ReLU

val model = Sequential[Float]()
model.add(new Reshape(Array(featureSize)))
model.add(new Linear(featureSize, classNum))
model.add(new ReLU[Float]())
model.add(new Linear(classNum, featureSize))
model.add(new Sigmoid[Float]())

val optimMethod = new Adagrad[Float](learningRate = 0.01, learningRateDecay
= 0.0, weightDecay = 0.0005)

val optimizer = Optimizer(
   model = model,
   dataset = trainDataSet,
   criterion = new MSECriterion[Float]()
)
```

```
optimizer.setOptimMethod(optimMethod).setEndWhen(Trigger.maxEpoch(param.max
Epoch)).optimize()
```

The following is the command used to execute the autoencoder example:

```
Aurobindos-MacBook-Pro-2:bigdl-rnn aurobindosarkar$
/Users/aurobindosarkar/Downloads/BigDL-master/scripts/bigdl.sh --
/Users/aurobindosarkar/Downloads/spark-2.1.0-bin-hadoop2.7/bin/spark-submit
--master local[2] --class
com.intel.analytics.bigdl.models.autoencoder.Train
/Users/aurobindosarkar/Downloads/BigDL-
master/spark/dist/target/bigdl-0.2.0-SNAPSHOT-spark-2.0.0-scala-2.11.8-mac-
dist/lib/bigdl-0.2.0-SNAPSHOT-jar-with-dependencies.jar -b 150 -f
/Users/aurobindosarkar/Downloads/mnist --maxEpoch 2 --checkpoint
/Users/aurobindosarkar/Downloads/mnist
```

The output generated by the example is as follows:

```
17/08/16 22:52:16 INFO utils.ThreadPool$: Set mkl threads to 1 on thread 1
17/08/16 22:52:17 INFO utils.Engine$: Auto detect executor number and
executor cores number
17/08/16 22:52:17 INFO utils.Engine$: Executor number is 1 and executor
cores number is 2
17/08/16 22:52:17 INFO utils.Engine$: Find existing spark context. Checking
the spark conf...
17/08/16 22:52:18 INFO optim.DistriOptimizer$: caching training rdd ...
17/08/16 22:52:19 INFO optim.DistriOptimizer$: Cache thread models...
17/08/16 22:52:19 INFO optim.DistriOptimizer$: model thread pool size is 1
17/08/16 22:52:19 INFO optim.DistriOptimizer$: Cache thread models... done
17/08/16 22:52:19 INFO optim.DistriOptimizer$: config {
weightDecay: 5.0E-4
learningRate: 0.01
maxDropPercentage: 0.0
computeThresholdbatchSize: 100
momentum: 0.9
warmupIterationNum: 200
dampening: 0.0
dropPercentage: 0.0
}
17/08/16 22:52:19 INFO optim.DistriOptimizer$: Shuffle data
17/08/16 22:52:19 INFO optim.DistriOptimizer$: Shuffle data complete. Takes
0.013076416s
17/08/16 22:52:19 INFO optim.DistriOptimizer$: [Epoch 1 0/60000][Iteration
1][Wall Clock 0.0s] Train 150 in 0.217233789seconds. Throughput is 690.5003
records/second. Loss is 1.2499084.
17/08/16 22:52:20 INFO optim.DistriOptimizer$: [Epoch 1
150/60000][Iteration 2][Wall Clock 0.217233789s] Train 150 in
0.210093679seconds. Throughput is 713.9672 records/second. Loss is
```

```
1.1829382.
17/08/16 22:52:20 INFO optim.DistriOptimizer$: [Epoch 1
300/60000][Iteration 3][Wall Clock 0.427327468s] Train 150 in
0.05808109seconds. Throughput is 2582.5962 records/second. Loss is
1.089432.
17/08/16 22:52:20 INFO optim.DistriOptimizer$: [Epoch 1
450/60000][Iteration 4][Wall Clock 0.485408558s] Train 150 in
0.053720011seconds. Throughput is 2792.2556 records/second. Loss is
0.96986365.
17/08/16 22:52:20 INFO optim.DistriOptimizer$: [Epoch 1
600/60000][Iteration 5][Wall Clock 0.539128569s] Train 150 in
0.052071024seconds. Throughput is 2880.681 records/second. Loss is
0.9202304.
.
.
.
17/08/16 22:52:45 INFO optim.DistriOptimizer$: [Epoch 2
59400/60000][Iteration 797][Wall Clock 26.151645532s] Train 150 in
0.026734804seconds. Throughput is 5610.6636 records/second. Loss is
0.5562006.
17/08/16 22:52:45 INFO optim.DistriOptimizer$: [Epoch 2
59550/60000][Iteration 798][Wall Clock 26.178380336s] Train 150 in
0.031001227seconds. Throughput is 4838.518 records/second. Loss is
0.55211174.
17/08/16 22:52:45 INFO optim.DistriOptimizer$: [Epoch 2
59700/60000][Iteration 799][Wall Clock 26.209381563s] Train 150 in
0.027455972seconds. Throughput is 5463.292 records/second. Loss is
0.5566905.
17/08/16 22:52:45 INFO optim.DistriOptimizer$: [Epoch 2
59850/60000][Iteration 800][Wall Clock 26.236837535s] Train 150 in
0.037863017seconds. Throughput is 3961.6494 records/second. Loss is
0.55880654.
17/08/16 22:52:45 INFO optim.DistriOptimizer$: [Epoch 2
59850/60000][Iteration 800][Wall Clock 26.236837535s] Epoch finished. Wall
clock time is 26374.372173ms
[Wall Clock 26.374372173s] Save model to
/Users/aurobindosarkar/Downloads/mnist/20170816_225219
```

Summary

In this chapter, we introduced deep learning in Spark. We discussed various types of deep neural networks and their application. We also explored a few code examples provided in the BigDL distribution. As this is a rapidly evolving area in Spark, presently, we expect these libraries to provide a lot more functionalities using Spark SQL and the DataFrame/Dataset APIs. Additionally, we also expect them to mature and become more stable over the coming months.

In the next chapter, we will shift our focus to tuning Spark SQL applications. We will cover key foundational aspects regarding serialization/deserialization using encoders and the logical and physical plans associated with query executions, and then present the details of the **cost-based optimization (CBO)** feature released in Spark 2.2. Additionally, we will present some tips and tricks that developers can use to improve the performance of their applications.

11
Tuning Spark SQL Components for Performance

In this chapter, we will focus on the performance tuning aspects of Spark SQL-based components. The Spark SQL Catalyst optimizer is central to the efficient execution of many, if not all, Spark applications, including **ML Pipelines**, **Structured Streaming**, and **GraphFrames**-based applications. We will first explain the key foundational aspects regarding serialization/deserialization using encoders and the logical and physical plans associated with query executions, and then present the details of the **cost-based optimization** (**CBO**) feature released in Spark 2.2. Additionally, we will present some tips and tricks that developers can use to improve the performance of their applications throughout the chapter.

More specifically, in this chapter, you will learn the following:

- Basic concepts essential to understanding performance tuning
- Understanding Spark internals that drives performance
- Understanding cost-based optimizations
- Understanding the performance impact of enabling whole-stage code generation

Introducing performance tuning in Spark SQL

Spark computations are typically in-memory and can be bottlenecked by the resources in the cluster: CPU, network bandwidth, or memory. In addition, although the data fits in memory, network bandwidth may be challenging.

Tuning Spark applications is a necessary step to reduce both the number and size of data transfer over the network and/or reduce the overall memory footprint of the computations.

In this chapter, we will focus our attention on Spark SQL Catalyst because it is key to deriving benefits from a whole set of application components.

Spark SQL is at the heart of major enhancements made to Spark recently, including **ML Pipelines**, **Structured Streaming**, and **GraphFrames**. The following figure illustrates the key role **Spark SQL** plays between the **Spark Core** and the higher-level APIs built on top of it:

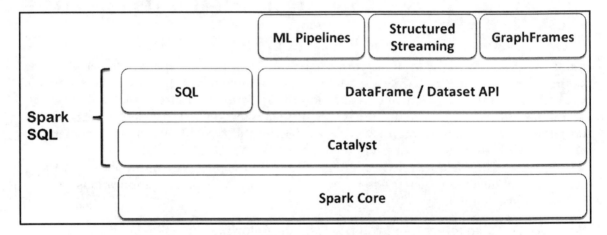

In the next several sections, we will cover the fundamental understanding required for tuning Spark SQL applications. We will start with the **DataFrame/Dataset** APIs.

Understanding DataFrame/Dataset APIs

A **Dataset** is a strongly typed collection of domain-specific objects that can be transformed parallelly, using functional or relational operations. Each Dataset also has a view called a **DataFrame**, which is not strongly typed and is essentially a Dataset of row objects.

Spark SQL applies structured views to the data from different source systems stored using different data formats. Structured APIs, such as the DataFrame/Dataset API, allows developers to use a high-level API to write their programs. These APIs allow them to focus on the "what" rather than the "how" of the data processing required.

Even though applying a structure can limit what can be expressed, in practice, structured APIs can accommodate the vast majority of computations required in application development. Also, it is these very limitations (imposed by structured APIs) that present several of the main optimization opportunities.

In the next section, we will explore encoders and their role in efficient serialization and deserialization.

Optimizing data serialization

The **Encoder** is the fundamental concept in the **serialization** and **deserialization** (SerDe) framework in Spark SQL 2.0. Spark SQL uses the SerDe framework for I/O resulting in greater time and space efficiencies. Datasets use a specialized encoder to serialize the objects for processing or transmitting over the network instead of using Java serialization or Kryo.

Encoders are required to support domain objects efficiently. These encoders map the domain object type, T, to Spark's internal type system, and `Encoder [T]` is used to convert objects or primitives of type T to and from Spark SQL's internal binary row format representation (using Catalyst expressions and code generation). The resulting binary structure often has a much lower memory footprint and is optimized for efficiency in data processing (for example, in a columnar format).

Efficient serialization is key to achieving good performance in distributed applications. Formats that are slow to serialize objects will significantly impact the performance. Often, this will be the first thing you tune to optimize a Spark application.

Encoders are highly optimized and use runtime code generation to build custom bytecode for serialization and deserialization. Additionally, they use a format that allows Spark to perform many operations, such as filtering and sorting, without requiring to be deserialized back to an object. As encoders know the schema of the records, they can offer significantly faster serialization and deserialization (compared to the default Java or Kryo serializers).

In addition to speed, the resulting serialized size of encoder output can also be significantly smaller, thereby reducing the cost of network transfers. Furthermore, the serialized data is already in the Tungsten binary format, which means that many operations can be executed in place, without needing to materialize the object. Spark has built-in support for automatically generating encoders for primitive types, such as String and Integer, and also case classes.

Here, we present an example of creating a custom encoder for the Bid records from Chapter 1, *Getting Started with Spark SQL*. Note that the encoders for most common types are automatically provided by importing spark.implicits._, and the default encoders are already imported in Spark shell.

First, let's import all the classes we need for the code in this chapter:

```
scala> import org.apache.spark.sql._
scala> import org.apache.spark.sql.types._
scala> import org.apache.spark.sql.functions._
scala> import org.apache.spark.sql.streaming._
scala> import spark.implicits._
scala> import spark.sessionState.conf
scala> import org.apache.spark.sql.internal.SQLConf.SHUFFLE_PARTITIONS
scala> import org.apache.spark.sql.Encoders
scala> import org.apache.spark.sql.catalyst.encoders.ExpressionEncoder
```

Next, we will define a case class for our domain object for Bid records in the input Dataset:

```
scala> case class Bid(bidid: String, timestamp: String, ipinyouid: String,
useragent: String, IP: String, region: Integer, cityID: Integer,
adexchange: String, domain: String, turl: String, urlid: String, slotid:
String, slotwidth: String, slotheight: String, slotvisibility: String,
slotformat: String, slotprice: String, creative: String, bidprice: String)
```

Next, we will create an Encoder object using the case class from the preceding step, as shown:

```
scala> val bidEncoder = Encoders.product[Bid]
```

The schema can be accessed using the schema property, as follows:

```
scala> bidEncoder.schema
```

We use the implementation of ExpressionEncoder (the only implementation of an encoder trait available in Spark SQL 2), as illustrated:

```
scala> val bidExprEncoder = bidEncoder.asInstanceOf[ExpressionEncoder[Bid]]
```

Here are the serializer and the deserializer parts of the encoder:

```
scala> bidExprEncoder.serializer

scala> bidExprEncoder.namedExpressions
```

Next, we will read in our input Dataset, as demonstrated:

```
scala> val bidsDF =
spark.read.format("csv").schema(bidEncoder.schema).option("sep",
"\t").option("header",
false).load("file:///Users/aurobindosarkar/Downloads/make-ipinyou-data-
master/original-data/ipinyou.contest.dataset/bidfiles")
```

We will then display a Bid record, as follows, from our newly created DataFrame:

```
scala> bidsDF.take(1).foreach(println)

[e3d962536ef3ac7096b31fdd1c1c24b0,20130311172101557,37a6259cc0c1dae299a7866
489dff0bd,Mozilla/4.0 (compatible; MSIE 8.0; Windows NT 6.1; Trident/4.0;
QQDownload 734; SLCC2; .NET CLR 2.0.50727; .NET CLR 3.5.30729; .NET CLR
3.0.30729; eSobiSubscriber 2.0.4.16;
MAAR),gzip(gfe),gzip(gfe),219.232.120.*,1,1,2,DF9blS9bQqsIFYB4uA5R,b6c5272d
fc63032f659be9b786c5f8da,null,2006366309,728,90,1,0,5,5aca4c5f29e59e425c7ea
657fdaac91e,300]
```

For convenience, we can use the record from the preceding step to create a new record as in the Dataset[Bid]:

```
scala> val bid =
Bid("e3d962536ef3ac7096b31fdd1c1c24b0","20130311172101557","37a6259cc0c1dae
299a7866489dff0bd","Mozilla/4.0 (compatible; MSIE 8.0; Windows NT 6.1;
Trident/4.0; QQDownload 734; SLCC2; .NET CLR 2.0.50727; .NET CLR 3.5.30729;
.NET CLR 3.0.30729; eSobiSubscriber 2.0.4.16;
MAAR),gzip(gfe),gzip(gfe)","219.232.120.*",1,1,"2","","DF9blS9bQqsIFYB4uA5R
,b6c5272dfc63032f659be9b786c5f8da",null,"2006366309","728","90","1","0","5"
,"5aca4c5f29e59e425c7ea657fdaac91e","300")
```

We will then serialize the record to the internal representation, as shown:

```
scala> val row = bidExprEncoder.toRow(bid)
```

Spark uses InternalRows internally for I/O. So, we deserialize the bytes to a JVM object, that is, a Scala object, as follows. However, we need to import Dsl expressions, and explicitly specify DslSymbol, as there are competing implicits in the Spark shell:

```
scala> import org.apache.spark.sql.catalyst.dsl.expressions._

scala> val attrs = Seq(DslSymbol('bidid).string,
DslSymbol('timestamp).string, DslSymbol('ipinyouid).string,
DslSymbol('useragent).string, DslSymbol('IP).string,
DslSymbol('region).int, DslSymbol('cityID).int,
DslSymbol('adexchange).string, DslSymbol('domain).string,
DslSymbol('turl).string, DslSymbol('urlid).string,
```

```
DslSymbol('slotid).string, DslSymbol('slotwidth).string,
DslSymbol('slotheight).string, DslSymbol('slotvisibility).string,
DslSymbol('slotformat).string, DslSymbol('slotprice).string,
DslSymbol('creative).string, DslSymbol('bidprice).string)
```

Here, we retrieve the serialized `Bid` object:

```
scala> val getBackBid = bidExprEncoder.resolveAndBind(attrs).fromRow(row)
```

We can verify that the two objects are the same, as shown:

```
scala> bid == getBackBid
res30: Boolean = true
```

In the next section, we will shift our focus to Spark SQL's Catalyst optimizations.

Understanding Catalyst optimizations

We briefly explored the Catalyst optimizer in `Chapter 1`, *Getting Started with Spark SQL*. Basically, Catalyst has an internal representation of the user's program, called the **query plan**. A set of transformations is executed on the initial query plan to yield the optimized query plan. Finally, through Spark SQL's code generation mechanism, the optimized query plan gets converted to a DAG of RDDs, ready for execution. At its core, the Catalyst optimizer defines the abstractions of users' programs as trees and also the transformations from one tree to another.

In order to take advantage of optimization opportunities, we need an optimizer that automatically finds the most efficient plan to execute data operations (specified in the user's program). In the context of this chapter, Spark SQL's Catalyst optimizer acts as the interface between the user's high-level programming constructs and the low-level execution plans.

Understanding the Dataset/DataFrame API

A Dataset or a DataFrame is typically created as a result of reading from a data source or the execution of a query. Internally, queries are represented by trees of operators, for example, logical and physical trees. Internally, a Dataset represents a logical plan that describes the computation required to produce the data. When an action is invoked, Spark's query optimizer optimizes the logical plan and generates a physical plan for efficient execution in a parallel and distributed manner.

A query plan is used describe a data operation such as aggregate, join, or filter, to generate a new Dataset using different kinds of input Datasets.

The first kind of query plan is the logical plan, and it describes the computation required on the Datasets without specifically defining the mechanism of conducting the actual computation. It gives us an abstraction of the user's program and allows us to freely transform the query plan, without worrying about the execution details.

A query plan is a part of Catalyst that models a tree of relational operators, that is, a structured query. A query plan has a `statePrefix` that is used when displaying a plan with ! to indicate an invalid plan, and ' to indicate an unresolved plan. A query plan is invalid if there are missing input attributes and children subnodes are non-empty, and it is unresolved if the column names have not been verified and column types have not been looked up in the catalog.

As a part of the optimizations, the Catalyst optimizer applies various rules to manipulate these trees in phases. We can use the explain function to explore the logical as well as the optimized physical plan.

Now, we will present a simple example of three Datasets and display their optimization plans using the `explain()` function:

```scala
scala> val t1 = spark.range(7)
scala> val t2 = spark.range(13)
scala> val t3 = spark.range(19)

scala> t1.explain()
== Physical Plan ==
*Range (0, 7, step=1, splits=8)

scala> t1.explain(extended=true)
== Parsed Logical Plan ==
Range (0, 7, step=1, splits=Some(8))

== Analyzed Logical Plan ==
id: bigint
Range (0, 7, step=1, splits=Some(8))

== Optimized Logical Plan ==
Range (0, 7, step=1, splits=Some(8))

== Physical Plan ==
*Range (0, 7, step=1, splits=8)

scala> t1.filter("id != 0").filter("id != 2").explain(true)
== Parsed Logical Plan ==
'Filter NOT ('id = 2)
+- Filter NOT (id#0L = cast(0 as bigint))
   +- Range (0, 7, step=1, splits=Some(8))
```

```
== Analyzed Logical Plan ==
id: bigint
Filter NOT (id#0L = cast(2 as bigint))
+- Filter NOT (id#0L = cast(0 as bigint))
   +- Range (0, 7, step=1, splits=Some(8))

== Optimized Logical Plan ==
Filter (NOT (id#0L = 0) && NOT (id#0L = 2))
+- Range (0, 7, step=1, splits=Some(8))

== Physical Plan ==
*Filter (NOT (id#0L = 0) && NOT (id#0L = 2))
+- *Range (0, 7, step=1, splits=8)
```

Analyzed logical plans result from applying the Analyzer's check rules on the initial parsed plan. Analyzer is a logical query plan Analyzer in Spark SQL that semantically validates and transforms an unresolved logical plan to an analyzed logical plan (using logical evaluation rules):

```
scala> spark.sessionState.analyzer
res30: org.apache.spark.sql.catalyst.analysis.Analyzer =
org.apache.spark.sql.hive.HiveSessionStateBuilder$$anon$1@21358f6c
```

Enable TRACE or DEBUG logging levels for the respective session-specific loggers to see what happens inside the Analyzer. For example, add the following line to conf/log4j properties:

```
log4j.logger.org.apache.spark.sql.hive.HiveSessionStateBuilder$$anon$1=DEBU
G scala> val t1 = spark.range(7)
17/07/13 10:25:38 DEBUG HiveSessionStateBuilder$$anon$1:
=== Result of Batch Resolution ===
!'DeserializeToObject unresolveddeserializer(staticinvoke(class
java.lang.Long, ObjectType(class java.lang.Long), valueOf,
upcast(getcolumnbyordinal(0, LongType), LongType, - root class:
"java.lang.Long"), true)), obj#2: java.lang.Long   DeserializeToObject
staticinvoke(class java.lang.Long, ObjectType(class java.lang.Long),
valueOf, cast(id#0L as bigint), true), obj#2: java.lang.Long
 +- LocalRelation <empty>, [id#0L]
+- LocalRelation <empty>, [id#0L]
t1: org.apache.spark.sql.Dataset[Long] = [id: bigint]
```

The Analyzer is a Rule Executor that defines the logical plan evaluation rules for resolving and modifying the same. It resolves unresolved relations and functions using the session catalog. The optimization rules for fixed points and the one-pass rules (the once strategy) in the batch are also defined here.

In the logical plan optimization phase, the following set of actions is executed:

- Rules convert logical plans into semantically equivalent ones for better performance
- Heuristic rules are applied to push down predicated columns, remove unreferenced columns, and so on
- Earlier rules enable the application of later rules; for example, merge query blocks enable global join reorder

`SparkPlan` is the Catalyst query plan for physical operators that are used to build the physical query plan. Upon execution, the physical operators produce RDDs of rows. The available logical plan optimizations can be extended and additional rules can be registered as experimental methods.

```
scala> t1.filter("id != 0").filter("id != 2")
17/07/13 10:43:17 DEBUG HiveSessionStateBuilder$$anon$1:
=== Result of Batch Resolution ===
!'Filter NOT ('id = 0)
Filter NOT (id#0L = cast(0 as bigint))
 +- Range (0, 7, step=1, splits=Some(8))
+- Range (0, 7, step=1, splits=Some(8))
...

17/07/13 10:43:17 DEBUG HiveSessionStateBuilder$$anon$1:
=== Result of Batch Resolution ===
!'Filter NOT ('id = 2)
Filter NOT (id#0L = cast(2 as bigint))
 +- Filter NOT (id#0L = cast(0 as bigint))
   +- Filter NOT (id#0L = cast(0 as bigint))
    +- Range (0, 7, step=1, splits=Some(8))
   +- Range (0, 7, step=1, splits=Some(8))
```

Understanding Catalyst transformations

In this section, we will explore Catalyst transformations in detail. Transformations in Spark are pure functions, that is, a tree is not mutated during the transformation (instead, a new one is produced). In Catalyst, there are two kinds of transformations:

- In the first type, the transformation does not change the type of the tree. Using this transformation, we can transform an expression to another expression, a logical plan to another logical plan, or a physical plan to another physical plan.

- The second type of transformation changes a tree from one kind of tree to another. For example, this type of transformation is used to change a logical plan to a physical plan.

A function (associated with a given tree) is used to implement a single rule. For example, in expressions, this can be used for constant folding optimization. A transformation is defined as a partial function. (Recall that a partial function is a function that is defined for a subset of its possible arguments.) Typically, case statements figure out whether a rule is triggered or not; for example, the predicate filter is pushed below the JOIN node as it reduces the input size of JOIN; this is called the **predicate pushdown**. Similarly, a projection is performed only for the required columns used in the query. This way, we can avoid reading unnecessary data.

Often, we need to combine different types of transformation rule. A Rule Executor is used to combine multiple rules. It transforms a tree to another tree of the same type by applying many rules (defined in batches).

There are two approaches used for applying rules:

- In the first approach, we apply the rule repeatedly until the tree does not change any more (called the fixed point)
- In the second type, we apply all the rules in a batch, only once (the once strategy)

Next, we look at the second type of transformation, in which we change from one tree to another kind of tree: more specifically, how Spark transforms a logical plan to a physical plan. A logical plan is transformed to a physical plan by applying a set of strategies. Primarily, a pattern matching approach is taken for these transformations. For example, a strategy converts the logical project node to a physical project node, a logical Filter node to a physical Filter node, and so on. A strategy may not be able to convert everything, so mechanisms are built-in to trigger other strategies at specific points in the code (for example, the planLater method).

The optimization process comprises of three steps:

1. Analysis (Rule Executor): This transforms an unresolved logical plan to a resolved logical plan. The unresolved to resolved state uses the Catalog to find where Datasets and columns come from and the types of column.
2. Logical Optimization (Rule Executor): This transforms a resolved logical plan to an optimized logical plan.

3. Physical Planning (Strategies+Rule Executor): This consists of two phases:
   - Transforms an optimized logical plan to a physical plan.
   - Rule Executor is used to adjust the physical plan to make it ready for execution. This includes how we shuffle the data and how we partition it.

As shown in the following example, an expression represents a new value, and it is computed based on its input values, for example, adding a constant to each element within a column, such as `1 + t1.normal`. Similarly, an attribute is a column in a Dataset (for example, `t1.id`) or a column generated by a specific data operation, for example, v.

The output has a list of attributes generated by this logical plan, for example, id and v. The logical plan also has a set of invariants about the rows generated by this plan, for example, `t2.id > 5000000`. Finally, we have statistics, the size of the plan in rows/bytes, per column stats, for example, min, max, and the number of distinct values, and the number of null values.

The second kind of query plan is the physical plan, and it describes the required computations on Datasets with specific definitions on how to conduct the computations. A physical plan is actually executable:

```scala
scala> val t0 = spark.range(0, 10000000)
scala> val df1 = t0.withColumn("uniform", rand(seed=10))
scala> val df2 = t0.withColumn("normal", randn(seed=27))
scala> df1.createOrReplaceTempView("t1")
scala> df2.createOrReplaceTempView("t2")

scala> spark.sql("SELECT sum(v) FROM (SELECT t1.id, 1 + t1.normal AS v FROM
t1 JOIN t2 WHERE t1.id = t2.id AND t2.id > 5000000) tmp").explain(true)
```

All the plans for the preceding query are displayed in the following code block. Note our annotations in the parsed logical plan, reflecting parts of the original SQL query:

```
== Parsed Logical Plan ==
'Project [unresolvedalias('sum('v), None)] ------------------> SELECT
sum(v)
+- 'SubqueryAlias tmp
   +- 'Project ['t1.id, (1 + 't1.normal) AS v#79] ----------->        SELECT
t1.id,
                                                             1 +
t1.normal as v
      +- 'Filter (('t1.id = 't2.id) && ('t2.id > 5000000))---> WHERE t1.id
= t2.id,
                                                             t2.id >
5000000
```

```
                   +- 'Join Inner -------------------------------------> t1 JOIN t2
                      :- 'UnresolvedRelation `t1`
                      +- 'UnresolvedRelation `t2`


== Analyzed Logical Plan ==
sum(v): double
Aggregate [sum(v#79) AS sum(v)#86]
+- SubqueryAlias tmp
   +- Project [id#10L, (cast(1 as double) + normal#13) AS v#79]
      +- Filter ((id#10L = id#51L) && (id#51L > cast(5000000 as bigint)))
         +- Join Inner
            :- SubqueryAlias t1
            :  +- Project [id#10L, randn(27) AS normal#13]
            :     +- Range (0, 10000000, step=1, splits=Some(8))
            +- SubqueryAlias t2
               +- Project [id#51L, rand(10) AS uniform#54]
                  +- Range (0, 10000000, step=1, splits=Some(8))


== Optimized Logical Plan ==
Aggregate [sum(v#79) AS sum(v)#86]
+- Project [(1.0 + normal#13) AS v#79]
   +- Join Inner, (id#10L = id#51L)
      :- Filter (id#10L > 5000000)
      :  +- Project [id#10L, randn(27) AS normal#13]
      :     +- Range (0, 10000000, step=1, splits=Some(8))
      +- Filter (id#51L > 5000000)
         +- Range (0, 10000000, step=1, splits=Some(8))


== Physical Plan ==
*HashAggregate(keys=[], functions=[sum(v#79)], output=[sum(v)#86])
+- Exchange SinglePartition
   +- *HashAggregate(keys=[], functions=[partial_sum(v#79)],
output=[sum#88])
      +- *Project [(1.0 + normal#13) AS v#79]
         +- *SortMergeJoin [id#10L], [id#51L], Inner
            :- *Sort [id#10L ASC NULLS FIRST], false, 0
            :  +- Exchange hashpartitioning(id#10L, 200)
            :     +- *Filter (id#10L > 5000000)
            :        +- *Project [id#10L, randn(27) AS normal#13]
            :           +- *Range (0, 10000000, step=1, splits=8)
            +- *Sort [id#51L ASC NULLS FIRST], false, 0
               +- Exchange hashpartitioning(id#51L, 200)
                  +- *Filter (id#51L > 5000000)
                     +- *Range (0, 10000000, step=1, splits=8)
```

You can use Catalyst's API to customize Spark to roll out your own planner rules.

 For more details on the Spark SQL Catalyst optimizer, refer
to `https://spark-summit.org/2017/events/a-deep-dive-into-spark-sq`
`ls-catalyst-optimizer/`.

Visualizing Spark application execution

In this section, we will present the key details of the SparkUI interface, which is indispensable for tuning tasks. There are several approaches to monitoring Spark applications, for example, using web UIs, metrics, and external instrumentation. The information displayed includes a list of scheduler stages and tasks, a summary of RDD sizes and memory usage, environmental information, and information about the running executors.

This interface can be accessed by simply opening `http://<driver-node>:4040` (`http://localhost:4040`) in a web browser. Additional `SparkContexts` running on the same host bind to successive ports: 4041, 4042, and so on.

 For a more detailed coverage of monitoring and instrumentation in Spark,
refer to `https://spark.apache.org/docs/latest/monitoring.html`.

We will explore Spark SQL execution visually using two examples. First, we create the two sets of Datasets. The difference between the first set (`t1`, `t2`, and `t3`) and the second set (`t4`, `t5`, and `t6`) of `Dataset[Long]` is the size:

```scala
scala> val t1 = spark.range(7)
scala> val t2 = spark.range(13)
scala> val t3 = spark.range(19)
scala> val t4 = spark.range(1e8.toLong)
scala> val t5 = spark.range(1e8.toLong)
scala> val t6 = spark.range(1e3.toLong)
```

We will execute the following JOIN query against two sets of Datasets to visualize the Spark jobs information in the SparkUI dashboard:

```scala
scala> val query = t1.join(t2).where(t1("id") ===
t2("id")).join(t3).where(t3("id") === t1("id")).explain()
== Physical Plan ==
*BroadcastHashJoin [id#6L], [id#12L], Inner, BuildRight
:- *BroadcastHashJoin [id#6L], [id#9L], Inner, BuildRight
:  :- *Range (0, 7, step=1, splits=8)
:  +- BroadcastExchange HashedRelationBroadcastMode(List(input[0, bigint,
false]))
:     +- *Range (0, 13, step=1, splits=8)
+- BroadcastExchange HashedRelationBroadcastMode(List(input[0, bigint,
false]))
   +- *Range (0, 19, step=1, splits=8)
query: Unit = ()

scala> val query = t1.join(t2).where(t1("id") ===
t2("id")).join(t3).where(t3("id") === t1("id")).count()
query: Long = 7
```

The following screenshot displays the event timeline:

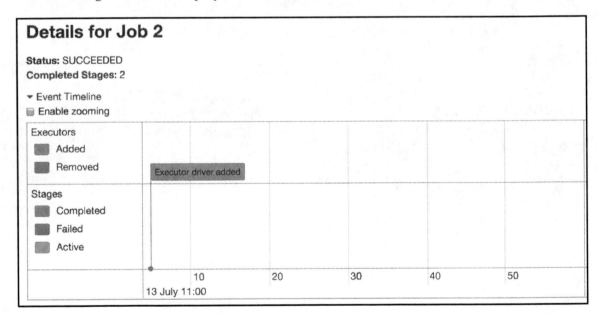

The generated **DAG Visualization** with the stages and the shuffles (**Exchange**) is shown next:

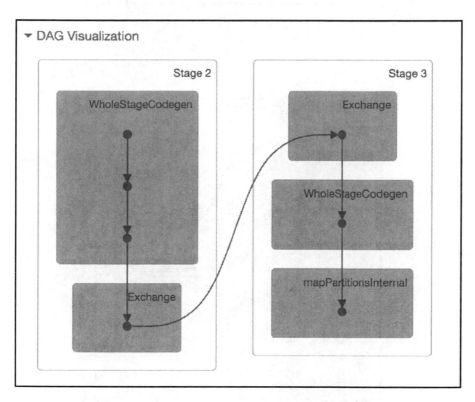

A summary of the job, including execution duration, successful tasks, and the total number of tasks, and so on, is displayed here:

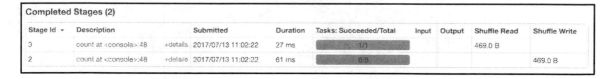

Stage Id ▾	Description	Submitted	Duration	Tasks: Succeeded/Total	Input	Output	Shuffle Read	Shuffle Write
3	count at <console>:48 +details	2017/07/13 11:02:22	27 ms	1/1			469.0 B	
2	count at <console>:48 +details	2017/07/13 11:02:22	61 ms	8/8				469.0 B

Completed Stages (2)

Click on the **SQL** tab to see the detailed execution flow, as demonstrated:

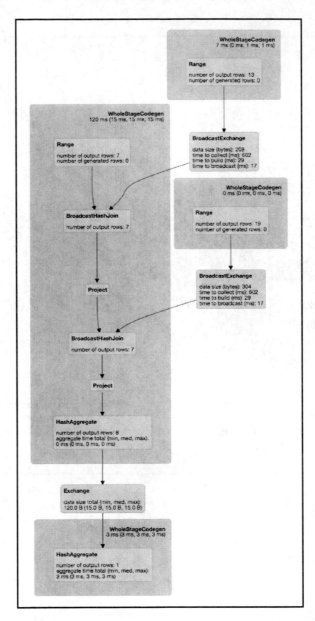

Next, we will run the same queries on the set of larger Datasets. Note that the
`BroadcastHashJoin` in the first example now changes to `SortMergeJoin` due to the
increased size of the input Datasets:

```scala
scala> val query = t4.join(t5).where(t4("id") ===
t5("id")).join(t6).where(t4("id") === t6("id")).explain()
== Physical Plan ==
*BroadcastHashJoin [id#72L], [id#78L], Inner, BuildRight
:- *SortMergeJoin [id#72L], [id#75L], Inner
:  :- *Sort [id#72L ASC NULLS FIRST], false, 0
:  :  +- Exchange hashpartitioning(id#72L, 200)
:  :     +- *Range (0, 100000000, step=1, splits=8)
:  +- *Sort [id#75L ASC NULLS FIRST], false, 0
:     +- ReusedExchange [id#75L], Exchange hashpartitioning(id#72L, 200)
+- BroadcastExchange HashedRelationBroadcastMode(List(input[0, bigint,
false]))
   +- *Range (0, 1000, step=1, splits=8)
query: Unit = ()
```

The execution DAG is shown in the following figure:

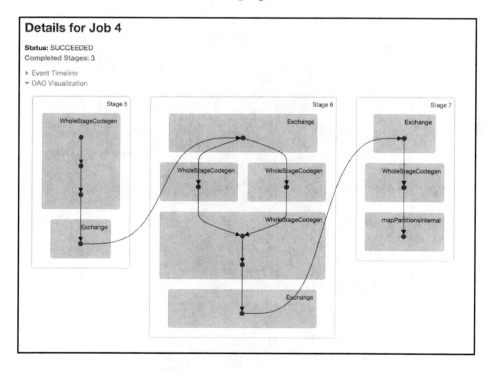

The job execution summary is, as shown:

Completed Stages (3)								
Stage Id ▾	Description	Submitted	Duration	Tasks: Succeeded/Total	Input	Output	Shuffle Read	Shuffle Write
7	count at <console>:48 +details	2017/07/13 11:11:52	14 ms	1/1			11.5 KB	
6	count at <console>:48 +details	2017/07/13 11:11:37	15 s	200/200			959.8 MB	11.5 KB
5	count at <console>:48 +details	2017/07/13 11:11:30	6 s	6/6				479.9 MB

The SQL execution details are shown in the following figure:

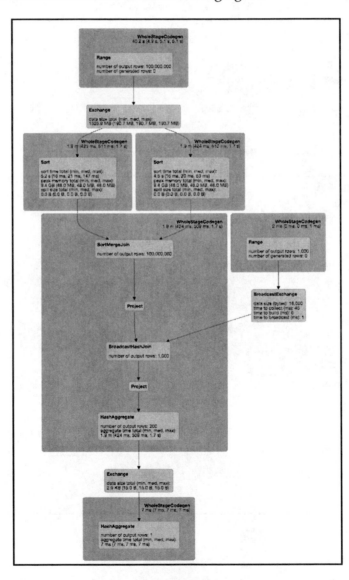

In addition to displaying in the UI, metrics are also available as JSON data. This gives developers a good way to create new visualizations and monitoring tools for Spark. The REST endpoints are mounted at `/api/v1`; for example, they would typically be accessible at `http://localhost:4040/api/v1`. These endpoints have been strongly versioned to make it easier to develop applications using them.

Exploring Spark application execution metrics

Spark has a configurable metrics system based on the `Dropwizard Metrics` library. This allows users to report Spark metrics to a variety of sinks, including `HTTP`, `JMX`, and `CSV` files. Spark's metrics corresponding to Spark components include the Spark standalone master process, applications within the master that report on various applications, a Spark standalone worker process, Spark executor, the Spark driver process, and the Spark shuffle service.

The next series of screenshots contain details, including summary metrics and the aggregated metrics by executors for one of the stages of the JOIN query against the larger Datasets:

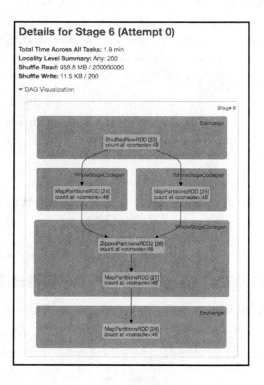

The summary metrics for the completed tasks is, as shown:

Metric	Min	25th percentile	Median	75th percentile	Max
Summary Metrics for 200 Completed Tasks					
Duration	0.4 s	0.5 s	0.5 s	0.6 s	2 s
GC Time	0 ms	9 ms	12 ms	22 ms	0.5 s
Shuffle Read Size / Records	4.8 MB / 996224	4.8 MB / 999172	4.8 MB / 1000060	4.8 MB / 1000926	4.8 MB / 1003388
Shuffle Write Size / Records	56.0 B / 1	59.0 B / 1	59.0 B / 1	59.0 B / 1	59.0 B / 1

The aggregated metrics by Executor is, as shown:

Executor ID ▲	Address	Task Time	Total Tasks	Failed Tasks	Killed Tasks	Succeeded Tasks	Shuffle Read Size / Records	Shuffle Write Size / Records	Blacklisted
▼ Aggregated Metrics by Executor									
driver	192.168.1.110:54752	2.0 min	200	0	0	200	959.8 MB / 200000000	11.5 KB / 200	0

Using external tools for performance tuning

External monitoring tools are often used to profile the performance of Spark jobs in large-sized `Spark clusters`. For example, Ganglia can provide an insight into overall cluster utilization and resource bottlenecks. Additionally, the `OS profiling` tools and `JVM` utilities can provide fine-grained profiling on individual nodes and for working with `JVM` internals, respectively.

 For more details on visualizing Spark application execution, refer to https://databricks.com/blog/2015/06/22/understanding-your-spark-application-through-visualization.html.

In the next section, we will shift our focus to the new cost-based optimizer released in Spark 2.2.

Cost-based optimizer in Apache Spark 2.2

In Spark, the optimizer's goal is to minimize end-to-end query response time. It is based on two key ideas:

Pruning unnecessary data as early as possible, for example, filter pushdown and column pruning.

Minimizing per-operator cost, for example, broadcast versus shuffle and optimal join order.

Till Spark 2.1, Catalyst was essentially a rule-based optimizer. Most Spark SQL optimizer rules are heuristic rules: `PushDownPredicate`, `ColumnPruning`, `ConstantFolding`, and so on. They do not consider the cost of each operator or selectivity when estimating `JOIN` relation sizes. Therefore, the `JOIN` order is mostly decided by its position in `SQL queries` and the physical join implementation is decided based on heuristics. This can lead to suboptimal plans being generated. However, if the cardinalities are known in advance, more efficient queries can be obtained. The goal of the CBO optimizer is to do exactly that, automatically.

Huawei implemented the CBO in Spark SQL initially; after they open sourced their work, many other contributors, including Databricks, worked to finish its first version. The CBO-related changes to Spark SQL, specifically the major entry points into Spark SQL's data structure and workflow, have been designed and implemented in a non-intrusive manner.

A configuration parameter, `spark.sql.cbo`, can be used to enable/disable this feature. Currently (in Spark 2.2), the default value is false.

 For more details, refer to Huawei's design document available at `https://issues.apache.org/jira/browse/SPARK-16026`.

Spark SQL's Catalyst optimizer has many rule-based optimization techniques implemented, for example, predicate pushdown to reduce the number of the qualifying records before a join operation is performed, and project pruning to reduce the number of the participating columns before further processing. However, without detailed column statistical information on data distribution, it is difficult to accurately estimate the filter factor and cardinality, and thus the output size of a database operator. With inaccurate and/or misleading statistics, the optimizer can end up choosing suboptimal query execution plans.

In order to improve the quality of query execution plans, the Spark SQL optimizer has been enhanced with detailed statistical information. A better estimate of the number of output records and the output size (for each database operator) helps the optimizer choose a better query plan. The CBO implementation collects, infers, and propagates `table / column` statistics on `source / intermediate` data. The query tree is annotated with these statistics. Furthermore, it also calculates the cost of each operator in terms of the number of output rows, the output size, and so on. Based on these cost calculations, it picks the most optimal query execution plan.

Understanding the CBO statistics collection

The `Statistics` class is the key data structure holding statistics information. This data structure is referenced when we execute statistics collection SQL statements to save information into the system catalog. This data structure is also referenced when we fetch statistics information from the system catalog to optimize a query plan.

CBO relies on detailed statistic to optimize a query execution plan. The following SQL statement can be used to collect `table-level` statistics, such as the number of rows, number of files (or HDFS data blocks), and table size (in bytes). It collects `table-level` statistics and saves them in the `meta-store`. Before 2.2, we only had the table size and not the number of rows:

```
ANALYZE TABLE table_name COMPUTE STATISTICS
```

Similarly, the following SQL statement can be used to collect column level statistics for the specified columns. The collected information includes the maximal column value, minimal column value, number of distinct values, number of null values, and so on. It collects column level statistics and saves them in the `meta-store`. Typically, it is executed only for columns in the WHERE and the GROUP BY clauses:

```
ANALYZE TABLE table_name COMPUTE STATISTICS FOR COLUMNS column-name1,
column-name2, ....
```

The given SQL statement displays the metadata, including table level statistics of a table in an extended format:

```
DESCRIBE EXTENDED table_name
```

The `customers` table is created in a later section of this chapter:

```
scala> sql("DESCRIBE EXTENDED customers").collect.foreach(println)
[# col_name,data_type,comment]
[id,bigint,null]
[name,string,null]
[,,]
[# Detailed Table Information,,]
[Database,default,]
[Table,customers,]
[Owner,aurobindosarkar,]
[Created,Sun Jul 09 23:16:38 IST 2017,]
[Last Access,Thu Jan 01 05:30:00 IST 1970,]
[Type,MANAGED,]
[Provider,parquet,]
[Properties,[serialization.format=1],]
[Statistics,1728063103 bytes, 200000000 rows,]
```

```
[Location,file:/Users/aurobindosarkar/Downloads/spark-2.2.0-bin-
hadoop2.7/spark-warehouse/customers,]
[Serde
Library,org.apache.hadoop.hive.ql.io.parquet.serde.ParquetHiveSerDe,]
[InputFormat,org.apache.hadoop.hive.ql.io.parquet.MapredParquetInputFormat,
]
[OutputFormat,org.apache.hadoop.hive.ql.io.parquet.MapredParquetOutputForma
t,]
```

The following SQL statement can be used to display statistics in the optimized logical plan:

```
EXPLAIN COST SELECT * FROM table_name WHERE condition
```

Statistics collection functions

Statistics are collected using a set of functions, for example, the row count is actually obtained by running a SQL statement, such as `select count(1) from table_name`. Using SQL statement to get row count is fast as we are leveraging Spark SQL's execution parallelism. Similarly, the `analyzeColumns` function gets the basic statistics information for a given column. The basic statistics, such as `max`, `min`, and `number-of-distinct-values`, are also obtained by running SQL statements.

Filter operator

A filter condition is the predicate expression specified in the WHERE clause of a SQL select statement. The predicate expression can be quite complex when we evaluate the overall filter factor.

There are several operators for which the filter cardinality estimation is executed, for example, between the AND, OR, and NOT logical expressions, and also for logical expressions such as =, <, <=, >, >=, and `in`.

For the filter operator, our goal is to compute the filter to find out the portion of the previous (or child) operator's output after applying the filter condition. A filter factor is a double number between 0.0 and 1.0. The number of output rows for the filter operator is basically the number of its `child node`'s output times the filter factor. Its output size is its `child node`'s output size times the filter factor.

Join operator

Before we compute the cardinality of a two-table join output, we should already have the output cardinalities of its `child nodes` on both sides. The cardinality of each join side is no longer the number of records in the original join table. Rather, it is the number of qualified records after applying all execution operators before this join operator.

If a user collects the `join column` statistics, then we know the number of distinct values for each `join column`. Since we also know the number of records on the join relation, we can tell whether or not `join column` is a unique key. We can compute the ratio of a number of distinct values on `join column` over the number of records in join relation. If the ratio is close to `1.0` (say greater than `0.95`), then we can assume that the `join column` is unique. Therefore, we can precisely determine the number of records per distinct value if a `join column` is unique.

Build side selection

The CBO can select a good physical strategy for an execution operator. For example, CBO can choose the `build side` selection for a `hash join` operation. For two-way hash joins, we need to choose one operand as `build side` and the other as `probe side`. The approach chooses the lower-cost child as the `build side` of `hash join`.

Before Spark 2.2, the build side was selected based on original table sizes. For the following Join query example, the earlier approach would have selected `BuildRight`. However, with CBO, the `build side` is selected based on the estimated cost of various operators before the join. Here, `BuildLeft` would have been selected. It can also decide whether or not a broadcast join should be performed. Additionally, the execution sequence of the database operators for a given query can be rearranged. `cbo` can choose the best plan among multiple candidate plans for a given query. The goal is to select the candidate plan with the lowest cost:

```scala
scala> spark.sql("DROP TABLE IF EXISTS t1")
scala> spark.sql("DROP TABLE IF EXISTS t2")
scala> spark.sql("CREATE TABLE IF NOT EXISTS t1(id long, value long) USING
parquet")
scala> spark.sql("CREATE TABLE IF NOT EXISTS t2(id long, value string)
USING parquet")
scala> spark.range(5E8.toLong).select('id, (rand(17) * 1E6) cast
"long").write.mode("overwrite").insertInto("t1")
scala> spark.range(1E8.toLong).select('id, 'id cast
"string").write.mode("overwrite").insertInto("t2")
```

```
scala> sql("SELECT t1.id FROM t1, t2 WHERE t1.id = t2.id AND t1.value =
100").explain()
== Physical Plan ==
*Project [id#79L]
+- *SortMergeJoin [id#79L], [id#81L], Inner
   :- *Sort [id#79L ASC NULLS FIRST], false, 0
   :  +- Exchange hashpartitioning(id#79L, 200)
   :     +- *Project [id#79L]
   :        +- *Filter ((isnotnull(value#80L) && (value#80L = 100)) &&
isnotnull(id#79L))
   :           +- *FileScan parquet default.t1[id#79L,value#80L] Batched:
true, Format: Parquet, Location:
InMemoryFileIndex[file:/Users/aurobindosarkar/Downloads/spark-2.2.0-bin-
hadoop2.7/spark-warehouse..., PartitionFilters: [], PushedFilters:
[IsNotNull(value), EqualTo(value,100), IsNotNull(id)], ReadSchema:
struct<id:bigint,value:bigint>
   +- *Sort [id#81L ASC NULLS FIRST], false, 0
      +- Exchange hashpartitioning(id#81L, 200)
         +- *Project [id#81L]
            +- *Filter isnotnull(id#81L)
               +- *FileScan parquet default.t2[id#81L] Batched: true,
Format: Parquet, Location:
InMemoryFileIndex[file:/Users/aurobindosarkar/Downloads/spark-2.2.0-bin-
hadoop2.7/spark-warehouse..., PartitionFilters: [], PushedFilters:
[IsNotNull(id)], ReadSchema: struct<id:bigint>
```

In the next section, we will explore CBO optimization in multi-way joins.

Understanding multi-way JOIN ordering optimization

Spark SQL optimizer's heuristics rules can transform a SELECT statement into a query plan with the following characteristics:

- The filter operator and project operator are pushed down below the join operator, that is, both the filter and project operators are executed before the join operator
- Without subquery block, the join operator is pushed down below the aggregate operator for a select statement, that is, a join operator is usually executed before the aggregate operator

With this observation, the biggest benefit we can get from CBO is multi-way join ordering optimization. Using a dynamic programming technique, we try to get the globally optimal join order for a multi-way join query.

For more details on multi-way join reordering in Spark 2.2, refer to `https://spark-summit.org/2017/events/cost-based-optimizer-in-apache-spark-22/`.

Clearly, the join cost is the dominant factor in choosing the best join order. The cost formula is dependent on the implementation of the Spark SQL execution engine.

The join cost formula in Spark is as follows:

*weight * cardinality + size * (1 - weight)*

The weight in the formula is a tuning parameter configured via the `spark.sql.cbo.joinReorder.card.weight` parameter (the default value is `0.7`). The cost of a plan is the sum of the costs of all intermediate tables. Note that the current cost formula is very coarse and subsequent versions of Spark are expected to have a more fine-grained formula.

For more details on reordering the joins using a dynamic programming algorithm, refer to the paper by Selinger et al, at `http://citeseerx.ist.psu.edu/viewdoc/download?doi=10.1.1.129.5879&rep=rep1&type=pdf`.

First, we put all the items (basic joined nodes) into level 1, then we build all two-way joins at level 2 from plans at level 1 (single items), then build all three-way joins from plans at previous levels (two-way joins and single items), then four-way joins and so on, until we have built all n-way joins, and pick the best plan among them at each stage.

When building m-way joins, we only keep the best plan (with the lowest cost) for the same set of m items. For example, for three-way joins, we keep only the best plan for items {A, B, C} among plans (A J B) J C, (A J C) J B, and (B J C) J A.

One drawback of this algorithm is the assumption that a lowest cost plan can only be generated among the lowest cost plans from its previous levels. In addition, because the decision to choose a sorted-merge join, which preserves the order of its input, versus other join methods is done in the query planner phase, we do not have this information to make a good decision in the optimizer.

Next, we present an extended example of a multi-way join with the `cbo` and `joinReorder` parameters switched off and switched on to demonstrate the speed improvements:

```scala
scala> sql("CREATE TABLE IF NOT EXISTS customers(id long, name string)
USING parquet")
scala> sql("CREATE TABLE IF NOT EXISTS goods(id long, price long) USING
```

```
parquet")
scala> sql("CREATE TABLE IF NOT EXISTS orders(customer_id long, good_id
long) USING parquet")

scala> import org.apache.spark.sql.functions.rand

scala> spark.sql("CREATE TABLE IF NOT EXISTS customers(id long, name
string) USING parquet")
scala> spark.sql("CREATE TABLE IF NOT EXISTS goods(id long, price long)
USING parquet")
scala> spark.sql("CREATE TABLE IF NOT EXISTS orders(customer_id long,
good_id long) USING parquet")

scala> spark.range(2E8.toLong).select('id, 'id cast
"string").write.mode("overwrite").insertInto("customers")

scala> spark.range(1E8.toLong).select('id, (rand(17) * 1E6 + 2) cast
"long").write.mode("overwrite").insertInto("goods")
spark.range(1E7.toLong).select(rand(3) * 2E8 cast "long", (rand(5) * 1E8)
cast "long").write.mode("overwrite").insertInto("orders")
```

We define a function benchmark to measure the execution time of our queries:

```
scala> def benchmark(name: String)(f: => Unit) {
     |       val startTime = System.nanoTime
     |       f
     |       val endTime = System.nanoTime
     |       println(s"Time taken with $name: " + (endTime -
     |             startTime).toDouble / 1000000000 + " seconds")
     | }
```

In the first example, as shown, we switch off the cbo and joinReorder parameters:

```
scala> val conf = spark.sessionState.conf

scala> spark.conf.set("spark.sql.cbo.enabled", false)

scala> conf.cboEnabled
res1: Boolean = false

scala> conf.joinReorderEnabled
res2: Boolean = false

scala> benchmark("CBO OFF & JOIN REORDER DISABLED"){ sql("SELECT name FROM
customers, orders, goods WHERE customers.id = orders.customer_id AND
orders.good_id = goods.id AND goods.price > 1000000").show() }
```

The following is the output on the command line:

```
+---------+
|    name|
+---------+
| 33270267|
|123904911|
|174393361|
|161741766|
|159902261|
|  2386203|
+---------+

Time taken with CBO OFF & JOIN REORDER DISABLED: 51.440248589 seconds
```

In the next example, we switch on `cbo` but keep the `joinReorder` parameter disabled:

```scala
scala> spark.conf.set("spark.sql.cbo.enabled", true)
scala> conf.cboEnabled
res11: Boolean = true
scala> conf.joinReorderEnabled
res12: Boolean = false

scala> benchmark("CBO ON & JOIN REORDER DIABLED"){ sql("SELECT name FROM
customers, orders, goods WHERE customers.id = orders.customer_id AND
orders.good_id = goods.id AND goods.price > 1000000").show() }
```

The following is the output on the command line:

```
+---------+
|    name|
+---------+
|174393361|
| 33270267|
|123904911|
|  2386203|
|161741766|
|159902261|
+---------+

Time taken with CBO ON & JOIN REORDER DISABLED: 42.191017053 seconds
```

Note the slight improvement in the execution time of the query with the `cbo` parameter enabled.

In the final example, we switch on both the `cbo` and `joinReorder` parameters:

```scala
scala> spark.conf.set("spark.sql.cbo.enabled", true)
scala> spark.conf.set("spark.sql.cbo.joinReorder.enabled", true)
```

```
scala> conf.cboEnabled
res2: Boolean = true
scala> conf.joinReorderEnabled
res3: Boolean = true

scala> benchmark("CBO ON & JOIN REORDER ENABLED"){ sql("SELECT name FROM
customers, orders, goods WHERE customers.id = orders.customer_id AND
orders.good_id = goods.id AND goods.price > 1000000").show()}
```

The following is the output on the command line:

```
+---------+
|    name|
+---------+
|  2386203|
| 33270267|
|159902261|
|161741766|
|174393361|
|123904911|
+---------+

Time taken with CBO ON & JOIN REORDER ENABLED: 7.099971757 seconds
```

Note the substantial improvement in the execution time of the query with both the parameters enabled.

In the next section, we will examine performance improvements achieved for various JOINs using whole-stage code generation.

Understanding performance improvements using whole-stage code generation

In this section, we first present a high-level overview of whole-stage code generation in Spark SQL, followed by a set of examples to show improvements in various JOINs using Catalyst's code generation feature.

After we have an optimized query plan, it needs to be converted to a DAG of RDDs for execution on the cluster. We use this example to explain the basic concepts of Spark SQL whole-stage code generation:

```
scala> sql("select count(*) from orders where customer_id =
26333955").explain()
```

```
== Optimized Logical Plan ==
Aggregate [count(1) AS count(1)#45L]
+- Project
   +- Filter (isnotnull(customer_id#42L) && (customer_id#42L =
          26333955))
      +- Relation[customer_id#42L,good_id#43L] parquet
```

The preceding optimized logical plan can be viewed as a sequence of **Scan, Filter, Project,** and **Aggregate** operations, as shown in the following figure:

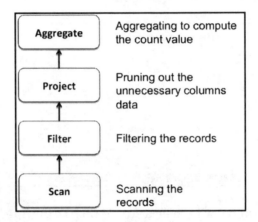

Traditional databases will typically execute the preceding query based on the Volcano Iterator Model, in which each operator implements an iterator interface, and consumes records from its input operator and outputs records to the operator that is sequenced after it. This model makes it easy to add new operators independent of their interactions with other operators. It also promotes composability of operators. However, the Volcano Model is inefficient because it involves execution of many virtual function calls, for example, three calls are executed for each record in the `Aggregate` function. Additionally, it requires extensive memory accesses (due to reads/writes in each operator as per the iterator interface). It is also challenging to leverage modern CPU features, such as pipelining, prefetching, and branch prediction, on the Volcano model.

Instead of generating iterator code for each operator, Spark SQL tries to generate a single function for the set of operators in the SQL statement. For example, the pseudo-code for the preceding query might look something like the following. Here, the `for` loop reads over all the rows (Scan operation), the if-condition roughly corresponds to the Filter condition, and the aggregate is essentially the count:

```
long count = 0;
for (customer_id in orders) {
   if (customer_id == 26333955) {
```

```
        count += 1;
    }
}
```

Note that the simple code mentioned has no virtual function calls and the count variable getting incremented is available in the CPU registers. This code is easily understood by compilers and therefore modern hardware can be leveraged to speed up queries like this one.

The key ideas underlying whole-stage code generation include the fusing together of operators, the identification of chains of operators (stages), and the compilation of each stage into a single function. This results in code generation that mimics hand-written optimized code for the execution of the query.

 For more details on compiling query plans on modern hardware, refer to http://www.vldb.org/pvldb/vol4/p539-neumann.pdf.

We can use EXPLAIN CODEGEN to explore the code generated for a query, as shown:

```
scala> sql("EXPLAIN CODEGEN SELECT name FROM customers, orders, goods WHERE
customers.id = orders.customer_id AND orders.good_id = goods.id AND
goods.price > 1000000").take(1).foreach(println)
[Found 6 WholeStageCodegen subtrees.
== Subtree 1 / 6 ==
*Project [id#11738L]
+- *Filter ((isnotnull(price#11739L) && (price#11739L > 1000000)) &&
isnotnull(id#11738L))
   +- *FileScan parquet default.goods[id#11738L,price#11739L] Batched:
true, Format: Parquet, Location:
InMemoryFileIndex[file:/Users/aurobindosarkar/Downloads/spark-2.2.0-bin-
hadoop2.7/spark-warehouse..., PartitionFilters: [], PushedFilters:
[IsNotNull(price), GreaterThan(price,1000000), IsNotNull(id)], ReadSchema:
struct<id:bigint,price:bigint>

Generated code:
/* 001 */ public Object generate(Object[] references) {
/* 002 */    return new GeneratedIterator(references);
/* 003 */ }
...
== Subtree 6 / 6 ==
*Sort [id#11734L ASC NULLS FIRST], false, 0
+- Exchange hashpartitioning(id#11734L, 200)
   +- *Project [id#11734L, name#11735]
      +- *Filter isnotnull(id#11734L)
         +- *FileScan parquet default.customers[id#11734L,name#11735]
```

```
Batched: true, Format: Parquet, Location:
InMemoryFileIndex[file:/Users/aurobindosarkar/Downloads/spark-2.2.0-bin-
hadoop2.7/spark-warehouse..., PartitionFilters: [], PushedFilters:
[IsNotNull(id)], ReadSchema: struct<id:bigint,name:string>

Generated code:
/* 001 */ public Object generate(Object[] references) {
/* 002 */   return new GeneratedIterator(references);
/* 003 */ }
...
]
```

Here, we present a series of JOIN examples with whole-stage code generation switched off and subsequently switched on to see the significant impact on execution performance.

 The examples in this section have been taken from the JoinBenchmark.scala class available at https://github.com/apache/spark/blob/master/sql/core/src/test/scala/org/apache/spark/sql/execution/benchmark/JoinBenchmark.scala.

In the following example, we present the details of obtaining the execution times for the JOIN operations with long values:

```
scala> spark.conf.set("spark.sql.codegen.wholeStage", false)

scala> conf.wholeStageEnabled
res77: Boolean = false

scala> val N = 20 << 20
N: Int = 20971520

scala> val M = 1 << 16
M: Int = 65536

scala> val dim = broadcast(spark.range(M).selectExpr("id as k", "cast(id as
string) as v"))

scala> benchmark("Join w long") {
     |    spark.range(N).join(dim, (col("id") % M) === col("k")).count()
     | }
Time taken in Join w long: 2.612163207 seconds

scala> spark.conf.set("spark.sql.codegen.wholeStage", true)

scala> conf.wholeStageEnabled
res80: Boolean = true
```

```
scala> val dim = broadcast(spark.range(M).selectExpr("id as k", "cast(id as
string) as v"))

scala> benchmark("Join w long") {
     |     spark.range(N).join(dim, (col("id") % M) === col("k")).count()
     | }
Time taken in Join w long: 0.777796256 seconds
```

For the following set of examples, we present only the essentials for obtaining their execution times with and without whole-stage code generation. Refer to the preceding example and follow the same sequence of steps to replicate the following examples:

```
scala> val dim = broadcast(spark.range(M).selectExpr("id as k", "cast(id as
string) as v"))
scala> benchmark("Join w long duplicated") {
     |        val dim = broadcast(spark.range(M).selectExpr("cast(id/10 as
long) as k"))
     |           spark.range(N).join(dim, (col("id") % M) === col("k")).count()
     | }
Time taken in Join w long duplicated: 1.514799811 seconds
Time taken in Join w long duplicated: 0.278705816 seconds

scala> val dim3 = broadcast(spark.range(M).selectExpr("id as k1", "id as
k2", "cast(id as string) as v"))
scala> benchmark("Join w 2 longs") {
     |        spark.range(N).join(dim3, (col("id") % M) === col("k1") &&
(col("id") % M) === col("k2")).count()
     | }
Time taken in Join w 2 longs: 2.048950962 seconds
Time taken in Join w 2 longs: 0.681936701 seconds

scala> val dim4 = broadcast(spark.range(M).selectExpr("cast(id/10 as long)
as k1", "cast(id/10 as long) as k2"))
scala> benchmark("Join w 2 longs duplicated") {
     |        spark.range(N).join(dim4, (col("id") bitwiseAND M) === col("k1")
&& (col("id") bitwiseAND M) === col("k2")).count()
     | }
Time taken in Join w 2 longs duplicated: 4.924196601 seconds
Time taken in Join w 2 longs duplicated: 0.818748429 seconds

scala> val dim = broadcast(spark.range(M).selectExpr("id as k", "cast(id as
string) as v"))
scala> benchmark("outer join w long") {
     |        spark.range(N).join(dim, (col("id") % M) === col("k"),
"left").count()
     | }
Time taken in outer join w long: 1.580664228 seconds
Time taken in outer join w long: 0.280608235 seconds
```

```
scala> val dim = broadcast(spark.range(M).selectExpr("id as k", "cast(id as
string) as v"))
scala> benchmark("semi join w long") {
     |       spark.range(N).join(dim, (col("id") % M) === col("k"),
"leftsemi").count()
     | }
Time taken in semi join w long: 1.027175143 seconds
Time taken in semi join w long: 0.180771478 seconds

scala> val N = 2 << 20
N: Int = 2097152
scala> benchmark("merge join") {
     |       val df1 = spark.range(N).selectExpr(s"id * 2 as k1")
     |       val df2 = spark.range(N).selectExpr(s"id * 3 as k2")
     |       df1.join(df2, col("k1") === col("k2")).count()
     | }
Time taken in merge join: 2.260524298 seconds
Time taken in merge join: 2.053497825 seconds

scala> val N = 2 << 20
N: Int = 2097152
scala> benchmark("sort merge join") {
     |       val df1 = spark.range(N).selectExpr(s"(id * 15485863) % ${N*10}
as k1")
     |       val df2 = spark.range(N).selectExpr(s"(id * 15485867) % ${N*10}
as k2")
     |       df1.join(df2, col("k1") === col("k2")).count()
     | }
Time taken in sort merge join: 2.481585466 seconds
Time taken in sort merge join: 1.992168281 seconds
```

As an exercise, use the examples in this section to explore their logical and physical plans, and also view and understand their execution using SparkUI.

There are several Spark SQL parameter settings used in tuning tasks. SQLConf is an internal key-value configuration store for parameters and hints used in Spark SQL. In order to print all the current values of these parameters, use the following statement:

```
scala> conf.getAllConfs.foreach(println)
(spark.driver.host,192.168.1.103)
(spark.sql.autoBroadcastJoinThreshold,1000000)
(spark.driver.port,57085)
(spark.repl.class.uri,spark://192.168.1.103:57085/classes)
(spark.jars,)
(spark.repl.class.outputDir,/private/var/folders/tj/prwqrjj16jn4k5jh6g91rwt
c0000gn/T/spark-9f8b5ba4-e8f4-4c60-b01b-30c4b71a06e1/repl-
ae75dedc-703a-41b8-b949-b91ed3b362f1)
(spark.app.name,Spark shell)
```

```
(spark.driver.memory,14g)
(spark.sql.codegen.wholeStage,true)
(spark.executor.id,driver)
(spark.sql.cbo.enabled,true)
(spark.sql.join.preferSortMergeJoin,false)
(spark.submit.deployMode,client)
(spark.master,local[*])
(spark.home,/Users/aurobindosarkar/Downloads/spark-2.2.0-bin-hadoop2.7)
(spark.sql.catalogImplementation,hive)
(spark.app.id,local-1499953390374)
(spark.sql.shuffle.partitions,2)
```

You can also use the following statement to list the extended set of all the defined configuration parameters:

```scala
scala> conf.getAllDefinedConfs.foreach(println)
```

Summary

In this chapter, we presented the foundational concepts related to tuning a Spark application, including data serialization using encoders. We also covered the key aspects of the cost-based optimizer introduced in Spark 2.2 to optimize Spark SQL execution automatically. Finally, we presented some examples of JOIN operations, and the improvements in execution times as a result of using whole-stage code generation.

In the next chapter, we will explore application architectures that leverage Spark modules and Spark SQL in real-world applications. We will also describe the deployment of some of the main processing models being used for batch processing, streaming applications, and machine learning pipelines.

12
Spark SQL in Large-Scale Application Architectures

In this book, we started with the basics of Spark SQL and its components, and its role in Spark applications. Later, we presented a series of chapters focusing on its usage in various types of applications. With DataFrame/Dataset API and the Catalyst optimizer at the heart of Spark SQL, it is no surprise that it plays a key role in all applications based on the Spark technology stack. These applications include large-scale machine learning, large-scale graphs, and deep learning applications. Additionally, we presented Spark SQL-based Structured Streaming applications that operate in complex environments as continuous applications. In this chapter, we will explore application architectures that leverage Spark modules and Spark SQL in real-world applications.

More specifically, we will cover key architectural components and patterns in large-scale applications that architects and designers will find useful as a starting point for their specific use-cases. We will describe the deployment of some of the main processing models being used for batch processing, streaming applications, and machine learning pipelines. The underlying architecture for these processing models is required to support ingesting very large volumes of various types of data arriving at high velocities at one end, while making the output data available for use by analytical tools, and reporting and modeling software at the other end. Additionally, we will present supporting code using Spark SQL for monitoring, troubleshooting, and gathering/reporting metrics.

We will cover the following topics in this chapter:

- Understanding Spark-based batch and stream processing architectures
- Understanding Lambda and Kappa Architectures
- Implementing scalable stream processing with structured streaming
- Building robust **Extract-Transform-Load** (ETL) pipelines using Spark SQL

- Implementing a scalable monitoring solution using Spark SQL
- Deploying Spark machine learning pipelines
- Using cluster managers: Mesos and Kubernetes

Understanding Spark-based application architectures

Apache Spark is an emerging platform that leverages distributed storage and processing frameworks to support querying, reporting, analytics, and intelligent applications at scale. Spark SQL has the necessary features, and supports the key mechanisms required, to access data across a diverse set of data sources and formats, and prepare it for downstream applications either with low-latency streaming data or high-throughput historical data stores. The following figure shows a high-level architecture that incorporates these requirements in typical Spark-based batch and streaming applications:

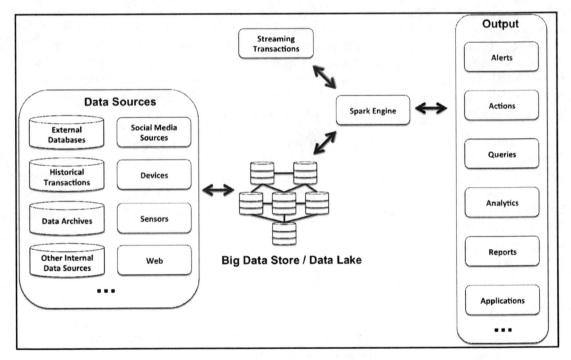

Additionally, as organizations start employing big data and NoSQL-based solutions across a number of projects, a data layer comprising RDBMSes alone is no longer considered the best fit for all the use-cases in a modern enterprise application. RDBMS-only based architectures illustrated in the following figure are rapidly disappearing across the industry, in order to meet the requirements of typical big-data applications:

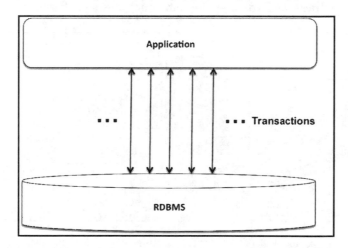

A more typical scenario comprising of multiple types of data store is shown in the next figure. Applications today use several types of data store that represent the best fit for a given set of use cases. Using multiple data storage technologies, chosen based on the way, data is being used by applications, is called **polyglot persistence**. Spark SQL is an excellent enabler of this and other similar persistence strategies in the cloud or on-premise deployments:

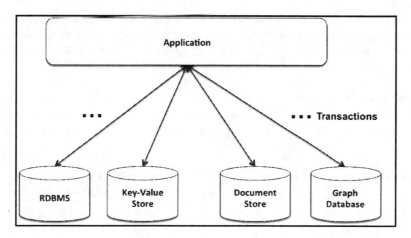

Additionally, we observe that only a small fraction of real-world ML systems are composed of ML code (the smallest box in the following figure). However, the infrastructure surrounding this ML code is vast and complex. Later in this chapter, we will use Spark SQL to create some of the key parts in such applications, including scalable ETL pipelines and monitoring solutions. Subsequently, we will also discuss the production deployment of machine learning pipelines, and the use of cluster managers such as Mesos and Kubernetes:

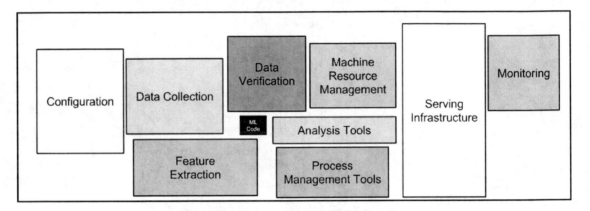

Reference: "Hidden Technical Debt in Machine Learning Systems." Google NIPS 2015

In the next section, we will discuss the key concepts and challenges in Spark-based batch and stream processing architectures.

Using Apache Spark for batch processing

Typically, batch processing is done on huge volumes of data to create batch views in order to support ad hoc querying and MIS reporting functionality, and/or to apply scalable machine learning algorithms for classification, clustering, collaborative filtering, and analytics applications.

Due to the data volume involved in batch processing, these applications are typically long-running jobs and can easily extend over hours, days, or weeks, for example, aggregation queries such as count of daily visitors to a page, unique visitors to a website, and total sales per week.

Increasingly, Apache Spark is becoming popular as the engine for large-scale data processing. It can run programs up to 100x faster than Hadoop MapReduce in memory, or 10x faster on disk. An important reason for the rapid adoption of Spark is the common/similar coding required to address both batch and stream processing requirements.

In the next section, we will introduce the key characteristics and concepts of stream processing.

Using Apache Spark for stream processing

Most modern businesses are trying to deal with high data volumes (and associated rapid and unbounded growth of such data), combined with low-latency processing requirements. Additionally, higher value is being associated with near real-time business insights derived from real-time streaming data than traditional batch processed MIS reports. In contrast to streaming systems, the traditional batch processing systems were designed to process large amounts of a set of bounded data. Such systems are provided with all the data they need at the beginning of the execution. As the input data grows continuously, the results provided by such batch systems become dated, quickly.

Typically, in stream processing, data is not collected over significant time periods before triggering the required processing. Commonly, the incoming data is moved to a queuing system, such as Apache Kafka or Amazon Kinesis. This data is then accessed by the stream processor, which executes certain computations on it to generate the resulting output. A typical stream processing pipeline creates incremental views, which are often updated based on the incremental data flowing into the system.

The incremental views are made available through a **Serving Layer** to support querying and real-time analytics requirements, as shown in the following diagram:

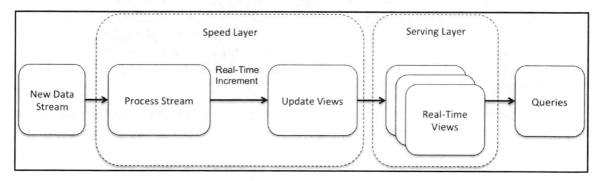

There are two types of time that are important in stream processing systems: event time and processing time. Event time is the time at which the events actually occurred (at source), while processing time is the time when the events are observed in the processing system. Event time is typically embedded in the data itself, and for many use cases, it is the time you want to operate on. However, extracting event time from data, and handling late or out-of-order data can present significant challenges in streaming applications. Additionally, there is a skew between the event times and the processing times due to resource limitations, the distributed processing model, and so on. There are many use cases requiring aggregations by event time; for example, the number of system errors in one-hour windows.

There can be other issues as well; for example, in windowing functionality, we need to determine whether all the data for a given event time has been observed yet. These systems need to be designed in a manner that allow them to function well in uncertain environments. For example, in Spark Structured Streaming, event-time, window-based aggregation queries can be defined consistently for a data stream because it can handle late arriving data, and update older aggregates appropriately.

Fault tolerance is crucial when dealing with large data streaming applications, for example, a stream processing job that keeps a count of all the tuples it has seen so far. Here, each tuple may represent a stream of user activity, and the application may want to report the total activity seen so far. A node failure in such a system can result in an inaccurate count because of the unprocessed tuples (on the failed node).

A naive way to recover from this situation would be to replay the entire Dataset. This is a costly operation given the size of data involved. Checkpointing is a common technique used to avoid reprocessing the entire Dataset. In the case of failures, the application data state is reverted to the last checkpoint, and the tuples from that point on, are replayed. To prevent data loss in Spark Streaming applications, a **write-ahead log (WAL)** is used, from which data can be replayed after failures.

In the next section, we will introduce the Lambda architecture, which is a popular pattern implemented in Spark-centric applications, as it can address requirements of both, batch and stream processing, using very similar code.

Understanding the Lambda architecture

The Lambda architectural pattern attempts to combine the best of both worlds--batch processing and stream processing. This pattern consists of several layers: **Batch Layer** (ingests and processes data on persistent storage such as HDFS and S3), **Speed Layer** (ingests and processes streaming data that has not been processed by the **Batch Layer** yet), and the **Serving Layer** (combines outputs from the **Batch** and **Speed Layers** to present merged results). This is a very popular architecture in Spark environments because it can support both the **Batch** and **Speed Layer** implementations with minimal code differences between the two.

The given figure depicts the Lambda architecture as a combination of batch processing and stream processing:

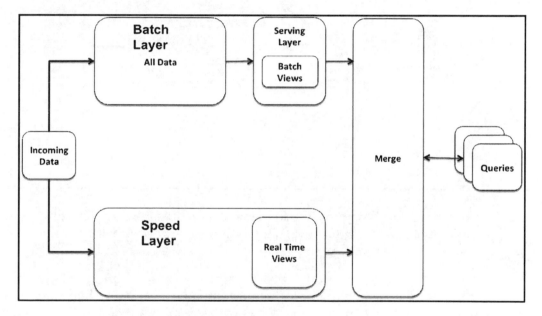

The next figure shows an implementation of the Lambda architecture using AWS Cloud services (**Amazon Kinesis**, **Amazon S3** Storage, **Amazon EMR**, **Amazon DynamoDB**, and so on) and Spark:

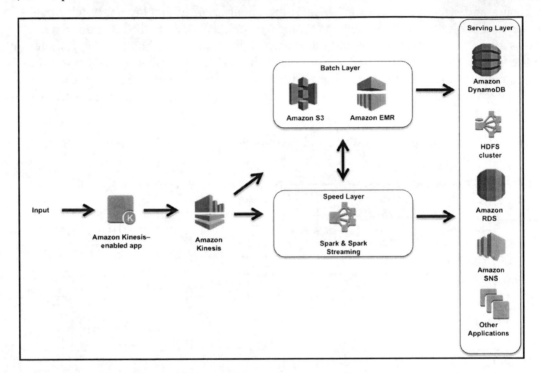

For more details on the AWS implementation of Lambda architecture, refer to https://d0.awsstatic.com/whitepapers/lambda-architecure-on-for-batch-aws.pdf.

In the next section, we will discuss a simpler architecture called Kappa Architecture, which dispenses with the **Batch Layer** entirely and works with stream processing in the **Speed Layer** only.

Understanding the Kappa Architecture

The **Kappa Architecture** is simpler than the Lambda pattern as it comprises the Speed and Serving Layers only. All the computations occur as stream processing and there are no batch re-computations done on the full Dataset. Recomputations are only done to support changes and new requirements.

Typically, the incoming real-time data stream is processed in memory and is persisted in a database or HDFS to support queries, as illustrated in the following figure:

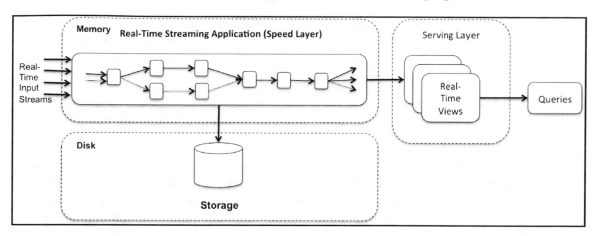

The Kappa Architecture can be realized by using Apache Spark combined with a queuing solution, such as Apache Kafka. If the data retention times are bound to several days to weeks, then Kafka could also be used to retain the data for the limited period of time.

In the next few sections, we will introduce a few hands-on exercises using Apache Spark, Scala, and Apache Kafka that are very useful in the real-world applications development context. We will start by using Spark SQL and Structured Streaming to implement a few streaming use cases.

Design considerations for building scalable stream processing applications

Building robust stream processing applications is challenging. The typical complexities associated with stream processing include the following:

- **Complex Data**: Diverse data formats and the quality of data create significant challenges in streaming applications. Typically, the data is available in various formats, such as JSON, CSV, AVRO, and binary. Additionally, dirty data, or late arriving, and out-of-order data, can make the design of such applications extremely complex.

- **Complex workloads**: Streaming applications need to support a diverse set of application requirements, including interactive queries, machine learning pipelines, and so on.

- **Complex systems**: With diverse storage systems, including Kafka, S3, Kinesis, and so on, system failures can lead to significant reprocessing or bad results.

Steam processing using Spark SQL can be fast, scalable, and fault-tolerant. It provides an extensive set of high-level APIs to deal with complex data and workloads. For example, the data sources API can integrate with many storage systems and data formats.

 For a detailed coverage of building scalable and fault-tolerant structured streaming applications, refer to `https://spark-summit.org/ 2017/events/easy-scalable-fault-tolerant-stream-processing-with- structured-streaming-in-apache-spark/`.

A streaming query allows us to specify one or more data sources, transform the data using DataFrame/Dataset APIs or SQL, and specify various sinks to output the results. There is built-in support for several data sources, such as files, Kafka, and sockets, and we can also combine multiple data sources, if required.

The Spark SQL Catalyst optimizer figures out the mechanics of incrementally executing the transformations. The query is converted to a series of incremental execution plans that operate on the new batches of data. The sink accepts the output of each batch and the updates are completed within a transaction context. You can also specify various output modes (**Complete**, **Update**, or **Append**) and triggers to govern when to output the results. If no trigger is specified, the results are continuously updated. The progress of a given query, and restarts after failures are managed by persisting checkpoints.

Spark structured streaming enables streaming analytics without having to worry about the complex underlying mechanisms that make streaming work. In this model, the input can be thought of as data from an append-only table (that grows continuously). A trigger specifies the time interval for checking the input for the arrival of new data and the query represents operations such as map, filter, and reduce on the input. The result represents the final table that is updated in each trigger interval (as per the specified query operation).

 For detailed illustrations on structured streaming internals, check out `http://spark.apache.org/docs/latest/structured-streaming- programming-guide.html`.

We can also execute sliding window operations on streaming data. Here, we define aggregations over a sliding window, in which we group the data and compute appropriate aggregations (for each group).

In the next section, we will discuss Spark SQL features that can help in building robust ETL pipelines.

Building robust ETL pipelines using Spark SQL

ETL pipelines execute a series of transformations on source data to produce cleansed, structured, and ready-for-use output by subsequent processing components. The transformations required to be applied on the source will depend on nature of the data. The input or source data can be structured (RDBMS, Parquet, and so on), semi-structured (CSV, JSON, and so on) or unstructured data (text, audio, video, and so on). After being processed through such pipelines, the data is ready for downstream data processing, modeling, analytics, reporting, and so on.

The following figure illustrates an application architecture in which the input data from Kafka, and other sources such as application and server logs, are cleansed and transformed (using an ETL pipeline) before being stored in an enterprise data store. This data store can eventually feed other applications (via Kafka), support interactive queries, store subsets or views of the data in serving databases, train ML models, support reporting applications, and so on:

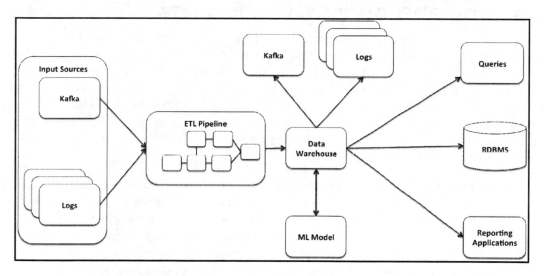

As the abbreviation (ETL) suggests, we need to retrieve the data from various sources (Extract), transform the data for downstream consumption (Transform), and transmit it to different destinations (Load).

Over the next few sections, we will use Spark SQL features to access and process various data sources and data formats for ETL purposes. Spark SQL's flexible APIs, combined with the Catalyst optimizer and tungsten execution engine, make it highly suitable for building end-to-end ETL pipelines.

In the following code block, we present a simple skeleton of a single ETL query that combines all the three (Extract, Transform, and Load) functions. These queries can also be extended to execute complex joins between tables containing data from multiple sources and source formats:

```
spark.read.json("/source/path") //Extract
.filter(...) //Transform
.agg(...) //Transform
.write.mode("append") .parquet("/output/path") //Load
```

In the next section, we will introduce a few criteria that can help you make appropriate choices regarding data formats to satisfy the requirements of your specific use cases.

Choosing appropriate data formats

In enterprise settings, the data is available in many different data sources and formats. Spark SQL supports a set of built-in and third-party connectors. In addition, we can also define custom data source connectors. Data formats include structured, semi-structured, and unstructured formats, such as plain text, JSON, XML, CSV, RDBMS records, images, and video. More recently, big data formats such as Parquet, ORC, and Avro are becoming increasingly popular. In general, unstructured formats such as plain text files are more flexible, while structured formats such as Parquet and AVRO are more efficient from a storage and performance perspective.

In the case of structured data formats, the data has a rigid, well-defined schema or structure associated with it. For example, columnar data formats make it more efficient to extract values from columns. However, this rigidity can make changes to the schema, or the structure, challenging. By contrast, unstructured data sources, such as free-form text, contain no markup or separators as in CSV or TSV files. Such data sources generally require some context around the data; for example, you need to know that the contents of files contain text from blogs.

Typically, we need many transformations and feature extraction techniques to interpret diverse Datasets. Semi-structured data is structured at a record level, but not necessarily across all the records. As a result, each data record contains the associated schema information as well.

The JSON format is probably the most common example of semi-structured data. JSON records are in a human-readable form, making it more convenient for development and debugging purposes. However, these formats suffer from parsing-related overheads, and are typically not the best choice for supporting the ad hoc querying functionality.

Often, applications will have to be designed to span and traverse across varied data sources and formats to efficiently store and process the data. For example, Avro is a good choice when access is required to complete rows of data, as in the case of access to features in an ML pipeline. In cases where flexibility in the schema is required, using JSON may be the most appropriate choice for the data format. Furthermore, in cases where the data does not have a fixed schema, it is probably best to use the plain text file format.

Transforming data in ETL pipelines

Typically, semi-structured formats such as JSON contain struct, map, and array data types; for example, request and/or response payloads for REST web services contain JSON data with nested fields and arrays.

In this section, we will present examples of Spark SQL-based transformations on Twitter data. The input Dataset is a file (cache-0.json.gz) containing 10 M tweets from a set of Datasets containing over 170 M tweets collected during the three months leading up to the 2012 US presidential elections. This file can be downloaded from https://datahub.io/dataset/twitter-2012-presidential-election.

Before starting with the following examples, start Zookeeper and the Kafka broker as described in Chapter 5, *Using Spark SQL in Streaming Applications*. Also, create a new Kafka topic, called tweetsa. We generate the schema from the input JSON Dataset, as shown. This schema definition will be used later in this section:

```scala
scala> val jsonDF =
spark.read.json("file:///Users/aurobindosarkar/Downloads/cache-0-json")

scala> jsonDF.printSchema()

scala> val rawTweetsSchema = jsonDF.schema

scala> val jsonString = rawTweetsSchema.json

scala> val schema = DataType.fromJson(jsonString).asInstanceOf[StructType]
```

Set up to read the streaming tweets from the Kafka topic (*tweetsa*), and then parse the JSON data using the schema from the previous step.

We select all the fields in the tweet by `specifying data.*` in this statement:

```scala
scala> val rawTweets =
spark.readStream.format("kafka").option("kafka.bootstrap.servers",
"localhost:9092").option("subscribe", "tweetsa").load()

scala> val parsedTweets = rawTweets.selectExpr("cast (value as string) as
json").select(from_json($"json", schema).as("data")).select("data.*")
```

You will need to use the following command repeatedly (as you work through the examples) to pipe the tweets contained in the input file to the Kafka topic, as illustrated:

```
Aurobindos-MacBook-Pro-2:kafka_2.11-0.10.2.1 aurobindosarkar$ bin/kafka-
console-producer.sh --broker-list localhost:9092 --topic tweetsa <
/Users/aurobindosarkar/Downloads/cache-0-json
```

Given the size of the input file, this can potentially result in space-related issues on your machine. If this happens, use appropriate Kafka commands to delete and recreate the topic (refer to `https://kafka.apache.org/0102/documentation.html`).

Here, we reproduce a section of the schema to help understand the structure we are working with over the next few examples:

```
root
 |-- contributors: array (nullable = true)
 |    |-- element: long (containsNull = true)
 ...
 |-- place: struct (nullable = true)
 ...
 |    |-- country: string (nullable = true)
 |    |-- country_code: string (nullable = true)
 ...
```

We can select specific fields from nested columns in the JSON string. We use the . (dot) operator to choose the nested field, as shown:

```scala
scala> val selectFields =
parsedTweets.select("place.country").where($"place.country".isNotNull)
```

Next, we write the output stream to the screen to view the results. You will need to execute the following statement after each of the transformations in order to view and evaluate the results. Also, in the interests of saving time, you should execute `s5.stop()`, after you have seen sufficient output on the screen. Alternatively, you can always choose to work with a smaller set of data extracted from the original input file:

```scala
scala> val s5 =
selectFields.writeStream.outputMode("append").format("console").start()
```

```
-----------------------------------------------------
Batch: 2
-----------------------------------------------------
+---------------+
|        country|
+---------------+
| United States|
|United Kingdom|
|         Brasil|
|         Brasil|
| United States|
| United States|
|         Brasil|
| United States|
| United States|
|United Kingdom|
|United Kingdom|
|      Argentina|
| United States|
| United States|
|         Brasil|
|United Kingdom|
| United States|
| United States|
| United States|
|   South Africa|
+---------------+
only showing top 20 rows
```

In the next example, we will flatten a struct using star (*) to select all the subfields in the struct:

```scala
scala> val selectFields =
parsedTweets.select("place.*").where($"place.country".isNotNull)
```

The results can be viewed by writing the output stream, as shown in the preceding example:

```
Batch: 2
+-------------+-------------------+---------------+------------+--------------------+-----------------+---------------+----------+--------------------+
|   attributes|       bounding_box|        country|country_code|           full_name|               id|           name|place_type|                 url|
+-------------+-------------------+---------------+------------+--------------------+-----------------+---------------+----------+--------------------+
| [null,null]|[WrappedArray(Wra...|  United States|          US|        Seaford, DE|b719350492e3ff2f|        Seaford|      city|http://api.twitte...|
| [null,null]|[WrappedArray(Wra...| United Kingdom|          GB|       Wigan, Wigan|e7e4fe93a6cfb48e|          Wigan|      city|http://api.twitte...|
| [null,null]|[WrappedArray(Wra...|         Brasil|          BR|   Bauru, São Paulo|77af3e46c7a19d54|          Bauru|      city|http://api.twitte...|
| [null,null]|[WrappedArray(Wra...|         Brasil|          BR|São Paulo, São Paulo|68e019afec7d0ba5|      São Paulo|      city|http://api.twitte...|
| [null,null]|[WrappedArray(Wra...|  United States|          US|        Boston, MA|67b98f17fdcf28be|         Boston|      city|http://api.twitte...|
| [null,null]|[WrappedArray(Wra...|  United States|          US|      New York, NY|274858690891a7938|       New York|      city|http://api.twitte...|
| [null,null]|[WrappedArray(Wra...|         Brasil|          BR|Foz do Iguaçu, Pa...|91f818a4abfb1d4d|  Foz do Iguacu|      city|http://api.twitte...|
| [null,null]|[WrappedArray(Wra...|  United States|          US|West Palm Beach, FL|03ee378d6ed2a73f|West Palm Beach|      city|http://api.twitte...|
| [null,null]|[WrappedArray(Wra...|  United States|          US|        Queens, NY|b6ea2e341ba4356f|         Queens|      city|http://api.twitte...|
| [null,null]|[WrappedArray(Wra...| United Kingdom|          GB|West Lothian, Wes...|5ef1506ee13006ae|   West Lothian|      city|http://api.twitte...|
| [null,null]|[WrappedArray(Wra...| United Kingdom|          GB|Westminster, London|548c2b8e3921a85a|    Westminster|   country|http://api.twitte...|
|        null|           Argentina|                AR|           Argentina|4d3b316fe2e52b29|      Argentina|      city|http://api.twitte...|
| [null,null]|[WrappedArray(Wra...|  United States|          US|  Citrus Heights, CA|a89175c4c91f45a3| Citrus Heights|      city|http://api.twitte...|
|[null,8144 Indian...|[WrappedArray(Wra...|  United States|          US|Coach USA, Highland|5fd07ec0b51fd138|      Coach USA|       poi|http://api.twitte...|
| [null,null]|           null|         Brasil|          BR|Rio de Janeiro, R...|97bcdfca1a2dca59|Rio de Janeiro|      city|http://api.twitte...|
| [null,null]|[WrappedArray(Wra...| United Kingdom|          GB|Lewes, East Sussex|016d3e5601d32304|          Lewes|      city|http://api.twitte...|
| [null,null]|[WrappedArray(Wra...|  United States|          US|     Manhattan, NY|086752cb03de1d5d|      Manhattan|      city|http://api.twitte...|
| [null,null]|[WrappedArray(Wra...|  United States|          US|      Kalamazoo, MI|413ef5a0d23bfe4f|      Kalamazoo|      city|http://api.twitte...|
| [null,null]|[WrappedArray(Wra...|  United States|          US|         Ohio, US|de599025188e2ee7|           Ohio|     admin|http://api.twitte...|
| [null,null]|[WrappedArray(Wra...|   South Africa|          ZA|  Pretoria, Gauteng|0e587c59401d0a27|       Pretoria|      city|http://api.twitte...|
+-------------+-------------------+---------------+------------+--------------------+-----------------+---------------+----------+--------------------+
only showing top 20 rows
```

We can use the struct function to create a new struct (for nesting the columns) as illustrated in the following code snippet. We can select a specific field or fields for creating the new struct. We can also nest all the columns using star (*), if required.

Here, we reproduce the section of the schema used in this example:

```
...
|    |-- id: long (nullable = true)
|    |-- id_str: string (nullable = true)
|    |-- in_reply_to_screen_name: string (nullable = true)
...
```

```
scala> val selectFields = parsedTweets.select(struct("place.country_code",
"place.name") as
'locationInfo).where($"locationInfo.country_code".isNotNull)
```

```
-------------------------------------------------
Batch: 2
-------------------------------------------------
+--------------------+
|        locationInfo|
+--------------------+
|        [US,Seaford]|
|          [GB,Wigan]|
|          [BR,Bauru]|
|      [BR,São Paulo]|
|         [US,Boston]|
|       [US,New York]|
|   [BR,Foz do Iguaçu]|
| [US,West Palm Beach]|
|        [US,Queens]|
|    [GB,West Lothian]|
|    [GB,Westminster]|
|      [AR,Argentina]|
|  [US,Citrus Heights]|
|      [US,Coach USA]|
|  [BR,Rio de Janeiro]|
|          [GB,Lewes]|
|      [US,Manhattan]|
|      [US,Kalamazoo]|
|           [US,Ohio]|
|       [ZA,Pretoria]|
+--------------------+
only showing top 20 rows
```

In the next example, we select a single array (or map) element using `getItem()`. Here, we are operating on the following part of the schema:

```
...
|       |-- entities: struct (nullable = true)
|       |    |-- hashtags: array (nullable = true)
|       |    |    |-- element: struct (containsNull = true)
|       |    |    |    |-- indices: array (nullable = true)
|       |    |    |    |    |-- element: long (containsNull = true)
|       |    |    |    |-- text: string (nullable = true)
|       |    |-- media: array (nullable = true)
|       |    |    |-- element: struct (containsNull = true)
...
|       |    |    |    |-- type: string (nullable = true)
|       |    |    |    |-- url: string (nullable = true)
```

```scala
scala> val selectFields = parsedTweets.select($"entities.hashtags" as
'tags).select('tags.getItem(0) as 'x).select($"x.indices" as
'y).select($"y".getItem(0) as 'z).where($"z".isNotNull)
```

```
------------------------------------------------
Batch: 1
------------------------------------------------
+---+
|  z|
+---+
| 87|
| 88|
|104|
| 84|
+---+
```

```scala
scala> val selectFields = parsedTweets.select($"entities.hashtags" as
'tags).select('tags.getItem(0) as 'x).select($"x.text" as
'y).where($"y".isNotNull)
```

```
------------------------------------------------
Batch: 1
------------------------------------------------
+-----------+
|          y|
+-----------+
|    florida|
|        USA|
|    florida|
|    florida|
|idonthateit|
|         OR|
|        USA|
|   Obama2012|
|      obama|
|       IFWT|
|       IFWT|
|       rtl4|
|       wrvt|
+-----------+
```

We can use the `explode()` function to create a new row for each element in an array, as shown. To illustrate the results of `explode()`, we first show the rows containing the arrays, and then show the results of applying the explode function:

```scala
scala> val selectFields = parsedTweets.select($"entities.hashtags.indices"
as 'tags).select(explode('tags))
```

The following output is obtained:

```
------------------------------------------
Batch: 1
------------------------------------------
+----------+
|      col|
+----------+
|   [87, 95]|
|   [88, 92]|
|  [93, 101]|
| [102, 110]|
| [104, 112]|
|   [84, 92]|
|   [69, 81]|
+----------+
```

Note the separate rows created for the array elements after applying the explode function:

```scala
scala> val selectFields =
parsedTweets.select($"entities.hashtags.indices".getItem(0) as
'tags).select(explode('tags))
```

The following is the output obtained:

```
------------------------------------------
Batch: 1
------------------------------------------
+---+
|col|
+---+
| 87|
| 95|
| 88|
| 92|
|104|
|112|
| 84|
| 92|
+---+
```

Spark SQL also has functions such as `to_json()`, to transform a `struct` to a JSON string, and `from_json()`, to convert a JSON string to a `struct`. These functions are very useful to read from or write to Kafka topics. For example, if the "value" field contains data in a JSON string, then we can use the `from_json()` function to extract the data, transform it, and then push it out to a different Kafka topic, and/or write it out to a Parquet file or a serving database.

In the following example, we use the `to_json()` function to convert a struct to a JSON string:

```scala
scala> val selectFields = parsedTweets.select(struct($"entities.media.type"
as 'x, $"entities.media.url" as 'y) as
'z).where($"z.x".isNotNull).select(to_json('z) as 'c)
```

```
-------------------------------------------
Batch: 2
-------------------------------------------
+--------------------+
|                   c|
+--------------------+
|{"x":["photo"],"y...|
|{"x":["photo"],"y...|
|{"x":["photo"],"y...|
|{"x":["photo"],"y...|
|{"x":["photo"],"y...|
|{"x":["photo"],"y...|
|{"x":["photo"],"y...|
|{"x":["photo"],"y...|
|{"x":["photo"],"y...|
|{"x":["photo"],"y...|
|{"x":["photo"],"y...|
|{"x":["photo"],"y...|
|{"x":["photo"],"y...|
|{"x":["photo"],"y...|
|{"x":["photo"],"y...|
|{"x":["photo"],"y...|
|{"x":["photo"],"y...|
|{"x":["photo"],"y...|
|{"x":["photo"],"y...|
|{"x":["photo"],"y...|
+--------------------+
only showing top 20 rows
```

We can use the `from_json()` function to convert a column containing JSON data into a `struct` data type. Further, we can flatten the preceding struct into separate columns. We show an example of using this function in a later section.

 For more detailed coverage of transformation functions, refer to https://databricks.com/blog/2017/02/23/working-complex-data-formats-structured-streaming-apache-spark-2-1.html.

Addressing errors in ETL pipelines

ETL tasks are usually considered to be complex, expensive, slow, and error-prone. Here, we will examine typical challenges in ETL processes, and how Spark SQL features assist in addressing them.

Spark can automatically infer the schema from a JSON file. For example, for the following JSON data, the inferred schema includes all the labels and the data types based on the content. Here, the data types for all the elements in the input data are longs by default:

test1.json

```
{"a":1, "b":2, "c":3}
{"a":2, "d":5, "e":3}
{"d":1, "c":4, "f":6}
{"a":7, "b":8}
{"c":5, "e":4, "d":3}
{"f":3, "e":3, "d":4}
{"a":1, "b":2, "c":3, "f":3, "e":3, "d":4}
```

You can print the schema to verify the data types, as shown:

```
scala>
spark.read.json("file:///Users/aurobindosarkar/Downloads/test1.json").print
Schema()
root
|-- a: long (nullable = true)
|-- b: long (nullable = true)
|-- c: long (nullable = true)
|-- d: long (nullable = true)
|-- e: long (nullable = true)
|-- f: long (nullable = true)
```

However, in the following JSON data, if the value of e in the third row and the value of b in the last row are changed to include fractions, and the value of f in the second-from-last row is enclosed in quotes, the inferred schema changes the data types of b and e to double, and f to string type:

```
{"a":1, "b":2, "c":3}
{"a":2, "d":5, "e":3}
{"d":1, "c":4, "f":6}
{"a":7, "b":8}
{"c":5, "e":4.5, "d":3}
{"f":"3", "e":3, "d":4}
{"a":1, "b":2.1, "c":3, "f":3, "e":3, "d":4}

scala>
```

```
spark.read.json("file:///Users/aurobindosarkar/Downloads/test1.json").print
Schema()
root
|-- a: long (nullable = true)
|-- b: double (nullable = true)
|-- c: long (nullable = true)
|-- d: long (nullable = true)
|-- e: double (nullable = true)
|-- f: string (nullable = true)
```

If we want to associate specific structure or data types to elements, we need to use a user-specified schema. In the next example, we use a CSV file with a header containing the field names. The field names in the schema are derived from the header, and the data types specified in the user-defined schema are used against them, as shown:

```
a,b,c,d,e,f
1,2,3,,,
2,,,5,3,
,,4,1,,,6
7,8,,,,f
,,5,3,4.5,
,,,4,3,"3"
1,2.1,3,3,3,4

scala> val schema = new StructType().add("a", "int").add("b", "double")

scala> spark.read.option("header",
true).schema(schema).csv("file:///Users/aurobindosarkar/Downloads/test1.csv
").show()
```

The following output is obtained:

```
+----+----+
|   a|   b|
+----+----+
|   1| 2.0|
|   2|null|
|null|null|
|   7| 8.0|
|null|null|
|null|null|
|   1| 2.1|
+----+----+
```

Issues can also occur in ETL pipelines due to file and data corruption. If the data is not mission-critical, and the corrupt files can be safely ignored, we can set `config property` `spark.sql.files.ignoreCorruptFiles` = `true`. This setting lets Spark jobs continue running even when corrupt files are encountered. Note that contents that are successfully read will continue to be returned.

In the following example, there is bad data for b in row 4. We can still read the data using the `PERMISSIVE` mode. In this case, a new column, called _corrupt_record, is added to the DataFrame, and the contents of the corrupted rows appear in that column with the rest of the fields initialized to nulls. We can focus on the data issues by reviewing the data in this column and initiate suitable actions to fix them. By setting the `spark.sql.columnNameOfCorruptRecord` property, we can configure the default name of the corrupted contents column:

```
{"a":1, "b":2, "c":3}
{"a":2, "d":5, "e":3}
{"d":1, "c":4, "f":6}
{"a":7, "b":{}}
{"c":5, "e":4.5, "d":3}
{"f":"3", "e":3, "d":4}
{"a":1, "b":2.1, "c":3, "f":3, "e":3, "d":4}

scala> spark.read.option("mode",
"PERMISSIVE").option("columnNameOfCorruptRecord",
"_corrupt_record").json("file:///Users/aurobindosarkar/Downloads/test1.json
").show()
```

```
+--------------------+----+----+----+----+----+----+
|     _corrupt_record|   a|   b|   c|   d|   e|   f|
+--------------------+----+----+----+----+----+----+
|                null|   1| 2.0|   3|null|null|null|
|                null|   2|null|null|   5| 3.0|null|
|                null|null|null|   4|   1|null|   6|
|      {"a":7, "b":{}}|null|null|null|null|null|null|
|                null|null|null|   5|   3| 4.5|null|
|                null|null|null|null|   4| 3.0|   3|
|                null|   1| 2.1|   3|   4| 3.0|   3|
+--------------------+----+----+----+----+----+----+
```

Now, we use the `DROPMALFORMED` option to drop all malformed records. Here, the fourth row is dropped due to the bad value for b:

```
scala> spark.read.option("mode",
"DROPMALFORMED").json("file:///Users/aurobindosarkar/Downloads/test1.json")
.show()
```

```
+----+----+----+----+----+----+
|  a|   b|   c|   d|   e|   f|
+----+----+----+----+----+----+
|   1| 2.0|   3|null|null|null|
|   2|null|null|   5| 3.0|null|
|null|null|   4|   1|null|   6|
|null|null|   5|   3| 4.5|null|
|null|null|null|   4| 3.0|   3|
|   1| 2.1|   3|   4| 3.0|   3|
+----+----+----+----+----+----+
```

For critical data, we can use the FAILFAST option to fail immediately upon encountering a bad record. For example, in the following example, due to the value of b in the fourth row, the operation throws an exception and exits immediately:

```
{"a":1, "b":2, "c":3}
{"a":2, "d":5, "e":3}
{"d":1, "c":4, "f":6}
{"a":7, "b":$}
{"c":5, "e":4.5, "d":3}
{"f":"3", "e":3, "d":4}
{"a":1, "b":2.1, "c":3, "f":3, "e":3, "d":4}

scala> spark.read.option("mode",
"FAILFAST").json("file:///Users/aurobindosarkar/Downloads/test1.json").show
()
```

In the following example, we have a record that spans two rows; we can read this record by setting the wholeFile option to true:

```
{"a":{"a1":2, "a2":8},
"b":5, "c":3}

scala> spark.read.option("wholeFile",true).option("mode",
"PERMISSIVE").option("columnNameOfCorruptRecord",
"_corrupt_record").json("file:///Users/aurobindosarkar/Downloads/testMultiL
ine.json").show()
+-----+---+---+
|    a|  b|  c|
+-----+---+---+
|[2,8]|  5|  3|
+-----+---+---+
```

 For more details on Spark SQL-based ETL pipelines and roadmaps, visit https://spark-summit.org/2017/events/building-robust-etl-pipelines-with-apache-spark/.

The preceding reference presents several higher-order SQL transformation functions, new formats for the DataframeWriter API, and a unified `Create Table` (as `Select`) constructs in Spark 2.2 and 2.3-Snapshot.

Other requirements addressed by Spark SQL include scalability and continuous ETL using structured streaming. We can use structured streaming to enable raw data to be available as structured data ready for analysis, reporting, and decision-making as soon as possible, instead of incurring the hours of delay typically associated with running periodic batch jobs. This type of processing is especially important in applications such as anomaly detection, fraud detection, and so on, where time is of the essence.

In the next section, we will shift our focus to building a scalable monitoring solution using Spark SQL.

Implementing a scalable monitoring solution

Building a scalable monitoring function for large-scale deployments can be challenging as there could be billions of data points captured each day. Additionally, the volume of logs and the number of metrics can be difficult to manage without a suitable big data platform with streaming and visualization support.

Voluminous logs collected from applications, servers, network devices, and so on are processed to provide real-time monitoring that help detect errors, warnings, failures, and other issues. Typically, various daemons, services, and tools are used to collect/send log records to the monitoring system. For example, log entries in the JSON format can be sent to Kafka queues or Amazon Kinesis. These JSON records can then be stored on S3 as files and/or streamed to be analyzed in real time (in a Lambda architecture implementation). Typically, an ETL pipeline is run to cleanse the log data, transform it into a more structured form, and then load it into files such as Parquet files or databases, for querying, alerting, and reporting purposes.

The following figure illustrates one such platform using **Spark Streaming Jobs**, a **Scalable Time Series Database** such as OpenTSDB or Graphite, and **Visualization Tools** such as Grafana:

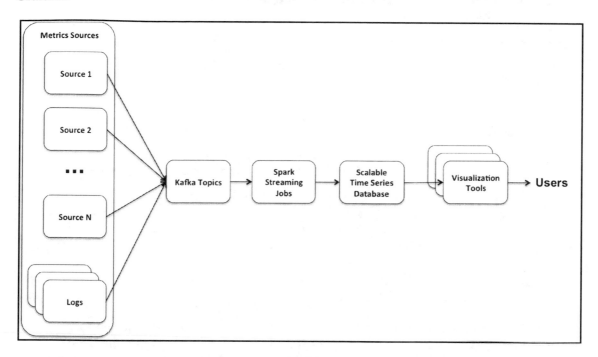

 For more details on this solution, refer to `https://spark-summit.org/2017/events/scalable-monitoring-using-apache-spark-and-friends/`.

Monitoring and troubleshooting problems are challenging tasks in large distributed environments comprising of several Spark clusters with varying configurations and versions, running different types of workloads. In these environments hundreds of thousands metrics may be received. Additionally, hundreds of MBs of logs are generated per second. These metrics need to be tracked and the logs analyzed for anomalies, failures, bugs, environmental issues, and so on to support alerting and troubleshooting functions.

The following figure illustrates an AWS-based data pipeline that pushes all the metrics and logs (both structured and unstructured) to Kinesis. A structured streaming job can read the raw logs from Kinesis and save the data as Parquet files on S3.

The structured streaming query can strip known error patterns and raise suitable alerts, if a new error type is observed. Other Spark batch and streaming applications can use these Parquet files to perform additional processing and output their results as new Parquet files on S3:

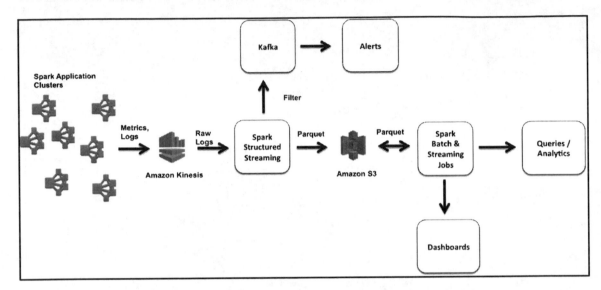

In this architecture, discovering issues from unstructured logs may be required to determine their scope, duration, and impact. **Raw Logs** typically contain many near-duplicate error messages. For efficient processing of these logs, we need to normalize, deduplicate, and filter out well-known error conditions to discover and reveal new ones.

 For details on a pipeline to process raw logs, refer to `https://spark-summit.org/2017/events/lessons-learned-from-managing-thousands-of-production-apache-spark-clusters-daily/`.

In this section, we will explore some of the features Spark SQL and Structured Streaming provide to create a scalable monitoring solution.

First, start the Spark shell with the Kafka packages:

```
Aurobindos-MacBook-Pro-2:spark-2.2.0-bin-hadoop2.7 aurobindosarkar$
./bin/spark-shell --packages org.apache.spark:spark-streaming-
kafka-0-10_2.11:2.1.1,org.apache.spark:spark-sql-kafka-0-10_2.11:2.1.1 --
driver-memory 12g
```

Download the traces for the month of July, 1995, containing HTTP requests to the NASA Kennedy Space Center WWW server in Florida from `http://ita.ee.lbl.gov/html/contrib/NASA-HTTP.html`.

Import the following packages for the hands-on exercises in this chapter:

```scala
scala> import org.apache.spark.sql.types._
scala> import org.apache.spark.sql.functions._
scala> import spark.implicits._
scala> import org.apache.spark.sql.streaming._
```

Next, define the schema for the records in the file:

```scala
scala> val schema = new StructType().add("clientIpAddress",
"string").add("rfc1413ClientIdentity", "string").add("remoteUser",
"string").add("dateTime", "string").add("zone",
"string").add("request","string").add("httpStatusCode",
"string").add("bytesSent", "string").add("referer",
"string").add("userAgent", "string")
```

For simplicity, we read the input file as a CSV file with a space separator, as follows:

```scala
scala> val rawRecords = spark.readStream.option("header",
false).schema(schema).option("sep", "
").format("csv").load("file:///Users/aurobindosarkar/Downloads/NASA")

scala> val ts = unix_timestamp(concat($"dateTime", lit(" "), $"zone"),
"[dd/MMM/yyyy:HH:mm:ss Z]").cast("timestamp")
```

Next, we create a DataFrame containing the log events. As the timestamp changes to the local time zone (by default) in the preceding step, we also retain the original timestamp with time zone information in the `original_dateTime` column, as illustrated:

```scala
scala> val logEvents = rawRecords.withColumn("ts", ts).withColumn("date",
ts.cast(DateType)).select($"ts", $"date", $"clientIpAddress",
concat($"dateTime", lit(" "), $"zone").as("original_dateTime"), $"request",
$"httpStatusCode", $"bytesSent")
```

We can check the results of the streaming read, as shown:

```
scala> val query =
logEvents.writeStream.outputMode("append").format("console").start()
```

```
-------------------------------------------------------
Batch: 0
-------------------------------------------------------
+-------------------+----------+------------------+------------------+--------------------+-------------+---------+
|                 ts|      date|     clientIpAddress|     original_dateTime|             request|httpStatusCode|bytesSent|
+-------------------+----------+------------------+------------------+--------------------+-------------+---------+
|1995-07-01 09:30:01|1995-07-01|       199.72.81.55|[01/Jul/1995:00:0...|GET /history/apol...|          200|     6245|
|1995-07-01 09:30:06|1995-07-01|unicomp6.unicomp.net|[01/Jul/1995:00:0...|GET /shuttle/coun...|          200|     3985|
|1995-07-01 09:30:09|1995-07-01|     199.120.110.21|[01/Jul/1995:00:0...|GET /shuttle/miss...|          200|     4085|
|1995-07-01 09:30:11|1995-07-01|   burger.letters.com|[01/Jul/1995:00:0...|GET /shuttle/coun...|          304|        0|
|1995-07-01 09:30:11|1995-07-01|     199.120.110.21|[01/Jul/1995:00:0...|GET /shuttle/miss...|          200|     4179|
|1995-07-01 09:30:12|1995-07-01|   burger.letters.com|[01/Jul/1995:00:0...|GET /images/NASA-...|          304|        0|
|1995-07-01 09:30:12|1995-07-01|   burger.letters.com|[01/Jul/1995:00:0...|GET /shuttle/coun...|          200|        0|
|1995-07-01 09:30:12|1995-07-01|     205.212.115.106|[01/Jul/1995:00:0...|GET /shuttle/coun...|          200|     3985|
|1995-07-01 09:30:13|1995-07-01|         d104.aa.net|[01/Jul/1995:00:0...|GET /shuttle/coun...|          200|     3985|
|1995-07-01 09:30:13|1995-07-01|     129.94.144.152|[01/Jul/1995:00:0...|       GET / HTTP/1.0|          200|     7074|
|1995-07-01 09:30:14|1995-07-01|unicomp6.unicomp.net|[01/Jul/1995:00:0...|GET /shuttle/coun...|          200|    40310|
|1995-07-01 09:30:14|1995-07-01|unicomp6.unicomp.net|[01/Jul/1995:00:0...|GET /images/NASA-...|          200|      786|
|1995-07-01 09:30:14|1995-07-01|unicomp6.unicomp.net|[01/Jul/1995:00:0...|GET /images/KSC-l...|          200|     1204|
|1995-07-01 09:30:15|1995-07-01|         d104.aa.net|[01/Jul/1995:00:0...|GET /shuttle/coun...|          200|    40310|
|1995-07-01 09:30:15|1995-07-01|         d104.aa.net|[01/Jul/1995:00:0...|GET /images/NASA-...|          200|      786|
|1995-07-01 09:30:15|1995-07-01|         d104.aa.net|[01/Jul/1995:00:0...|GET /images/KSC-l...|          200|     1204|
|1995-07-01 09:30:17|1995-07-01|     129.94.144.152|[01/Jul/1995:00:0...|GET /images/ksclo...|          304|        0|
|1995-07-01 09:30:17|1995-07-01|     199.120.110.21|[01/Jul/1995:00:0...|GET /images/launc...|          200|     1713|
|1995-07-01 09:30:18|1995-07-01|ppptky391.asahi-n...|[01/Jul/1995:00:0...|GET /facts/about_...|          200|     3977|
|1995-07-01 09:30:19|1995-07-01| net-1-141.eden.com|[01/Jul/1995:00:0...|GET /shuttle/miss...|          200|    34029|
+-------------------+----------+------------------+------------------+--------------------+-------------+---------+
only showing top 20 rows
```

We can save the streaming input to Parquet files, partitioned by date to support queries more efficiently, as demonstrated:

```
scala> val streamingETLQuery =
logEvents.writeStream.trigger(Trigger.ProcessingTime("2
minutes")).format("parquet").partitionBy("date").option("path",
"file:///Users/aurobindosarkar/Downloads/NASALogs").option("checkpointLocat
ion",
"file:///Users/aurobindosarkar/Downloads/NASALogs/checkpoint/").start()
```

We can read input so that the latest records are available first by specifying the `latestFirst` option:

```
val rawCSV = spark.readStream.schema(schema).option("latestFirst",
"true").option("maxFilesPerTrigger", "5").option("header",
false).option("sep", "
").format("csv").load("file:///Users/aurobindosarkar/Downloads/NASA")
```

We can also write out the output in the JSON format, partitioned by date, easily, as follows:

```
val streamingETLQuery =
logEvents.writeStream.trigger(Trigger.ProcessingTime("2
minutes")).format("json").partitionBy("date").option("path",
"file:///Users/aurobindosarkar/Downloads/NASALogs").option("checkpointLocat
ion",
"file:///Users/aurobindosarkar/Downloads/NASALogs/checkpoint/").start()
```

Now, we show the use of Kafka for input and output in streaming Spark applications. Here, we have to specify the format parameter as `kafka`, and the kafka broker and topic:

```
scala> val kafkaQuery = logEvents.selectExpr("CAST(ts AS STRING) AS key",
"to_json(struct(*)) AS
value").writeStream.format("kafka").option("kafka.bootstrap.servers",
"localhost:9092").option("topic", "topica").option("checkpointLocation",
"file:///Users/aurobindosarkar/Downloads/NASALogs/kafkacheckpoint/").start(
)
```

Now, we are reading a stream of JSON data from Kafka. The starting offset is set to the earliest to specify the starting point for our query. This applies only when a new streaming query is started:

```
scala> val kafkaDF =
spark.readStream.format("kafka").option("kafka.bootstrap.servers",
"localhost:9092").option("subscribe", "topica").option("startingOffsets",
"earliest").load()
```

We can print out the schema for records read from Kafka, as follows:

```
scala> kafkaDF.printSchema()
root
|-- key: binary (nullable = true)
|-- value: binary (nullable = true)
|-- topic: string (nullable = true)
|-- partition: integer (nullable = true)
|-- offset: long (nullable = true)
|-- timestamp: timestamp (nullable = true)
|-- timestampType: integer (nullable = true)
```

Next, we define the schema for input records, as shown:

```
scala> val kafkaSchema = new StructType().add("ts",
"timestamp").add("date", "string").add("clientIpAddress",
"string").add("rfc1413ClientIdentity", "string").add("remoteUser",
"string").add("original_dateTime", "string").add("request",
"string").add("httpStatusCode", "string").add("bytesSent", "string")
```

Next, we can specify the schema, as illustrated. The star * operator is used to select all the subfields in a struct:

```scala
scala> val kafkaDF1 = kafkaDF.select(col("key").cast("string"),
from_json(col("value").cast("string"),
kafkaSchema).as("data")).select("data.*")
```

Next, we show an example of selecting specific fields. Here, we set the outputMode to append so that only the new rows appended to the result table are written out to external storage. This is applicable only on queries where the existing rows in the result table are not expected to change:

```scala
scala> val kafkaQuery1 = kafkaDF1.select($"ts", $"date",
$"clientIpAddress", $"original_dateTime", $"request", $"httpStatusCode",
$"bytesSent").writeStream.outputMode("append").format("console").start()
```

```
----------------------------------------------------------------------
Batch: 0
----------------------------------------------------------------------
+-------------------+----------+-----------------+-----------------+----------------+-------------+---------+
|                 ts|      date|    clientIpAddress|original_dateTime|          request|httpStatusCode|bytesSent|
+-------------------+----------+-----------------+-----------------+----------------+-------------+---------+
|1995-07-01 09:30:01|1995-07-01|     199.72.81.55|[01/Jul/1995:00:0...|GET /history/apol...|          200|     6245|
|1995-07-01 09:30:06|1995-07-01|unicomp6.unicomp.net|[01/Jul/1995:00:0...|GET /shuttle/coun...|          200|     3985|
|1995-07-01 09:30:09|1995-07-01|    199.120.110.21|[01/Jul/1995:00:0...|GET /shuttle/miss...|          200|     4085|
|1995-07-01 09:30:11|1995-07-01|  burger.letters.com|[01/Jul/1995:00:0...|GET /shuttle/coun...|          304|        0|
|1995-07-01 09:30:11|1995-07-01|    199.120.110.21|[01/Jul/1995:00:0...|GET /shuttle/miss...|          200|     4179|
|1995-07-01 09:30:12|1995-07-01|  burger.letters.com|[01/Jul/1995:00:0...|GET /images/NASA-...|          304|        0|
|1995-07-01 09:30:12|1995-07-01|  burger.letters.com|[01/Jul/1995:00:0...|GET /shuttle/coun...|          200|        0|
|1995-07-01 09:30:12|1995-07-01|   205.212.115.106|[01/Jul/1995:00:0...|GET /shuttle/coun...|          200|     3985|
|1995-07-01 09:30:13|1995-07-01|        d104.aa.net|[01/Jul/1995:00:0...|GET /shuttle/coun...|          200|     3985|
|1995-07-01 09:30:13|1995-07-01|    129.94.144.152|[01/Jul/1995:00:0...|         GET / HTTP/1.0|          200|     7074|
|1995-07-01 09:30:14|1995-07-01|unicomp6.unicomp.net|[01/Jul/1995:00:0...|GET /shuttle/coun...|          200|    40310|
|1995-07-01 09:30:14|1995-07-01|unicomp6.unicomp.net|[01/Jul/1995:00:0...|GET /images/NASA-...|          200|      786|
|1995-07-01 09:30:14|1995-07-01|unicomp6.unicomp.net|[01/Jul/1995:00:0...|GET /images/KSC-l...|          200|     1204|
|1995-07-01 09:30:15|1995-07-01|        d104.aa.net|[01/Jul/1995:00:0...|GET /shuttle/coun...|          200|    40310|
|1995-07-01 09:30:15|1995-07-01|        d104.aa.net|[01/Jul/1995:00:0...|GET /images/NASA-...|          200|      786|
|1995-07-01 09:30:15|1995-07-01|        d104.aa.net|[01/Jul/1995:00:0...|GET /images/KSC-l...|          200|     1204|
|1995-07-01 09:30:17|1995-07-01|    129.94.144.152|[01/Jul/1995:00:0...|GET /images/ksclo...|          304|        0|
|1995-07-01 09:30:17|1995-07-01|    199.120.110.21|[01/Jul/1995:00:0...|GET /images/launc...|          200|     1713|
|1995-07-01 09:30:18|1995-07-01|ppptky391.asahi-n...|[01/Jul/1995:00:0...|GET /facts/about_...|          200|     3977|
|1995-07-01 09:30:19|1995-07-01|   net-1-141.eden.com|[01/Jul/1995:00:0...|GET /shuttle/miss...|          200|    34029|
+-------------------+----------+-----------------+-----------------+----------------+-------------+---------+
only showing top 20 rows
```

We can also specify read (not readStream) to read the records into a regular DataFrame:

```scala
scala> val kafkaDF2 =
spark.read.format("kafka").option("kafka.bootstrap.servers","localhost:9092
").option("subscribe", "topica").load().selectExpr("CAST(value AS STRING)
as myvalue")
```

We can now do all the standard DataFrame operations against this DataFrame; for example, we create a table and query it, as shown:

```scala
scala> kafkaDF2.registerTempTable("topicData3")

scala> spark.sql("select myvalue from topicData3").take(3).foreach(println)
```

```
[{"ts":"1995-07-01T09:30:01.000+05:30","date":"1995-07-
01","clientIpAddress":"199.72.81.55","rfc1413ClientIdentity":"-","remoteUser":"-
","original_dateTime":"[01/Jul/1995:00:00:01 -0400]","request":"GET /history/apollo/
HTTP/1.0","httpStatusCode":"200","bytesSent":"6245"}]
[{"ts":"1995-07-01T09:30:06.000+05:30","date":"1995-07-
01","clientIpAddress":"unicomp6.unicomp.net","rfc1413ClientIdentity":"-
","remoteUser":"-","original_dateTime":"[01/Jul/1995:00:00:06 -0400]","request":"GET
/shuttle/countdown/ HTTP/1.0","httpStatusCode":"200","bytesSent":"3985"}]
[{"ts":"1995-07-01T09:30:09.000+05:30","date":"1995-07-
01","clientIpAddress":"199.120.110.21","rfc1413ClientIdentity":"-","remoteUser":"-
","original_dateTime":"[01/Jul/1995:00:00:09 -0400]","request":"GET
/shuttle/missions/sts-73/mission-sts-73.html
HTTP/1.0","httpStatusCode":"200","bytesSent":"4085"}]
```

Then, we read the records from Kafka and apply the schema:

```scala
scala> val parsed =
spark.readStream.format("kafka").option("kafka.bootstrap.servers",
"localhost:9092").option("subscribe", "topica").option("startingOffsets",
"earliest").load().select(from_json(col("value").cast("string"),
kafkaSchema).alias("parsed_value"))
```

We can execute the following query to check the contents of the records:

```scala
scala> val query =
parsed.writeStream.outputMode("append").format("console").start()
```

```
-------------------------------------------
Batch: 0
-------------------------------------------
+--------------------+
|        parsed_value|
+--------------------+
|[1995-07-01 09:30...|
|[1995-07-01 09:30...|
|[1995-07-01 09:30...|
|[1995-07-01 09:30...|
|[1995-07-01 09:30...|
|[1995-07-01 09:30...|
|[1995-07-01 09:30...|
|[1995-07-01 09:30...|
|[1995-07-01 09:30...|
|[1995-07-01 09:30...|
|[1995-07-01 09:30...|
|[1995-07-01 09:30...|
|[1995-07-01 09:30...|
|[1995-07-01 09:30...|
|[1995-07-01 09:30...|
|[1995-07-01 09:30...|
|[1995-07-01 09:30...|
|[1995-07-01 09:30...|
|[1995-07-01 09:30...|
+--------------------+
only showing top 20 rows
```

We can select all the fields from the records, as follows:

```scala
scala> val selectAllParsed = parsed.select("parsed_value.*")
```

We can also select specific fields of interest from the DataFrame:

```scala
scala> val selectFieldsParsed = selectAllParsed.select("ts",
"clientIpAddress", "request", "httpStatusCode")
```

Next, we can use window operations, as demonstrated, and maintain counts for various HTTP codes. Here, we use `outputMode` set to `complete` since we want the entire updated result table to be written to the external storage:

```scala
scala> val s1 = selectFieldsParsed.groupBy(window($"ts", "10 minutes", "5
minutes"),
$"httpStatusCode").count().writeStream.outputMode("complete").format("conso
le").start()
```

```
-------------------------------------------
Batch: 0
-------------------------------------------
+--------------------+--------------+-----+
|              window|httpStatusCode|count|
+--------------------+--------------+-----+
|[1995-07-19 14:20...|           200|  220|
|[1995-07-21 02:35...|           404|    4|
|[1995-07-17 17:00...|           200|  318|
|[1995-07-23 09:00...|           304|   22|
|[1995-07-27 06:10...|           404|    2|
|[1995-07-15 16:35...|           404|    2|
|[1995-07-27 00:15...|           200|  574|
|[1995-07-14 20:55...|           302|   28|
|[1995-07-05 08:00...|           404|    1|
|[1995-07-18 20:10...|           404|    2|
|[1995-07-27 06:05...|           302|    8|
|[1995-07-18 09:00...|           404|    2|
|[1995-07-19 05:40...|           200|  367|
|[1995-07-10 09:30...|           200|  334|
|[1995-07-26 18:55...|           302|    3|
|[1995-07-13 06:25...|           304|   71|
|[1995-07-21 02:30...|           302|   18|
|[1995-07-14 17:40...|           404|    1|
|[1995-07-15 06:00...|           302|   18|
|[1995-07-06 13:30...|           200|  270|
+--------------------+--------------+-----+
only showing top 20 rows
```

Next, we show another example of using `groupBy` and computed counts for various page requests in these windows. This can be used to compute and report the top pages visited type metrics:

```scala
scala> val s2 = selectFieldsParsed.groupBy(window($"ts", "10 minutes", "5
minutes"),
$"request").count().writeStream.outputMode("complete").format("console").st
art()
```

```
-------------------------------------------------
Batch: 0
-------------------------------------------------
+--------------------+--------------------+-----+
|              window|             request|count|
+--------------------+--------------------+-----+
|[1995-07-04 01:20...|GET /software/win...|    1|
|[1995-07-12 09:30...|GET /shuttle/miss...|    5|
|[1995-07-13 00:30...|GET /images/launc...|    9|
|[1995-07-06 02:50...|GET /shuttle/tech...|    1|
|[1995-07-17 04:50...|GET /shuttle/miss...|    4|
|[1995-07-03 19:50...|GET /shuttle/miss...|    1|
|[1995-07-11 02:35...|GET /software/win...|    2|
|[1995-07-11 07:40...|GET /elv/DELTA/de...|    1|
|[1995-07-26 19:25...|GET /shuttle/coun...|    1|
|[1995-07-17 20:55...|GET /history/apol...|    1|
|[1995-07-24 02:20...|GET /history/gemi...|    1|
|[1995-07-01 23:30...|GET /shuttle/miss...|    3|
|[1995-07-18 00:50...|GET /history/apol...|    1|
|[1995-07-09 22:25...|GET /shuttle/miss...|    1|
|[1995-07-20 10:25...|GET /history/apol...|    2|
|[1995-07-15 01:25...|GET /shuttle/miss...|    1|
|[1995-07-07 12:55...|GET /cgi-bin/imag...|    1|
|[1995-07-13 12:05...|GET /shuttle/miss...|    1|
|[1995-07-13 19:15...|GET /shuttle/miss...|    1|
|[1995-07-19 20:20...|GET /shuttle/miss...|    2|
+--------------------+--------------------+-----+
only showing top 20 rows
```

Note that the examples presented earlier are instances of stateful processing. The counts have to be saved as a distributed state between triggers. Each trigger reads the previous state and writes the updated state. This state is stored in memory, and is backed by the persistent WAL, typically located on HDFS or S3 storage. This allows the streaming application to automatically handle data arriving late. Keeping this state allows the late data to update the counts of old windows.

However, the size of the state can increase indefinitely, if the old windows are not dropped. A watermarking approach is used to address this issue. A watermark is a moving threshold of how late data is expected to be and when to drop the old state. It trails behind the max seen event time. Data newer than watermark may be late, but is allowed into the aggregate, while data older than the watermark is considered "too late" and dropped. Additionally, windows older than the watermark are automatically deleted to limit the amount of intermediate state that is required to be maintained by the system.

A watermark specified for the previous query is given here:

```
scala> val s4 = selectFieldsParsed.withWatermark("ts", "10
minutes").groupBy(window($"ts", "10 minutes", "5 minutes"),
$"request").count().writeStream.outputMode("complete").format("console").st
art()
```

For more details on watermarking, refer to `https://databricks.com/blog/2017/05/08/event-time-aggregation-watermarking-apache-sparks-structured-streaming.html`.

In the next section, we will shift our focus to deploying Spark-based machine learning pipelines in production.

Deploying Spark machine learning pipelines

The following figure illustrates a machine learning pipeline at a conceptual level. However, real-life ML pipelines are a lot more complicated, with several models being trained, tuned, combined, and so on:

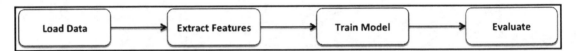

The next figure shows the core elements of a typical machine learning application split into two parts: the modeling, including model training, and the deployed model (used on streaming data to output the results):

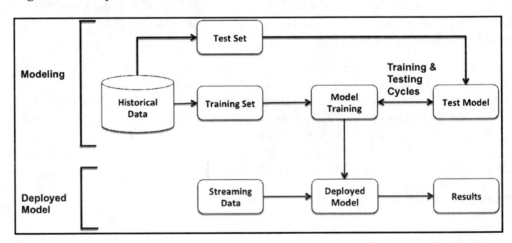

Typically, data scientists experiment or do their modeling work in Python and/or R. Their work is then reimplemented in Java/Scala before deployment in a production environment. Enterprise production environments often consist of web servers, application servers, databases, middleware, and so on. The conversion of prototypical models to production-ready models results in additional design and development effort that lead to delays in rolling out updated models.

We can use Spark MLlib 2.x model serialization to directly use the models and pipelines saved by data scientists (to disk) in production environments by loading them from the persisted model files.

In the following example (source: https://spark.apache.org/docs/latest/ml-pipeline. html), we will illustrate creating and saving a ML pipeline in Python (using pyspark shell) and then retrieving it in a Scala environment (using Spark shell).

Start the pyspark shell and execute the following sequence of Python statements:

```
>>> from pyspark.ml import Pipeline
>>> from pyspark.ml.classification import LogisticRegression
>>> from pyspark.ml.feature import HashingTF, Tokenizer
>>> training = spark.createDataFrame([
... (0, "a b c d e spark", 1.0),
... (1, "b d", 0.0),
... (2, "spark f g h", 1.0),
... (3, "hadoop mapreduce", 0.0)
... ], ["id", "text", "label"])
>>> tokenizer = Tokenizer(inputCol="text", outputCol="words")
>>> hashingTF = HashingTF(inputCol=tokenizer.getOutputCol(),
outputCol="features")
>>> lr = LogisticRegression(maxIter=10, regParam=0.001)
>>> pipeline = Pipeline(stages=[tokenizer, hashingTF, lr])
>>> model = pipeline.fit(training)
>>> model.save("file:///Users/aurobindosarkar/Downloads/spark-logistic-
regression-model")
>>> quit()
```

Start the Spark shell and execute the following sequence of Scala statements:

```
scala> import org.apache.spark.ml.{Pipeline, PipelineModel}
scala> import org.apache.spark.ml.classification.LogisticRegression
scala> import org.apache.spark.ml.feature.{HashingTF, Tokenizer}
scala> import org.apache.spark.ml.linalg.Vector
scala> import org.apache.spark.sql.Row

scala> val sameModel =
PipelineModel.load("file:///Users/aurobindosarkar/Downloads/spark-logistic-
regression-model")
```

Next, we create a `test` Dataset and run it through the ML pipeline:

```scala
scala> val test = spark.createDataFrame(Seq(
| (4L, "spark i j k"),
| (5L, "l m n"),
| (6L, "spark hadoop spark"),
| (7L, "apache hadoop")
| )).toDF("id", "text")
```

The results of running the model on the `test` Dataset are shown here:

```scala
scala> sameModel.transform(test).select("id", "text", "probability",
"prediction").collect().foreach { case Row(id: Long, text: String, prob:
Vector, prediction: Double) => println(s"($id, $text) --> prob=$prob,
prediction=$prediction")}

(4, spark i j k) --> prob=[0.15554371384424398,0.844456286155756],
prediction=1.0
(5, l m n) --> prob=[0.8307077352111738,0.16929226478882617],
prediction=0.0
(6, spark hadoop spark) --> prob=[0.06962184061952888,0.9303781593804711],
prediction=1.0
(7, apache hadoop) --> prob=[0.9815183503510166,0.018481649648983405],
prediction=0.0
```

The key parameters of the saved logistic regression model are read into a DataFrame, as illustrated in the following code block. Earlier, when the model was saved in the `pyspark` shell, these parameters were saved to a Parquet file located in a subdirectory associated with the final stage of our pipeline:

```scala
scala> val df =
spark.read.parquet("file:///Users/aurobindosarkar/Downloads/spark-logistic-
regression-
model/stages/2_LogisticRegression_4abda37bdde1ddf65ea0/data/part-00000-415b
f215-207a-4a49-985e-190eaf7253a7-c000.snappy.parquet")

scala> df.show()
```

The following output is obtained:

numClasses	numFeatures	interceptVector	coefficientMatrix	isMultinomial
2	262144	[-1.5906514317596...	1 x 262144 CSCMat...	false

```
scala> df.collect.foreach(println)
```

The output is, as shown:

```
[2,262144,[-1.5906514317596054],1  x 262144  CSCMatrix
(0,15554)  1.6097382089819763
(0,17222)  2.7668185824796496
(0,24152)  1.6097382089819763
(0,27526)  -1.9454856869974295
(0,28698)  2.7668185824796496
(0,30913)  -1.9454856869974295
(0,42633)  -2.381670949064051
(0,51505)  1.6097382089819763
(0,155117) -2.381670949064051
(0,227410) 2.7668185824796496
(0,234657) 3.28241759359622,false]
```

For more details on how to productionize ML models, refer to `https://spark-summit.org/2017/events/how-to-productionize-your-machine-learning-models-using-apache-spark-mllib-2x/`.

Understanding the challenges in typical ML deployment environments

Production deployment environments for ML models can be very diverse and complex. For example, models may need to be deployed in web applications, portals, real-time and batch processing systems, and as an API or a REST service, embedded in devices or in large legacy environments.

Additionally, enterprise technology stacks can comprise of Java Enterprise, C/C++, legacy mainframe environments, relational databases, and so on. The non-functional requirements and customer SLAs with respect to response times, throughput, availability, and uptime can also vary widely. However, in almost all cases, our deployment process needs to support A/B testing, experimentation, model performance evaluation, and be agile and responsive to business needs.

Typically, practitioners use various methods to benchmark and phase-in new or updated models to avoid high-risk, big bang production deployments.

In the next section, we will explore a few model deployment architectures.

Understanding types of model scoring architectures

The simplest model is to precompute model results using Spark (batch processing), save the results to a database, and then serve the results to web and mobile applications from the database. Many large-scale recommendation engines and search engines use this architecture:

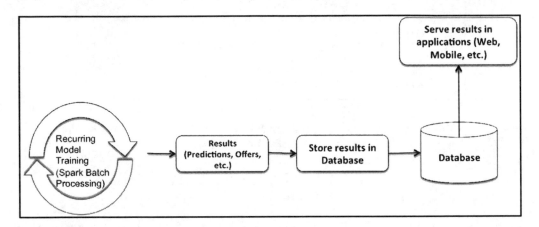

A second model scoring architecture computes the features and runs prediction algorithms using Spark Streaming. The prediction results can be cached using caching solutions, such as Redis, and can be made available via an API. Other applications can then use these APIs to obtain the prediction results from the deployed model. This option is illustrated in this figure:

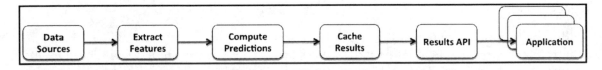

In a third architectural model, we can use Spark for model training purposes only. The model is then copied into the production environment. For example, we can load the coefficients and intercept of a logistic regression model from a JSON file. This approach is resource-efficient and results in a high-performing system. It is also a lot easier to deploy in existing or complex environments.

It is illustrated here:

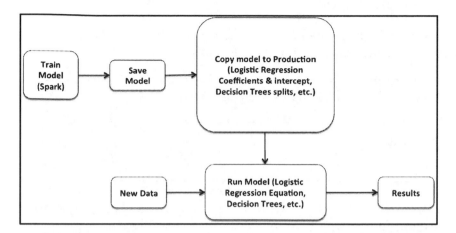

Continuing with our earlier example, we can read in the saved model parameters from a Parquet file and convert it to a JSON format that can, in turn, be conveniently imported into any application (inside or outside the Spark environment) and applied to new data:

```
scala> spark.read.parquet("file:///Users/aurobindosarkar/Downloads/spark-
logistic-regression-
model/stages/2_LogisticRegression_4abda37bdde1ddf65ea0/data/part-00000-415b
f215-207a-4a49-985e-190eaf7253a7-
c000.snappy.parquet").write.mode("overwrite").json("file:///Users/aurobindo
sarkar/Downloads/lr-model-json")
```

We can display the intercept, coefficients, and other key parameters using standard OS commands, as follows:

```
Aurobindos-MacBook-Pro-2:lr-model-json aurobindosarkar$ more part-00000-
e2b14eb8-724d-4262-8ea5-7c23f846fed0-c000.json
```

```
{"numClasses":2,"numFeatures":262144,"interceptVector":{"type":1,"values":[-
1.5906514317596054]},"coefficientMatrix":{"type":0,"numRows":1,"numCols":262144,"colPt
rs":[0,11],"rowIndices":[15554,17222,24152,27526,28698,30913,42633,51505,155117,227410
,234657],"values":[1.6097382089819763,2.7668185824796496,1.6097382089819763,-
1.9454856869974295,2.7668185824796496,-1.9454856869974295,-
2.381670949064051,1.6097382089819763,-
2.381670949064051,2.7668185824796496,3.28241759359622],"isTransposed":true},"isMultino
mial":false}
```

As models are becoming bigger and more complex, it can be challenging to deploy and serve them. Models may not scale well, and their resource requirements can become very expensive. Databricks and Redis-ML provide solutions to deploy the trained model.

In the Redis-ML solution, the model is applied to the new data directly in the Redis environment.

This can provide the required overall performance, scalability, and availability at a much lower price point than running the model in a Spark environment.

The following figure shows Redis-ML being used as a serving engine (implementing the third model scoring architectural pattern, as described earlier):

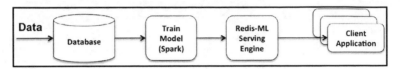

In the next section, we will briefly discuss using Mesos and Kubernetes as cluster managers in production environments.

Using cluster managers

In this section, we will briefly discuss Mesos and Kubernetes at a conceptual level. The Spark framework can be deployed through Apache **Mesos**, **YARN**, Spark Standalone, or the **Kubernetes** cluster manager, as depicted:

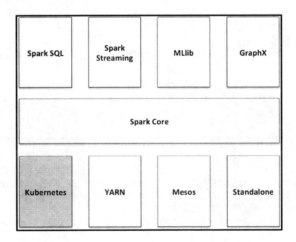

Mesos can enable easy scalability and replication of data, and is a good unified cluster management solution for heterogeneous workloads.

To use Mesos from Spark, the Spark binaries should be accessible by Mesos and the Spark driver configured to connect to Mesos. Alternatively, you can also install Spark binaries on all the Mesos slaves. The driver creates a job and then issues the tasks for scheduling, while Mesos determines the machines to handle them.

Spark can run over Mesos in two modes: coarse-grained (the default) and fine-grained (deprecated in Spark 2.0.0). In the coarse-grained mode, each Spark executor runs as a single Mesos task. This mode has significantly lower start up overheads, but reserves Mesos resources for the duration of the application. Mesos also supports dynamic allocation where the number of executors is adjusted based on the statistics of the application.

The following figure illustrates a deployment that collocates the **Mesos Master** and **Zookeeper** nodes. The **Mesos Slave** and **Cassandra Node** are also collocated for better data locality. In addition, the Spark binaries are deployed on all worker nodes:

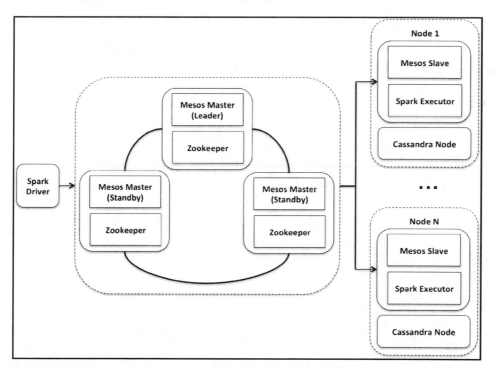

Another emerging Spark cluster management solution is Kubernetes, which is being developed as a native cluster manager for Spark. It is an open source system that can be used for automating the deployment, scaling, and management of containerized Spark applications.

The next figure depicts a high-level view of Kubernetes. Each node contains a daemon, called a **Kublet,** which talks to the **Master** node. The users also talks to the Master to declaratively specify what they want to run. For example, a user can request running a specific number of web server instances. The Master will take the user's request and schedule the workload on the nodes:

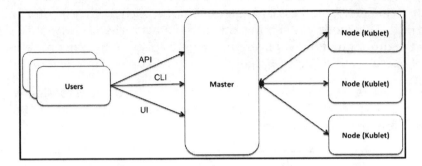

The nodes run one or more pods. A pod is a higher-level abstraction on containers, and each pod can contain a set of colocated containers. Each pod has its own IP address and can communicate with the pods in other nodes. The storage volumes can be local or network-attached. This can be seen in the following figure:

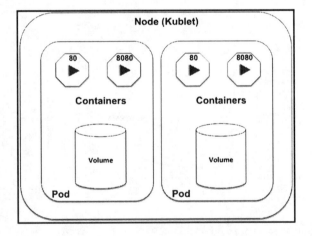

Kubernetes promotes resource sharing between different types of Spark workload to reduce operational costs and improve infrastructure utilization. In addition, several add-on services can be used out-of-the-box with Spark applications, including logging, monitoring, security, container-to-container communications, and so on.

For more details on Spark on Kubernetes, visit `https://github.com/apache-spark-on-k8s/spark`.

In the following figure, the dotted line separates Kubernetes from Spark. Spark Core is responsible for getting new executors, pushing new configurations, removing executors, and so on. The **Kubernetes Scheduler Backend** takes the Spark Core requests and converts them into primitives that Kubernetes can understand. Additionally, it handles all resource requests and all communications with Kubernetes.

Other services, such as a File Staging Server, can make your local files and JARs available to the Spark cluster, and the Spark shuffle service can store shuffle data for the dynamic allocation of resources; for example, it can enable elastically changing the number of executors in a particular stage. You can also extend the Kubernetes API to include custom or application-specific resources; for example, you can create dashboards to display the progress of jobs:

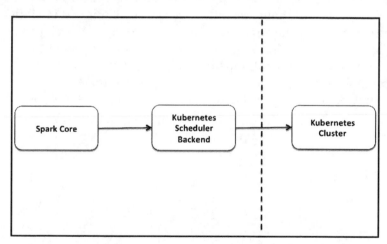

Kubernetes also provides useful administrative features to help manage clusters, for example, RBAC and namespace-level resource quotas, audit logging, monitoring node, pod, cluster-level metrics, and so on.

Summary

In this chapter, we presented several Spark SQL-based application architectures for building highly-scalable applications. We explored the main concepts and challenges in batch processing and stream processing. We discussed the features of Spark SQL that can help in building robust ETL pipelines. We also presented some code towards building a scalable monitoring application. Additionally, we explored an efficient deployment technique for machine learning pipelines, and some basic concepts involved in using cluster managers such as Mesos and Kubernetes.

In conclusion, this book attempts to help you build a strong foundation in Spark SQL and Scala. However, there are still many areas that you can explore in greater depth to build deeper expertise. Depending on your specific domain, the nature of data and problems could vary widely and your approach to solving them would typically encompass one or more areas described in this book. However, in all cases EDA and data munging skills will be required, and the more you practice, the more proficient you will become at it. Try downloading and working with different types of data covering structured, semi-structured and unstructured data. Additionally, read the references mentioned in all the chapters to get deeper insights into how other data science practitioners approach problems. Reference Apache Spark site for latest releases of the software, and explore other machine learning algorithms you could use in your ML pipelines. Finally, topics such as deep learning and cost-based optimizations are still evolving in Spark, try to keep up with the developments in these areas as they will be key to solving many interesting problems in the near future.

Index

2

20 Newsgroup Datasets
  reference link 334

A

Alternating Least Squares (ALS) 265
Amazon DynamoDB 392
Amazon EMR 392
Amazon Kinesis 392
Amazon S3 Storage 392
Apache Spark
  used, for batch processing 388
  used, for stream processing 389
Apache Zeppelin
  data, visualizing with 70, 71, 73
artificial neural network (ANN) 320
autoencoders 343
Avro files
  Spark, using with 55, 56

B

basic data analysis
  Spark SQL, using for 62
basic statistics
  computing 66, 67, 68
Batch Layer 392
batch
  processing, Apache Spark used 388
BigDL
  URL, for documentation 327
  working 325
Bucketizer
  using 181

C

CaffeOnSpark
  about 324
  reference link 324
Catalyst optimizations
  about 22, 23, 354
  Catalyst transformations 357
  Dataset/DataFrame APIs 354
  logical optimizations 22
  physical optimizations 22
Catalyst optimizer 21, 22
Catalyst transformations 23, 24, 27, 357
Chi-squared selector
  using 183
cluster managers
  using 424
CNAE-9 Data Set
  reference link 308
Comma-Separated values (CSV) 233
Communities and Crime Unnormalized Data Set
  reference link 240
Complex Event Processing (CEP) 124
convolutional neural network (ConvNet/CNN)
  about 328, 329
  used, for text classification 333
Cost-based Optimizer (CBO) 22
cost-based optimizer
  build side selection 372
  in Apache Spark 2.2 369
  reference link 369
  statistics collection 370
  statistics collection functions 371
custom data sources
  defining 58
  receiver, writing 142
  using, in Spark 58

D

DAG Visualization 363
data formats
  selecting 396
data munging tasks 232
data munging techniques
  aggregations, computing 87
  basic statistics, computing 87
  data combining, JOIN operation used 94
  dataset, augmenting 88
  exploring 85
  household electric consumption dataset, pre-processing 86
  miscellaneous processing steps, executing 89
  missing data, analyzing 92
  weather dataset, pre-processing 90
data munging
  about 83
  datasets 84
data outliers
  identifying 69
data preprocessing pipelines
  creating 284
data sources
  in Spark applications 38, 39
data
  pre-processing 162
  pre-processing, for machine learning 118
  preparing, for machine learning 117
  sampling, with DataFrame 75
  sampling, with Dataset API 75
  sampling, with RDD API 76
  sampling, with Spark SQL APIs 75
  transforming, in ETL pipelines 397
  visualizing, on map 261
  visualizing, with Apache Zeppelin 70, 71, 73
DataFrame APIs
  about 350
  data serialization, optimizing 351
DataFrame
  about 17, 18, 20
  data, sampling with 76
Dataset APIs
  about 350, 354

data, sampling with 76
Datasets 17, 18, 20, 39, 350
deep learning pipelines, in Spark
  reference link 328
deep learning, with Apache Spark
  reference link 328
deep learning
  about 321
  BigDL, working 325
  CaffeOnSpark 324
  deep learning pipelines 328
  DL4J 324
  hyperparameters, tuning 327
  in Spark 324
  reference link 321
  TensorFrames 325
deep neural networks
  Recurrent Neural Networks (RNNs) 337
  used, for language processing 337
diabetes dataset
  exploring 156
  reference link 155
DL4J
  about 324
  reference link 324
Domain-Specific Language (DSL) 200
domain-specific language (DSL) 17

E

EDGAR
  URL 276
edges
  visualizing 262
encoders
  using 180
errors
  addressing, in ETL pipelines 404
ETL pipelines
  building, Spark SQL used 395
  data formats, selecting 396
  data, transforming 397
  errors, addressing 404
Exploratory Data Analysis (EDA) 62
Extract-Transform-Load (ETL) 386

F

feature engineering
  about 150
  dimensionally reduction 152
  feature importance, estimating 152
  features, creating from raw data 151
  good features 153
  reference link 151
Federal Court of Australia (FCA)
  about 295
  reference link 295
filesystems 39

G

generic stop words list
  reference link 289
ggplot
  reference link 248
Global Reactive Power (GRP) 96
GloVe embedding
  reference link 333
  URL, for downloading 334
graph algorithms
  applying, GraphFrames used 206
graph applications
  GraphFrames, used 210
graph nodes
  visualizing 262
graph queries 197
GraphFrames
  about 350
  constructing 195
  loading 210
  partitioning 223
  physical execution plan, viewing 222
  saving 210
  used, for exploring graphs 195
  used, for graph applications 210
  used, for Motif analysis 199
  used, for processing subgraphs 206
graphs
  exploring, GraphFrames used 195
  processing, multiple types of relationships
    contained 218

I

Initial Data Analysis (IDA) 62
input Datasets
  data, training 334
  embedding 334

J

JSON data
  Spark, using with 52, 53, 55

K

Kafka-Spark integration 138
Kafka-Spark Structured Streaming 140
Kafka
  brokers 137
  concepts 137
  consumers 137
  Kafka-Spark integration 138
  Kafka-Spark Structured Streaming 141
  producers 137
  reference link 398
  topic 137
  URL 137
  used, with Spark Structured Streaming 137
  ZooKeeper concepts 138
Kappa Architecture 392, 393
Kolmogorov-Smirnov (KS) 270
Kubernetes 424
Kubernetes Scheduler Backend 427
Kublet 426

L

labels
  retrieving 185
Lambda architecture
  about 391
  Batch Layer 391
  reference link 392
  Speed Layer 391
large-scale graph applications 194
Latent Dirichlet Allocation (LDA)
  about 265
  reference link 294
Latent Semantic Analysis (LSA) 294

Lenet-5
  reference link 329
Logical Plans 21
Long Short-Term Memory (LSTM) 337

M

machine learning applications
  about 147
  developing 308
  pipeline application development process 149
  Spark ML pipelines 148
machine learning
  data, preparing 117
  pipeline, creating 119
  pipeline, executing 119
  SparkR, used 265
Mesos 424
missing data
  identifying 64
ML algorithm
  changing, in pipeline 178
ML pipeline
  reference link 419
ML Pipelines 350
MNIST database
  reference link 329
model scoring architecture
  types 422
mongo-spark-connector jar
  download link 50
MongoDB
  download link 47
  Spark, using with 47, 48, 50
monitoring and instrumentation
  reference link 361
Motif analysis
  GraphFrames, used 199
multi-way join ordering optimization 373
multi-way join recording
  reference link 373
MySQL
  reference 42

N

Naive Bayes classifiers
  using 298
Naive Bayes Text Classifiers
  reference link 299
neural networks
  about 320
  deep learning 321
  representation learning 321
  stochastic gradient descent (SGD) 323
normalizer
  using 184
NoSQL
  reference 41

O

OpenNLP
  URL, for downloading 339
operations 197
outlier 69
output sinks
  File Sink, used for saving output to partitioned table 133
  Foreach Sink, used for arbitrary computations 132
  Memory Sink, used for saving output to table 133
  using 131

P

Parquet files
  Spark, using with 57
performance improvements
  used, for whole-stage code generation 377
performance tuning
  in Spark SQL 349
Physical Plans 21
pipeline application development process
  about 149
  data cleansing 149
  data ingestion 149
  feature engineering 150
  model deployment 150
  model selection 150
  model training 150

model validation 150
preprocessing 149
pipeline stages
transformer 149
pivot tables
creating, Spark SQL used 78, 79, 80, 81
polyglot persistence 387
predicate pushdown 358
Principal Component Analysis (PCA)
about 179
reference link 180
used, to select features 180
Project Tungsten 27, 28, 29

Q

query plan 354
query plan, for modern hardware
reference link 379

R

raw logs
about 410
reference link 410
RDD API
data, sampling with 76
Real-Time Bidding Dataset
reference link 24
Rectified Linear Unit (ReLU) 329
Recurrent Neural Networks (RNNs)
about 337
reference link 339
Redis 38
relational databases
Spark, using with 40, 41, 43, 45, 46
representation learning 321
Resilient Distributed Datasets (RDDs) 15, 16, 17
Reuters-21578
reference link 288

S

scalable monitoring solution
implementing 408
reference link 409
scalable stream processing
complex data 393

complex systems 394
complex workloads 393
implementing, with structured streaming 393
Scalable Time Series Database 408
serialization and deserialization (SerDe) 351
Serving Layer 389
SNAP dataset
reference link 195
Spark application execution
external tools, used for performance tuning 368
metrics, exploring 367
visualizing 361
Spark applications
data sources 38, 39
Spark Core 350
Spark data sources
selecting 39, 40
Spark DataFrames
basic operations, executing 236
contents 233
merging 240
reading 232
SQL statements, executing 239
structure, exploring 233
writing 232
Spark machine learning pipelines
deploying 418
ML model, deployment environments, challenges
421
model scoring architecture, types 422
Spark ML classification model
data, pre-processing 162
diabetes dataset, exploring 156
implementing 154
ML algorithm, changing in pipeline 178
Spark ML pipeline, building 167
Spark ML clustering model
implementing 186
Spark ML pipeline
about 148
building 167
components 148
creating 173
datasets 148
estimator 149

model, selecting 175
pipeline stages 149
pipelines 148
predictions creating, PipelineModel used 174
Spark ML classifier, used 172
StringIndexer, used for indexing categorical
    features and labels 167
training, creating 173
VectorAssembler, used for assembling features
    into column 171
Spark ML tools 179
Spark ML utilities
    about 179
    Bucketizer, used 181
    Chi-squared selector, used 183
    encoders, used 180
    labels, retrieving 185
    normalizer, used 184
    Principal Component Analysis (PCA), used to
        select features 180
    VectorSlicer, used 182
Spark on Kubernetes
    reference link 427
Spark packages
    reference 38
Spark pipelines
    reference link 289
Spark SQL APIs
    data, sampling with 75
Spark SQL applications
    about 273
    machine learning application, developing 308
    Naive Bayes classifiers, used 298
    text analysis applications 274
    themes, in document corpuses 294
    used, for textual analysis 275
Spark SQL Catalyst optimizer
    reference link 361
Spark SQL concepts
    about 15
    Catalyst optimizer 21, 22
    DataFrame 21
    Dataset 17, 18, 19, 20, 21
    Project Tungsten 27, 28, 29
    Resilient Distributed Datasets (RDDs) 15, 16, 17

Spark SQL
    about 8, 9, 350
    ETL pipelines, building 395
    Structured Streaming internals 34, 35
    used, for creating pivot tables 78, 79, 80, 81
    used, in streaming applications 30, 31, 32, 34
    using, for basic data analysis 62
Spark streaming applications
    building 124
    dataset API, used in structured streaming 131
    output sinks, using 131
    sliding window-based functionality, implementing
        126
    streaming dataset, joining with static dataset 128
Spark Streaming Jobs 408
Spark Structured Streaming
    Kafka, used 137
spark-avro
    reference 57
Spark-based application architectures
    about 386
    Apache Spark, used for batch processing 388
    Apache Spark, used for stream processing 389
spark-ts package
    reference link 102
Spark
    custom data sources, defining 58
    custom data sources, using 58
    using, with Avro files 55, 56
    using, with JSON data 52, 53, 55
    using, with MongoDB 47, 48, 50
    using, with Parquet files 57
    using, with relational databases 40, 41, 43, 44,
        46
SparkR DataFrames 231
SparkR
    about 229
    architecture 230
    reference link 232
    used, for computing summary statistics 244
    used, for data visualization 248
    used, for EDA 232
    used, for machine learning 265
SparkSession 9, 10, 11, 12, 13, 14, 15
Speed Layer 392

statistics collection functions
  about 371
  filter operator 371
  join operator 372
stochastic gradient descent (SGD) 323
stop words
  reference link 101
stream
  processing, Apache Spark used 389
streaming application
  reference link 394
streaming data applications 123
strongly connected component (SCC) 206
Structured Streaming 350
Structured Streaming internals 34, 35
structured streaming internals
  reference link 394
structured streaming programming
  references 126
structured streaming
  scalable stream processing, implementing 393
subgraphs
  processing, GraphFrames used 206
supervised learning 328
Support Vector Machines (SVMs) 299

T

tennis tournament match statistics dataset
  reference link 242
TensorFrames
  about 325
  reference link 325
term frequency-inverse document frequency (tf-idf) 275
text analysis applications 274
textual analysis
  data preprocessing pipelines, creating 285
  readability, computing 280
  reference link 274
  Spark SQL, used 275
  textual data, preprocessing 275
textual data
  multiple input data files, processing 98
  munging 97
  stop words, removing 100

time series data
  basic statistics, computing 109
  data, loading 105
  data, persisting 105
  date fields, processing 105
  date-time index, defining 107
  missing data, handling 109
  munging 102
  pre-processing 103
  reference link 102
  TimeSeriesRDD object, used 107
transformation functions
  reference link 403
Transport for London (TfL)
  about 142
  reference link 142

U

Ubuntu
  reference link 263
User Defined Functions (UDFs)
  about 10, 242
  using 242
User Knowledge Modeling Data Set
  reference link 186

V

variable length records
  converting, to fixed-length records 111
  data, extracting from columns 114
  dealing 110
VectorSlicer
  using 182
Visualization Tools 408
visualizing Spark application execution
  reference link 368

W

watermarking approach
  about 417
  reference link 418
whole-stage code generation
  performance improvements 377
wine quality dataset
  reference link 265

Within Set Sum of Squared Errors (WSSSE) 188
Write-Ahead Log (WAL) 34
write-ahead log (WAL) 390

Y

YARN 424

Z

ZooKeeper concepts 138
  reference link 138

CPSIA information can be obtained
at www.ICGtesting.com
Printed in the USA
FFOW01n1817020118
44284672-43841FF